*France and the Africans 1944–1960*

# France and the Africans 1944–1960

## A POLITICAL HISTORY

Edward Mortimer

**WALKER AND COMPANY**
New York

First published in the United States of America in 1969 by Walker and Company, a division of the Walker Publishing Company, Inc.

Published simultaneously in Canada by The Ryerson Press, Toronto.

Library of Congress Catalog Card Number: 68–13985

Printed in the United States of America from type set in Great Britain.

# Contents

# Contents

# Contents

# Contents

# Key to abbreviations which recur in the text

AEF: Afrique Equatoriale Française
ALCAM: Assemblée Législative du Cameroun
AOF: Afrique Occidentale Française
ARCAM: Assemblée Représentative du Cameroun
AST: Action Sociale Tchadienne – Gaullist party in Tchad after 1953
ATCAM: Assemblée Territoriale du Cameroun
BAG: Bloc Africain de Guinée – anti-RDA party in Guinea 1954–8, led by Barry Diawadou
BDC: Bloc Démocratique Camerounais – Aujoulat's party
BDG: Bloc Démocratique Gabonais – Mba's party (RDA)
BDS: Bloc Démocratique Sénégalais – Senghor's party from 1948 to 1956
BPS: Bloc Populaire Sénégalais – ditto, 1956–8
CFTC: Confédération Française des Travailleurs Chrétiens – French Catholic group of trade unions
CGT: Confédération Générale du Travail – largest group of French trade unions, Communist-controlled
CGTA: Confédération Gézérale des Travailleurs Africains – African splinter-group from CGT, led by Sékou Touré (1956–7)
CPP: Convention People's Party – Nkrumah's party in Ghana
CUT: Comité d'Unité Togolaise – Ewe (later Togolese nationalist) party, led by Sylvanus Olympio
DSG: Démocratie Socialiste de Guinée – Socialist party in Guinea (1954–8), led by Barry III
E.E.C.: European Economic Community
FAC: Fonds d'Aide et de Co-opération (successor to FIDES)
FEANF: Fédération des Etudiants d'Afrique Noire en France
FIDES: Fonds d'Investissement pour le Développement Economique et Social – main channel for French overseas aid, 1946–58
FLN: Front de Libération Nationale – Algerian nationalist movement
FO: Force Ouvrière – Socialist group of French trade unions, which split off from the CGT in 1948
GIRT: Groupement des Intérêts Ruraux du Tchad – chiefs' party, founded 1957, led by Gontchomé Sahoulba
IOM: Indépendants d'Outre-Mer – see pp. 129–31
IPAS: Indépendants et Paysans d'Action Sociale – Conservative group in French parliament from 1956
JEUCAFRA: Jeunesse Camerounaise Française – pre-war pro-French movement in Cameroun

## Key to abbreviations

JUVENTO: either Juventus Togolensis or Justice-Union-Vigilance-Education-Nationalisme-Tenacité-Optimisme. Youth movement of the CUT, which however it opposed after 1959

MDV: Mouvement Démocratique Voltaïque–Gaullist, but anti-chief, party in eastern Upper Volta, led by Michel Dorange and Gérard Ouédraogo

MESAN: Mouvement d'Evolution Sociale en Afrique Noire–Boganda's party in Oubangui-Chari

MPEA: Mouvement Populaire d'Evolution Africaine–anti-RDA party in western Upper Volta, led by Nazi Boni

MPS: Mouvement Populaire Sénégalais–pro-Houphouët RDA section in Senegal, founded 1955

MRP: Mouvement Républicain Populaire–French christian democrat party

MSA: Mouvement Socialiste Africain–interterritorial movement formed by African Socialist parties in 1957

MUR: Mouvement Unifié de la Résistance–fellow-travellers' group in French parliament

N.Y.: New York (state)

PAI: Parti Africain de l'Indépendance–extreme left party in Senegal, founded 1957, led by Majhemout Diop

PCF: Parti Communiste Français

PDCI: Parti Démocratique de la Côte d'Ivoire (RDA section, led by Houphouët)

PDG: Parti Démocratique de Guinée (RDA section until 1958, led by Sékou Touré)

PPC: Parti Progressiste Congolais (RDA section until 1957, led by Tchicaya)

PPT: Parti Progressiste Tchadien (RDA section, led by Lisette)

PRA: Parti du Regroupement Africain–alliance of virtually all non-RDA parties (1958–9)

PRA-Sénégal: left-wing splinter-group from UPS, claiming fidelity to PRA line as defined at Cotonou Congress (1958)

PRD: Parti Républicain du Dahomey–Apithy's party from 1951

PSEMA: Parti Social d'Education des Masses Africaines–pro-chief party in eastern Upper Volta after 1954. Led by Conombo

PSP (or PPS): Parti Soudanais Progressiste–Sissoko's party, anti-RDA

PTP: Parti Togolais du Progrès–pro-French party led by Grunitzky

RDA: Rassemblement Démocratique Africain–largest group of African parties, founded 1946. Led by Houphouët

RI: Républicans Indépendants–a Conservative group in the French parliament (merged with Peasants in IPAS, 1956)

RPF: Rassemblement du Peuple Français–Gaullist party, 1947–53

RS: Républicains Sociaux–Gaullist parliamentary group 1953–8

SFIO: Section Française de l'Internationale Ouvrière–French Socialist party

T.O.M.: Territoires d'Outre-Mer (i.e. overseas territories)

UCPN: Union des Chefs et des Populations du Nord–pro-French chiefs' party in northern Togo

## Key to abbreviations

**UDD:** Union Démocratique Dahoméenne–Ahomadegbé's party, RDA section from 1956

**UDDIA:** Union Démocratique de Défense des Intérêts Africains–Youlou's party in Moyen-Congo, RDA section from 1957

**UDIT:** Union Démocratique Indépendante du Tchad–centre party, founded 1953, led by Jean-Baptiste

**UDS:** Union Démocratique Sénégalaise–Senegal section of RDA, which supported d'Arboussier against Houphouët after 1950

**UDSG:** Union Démocratique et Sociale du Gabon–Aubame's party

**UDSR:** Union Démocratique et Sociale de la Résistance–small centre-left group in National Assembly, led by Pleven

**UDT:** Union Démocratique Tchadienne–Gaullist party in Tchad, 1945–53

**UGTAN:** Union Générale des Travailleurs d'Afrique Noire–*see* p. 248

**UN:** United Nations

**UNIS:** Union Nigérienne des Indépendants et Sympathisants–anti-RDA party in Niger, led by Djermakoye until 1955

**UPC:** Union des Populations Camerounaises–nationalist party led by Um Nyobé

**UPS:** Union Progressiste Sénégalaise–ruling party in Senegal since 1958, led by Senghor and Lamine-Guèye

**US:** Union Soudanaise–Soudan section of RDA

**USA:** United States of America

**USC:** Union Sociale Camerounaise–Socialist party led by Okala

**USCC:** Union des Syndicats Confédérés du Cameroun–Cameroun section of CGT

**USSR:** Union of Soviet Socialist Republics

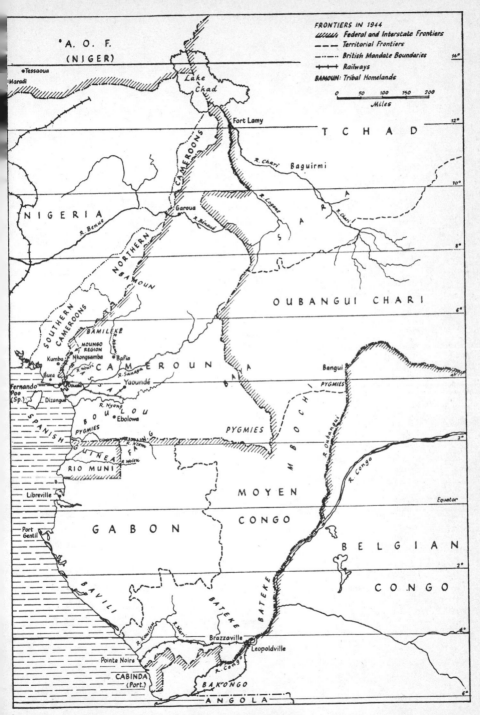

A.E.F. and Cameroun

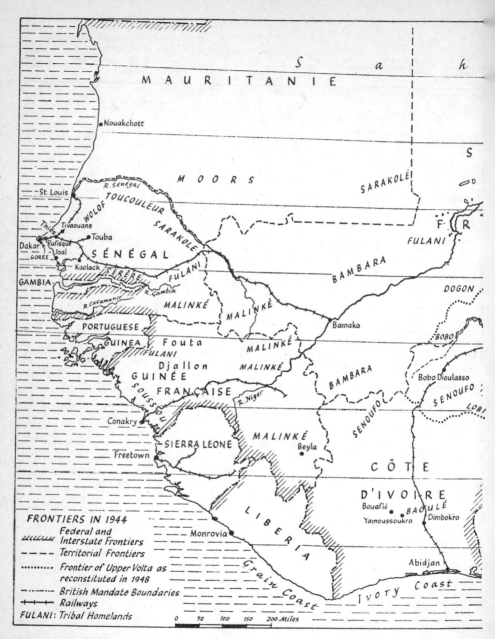

FRONTIERS IN 1944

Federal and
Interstate Frontiers
Territorial Frontiers
Frontier of Upper Volta as
reconstituted in 1948
British Mandate Boundaries
Railways
FULANI: Tribal Homelands

0    50   100   150   200 Miles

A.O.F.

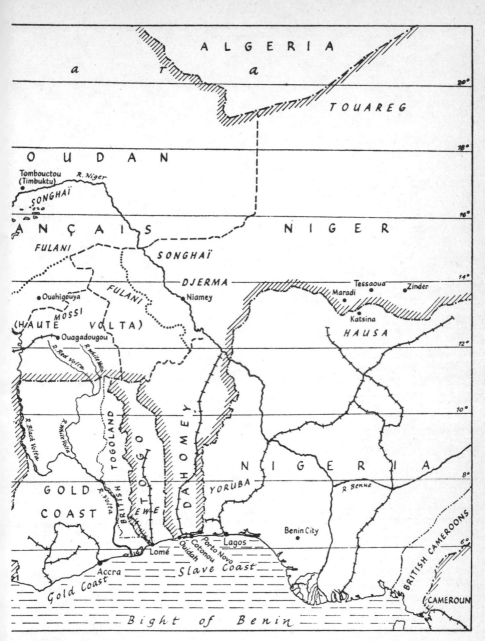

and Togo

France and French Africa

INTERNATIONAL FRONTIERS
AT END OF 1962

at the end of World War II

# Foreword

The sub-title of this book–'A Political History'– may seem super-flous. Its purpose is less to indicate what the book is than what it is not. It is intended to anticipate two criticisms which the reader might make.

The first is that the book neglects economic and social factors and concentrates on a series of political events which have little meaning when separated from their context. The second is that it is a bald narrative which fails to justify itself by any general analysis or con-clusions.

To both criticisms I plead guilty. This book was written in a very short time, almost on a whim. It attempts to say what happened but not, in any fundamental sense, why.

My motive for writing it can best be explained autobiographically. In 1962, at the age of 18, I was sent by Voluntary Service Overseas to Senegal–a country I had then barely heard of. Senegal had then been independent for a year and a half. While I was there I heard innumerable references to the time before independence, the events leading up to it, the different political parties involved and the different positions taken by their leaders at different times. The more I heard, the more confused I became. Often my informants seemed to be flatly contradicting each other.

After returning to England I read a certain number of books about French-speaking Africa, and my picture of the events leading to independence became a little clearer. But I was more and more intrigued by the close interconnection of French and African politics during this period, and by the consequent interaction of political events in different, and often quite dissimilar, African territories. I was also fascinated to see how late in the history of French Africa the politicians, including African politicians with genuine mass support, came to accept independence as the goal of their political development.

These points seemed to me to make a very important difference between French and British territories in Africa. They are, of course, points which have been made before. But they have been made principally by political scientists who were trying to analyse modern African societies and political structures. This analytical approach often leaves one's curiosity unsatisfied, and one's mind confused. One begins to feel (or I do, at least) that before answering complex questions one should attempt the simple ones: who was who, who said and did what, when, and where?

These are the questions which this book tries to answer. No doubt the reader who finishes it will find his curiosity is still unsatisfied and his mind is still confused. I hope so, and I hope he will go on to ask, 'why?', and perhaps to find out. But I also hope by then he will have in his mind a set of reasonably firm pegs (places, dates, people, *events*) on which to hang his findings.

In places, the book will probably strike the reader as anti-French. I do not claim to be exempt from that strange, atavistic *schadenfreude* which affects both French and English when discussing the failures of each other's colonial policy. But if I were to convey a sentiment to the reader, I should prefer that it were admiration for, or even envy of, the French. The idea of a multicontinental state in which Africans and French would eventually be equal partners may in retrospect seem absurd and impractical, but it was also noble; and I believe that if today relations between Africans and Frenchmen are easier and better than relations between Africans and Englishmen, that is not only due to the personality of General de Gaulle, but also to the memory of the Fourth Republic, in which France found it normal and reasonable to be represented by African deputies and governed by African ministers. Britain may have been more realistic in her colonial policy, but she was also more condescending. She would never have accepted the presence of Nkrumah or Kenyatta in the Macmillan cabinet—the idea seems delightfully absurd. Yet the equivalent is what France accepted. It may not have done much for the ordinary African's standard of living. But it was a gesture of confidence and respect; and these are what matter to a race that has endured many centuries of contempt, of all injuries the hardest to forgive.

# Foreword

NOTE ON THE TITLE

An apology is owed to any reader who opened this book hoping to find an account of what happened to Algeria, Tunisia, and Morocco. I do not dispute the right of the inhabitants of those countries to call themselves Africans, nor do I wish for one moment to suggest that events there were less important then those further south. (Most people would say that those in Algeria, at any rate, were *more* important.) But any attempt to include them would finally have burst the seams of my already overstretched chronological narrative.

The title of the book should really be 'France and the Black Africans'–i.e. the inhabitants of what the French call 'Afrique Noire'. Strictly, this term is synonymous with the American term 'sub-Saharan Africa'; but during the period covered by the book it was often used (I think almost unconsciously) in statements which can only make sense if we take it as meaning 'French tropical Africa'. I have taken the liberty of using it in this sense throughout the book.

Madagascar is *not* part of Africa. (If it were, the words 'et malgache' in 'Organisation commune africaine et malgache' (OCAM) would be redundant.) Somaliland[1] is, and deserves fuller treatment than I have given it. It got left out principally because it is so small and so far away from the other territories, but also because the most striking political events there have occurred since 1960 (some of them while I was actually writing the book). At the moment it is still a French 'territoire d'outre-mer', and it remains to be seen whether it will experience a political *dénouement* comparable to that of 1958–1960 in West and Equatorial Africa. In the much-criticised referendum of March 1967 there was a 60 per cent majority for maintaining the connection with France–but if anyone thinks that conclusive, let him read on.

NOTE ON PROPER NAMES

For the French Sudan (now Mali) I have adopted the French spelling, 'Soudan', in order to avoid confusion with the Anglo-Egyptian (now Republic of) Sudan. The spelling 'Cameroun' denotes that part of the former German colony which was placed under

[1] Since 1967 the official name of French Somaliland is 'Territoire Français des Afars et des Issas'.

French mandate in 1919. The parts mandated to Britain I refer to as 'the Cameroons' and I have reserved the form 'Cameroon' for the federal state created in 1962.

Otherwise I have left place-names in the form which seems to be most common in French, except where a different spelling is in current English usage (e.g. Timbuktu for Tombouctou). For names of persons I have used whatever spelling seems to be most common in French, except that where a name begins with two consonants (e.g. Mba) I have not put an apostrophe between them. This practice is condemned by Professor Alexandre, a leading French authority on African linguistics, who points out that in African languages these two initial consonants usually represent a single phoneme, and that to separate them therefore gives the worst possible guide to pronunciation.

Where a new character appears in the story, his name is given in bold type. The purpose of this is to reassure the reader who might otherwise wonder whether he was supposed to have heard of this character already.

NOTE ON SOURCES

This is a not a bibliography. I have given references for my material as fully as possible in the footnotes. A reader wishing to find the full title or place and date of publication of a work cited should consult the index under the author's name and then look up the first reference.

Here I want only to mention a few of the sources which I have found most useful, and which I think could be useful to anyone who wants to explore the subject further.

Of general works, it will be apparent to anyone who reads the footnotes that my debt to Dr Franz Ansprenger's *Politik im schwarzen Afrika* (Köln and Opladen 1961) is almost greater than can be decently admitted. This work, subtitled 'Die modernen politischen Bewegungen im Afrika französischer Prägung', covers substantially the same ground as my own, though with rather more detail on the social and economic background in Africa and perhaps rather less on the actual political events, particularly those in France in the earlier part of the period. Although written essentially for the West German public at a time when West Germany was just beginning to resume contact with Africa, it has as far as I know no rival, in either French or English. Certainly I would not claim that status for my own work. On the contrary, my guess is that if an English translation of Dr Ansprenger's had been available, no publisher would have thought mine worth looking at.

For the political history of Senegal, the Ivory Coast, Guinea and the Soudan (Mali), especially up to and including the mid-fifties, I have relied heavily on Ruth Schachter Morgenthau's *Political Parties in French-speaking West Africa* (London 1964). This was originally written as an Oxford D.Phil. thesis, and the author was fortunate enough to be able to spend a good deal of time in West Africa when she was writing it. She became friendly with a number of leading African politicians, notably Ouezzin Coulibaly, and can I think be regarded as the leading academic expert on the early history of the RDA sections in the Ivory Coast, Guinea and the Soudan. Her book also contains two very interesting chapters on 'West Africans in the French Parliament' and 'From AOF Federation to Sovereign Nations', which really gave me the idea for the present work.

A shorter, but also useful work, dealing with the same subject-matter from a journalist's angle is Ernest Milcent's *L'AOF entre en Scène* (Paris 1958). One should also mention the general surveys by Virginia Thompson and Richard Adloff, *French West Africa* (1958) and *The Emerging States of French Equatorial Africa* (1961). These devote relatively little space to politics, but contain a great deal of economic and geographical information.

Earlier works of considerable value are Michel Devèze, *La France d'Outre-Mer* (Paris 1948) and Jacques Richard-Molard, *Afrique Occidentale Française* (Paris 1952).

On French politics in the Fourth Republic the standard work in English is Philip Williams, *Crisis and Compromise* (London, 3rd ed. 1964 – the first edition was published in 1954 under the title *Politics in Post-War France*). For the constituent assemblies of 1945–6 this should be supplemented by Gordon Wright, *The Re-shaping of French Democracy* (1956) and for the events of 1958–60 by Philip Williams and Martin Harrison, *De Gaulle's Republic* (1960).

African politics after the Loi-Cadre are dealt with in some detail by André Blanchet in *L'Itinéraire des partis africains depuis Bamako* (Paris 1958), and Gil Dugué in *Vers les Etats-Unis d'Afrique* (Dakar 1960).

Apart from these my main sources were National Assembly debates in the *Journal Officiel*, and various newspapers published in Africa – notably the daily *Paris-Dakar* and the weekly *Afrique Nouvelle*, and some of the party papers: Lamine-Guèye's *L'AOF*, Senghor's *Condition Humaine*, Etcheverry's *Réveil* (and later *Afrique*

*Noire*), Zinsou's *L'Eveil du Bénin*, and Aujoulat's *Le Cameroun de demain*. I am extremely grateful to Dr Aujoulat for lending me a set of the latter, covering the period 1951 to 1956, as well as a large quantity of his private papers, both on Cameroun politics and on the IOM parliamentary group. The other papers I consulted mainly in the library of the Ministère de la France d'Outre-Mer, whose staff, especially Mme Morin, I should like to thank for their kindness and help.

A special word of thanks is owed to M. Max Jalade of the *Nouvelle Agence de Presse*, who not only gave me the benefit of his own extremely interesting reminiscences, but also put me in touch with others who were even more closely involved than himself in the events that I have tried to describe. For agreeing to see me and answer my questions I should like to thank: ex-President Sourou Migan Apithy, M. Robert Buron, M. Gérard Jaquet, M. Fernand Wibaux and M. Gaston Espinasse.

Mr Michael Crowder kindly allowed me to see page proofs of the second edition of his book, *Senegal* (London 1967) before publication, and also offered helpful information and advice at several stages in the book's composition. I have adopted some suggestions and corrections from Mrs Rita Cruise O'Brien, who read the manuscript on behalf of the publisher; and I am grateful also for the advice and interest of my friend Papa Kane, of the Ecole Nationale d'Economie Appliquée in Dakar.

Finally, I should like to thank Voluntary Service Overseas, which first sent me to Senegal in 1962, and All Souls College, Oxford, whose money enabled me to come to Paris in 1966, and whose liberality in interpreting its own statutes enabled me to stay there and finish this book.

Edward Mortimer

Paris, March 1968

# PART ONE

The World's Rebirth, 1944–1946

*Chapter 1*

# The Brazzaville Conference and its Background

## A. The Free French

On 30th January 1944, **Charles de Gaulle,** chairman of the Free French 'Committee of National Liberation', presided over the opening session of a conference in Brazzaville, French Equatorial Africa, which had been summoned to discuss French colonial policy, and particularly French policy in sub-Saharan Africa. That this event should receive priority among his many preoccupations, in the middle of a world war, and at a time when mainland France was in enemy hands, would have seemed odd to any pre-war French prime minister. It was an event of such apparent insignificance that the British press did not even bother to report it.

But de Gaulle had good reasons for being there. This conference was a turning-point in French colonial history, and colonial policy had never been so important to France as it was during the Second World War. Had there been no empire, there would have been no Free French territory. When de Gaulle in his broadcast of June 18th 1940 had declared that France was not finally defeated, he based this assertion not on the hope that she would eventually be liberated by her allies, but on the existence of a French empire as yet untouched by the German attack, from which France herself could continue the struggle. France's status as an imperial power thus became closely associated with her continued self-respect. The empire had been acquired partly to revive self-respect after the defeat of 1870: its existence helped self-respect to survive that of 1940. From inside France the reply to the 18th June appeal was necessarily muffled and of uncertain strength, but Cameroun and Equatorial Africa had officially accepted it by the end of August 1940. For two and a half years Brazzaville, capital of French Equatorial Africa, was also the provisional capital of what claimed to be the government of France. A force organised and equipped in Equatorial Africa crossed

27

the Sahara under General Leclerc and took part in the last stages of the North Africa campaign.

That the Free French regarded the empire as important, and Africa as particularly so, is therefore not very surprising. It enabled them to participate in, rather than merely benefit from, the Allied war effort. But Africa's importance to France had not only increased; its nature had changed. Before 1940, the essential fact had been that France ruled over very large areas of African territory; this proved that she was a great power. After 1940, the attitude of the inhabitants of this territory, and their attitude to France, began to matter too. Perhaps nothing did so much to salvage French self-respect after 1940 as the readiness of many Africans to regard themselves as Frenchmen and fight for France's liberation. Their confidence in France helped to restore France's confidence in herself.

So the Free French leaders of 1944 were striving, not merely to liberate French territory in Europe, but to recreate a French civilisation which had dramatically revealed itself as intercontinental. The nature of this civilisation was symbolised by the man who dominated the proceedings at Brazzaville: **Félix Eboué.** As governor of Tchad in 1940, Eboué had been the first in Africa to respond officially to the appeal of 18th June, and de Gaulle had subsequently appointed him Governor-General of French Equatorial Africa. He was by any standards an outstanding personality, but what made him particularly remarkable in the circumstances was that he was black. Not in fact an African by birth–he came from French Guiana–he was none the less incontestably both negro and French; both his existence and his position seemed to prove that the colonies could become, not merely subject to, but part of, France.

The stated object of the Brazzaville conference was 'to determine on what practical bases it would be possible to found stage by stage a French community including the territories of black Africa'.[1] It had first been hoped to deal with the empire as a whole, and to convene the governors of all colonies so far liberated. Practical difficulties restricted its scope to 'Afrique noire'–i.e. Africa south of the Sahara –but observers representing the governors of Morocco, Algeria and Tunisia were also present, and it was clear that the conclusions reached at Brazzaville would influence French colonial policy everywhere. The intention was, in de Gaulle's words, 'to choose nobly and liberally the road to the new era towards which she (France) intends to direct the sixty million men who find themselves involved in the

[1] Charles de Gaulle, War Memoirs, Vol. II (*L'Unité, 1942–1944*, Paris 1956).

destiny of her forty-two million children,' and he went on to make it clear that one of the principal reasons for France's preoccupation with this problem was that 'in the extremity to which a temporary defeat had reduced her, it was in her overseas territories, none of whose population in any part of the world, wavered for a single moment in their magnificent loyalty,[1] that she found her refuge and the starting-point for her liberation, and as a result of this there is from now on a permanent bond between the Mother Country and the Empire.'[2]

## B. International Considerations

Even if de Gaulle had not been moved by genuine gratitude to the Africans for their part in the war effort, he would almost certainly have felt it necessary to make some re-statement of colonial policy before the end of the war, in order to forestall any possible dismemberment of France's empire by her victorious allies. In 1919 only the defeated powers had been deprived of their colonies, but the international climate had changed since then, and the Second World War called the very existence of colonialism into question.

In the first place, the spectacular reverses suffered at the beginning of the war by the two main colonial powers effectively destroyed their semi-conscious assumption that they had a natural right to rule the 'uncivilised' world. In Africa this assumption had been strengthened by a widespread acceptance of it even among the natives–to the extent at least that white power was assumed to be invincible. The collapse of France in 1940, and the subsequent struggle for French loyalty between rival authorities, deprived the Frenchman in Africa of much of his prestige. Certainly black Africans did not immediately revolt against France; on the contrary, they rallied to her defence. But the realisation that she actually needed their help, that they were no longer being lectured like children but appealed to as brothers, was clearly going to make it difficult to retain an authoritarian system of government after the peace.

The British, too, had to accept that the war marked the end of the old colonial era. For them the traumatic experience came in the Far East, and significantly it was a defeat of whites by non-whites. The

[1] This sounded good but was not strictly true. Both Vietnamese and Tunisian nationalist movements took some advantage of France's plight. Also, in many parts of the empire, including West Africa and Somaliland, the population had followed the lead of its rulers in being loyal to Pétain rather than de Gaulle.

[2] de Gaulle, ibid.

fall of Singapore was described by *The Times* as 'the greatest blow which has befallen the British Empire since the loss of the American colonies . . . British dominion in the Far East can never be restored – nor will there be any desire to restore it – in its former guise'. Traditional British colonialism stood condemned by the fact that in the face of Japanese invasion, 'the bulk of the Asiatic population remained spectators from start to finish'. In the light of this, British politicians were forced to re-examine their colonial policy in Africa as well. 'Will the same be true of the African population? Will they also remain spectators if Japan should reach the shores of Africa one day?,' asked an M.P. in a debate on the use of forced labour in Kenya. 'If we pursue the sort of policy in Kenya which has been suggested, we shall undoubtedly find that the inhabitants of Kenya will not only be spectators but will not help us and may even help the enemy.'[1] Meanwhile Churchill, once the passionate defender of British India, could be heard promising independence in return for Indian co-operation in the war. Not surprisingly, many British people began to feel that the peace conference would be the moment to wind up the old colonial system.

But it was in the United States that this feeling was really widespread. Many Americans took literally the war aim stated in Article 3 of the Atlantic Charter: 'they respect the right of all peoples to choose the form of government under which they live; and they wish to see sovereign rights restored to those who have been forcibly deprived of them'. This implied some very radical changes if applied to Africa – and Roosevelt insisted that the Charter applied to the whole world. In the view of many Americans, such changes were in any case overdue. Conscious both of their own past as an oppressed colonial people, and of the large minority of negroes in their midst, they were anxious to see the African peoples progress towards self-government. The British were relatively well-placed to respond to this challenge, having always proposed self-government as the eventual, even if distant, goal of colonial development. Even so, Margery Perham, who was sent on a lecture tour to explain British policy in Africa to Americans at the end of the war, met with a predominantly hostile or uncomprehending reception.[2] It was all the more necessary for the French, whose status as a great power was much less certain, and whose colonial policy had never been devolutionary even in

[1] See *The Atlantic Charter and Africa from an American Standpoint* (New York 1943).
[2] M. Perham, *The Colonial Reckoning* (London 1963).

theory, to redefine their empire in terms acceptable to American opinion.

Even more uncompromisingly anti-imperialist, though herself a successfully disguised colonial power,[1] was the other great Allied power, the Soviet Union. And the Soviet attitude was particularly important to France because it dictated that of the French Communist Party (PCF), a group whose prestige and following were greatly increased by its role in the wartime resistance. Any French government would be forced to take some account of Stalin's views on colonialism. Stalin favoured the separation of colonies from their mother countries, even under a 'bourgeois' national leadership, because he accepted Lenin's theory that colonies are a necessary outlet for capital in the 'putrefying' stage of industrial capitalism. The independence of the colonies would therefore bring on the final crisis of capitalism at home and so facilitate the proletarian revolution. Hence communist support for 'wars of national liberation', and the identification of the interests of colonial nationalists with those of the proletariat at home. French communists were already setting up 'Study Groups' in African colonies to help create a national consciousness and a sense of solidarity against exploitation by French capitalists. This was yet another threat which could only be met by extensive colonial reform. The French empire could only survive if it succeeded in clearing itself of the charge of 'Imperialist exploitation'.[2]

## C. French Imperial Theory. 'Assimilation'

Such were the main pressures which led to radical change in the relationship between France and her African colonies during and after 1944. But before we describe or assess that change, we must make a brief survey of previous French policy in Africa.

French and British rule in Africa were less different in practice than has sometimes been suggested, but the ideas that governed the thinking of French and British about Africa, especially in the thinking of those who were not themselves directly involved in governing Africa, *were* different. Both, it is true, were anxious to spread

[1] The present-day Soviet Union, commonly referred to as 'Russia', contains a number of Asiatic Moslem countries conquered by Russian armies in the nineteenth century.

[2] The PCF's attitude is described in greater detail below, pages 72–3 and 80. See also M. H. Fabré, *Le Séparatisme Colonial Stalinien et ses manifestations dans l'ordre juridique international* (*Pénant*, April–May 1954).

'civilisation', in the sense of putting an end to tribal war, human sacrifice and the slave trade; and many people in both countries associated this negative task with the positive one of spreading trade and the Christian religion. But only in France was this idea of 'civilisation' associated with that of citizenship. Only France expected to 'assimilate' its colonial subjects to the point where, not only culturally but legally and politically, they would actually be Frenchmen.

The origins of this idea of assimilation have been traced as far back as Louis XIV, who remarked to a prince from the Ivory Coast who had spent a year at his court: 'there is no longer any difference between you and me, except that you are black and I am white.'[1] Certainly well before the end of the eighteenth century the French-speaking Africans living in Saint-Louis and Gorée (Senegal) were describing themselves as Frenchmen and objecting in that capacity to their treatment by British conquerors during the Seven Years' War. Soon afterwards they took the 1789 Declaration of Rights to apply to them and became embarrassingly fervent Jacobins.[2] At a moment when France was fighting to extend the privilege of French citizenship to the oppressed peoples of Europe, it seemed logical to extend it also to her non-European subjects. All had been slaves under the Bourbon tyranny–so ran the argument– and all should now be free citizens of the French republic. Thus in February 1794 Danton and Delacroix succeeding in persuading the Convention to vote not only the abolition of slavery but at the same time that 'all men, without distinction of colour, who live in the colonies, are French citizens and enjoy all the rights guaranteed by the Constitution.'[3]

This law was repealed by Napoleon[4] before it could have much practical effect, but the ideal which it embodied was not forgotten. As long as the colonial empire was limited to a few small coastal settlements, in which the native population was more or less urbanised and de-tribalised, it was not unreasonable to hope that the ideal could be realised. When slavery was again abolished in 1848, the colonies were given representation in the French National Assembly

[1] Quoted in Franz Ansprenger, *Politik im schwarzen Afrika*, p. 42.
[2] See J. D. Hargreaves, 'Assimilation in Late Eighteenth-century Senegal', *Journal of African History*, 1964.
[3] Loi du 16 pluviôse, An II. Robespierre, when making notes for the indictment against Danton, noted that he had introduced 'a law tending to provoke the dissolution of the empire'. (See H. Morse Stephens (ed.), *Orators of the French Revolution* Vol. II.)
[4] Loi du 16 floréal, An IX.

–this was, as it were, the French reply to any possible cry of 'no taxation without representation' from the colonists. At this time the only French possessions in sub-Saharan Africa were three minute trading-stations in Gabon and the Ivory Coast and the two settlements of Saint-Louis (at the mouth of the Senegal River) and Gorée, an island in what is now the harbour of Dakar. The African inhabitants of Saint-Louis and Gorée, and later also those of Dakar and nearby Rufisque, voted in elections for a deputy from Senegal to the National Assembly in both Second and Third Republics. Although nominally deprived of their citizenship in 1857, they continued to enjoy the political rights of French citizens, and indeed were usually known as such. Though the majority of the electorate there was negro, until 1914 the deputy for Senegal was always either European or mulatto.

By 1914, however, Senegal was no longer a tenuous French foothold on an unknown continent, but the gateway to a French African Empire of some seven million square kilometers. This vast hinterland was not represented in the French parliament, and probably few Frenchmen seriously expected that its entire population could ever be assimilated to the point of full French citizenship. Some attempts were made to produce an alternative colonial theory which would meet this new situation: Lyautey, founder of the French Protectorate in Morocco, favoured a policy similar to Lord Lugard's 'indirect rule'–building up and working through the power of traditional native rulers. Perhaps more influential was Jules Harmand's idea of a *politique d'association*. Harmand's book, *Domination et Colonisation*, published in 1910, derided the assimilation policy as a bankrupt attempt to extend to 'dominations'–i.e. possessions with a predominantly non-European subject population –principles which could only apply to 'colonies' in the old sense of settlements of emmigrants from the mother country. In any case, Harmand thought, it was nonsense to pretend that either sort of possession was 'an integral part of the national territory'; they were merely part of the nation's *property*. They should not be represented in Parliament, but governed on an authoritarian, paternalistic principle by Governors who, as delegates of the national government, would have a virtually free hand, would be 'heads or presidents of States rather than administrative functionaries'. Harmand summed up his system as 'the largest amount of administrative, economic and financial independence that is compatible with the greatest possible political dependence'.

Harmand was influential in the sense that many people read his book and agreed with much of what he said, and that before 1940 a paternalistic attitude to colonial subjects, particularly Africans, was more common than an egalitarian one. But if assimilation was soft-pedalled, it was never officially abandoned; and certainly no serious attempt was ever made to put 'association' into practice. The French empire remained highly centralised and was considered by most Frenchmen to be, like the Republic itself, a heritage to be preserved, one and indivisible.

### D. The League of Nations Mandates

In other words, French imperialism was pointing in a different direction from British, even if before 1940 both remained largely static. Consequently it was in different directions that they started developing after 1940. A British imperialist, if he thought in terms of progress, would think of it as an advance towards self-government; for a French imperialist, progress would imply closer integration with the mother country, and political maturity would mean not the rule of Africans by Africans—which after all had existed before the imperial power arrived—but the participation of Africans as Frenchmen in the government of a greater France.

Such a conception of progress certainly involved grave, perhaps insuperable, difficulties in practice; they form the main subject of this book. In principle, however, it was unobjectionable as long as one argued in a purely French context—that is to say, in one in which the superiority of French culture and French nationality as against any other was taken for granted. It was less likely to gain adherents in an international context, where individual nations were seen merely as agents of a broader community into which backward peoples were to be initiated. In this latter context it would cease to be obvious that such peoples could best reach civilisation via French nationality, and the Anglo-Saxon idea that they should eventually be members of the civilised community in their own right was more likely to be accepted.

Such an international context for imperial expansion, or at least for public discussion of it, existed right from the beginning of the scramble for Africa. The Belgian Congo was explored and conquered by the agents of Leopold II under the banner of an 'International African Association' with ostensibly humanitarian aims. More genuinely international were the Berlin and Brussels Conferences of 1885 and 1890, at which an international civilising mission was clearly recognised by all the great imperial powers, and this mission was already thought of as analogous to trusteeship or guardianship. Thus a French parliamentarian was able to say of the Brussels Conference: 'France had only to remain faithful to her own principles in presenting to the Conference proposals which were really tutelary . . .'[1] In so far as France's own principles involved assimilation, this statement was inaccurate; for tutelage is normally understood as temporary and revocable, not a complete and permanent absorption of the ward into the guardian's personality.

Since the Berlin and Brussels conferences set up no international authority to which France could be held accountable for her fulfilment of the civilising mission, such theoretical contradictions could easily be ignored. But the problem became more real with the creation of the League of Nations Mandate system in 1919.

During the First World War both the German and the Turkish colonial empires were conquered by the Allies, and at the end of it no one was disposed simply to hand them back. It was not, however, thought proper to treat them openly as spoils of war, and the *de facto* partition between the Allies was therefore legitimised by 'mandates' from the newly formed League of Nations. There were to be three different sorts, christened imaginatively by Lord Milner 'A', 'B' and 'C'. Type A, intended for the Arab states, provisionally recognised their independence but assigned them a Mandatory to 'guide their administration until the moment when they will be capable of governing themselves'. Type C, intended for South West Africa and the German colonies in the Pacific, authorised the Mandatory to administer them under its own laws and 'as an integral part of its own territory'.

In between these two came Type B, which covered the German colonies of tropical Africa; here the Mandatory was to 'assume the administration of the territory on conditions which, with the prohibition of abuses, such as the slave trade and the sale of firearms and alcohol, will guarantee freedom of conscience and religion . . .' etc. It was on these terms that France and Britain obtained confirmation of their partition of the Cameroons and Togoland. But whereas the British merged the administration of their sectors with that of Nigeria and the Gold Coast respectively, the French did not

[1] See League of Nations pamphlet *Le Système des Mandats. Origine, principes et applications* (Geneva 1954).

bring Cameroun into the federation of French Equatorial Africa (AEF) or Togo into that of French West Africa (AOF).[1] The reason for this seems clear. The Covenant spoke of the mandated territories as being 'not *yet* able to stand by themselves' and obliged the mandatory powers to make annual reports to the League on their progress. The juridical implications of this were not at all certain, but seemed to be that the mandate conferred something less than full sovereignty, and that its eventual, if remote, goal was self-government for the mandated territory. Territories accepted on such terms could not be legally integrated into the French Republic without damaging its indivisibility; they could not be assimilated to French Africa without jeopardising the hoped-for assimilation of French Africa into France itself. Even without legal integration – as we shall see – their very existence, and their inevitably close contacts with adjacent French territories, tended to have this effect.

### E. Realities of French Rule in Africa

If assimilation remained the ideal, at least to those who accepted the Jacobin tradition, it was still in 1940 very far from being the reality of French rule in Afrique Noire. Only the Four Communes of Senegal were represented in the French parliament. Rural Senegal, and all other Black African territories in their entirety, were a purely executive responsibility; the government could legislate for them by decree, without reference to Parliament. And as French governments during the Third Republic tended to be weak and of short duration, real power slipped into the hands of the Governors-General of AOF and AEF, heads of centralised authoritarian hierarchies running down through the territorial governors to *commandants de cercle* and *chefs de subdivision* and then to native authorities appointed by the French administration: *chefs de canton* and *chefs de village*.[2]

The key figure in the French colonial system was the *commandant de cercle* – roughly the equivalent of the British District Commissioner. He carried a general responsibility for everything in his area: roads,

[1] Although Togo and Dahomey were jointly administered for a time after the economic depression of 1929. (See R. Cornevin, *Histoire du Togo* (2nd ed., Paris 1962) and *Histoire du Dahomey* (Paris 1962).)

[2] The office of *chef de canton* was invented by the French, and often corresponded to nothing at all in the traditional structure of the African society on which it was imposed. Its holder's standing with the French officials above him depended principally on his efficiency and punctuality in supplying the tax-quota. If he did this regularly, he was usually not strictly supervised and his methods of assessing and collecting taxes were not investigated.

justice, health services, police, agricultural development, etc. Under him the African chiefs were supposed to represent a traditional native authority. Up to a point they did, but in many cases the chief recognised by the French was not the true chief in African eyes, but a man of straw put forward as a buffer between the village and the administration. This was not surprising, since chiefs were usually treated with scant respect by French officials, and often deposed or punished in person for their 'subjects' 'misdemeanours, such as failure to pay taxes or provide the labour force for public works. Nor was their popularity or prestige increased by the fact that they supplemented their miserably low wages by taking a percentage of the taxes they collected, and often by collecting illegal supplementary taxes.[1]

One feature of French administration particularly resented by the Africans was the *indigénat*. This was the name of the group of provisions in the criminal code which permitted administrators to impose punishments on African subjects without reference to a court of law. It was in fact an intentionally arbitrary weapon for use by the administration against any African who was troublesome. As codified in 1924 it authorised for some cases punishments as heavy as deportation, or in Cameroun imprisonment for as much as ten years. By 1940 it was normally restricted to five days' imprisonment or 100 francs' fine. Even so it remained a keenly felt grievance for many Africans, who understandably disliked being subjected to this schoolmasterly discipline.

Separate from the *indigénat*, though often confused with it, was the 'native penal code'. This was at least administered by courts of law, but it created a large category of actions which were quite legal for French citizens, but became criminal offences carrying heavy penalties when committed by African 'subjects'.

There were so-called 'native courts' for both civil and criminal cases at the level of the subdivision and the *cercle*. But since they were presided over by a French administrator and could inflict penalties up to and including death or penal servitude for life, Africans could hardly welcome them as an opportunity to manage their own affairs.

However, undoubtedly the worst abuse of French pre-war colonial rule was the widespread use of forced labour. The most notorious examples were those resulting from the rule of large concessionary

---

[1] See J. Suret-Canale, 'Fin de la Chefferiel en Guinée', *Journal of African History*, 1966.

companies in AEF, which were exposed by André Gide in his *Voyage au Congo* (1927). The public outcry in France which followed the publication of this work hastened the end of the system of granting territorial concessions. But it was by no means the end of forced labour as such; it continued to be used legally by the administration and illegally by private enterprise (usually with the administration's connivance) in many different parts of French Africa.[1] The conditions in which it was performed were often apalling. A particularly high mortality rate was noted among workers on the Brazzaville Pointe-Noire railway in Moyen-Congo; while on the Ivory Coast cocoa and coffee plantations 'the whip and the stick were in current practice'.[2] Here the evil was accentuated by the forced transportation of the workers from their more populous homeland of Upper Volta to the thinly populated plantation areas; and from 1937 onwards it got worse as demand for the plantation products rose, while the supply of workers began to decline.

To a large extent the use of forced labour was an almost inevitable result of the chronic shortage of funds from which the pre-war French administration in Africa suffered. The official view in Paris was that once conquered and pacified, colonies should be expected to live of their own. Since 1900 both AOF and AEF had been financially 'autonomous'– that is, they had their own budgets; only military expenditure was underwritten by France, along with such loans as might be necessary in times of crisis. The territorial concessions system in AEF was an attempt to bribe private enterprise into bearing the initial costs of economic development. It failed largely because the companies were anxious for quick results, and therefore concentrated on extracting raw materials as fast as possible by methods which were not only brutal but in the long run inefficient since the available labour force was terrorised, antagonised and sometimes literally destroyed.

By and large, the French had come off with the poorer and less populous bits of Africa in the grand scramble, and probably they could never have made imperialism there a very profitable venture. At all events, until 1944 they quite failed to realise how large an initial outlay was required before any visible return could be expected. French Black Africa remained a land of bad roads, few

[1] The main instrument for forcing Africans to work was taxation. A subsistence farmer had either to go and work for a wage in order to pay his taxes or, because he had no money, be conscripted for work by the administration.

[2] R. S. Morgenthau, *Political Parties in French-speaking West Africa* (Oxford 1964), p. 4, quoting a report of 1931.

railways, no industry to speak of, and in most places primitive peasant agriculture.

Theoretically, the assimilation policy meant that any French colonial 'subject' could be 'naturalised' as a full French citizen. In practice, even those who reached a high enough level of education usually did not attempt to avail themselves of this privilege, largely because, except in the Four Communes, French citizenship was incompatible with the retention of one's 'personal status'– i.e. the right to live by African customary law as opposed to the French *code civil*. There was a certain logic in this from a strict assimilationist point of view: if you were going to be a Frenchman politically you should behave like one socially and accept such institutions as monogamy and French inheritance laws. But its effect underlined the failure of assimilation, for on these terms assimilation was not a saleable commodity; and so, outside the Four Communes, 'citizen' remained virtually synonymous with 'European'.

If assimilation meant anything, it should have involved the spreading of French education. Yet here again the close-fistedness of the French government overcame its ideological generosity. In 1945 only five per cent of Africans in the relevant age-group were receiving primary education. (In 1947 the figure reached ten per cent for Dahomey–where there were most mission schools–and 12·4 per cent for Senegal, but it was still only 1·3 per cent in Guinea.)[1] For secondary education the percentage was of course far smaller, and except in Senegal there were no university graduates at all. Again, it was only in Senegal that the few who were educated had any say in how they were governed. The Four Communes, as well as being the only area represented by a deputy in Paris, were the only towns in Afrique Noire with elected town councils; and Senegal was the only colony with an elected colonial council.

## F. The Beginnings of Modern African Politics

(a) *Among the 'Subjects':* Outside Senegal there was therefore no electoral politics before 1940. But there were one or two semi-political or political movements.

MATSOUANISM: **André Matsoua** was the leader of an *amicaliste* movement which spread rapidly among the ba-Lari (a sub-group of the ba-Kongo tribe) in and around Brazzaville after 1928. He

[1] Table in Ansprenger, op. cit.

himself was an educated man (*évolué*) who had worked for some time in Paris; he protested against specific French abuses like the *indigénat* and the government's failure to promote economic development in AEF. But his followers tended to regard him more as a religious than as a political leader, and their chief form of protest was passive resistance against all Western innovations. They refused to co-operate with the administration in agricultural reform, social security, censuses, labour recruitment, or indeed anything.

GABONESE GROUPS: Libreville, capital of Gabon, was founded in 1848 as a settlement for freed slaves. Though less advanced than the Senegalese Communes, and lacking their political privileges, it did have an older tradition of French civilisation and a longer experience of urban life, than any other town outside Senegal. In 1920 a group of young *évolués* did actually found a political party, the *Jeune Gabonais*. But it was not a success. The administration opposed it; it was weakened by internal dissensions; and improvements in the economic situation cut some of the ground from under it. After a few years all that remained was the knowledge that an African élite existed and was capable of organising itself.

The dominant tribe in Gabon was the Fang, who adapted readily to Western methods and spread rapidly after French rule was imposed on the interior in the late nineteenth century. In the Libreville area they came into conflict with the Mpongwe and other coastal groups which had been the original allies of the French. At the same time, different Fang sub-groups lost contact with each other as they spread out, and the authority of the traditional chiefs declined. Leadership passed to the most Westernised elements—wage-earners and educated men. One of the latter was **Léon Mba,** a civil servant born in Libreville who decided to specialise in the study of Fang customary law. The French made him a *chef de canton*, then (in 1934) dismissed him because he supported a movement to rebuild the unity of the tribe – the 'Bwiti cult' – which they suspected of being anti-French. In fact it was more religious than political, but Mba gained from it a prestige which he was later to turn to political account.[1]

[1] See Virginia Thompson and Richard Adloff, *The Emerging States of French Equatorial Africa* (London 1960).

DAHOMEY:[1] The case of southern Dahomey is altogether special. It had more in common, and closer contacts, with nearby Lagos than any other parts of AOF. (See p. 194.) Intensive missionary activity in the ports of Ouidah, Porto Novo and Cotonou, the existence of a coastal élite of liberated slaves from Brazil and their descendents, a long history of contact with Europeans through the slave trade, a tradition of political organisation inherited from the kingdoms of Porto Novo (which became a French protectorate in 1882–1883) and Abomey (whose last independent King, Behanzin, was deported to Martinique in 1894)–all these circumstances contributed to the early growth of political consciousness in Dahomey.

Before and during the First World War, political protest focused on the person of Governor **Charles Noufflard.** His opponents among the Dahomeyan population–notably **Tovalou Quenum,** a Porto Novo businessman, and **Louis Hunkanrin,** who taught at a government school in Ouidah until dismissed for indiscipline in 1910 – took advantage of their Senegalese connections to publish attacks on him in Dakar and Paris newspapers. In 1914 Hunkanrin formed a Dahomeyan branch of the *Ligue des Droits de l'Homme,* which bombarded the Government-General in Dakar with complaints about Noufflard's administration, and in December of that year he had to flee the territory, only to continue his campaign against Noufflard from beyond the Nigerian frontier. Next year two other teachers in Ouidah, **Paul Hazoumé** and **Emile Zinsou Bodé,** started a clandestine monthly, *Le Récadaire de Behanzin,* whose *raison d'être* was likewise to attack Noufflard. The offending governor was finally removed in 1917 after a Government-General investigation.

In 1918 Hunkanrin returned to French territory as a protégé of **Blaise Diagne,** whom he had helped in the Senegal election of 1914 (see below page 43), and was given a job in Paris, in charge of colonial troops. But his presence at anarchist meetings and his contributions to anti-colonialist journals soon lost him the favour of the government, and in 1920 he was court-martialled at Dakar and imprisoned for six months, after which he was returned to Dahomey, demobilised and given a further sentence of three years' imprisonment and five years' banishment from Porto Novo (the territorial capital). This did not prevent him from continuing to agitate, now in alliance with elements

[1] This section is based mainly on John Ballard, 'The Porto Novo Incidents of 1923: Politics in the Colonial Era' in *Odu,* July 1965. (French translation in *Etudes Dahoméennes,* of the same date.)

that were opposed by the French, both in the Porto Novo royal family and in the Moslem community.

Anti-colonial literature was regularly forwarded to Dahomey from Paris by friends of Hunkanrin's and Quenum's and from the end of 1920 onwards there were also constant attacks on Noufflard's successor, Governor **Fourn,** in the local paper, *Le Guide du Dahomey*. The *Ligue des Droits de l'Homme* was revived and used as a cover for political activities (as also happened in Gabon), working in alliance with a local branch of the *Comite Franco-Musulman*. All this activity culminated in the great strikes and incidents of February-March 1923, whose immediate origin was a sharp increase in taxes. The declared aims of the strikers were: the restoration of the protectorate in place of the direct colonial rule to which Dahomey had been subject since 1900; the reduction of taxes; the replacement of the official king of Porto Novo by a rival claimant, **Sognigbé**; the release of Hunkanrin; the removal of Governor Fourn and his chief assistant, Maria. Telegrams were sent to the French *Ligue des Droits de l'Homme* and to an opposition newspaper in Senegal, *L'AOF*, comparing the reprisal measures adopted by Fourn and Maria to 'boche atrocities during the war'– a propaganda line which was to be much favoured by Africans after World War Two. Eventually six of the movements' leaders, including Hunkanrin, Sognigbé, and the leaders of both the *Ligue* and the *Comite Franco-Musulman*, were sentenced to ten years' internment in Mauritania. Only Hunkanrin survived the experience.

That was the end of the radical phase in Dahomeyan politics, but individual Dahomeyans retained links with the *Association Pan-Africaine* in Paris, where a son of Behanzin was a prominent figure in the anti-colonial movement of the twenties.[1] Many Dahomeyans benefited from a clause in the second Loi Diagne (see below) which gave citizenship to educated Africans who had done military service in Europe, and by 1945 Dahomey was the only territory besides Senegal where a majority of the 'citizens' were African. From 1928 onwards the election of African delegates to the territorial administrative council stimulated political activity both in the press and in electoral committees; and some veterans of the early struggles– notably Hunkanrin himself and Paul Hazoumé–lived on to take part in the politics of the postwar era.

[1] I was told this by Mr James Spiegler of Nuffield College, Oxford.

TOGO AND CAMEROUN: In the Mandated territories political activity first arose from the tension between the German- and French-educated élites. The former naturally tended to favour a return to German rule so that they could regain their previous privileged position. The *Bund der Deutschen Togoländer* was sending petitions in this respect to the League of Nations from 1929 onwards. When Hitler began to demand the restitution of German colonies, the French responded by encouraging the formation of pro-French groups: a *Cercle des Amitiés Françaises* was formed in Lomé (capital of Togo) in 1936, and *Jeunesse Camerounaise Française* (JEUCAFRA) in 1937. The latter actually demanded that Cameroun be made formally a French colony and fully integrated into AEF. Both these groups represented a tiny élite of clerks and small business-men in the coastal towns (Lomé and Douala). Their African leaders were respectively **Sylvanus Olympio,** a local representative of the United Africa Company, and **Paul Soppo Priso,** an independent building contractor.[1]

(b) *Among the 'citizens' of coastal Senegal:* The inhabitants of the Senegalese Four Communes were in every respect a privileged group in French Africa. For them alone assimilation was a reality, in the first place because of their comparatively easy access to French education, including secondary education. (In Saint-Louis, for example, two-thirds of the 230 pupils at the lycée in 1936 were Africans.) A number of outstanding pupils were even able to go to France for higher-level courses. Veterinary science was the subject thought most suitable for Africans by the government, but some did succeed in taking university degrees in such subjects as law and French literature.[2]

Although the natives–*originaires*– of the Four Communes had voting rights, until the First World War their status as citizens was not established, and the administration seemed to be trying to whittle away their privileges. They reacted against these attempts and in 1914 elected, for the first time, a black African as their representative in the Chamber of Deputies: Blaise Diagne.[3] Asserting the readiness

[1] See R. Cornevin, *Histoire du Togo* (2nd ed., Paris 1962), and Father Engelbert Mveng's *Histoire du Cameroun* (Paris 1963).

[2] Morgenthau, op. cit., p. 11.

[3] See G. Wesley Johnson, 'Blaise Diagne and the beginning of African politics in Senegal' (*Africa*, 1966) for an excellent account of the election campaign, vigorously conducted by the various white candidates with methods reminiscent of the great Duke of Newcastle. Diagne's victory came as a complete shock to the administration.

of his compatriots to accept the military obligations of citizenship as well as its privileges, Diagne promised to recruit forces in West Africa for the war. In return Parliament confirmed by laws of 1915 and 1916 that all natives of the Four Communes and their descendants were automatically full French citizens without having to renounce their 'personal status' or fulfil any other qualifications.[1]

From this time onwards the distinction between citizens and subjects in Senegal became almost as important as that between Africans and Europeans. The subjects remained excluded from electoral politics. It is true that from 1920 they were represented on the colonial council, but only through the chiefs, who were appointed and controlled by the administration. Only in 1939, as a further war recruiting measure, was direct representation extended to subjects who had completed their military service.[2]

Meanwhile the citizens were increasingly politicised. Blaise Diagne was rewarded for his recruiting activities with a junior portfolio in the Ministry of Colonies. In the Chamber of Deputies he belonged to a series of different Socialist groups, but in Senegal his followers were known simply as 'Diagnistes', and he owed his continued re-election entirely to his personal prestige. Some of the younger Senegalese *évolués* became critical of his inertia. In 1925 he was defeated in the Saint-Louis mayoral election by a young radical lawyer, **Amadou Lamine-Guèye,** who had connections with Socialists in France. Later Lamine-Guèye, in co-operation with the president of the Dakar Chamber of Commerce (a European), started a *Parti Socialiste Senegalais.* In the general elections of 1928 and 1932 they supported a rival candidate, **Galandou Diouf,** against Diagne–but unsuccessfully.[3] Then in 1934 Diagne died; there was a by-election which Diouf won, supported by the former Diagnistes but now opposed by Lamine-Guèye.

This result was repeated in the general election of 1936; but this time the victory of the Popular Front brought Lamine-Guèye's friends to power in France; a Socialist, **Marius Moutet,** became Minister of Colonies. In Dakar Lamine-Guèye organised a local 'Popular Front Committee' which gave Moutet an enthusiastic welcome when he visited Senegal. Immediately afterwards a Senegalese section of the French Socialist party (SFIO: *Section Française*

[1] Ansprenger, op. cit., p. 43.
[2] Kenneth Robinson, 'Political Development in French West Africa' in *Africa in the Modern World*, ed. Calvin Stillmann (Chicago 1955).
[3] The administration apparently rigged these elections in Diagne's favour. (I owe this information to Mrs Rita Cruise O'Brien.)

*de l'Internationale Ouvrière*) was formed. Lamine-Guèye was its political director. He himself was a showpiece of successful assimilation: a qualified barrister and Doctor of Law, on familiar terms with many French left-wing politicians and intellectuals. His political programme was by no means anti-French, but rather a demand for more–and more genuine–assimilation; he wanted to see citizen privileges extended to the subject. Yet his personal following was confined to the existing citizen body, and was strongest among the educated middle-class–so that paradoxically the Socialist party in Senegal tended to become a party of privilege. As so often in the future, an apparently ideological French party label was used to disguise a loose coalition of interests held together by ethnic and personal loyalties.[1]

## G. French Policy from 1936 to 1944

*The Popular Front:* Moutet was not the only member of the Popular Front government who was interested in colonial affairs. **Léon Blum,** the prime minister, had himself helped to publicise Gide's revelations about the atrocities in AEF, and his reform programme included provisions to help colonial subjects: it was made easier for them to qualify for citizenship and possible for some in AOF to join trade unions. But plans to abolish forced labour and reform the *indigénat* remained on the drawing-board (like much of the Front's internal programme). Nonetheless, Africans continued to have faith in France–to judge at least from the enthusiastic response to the recruiting campaign of 1939. That faith was shaken but not broken by the armistice of 1940 and the events which followed it.

*The Vichy Régime in West Africa:* In AOF and Togo the French administration accepted the armistice and did not rally to de Gaulle until November 1942, after the Allied invasions of North Africa. For nearly two and a half years, therefore, these countries were controlled by the Vichy government. During this period republican ideals, including assimilation, were abandoned. Africans had some good reasons to regret the change. For the first time racial discrimination was openly and methodically practised in shops, trains and hotels. In Senegal various democratic institutions were suppressed– as were the advisory *conseils d'administration* in the other colonies.

---

[1] Morgenthau, pp. 132–3. I am told there is a valid comparison with municipal politics in the United States.

A number of Senegalese citizens were arrested for conspiring with left-wing Frenchmen to overthrow the régime. The African conspirators were quickly executed, while the Europeans were allowed to escape and then condemned *in absentia*.[1]

But these changes mainly affected the educated minority, and especially the citizens. The mass of the population had never been treated as equals by Europeans anyway, and they were used to authoritarian government. From the economic point of view they may even have benefited from Vichy rule, since it meant that African producers remained in contact with their markets in metropolitan France, and profited to some extent from a rise in prices resulting from shortages in Europe.

Vichy's official African policy was one of benevolent paternalism. Some efforts were made to improve vocational training, provide assistance for peasant cultivators and promote industrialisation. There was even an attempt to win over some educated Africans: the Governor-General sponsored a youth weekly, *Dakar-Jeunes*, in whose pages appeared strongly pro-French items by, among others, **Ouezzin Coulibaly** and **Mamadou Dia**. Coulibaly, born in Upper Volta, was at this time a professor at the famous Ecole Normale William Ponty near Dakar – a teacher-training college which provided the nearest thing to higher education available in Afrique Noire. Dia was a Senegalese subject schoolmaster, himself trained at the Ecole Ponty. Both these men had important political careers ahead of them. It is of some interest that the Vichy régime should have encouraged them to express themselves in print.[2]

Vichy's colonial policy has probably had a worse press than it deserved, partly because those who agitated for colonial reform after the Liberation often associated with Vichy, for propaganda purposes, abuses that had existed long before 1940. Some abuses got worse owing to the difficult conditions created by the war – but this is probably truer of the period after West Africa came back into the war on the Gaullist side than of the Vichy period itself. The Gaullists never succeeded in arousing the same enthusiasm in West as they did in Equatorial Africa, where they were in control from the start. Marshal Pétain, on the other hand, was the object of much genuine loyalty, especially among veterans who had served under him in the

---

[1] This is stated by Lamine-Guèye in his autobiography, *Itinéraire Africain* (Paris 1966), but disputed by the British scholar Michael Crowder in *Senegal* (London 1967), p. 40.
[2] Crowder, op. cit., pp. 39–41.

former war. The government successfully exploited this loyalty. In Senegal its task was facilitated by de Gaulle's unsuccessful bombardment of Dakar in 1940, in which a number of Africans were killed, while others survived to be proud of their resistance.[1]

According to postwar French writers,[2] some African chiefs fled to British or Free French territory to escape from Vichy rule. The chief of Porto Novo is supposed to have committed suicide in protest against the Governor-General's policy in Dahomey; the Moro Naba (king of the powerful Mossi tribe in eastern Upper Volta and one of the few dynastic leaders whom French administration had left with some real power) is said to have killed himself after instructing his son not to assume the throne 'until the true French come back'. How much one should believe this sort of story it is difficult to say. It may be that some administrators felt freer to pursue racialist or oppressive policies under an anti-semitic French government than they did under a republican one. But certainly the harshness of Vichy rule was exaggerated by subsequent Gaullist propaganda. The episode's real importance lies in the fact that it revealed France's internal divisions to Africans, and obliged Frenchmen of one side to try and prove that they were better and more generous colonial rulers than Frenchmen of the other. Both in AEF in 1940 and in AOF in 1942–43, adhesion to Free France was followed by changes in administrative personnel and a swing to the left in colonial policy.

*Eboué's Administration in Equatorial Africa:* in AEF this change was closely associated with the Governor-Generalship of Felix Eboué. Although himself the perfect example of the end-product of assimilation–the black Frenchman–Eboué was by no means a thoroughgoing assimilationist in his own views on Africa. He belonged rather to the Lyautey school, insisting on respect for traditional societies and rulers. The attempt to 'recreate native society in our own image with our own habits of mind' must, he said, be given up. Instead 'its natural institutions must be respected'. Moreover, 'every society has a ruling class, born to rule, without which nothing can be done. We must have it on our side'. More care should be taken to see that

[1] Later, when the Free French gained control, they had to explain AOF's re-entry into the war by telling schoolchildren that the good old Marshal had been made a prisoner and the soldiers were going to France to set him free (ibid., p. 41).

[2] Notably Jacques-Richard Molard, *Afrique Occidentale Française* (3rd ed., Paris 1956).

the chief recognised by the administration was the legitimate one accepted by the tribe. This done, the chief must be recognised also in a diplomatic sense, and treated with proper respect, not as a subordinate. 'The chief is not a civil servant, but an aristocrat.'

This cosseting of the traditional élite was not intended merely as a way of keeping the population under control, for Eboué insisted that the latter's interests must always have priority. 'Let us not forget that all of us, missionaries, settlers, businessmen, industrialists and civil servants ... we are all here *for the natives' sake.*' His objection to assimilation was that he thought any attempt to assimilate everyone at once would only result in the destruction of African culture without replacing it with anything else. 'Instead of creating by contact with us a crowd of proletarians more or less clothed and more or less French-speaking, we shall do better to create an élite, and first of all an élite of chiefs and notables.' Nor did he ignore the existence of an embryonic élite of *évolués*-though in AEF this was still numerically minute. To give some expression to its aspirations, he created a new status of *notable évolué*, in between citizen and subject. Those qualifying for this status would in a few of the more advanced towns be allowed to elect the town council, which however was to have a European official at its head and would not have its own budget. Perhaps not surprisingly, this concession met with little enthusiasm among those to whom it was directed, and except for a few civil servants almost no one applied for the new status.

But the details of Eboué's programme are less important than the fact of its existence. In many of his views–not least in his opinion that 'the native has a way of life, laws, and a country [*patrie*–which almost implies nationality] different from our own'–he was neither typical nor influential. But he did make some Frenchmen aware of the need for colonial reform of some sort and he promoted junior administrators of liberal views.[1]

*Liberation and the War Effort:* If de Gaulle himself insisted on the debt of gratitude which France owed to Africa, this was all the more keenly felt by those directly involved in the African war effort. The effort was not only military (100,000 Africans fought in the Free French armies, of which at one point they formed more than half), but also economic–and the economic effects were felt by almost the

[1] Ansprenger, op. cit., pp. 56–9. Quotations from Eboué, *La Nouvelle Politique Indigène pour L'AEF* (Algiers 1945).

whole population. Superficially, AEF and Cameroun gained unprecedented prosperity from their involvement in the war.[1] Exports in various products needed by the Allies boomed (notably in diamonds, coffee, cotton and palm-oil), and much foreign currency was brought in by Allied troops on the way to the Middle East. But the principal beneficiaries were the businessmen and the government; the African economy was not equipped to deal with the expansion of demand, and to mobilise the required labour-force administrators had to revive some of the worse practices of the concessionary companies.[2]

Particularly heavy burdens were imposed on West Africa when it too was brought into the war in 1943. Exorbitant demands were made for the rubber and other commodities on the basis of inaccurate pre-war statistics, with the result that many districts were asked to supply resources that they simply did not have, and often the inhabitants had to buy them elsewhere in order to re-sell, at a loss, to the administration. A much-quoted story is that of the *commandant de cercle* who replied to one government demand with the simple telegram: 'Honey agreed Stop Send bees.' The distress involved was aggravated by the collapse of prices, which fell suddenly from the inflated levels prevailing in Axis-controlled Europe to those of the world—that is the Allied—market.[3]

All of this was watched with bitter amusement by the European population, much of which had been in sympathy with Vichy. Once in control of Dakar, the Free French authorities did little to conciliate them; on the contrary, there were numerous arrests and reprisals—a spectacle which must have helped to undermine French prestige in African eyes. At the same time some left-wing teachers and administrators who had come to Africa at the time of the Popular Font were promoted, and many new ones arrived, especially Communists. It was from these men that many young *évolués* in West Africa received their first political education.[4]

## H. The Brazzaville Recommendation[5]

Such was the confused and fluid situation when the *Conférence Africaine Française* met at Brazzaville. Despite its name, no Africans

[1] Eboué, *L'AEF et la Guerre* (Brazzaville 1943).
[2] H. Zieglé, *L'Afrique Equatoriale Française* (Paris 1952).
[3] Richard Molard, op. cit.     [4] Morgenthau, pp. 22–7.
[5] For all this section see *La Conférence Africaine Française*, a booklet published by the Commissariat aux Colonies, Algiers 1944.

were actually members of it. It was a gathering of Frenchmen—colonial governors and officials, parliamentarians, a few trades unionists, and a bishop—who for one reason or another were considered qualified to make plans for Africa. Only Eboué thought of seeking the opinion of Africans themselves. He read a report which included documents submitted by various *évolué* groups in Brazzaville and two longish statements from **Fily-Dabo Sissoko,** a teacher and *chef de canton* from AOF, entitled 'Evolution and Colonisation in AOF' and 'Evolution at Work'. These tended to reinforce Eboué's own anti-assimilationist stand, by arguing that there was a distinct African culture which assimilation should not be allowed to smother.

The recommendations which emerged from the Conference suffered from a certain lack of precision which partly concealed an uneasy compromise between Eboué and the assimilationists. On social questions, the Conference declared that 'respect for, and the progress of, native life will be the foundation of our entire colonial policy, and we must submit absolutely to the necessities which that involves. The natives will be neither interchangeable, nor subject to eviction and arbitrary corvées.' More jobs should be open to Africans, especially in the administration, 'but for the time being the higher grades carrying authority can only be open to French citizens'. This qualification seemed to dispel the hope that the declared objective of 'giving the native élite as soon as possible the opportunity to measure its abilities against the harsh realities of management and command', would immediately be realised. On the question of citizenship, the *notable évolué* status which Eboué had introduced in AEF was recommended as a model for other African territories, with the suggestion that it might be extended to include artisans and skilled workers. The establishment of a uniform African penal code was recommended—but the liberal potential of this was limited, since the new code was to be based on the existing one in AOF. The *indigénat* punishments were to be suppressed—but not till the end of the war. The 'absolute superiority of the freedom of labour' was unanimously affirmed—but a delay of five years was allowed for its establishment in practice, and even then young men were still to be liable for a year's conscripted labour in lieu of military service. On the other hand, a pension scheme was called for, along with a six- (as opposed to seven-) day week, an eight-hour day, and a specialised colonial section of the Labour Inspection service. Trade unions might also be encouraged.

In the political recommendations the assimilationist element was more clearly in evidence. One point was settled firmly right at the start: 'The objectives of the work of civilisation accomplished by France in the colonies exclude any idea of autonomy, any possibility of evolution outside the French imperial bloc; the constitution of 'self-governments' (*sic*) in the colonies, even in the distant future, is to be excluded.' It was considered desirable that 'the political power of France be exercised with precision and rigour in all the lands of her Empire', but 'it is also desirable that the colonies should enjoy a large measure of administrative and economic freedom; ... the colonial peoples should experience this freedom personally and their responsibility should be gradually formed and elevated until they can be associated with the management of public affairs in their country'. How this could be achieved without any sort of political autonomy was not explained. Likewise the representation of the colonies in the new French Constitution (for it was generally assumed that France would have a new constitution after the Liberation) was left to a hypothetical committee of experts to work out. The Conference did, however, insist that the colonies should be represented in the forthcoming Constituent Assembly and that such representation should correspond to 'the importance of the colonies in the French community, an importance which can no longer be questioned after their services to the nation during this war'. Only there was no suggestion as to how this importance could be measured in terms of seats per million of population–except that it would involve much fuller representation than under the Third Republic. Yet the Conference would not be satisfied by a mere increase in the number of colonial senators and deputies; it wanted to see a new body, a 'Colonial Parliament, or preferably Federal Assembly' whose function would be 'to strengthen and guarantee the unbreakable political unity of the French world, while respecting the local life and freedom of each of the territories . . .' A clear distinction would be called for between the powers of the central government and those of the individual colonies.

Within the colonies, the old *conseils d'administration* were to be replaced, on the one hand by a subdivisional and regional council of 'native notables', representing the traditional élite, and on the other by representative assemblies containing both Europeans and natives, elected by universal suffrage 'wherever such a possibility is recognised'. These assemblies should be allowed to vote the colonial budget but in other matters were to remain advisory.

This last recommendation, at least, involved a new and bold step towards democratisation; and even if the general tenor of the provisions was less than revolutionary, it was nonetheless clear that reform was now genuinely intended. Perhaps the most important feature of the Conference was its readiness to recommend measures – such as rapid extension of education, and state aid to new industries – which would involve the expenditure in Africa of considerable sums of French public money; for this perhaps more than any political reform was to change the face of French Africa after the war. But politically too it was significant. By insisting both that Africans were indissolubly linked to France and that they had a right to representative government, it set a constitutional problem which was to perplex both Africans and Frenchmen for the next sixteen years; and by insisting that Africans should be represented in the Constituent Assembly of the Fourth Republic it ensured (unintentionally) that the French Parliament itself would be the forum in which this problem was discussed.

# Chapter 2

# The Provisional Government

## A. Application of the Brazzaville Proposals

De Gaulle's government wasted little time in pushing ahead with some of the social and technical reforms which the Conference had recommended. In Cameroun the recommendations on labour reform had actually been anticipated by a decree of 7th January 1944, which set up a special labour department (*office du travail*), enrolled a number of administrators and doctors as labour inspectors, applied metropolitan regulations to local working conditions, inaugurated a social security scheme, and forbade the much-abused practice of paying workers in kind. Between February and August 1944 a whole series of decrees applied these and other reforms to other colonies. Specialised agricultural services were set up to improve production of such commodities as rice, timber and cellulose. Wireless and telegraphic communications between the colonies were re-organised. Mobile hygiene and preventive medicine units were created. The promised uniform native penal code for all Africa was published; a new system of recruitment and training for colonial administrators was introduced; and the various sytems of native customary jurisdiction were drastically reorganised. Taxation in kind and compulsory corvées were abolished. Finally, the formation of trade unions was authorised in all the Black African territories. Numerous French trade unionists, many of them Communist, immediately set to work to organise African labour. Admittedly the urban workers affected by this were numerically a tiny minority living in the midst of an overwhelming majority of subsistence farmers; but in many territories this minority, precisely because of its precocious political awareness, was to play a crucial political rôle.

As for educational problems, they were the subject of a special conference at Dakar in July 1944, which produced a twenty-year plan for AOF: 50,000 new primary schools and 200 upper primary schools were to be built, as well as 75 'écoles normales africaines' to train 50,000 extra teachers.[1]

## B. Towards a Constitutional Formula

All this went on while the liberation of France herself from the Germans was still in progress. Political reform would have to wait till the end of the war. But even during these months decisions were taken which would inevitably influence Africa's political future. An *ordonnance* of 7th March 1944 laid down that henceforward the Algerian Moslems should have the same rights and obligations as non-Moslem Frenchmen, whatever their personal status. But at the same time it introduced a 'double-college' voting system: only certain privileged categories of Moslem were admitted to the first college, in which they were safely outnumbered by Europeans; the remainder would vote in the second college which would only have two fifths of the seats in the local and municipal councils. The European minority was thus assured of majority representation. The system seemed to point the way to an empire notionally democratised but in fact still dominated by France–which was precisely what was to emerge in 1946. Another example of this ambiguity was the so-called Representative Council created in Madagascar in April 1945; thirty of its sixty members had to be French citizens, and only twenty of them were actually elected.

What of the federal constitution of the empire as a whole, at which the Brazzaville Conference had hinted? The Free French leaders made some attempts to define it, in order to deal with the problem of Indo-China; they realised that, once liberated from the Japanese, the peoples of Indo-China would no longer tolerate straightforward subordination to France. Already in December 1943 de Gaulle had spoken of giving them 'a new political status within the French community, by which, in the framework of the Indo-Chinese federal organisation, the liberties of the different countries of the Union will be extended and consecrated, and the liberal character of their institutions will be accented without destroying the character of Indo-Chinese civilisation and traditions.' In March 1945 **Paul Giacobbi,** Minister of Colonies in the Provisional Government (which was now actually governing France), made a less mystical and more definite statement of policy: 'The Indo-Chinese Federation

[1] M. Devèze, *La France d'Outre-Mer* (Paris 1948).

will form, with France and the other parts of the Community, a French Union, whose external interests will be represented by France . . . The inhabitants of the Indo-Chinese Federation will be Indo-Chinese citizens and citizens of the French Union without discrimination as to race or religion, and with equal rights. They will have access to all positions and all federal employments in Indo-China and in the Union'.[1] The idea of a French Union, in which all would be equal citizens while remaining citizens of their individual countries, seemed to many Frenchmen a bold and splendid one. The liberal colonial theorist **Robert Delavignette**[2] ecstatically hailed Giacobbi's speech as comparable to 'the famous edict of Caracalla' which in A.D. 212 had conferred Roman citizenship on all free inhabitants of the Roman Empire, without affecting the status of their different communities. (Cf. the remark made by one of the assimilationist speakers at Brazzaville: 'we are heading for Empire in the Roman sense, and not for Empire in the Anglo-Saxon sense.')[3]

Delavignette noted in passing that there was a *prima facie* contradiction between Giacobbi's proposals and the Brazzaville exclusion of 'self-governments'–for what was offered to the Indo-Chinese colonies amounted to just that. In fact a federal French Union could only be built up of more or less autonomous components, and it began to look as though this solution would be accepted as the goal of colonial development, tainted with Anglo-Saxon precedent though it was. (Delavignette openly relished the idea of beating Britain to it in creating the first 'Dominion' with a predominantly non-European population.) At the Conference of San Francisco in the summer of 1945 the French delegates allowed 'self-government' to be written into the United Nations Charter, as an aim not only of the Trusteeship system which was to replace the League of Nations Mandates, but of all colonial responsibilities (Article 73), contenting themselves with the addition, in Article 76 (whose terms they knew would eventually be applied to Togo and Cameroun), of the words 'as may be appropriate to the particular circumstances of each territory and its peoples and the freely expressed wishes of the people concerned.'[4]

---

[1] Devèze, op. cit.
[2] In *Esprit*, 1st July 1945.
[3] *La Conférence Africaine Française* (op. cit.).
[4] Dupuy, 'San Francisco et la Charte des Nations Unies' (Paris 1945).

## C. Preparations for the Constituent Assembly

The government accepted the Brazzaville recommendation that the colonies should be represented in the Constituent Assembly. On 20th February 1945 it set up a special commission to consider how this representation should be organised. The chairman was **Gaston Monnerville,** a mulatto from Guiana who had sat in the Chamber of Deputies before 1940.[1] Two black Africans were co-opted on to the commission: **Léopold Sédar Senghor** of Senegal and **Sourou Migan Apithy** of Dahomey. Both were Catholics educated in mission schools, and both had been in Europe since the beginning of the war. Senghor indeed had lived in France almost continuously since 1928, first as student, then as secondary school teacher, and after war broke out as a private in the French army. He spent the years 1940 to 1942 in a German prisoner of war camp.[2] By 1945 he had already acquired a reputation as a poet and grammarian; he was the only African who had achieved the rank of *agrégé*—France's highest teaching qualification, awarded on the results of an intensely competitive examination. Apithy was a younger man (thirty-one, Senghor was thirty-eight) and in absolute terms less distinguished—but the very fact that he had studied in Paris made him almost unique among Dahomeyans; he was by training an accountant, economist and lawyer. Both these men were chosen principally because they were on the spot, and both took care to emphasise that they had no claim to represent anybody, but on the contrary were quite out of touch with the current situation in Africa. Nonetheless they felt entitled to react strongly when the commission was confronted with a draft project which divided the territories of the empire into three categories:

(i)   States—the former protectorates.
(ii)  Departments of the French Republic.
(iii) 'Countries over which France must continue to exercise its domination'.

Into this last category fell the territories of Afrique Noire. Apithy was astounded that the French, who had just liberated themselves, with African help, from German 'domination', should now expect Africans to accept the continued domination of France. He also

---

[1] Devèze, op. cit.
[2] In 1942 he was released and went back to teaching. See A. Guibert, *Léopold Sédar Senghor* (Paris 1962).

protested against the proposal that representatives from Africa to the Constituent Assembly should be elected on the 'double college' system already in use for local elections in Algeria–i.e. with a special electoral roll for the tiny minority of French 'citizens'. It was time, he suggested, that all inhabitants of the overseas territories were recognised as equal in rights, whatever their colour or status. This was already the case in metropolitan France, but not in the territories themselves–with the ridiculous result that he himself, for example, had the right to practise law in Paris, but not in his native Dahomey. A Vietnamese member of the commission made a similar protest, and Senghor (who was absent from the relevant session) later associated himself with that of Apithy.[1] Monnerville and the majority of the commission were in sympathy with their views; and the commission therefore recommended a single electoral roll and a much larger number of overseas deputies than there had been in the parliament of the Third Republic. If it was decided to call a single-chamber Constituent Assembly, it should contain 95 colonial deputies; if there were two chambers, the lower one should have 66 representatives from the colonies, distributed in approximate proportion to the population, and the Senate 29 (one from each territory). Similar suggestions came independently from various Resistance organisations. None of them envisaged an overseas representation of more than about one fifth of the total number of deputies–remarkably moderate when one considers that the total population of the colonies outnumbered that of France itself. But the minority of the commission, and a number of politicians close to de Gaulle himself, considered that they went too far. The main argument used against them was that in practice deputies elected by colonial 'subjects' would prove less representative of the population than of the administrators who organised the election. Monnerville derided this suggestion, but the early electoral history of many African territories was to show that it was far from absurd.

In any case, for this or other reasons, the government eventually decided to retain the 'double college' system, and to provide for only 33 colonial deputies in a total Assembly of 586. A referendum was to be held simultanously with the election, by which the French people was asked to grant the Assembly constituent powers. In this referendum only French citizens could vote; in the election itself 'subjects' might vote as well. But should the suffrage be universal?

[1] Apithy, *Au Service de mon pays* (Montrouge 1957) and a personal conversation with the author.

TABLE I

**The Franchise,** October 1945

| Constituency | A<br>Estimated total pop. mid-1946 († = mid-1947) | B<br>Entitled to vote | C<br>B as % of A | D<br>Actually voting | E<br>Entitled to vote under universal suffrage 1957 (* = Togo election 1958) |
|---|---|---|---|---|---|
| SENEGAL AND MAURITANIA | 2,392,000 | 69,500 | 2·9 | 47,100 | 1,440,000 |
| SOUDAN AND NIGER | 5,965,000 | 34,900 | 0·6 | 27,600 | 3,324,000‡ |
| IVORY COAST | 4,056,000 | 35,100 | 0·9 | 28,600 | 1,483,000‡ |
| GUINEA | 2,125,000 | 18,100 | 0·9 | 14,000 | 1,376,000 |
| DAHOMEY AND TOGO | 2,378.000 | 12,900 | 0·2 | 10,200 | 1,163,800* |
| AOF AND TOGO Total | 16,916,000 | 172,500 | 1·0 | 127,500 | 10,692,300 |
| GABON AND MOYEN-CONGO | 1,054,000† | 8,000 | 0·8 | 5,900 | 644,200 |
| TCHAD AND OUBANGUI-CHARI | 3,077,000† | 8,300 | 0·3 | 6,100 | 1,816,100 |
| AEF Total | 3,984,000 | 16,300 | 0·4 | 12,000 | 2,460,300 |
| CAMEROUN | 2,820,000 | 14,200 | 0·5 | 11,400 | 942,300 (Dec. 1956) |
| AFR. NOIRE Total | 23,720,000 | 203,000 | 0·9 | 150,900 | 14,094,900 |

‡ (Column E, Soudan, Niger and Ivory Coast): To these totals can be added a further 1,905,000 registered voters in Upper Volta, whose territory was in 1945 still divided between Ivory Coast, Soudan and Niger. Thus the four territories combined had an electorate of 6,712,000 in 1957, as against 70,000 in 1945.

See p. 59 for *Note* to Table.

'This question seemed rhetorical to those who considered the state of illiteracy which still characterised the great majority of the inhabitants, and especially their lack of any modern political experience.' Such was the opinion of **Michel Devèze,** a writer who himself became an MRP (Christian Democrat) member of the Constituent Assembly. It seems also to have been that of de Gaulle's government, which in its *Ordonnance* of 22nd August 1945 provided for an African franchise so restrictive that it allowed the vote to only 203,000 people in the whole of Afrique Noire–less than one per cent of the population. (See Table I.)

These 203,000–citizens and subjects combined–had 16 deputies between them. But even within this electorate the seats were not equally distributed. As Devèze put it: 'that would have involved a risk of smothering the voice of the French minority, whose rôle was of capital importance in the evolution of the country'.[1] In each African constituency, therefore, there were two seats, one reserved for the 'first college' (Citizens), and one for the 'second college' (Subjects); i.e. in most territories half the representation was automatically reserved for the tiny European population. Only in Senegal, where the 44,000 inhabitants of the Four Communes were all 'citizens', did the first college contain anything like half the total. In the rest of Afrique Noire 17,000 first college electors (nearly all Europeans) had seven deputies between them, while another seven were shared between 117,000 African 'subjects'.

*Note:* The population figures in column A are now thought to have been underestimated. Probably, therefore, the percentages in column C should be even lower. Column E gives the number of registered voters at the first elections held under full universal suffrage, namely the territorial elections of March 1957 in AOF and AEF, those of December 1956 in Cameroun, and those of April 1958 in Togo. A comparison of column E with column B shows, perhaps more clearly than the percentages, how very restricted the 1945 franchise was. Those qualified were: *notables évolués* (as defined by Eboué's reforms); members and ex-members of local or municipal assemblies, chambers of commerce etc.; holders of various military or civil decorations; civil servants; holders of certificates of primary education; recognised officials in native courts; ministers of religion; former officers or NCOs, and any ex-serviceman who had been on active service outside his home territory during either world war, or had volunteered, or drew an army pension; registered tradesmen qualified to vote in chamber of commerce elections; and tribal rulers. Of course many of these categories overlapped almost completely with each other, which explains why they contained so few people altogether.

*Sources:* Population figures from United Nations Statistical Year Book 1948. Registered and actual voters from F. Ansprenger, *Politik im schwarzen Afrika.*

[1] Devèze, op. cit.

## D. The Election Campaign of 1945

The elections were fixed for 21st October 1945. For two months preceding that date the tiny élite of African voters looked about for men able to represent it in discussion about the future relationship between Africa and France. The thirteen territories of Afrique Noire were grouped into eight parliamentary constituencies: i.e. only three territories (Ivory Coast, Guinea and Cameroun) were allowed a whole constituency to themselves. The remainder were grouped in pairs.

*Senegal:* Senegal was grouped with Mauritania; but Mauritania had so few inhabitants qualified to vote that this made little practical difference. To all intents and purposes the double college system created two separate constituencies in Senegal: the coastal towns inhabited by the 'citizens' on the one hand, and the rural hinterland of the 'subjects' on the other. As it happened, the elections found Senegal at a moment of unusually good relations between the two. The Vichy régime and the war had reduced both to a common level of suffering. Discontent turned to fury after an ugly incident in November 1944. Some African soldiers, who had fought for France during 1939–40 and subsequently been imprisoned by the Germans, had just been repatriated to a camp at Tiaroye, outside Dakar. They had been promised their arrears of pay on arrival at Dakar, and when these were not forthcoming they refused an order to embark in lorries for Bamako. This was taken as mutiny and the officers opened fire; some forty African soldiers were killed, and at least as many wounded. To make matters worse, some of the survivors were sentenced to ten years' imprisonment by the Dakar Military Tribunal in March 1945. The 'massacre of Tiaroye' was seen in Senegal as an intolerable example of French ingratitude; many believed that de Gaulle (the aggressor of 1940) had ordered the shooting personally. This was certainly untrue, but his government handled the affair clumsily. It was also supremely tactless in its handling of the 'citizens' ' voting rights. It had been decided, in view of the important rôle played by women in the Resistance, that women should now be allowed to vote in France (only men had voted under the Third Republic). But by decree of 19th February 1945 this privilege was extended to Senegal only for European women, and not for native *citoyennes*–a distinction which, since Blaise Diagne's laws of 1915 and 1916, it ought to have been legally impossible to draw. It implied that African 'citizens', like African 'subjects', were not automatically included in universal suffrage, and thereby helped to unite both categories in resentment of their inequality with Europeans.

At such a moment there could be little doubt where to look for leadership. Galandou Diouf had died in 1941, and Maître Lamine-Guèye, now fifty-three years old, was clearly the most politically experienced man in Afrique Noire. It was he who appeared in court for the Tiaroye victims, and he who flew to Paris and persuaded the government to allow Senegalese *citoyennes* to vote after all.[1] In July he was elected mayor of Dakar, a post he was to hold continuously for the next sixteen years. He was also the leader of Senegal's only political party, the SFIO. He realised, however, that it was not the moment for party politics, but rather for a popular front. He therefore formed in Dakar a *comité d'entente* which included not only Socialists but members of the Communist Study Group and of the Gaullist 'Franco-African Study Committee', and representatives of other, intermediate political groups. All agreed to fight the election as an African Bloc, which in reality meant that they agreed to support the Socialist candidates.[2] These were Lamine-Guèye himself for the first college, and Senghor for the second. Senghor was something of a surprise choice, since he had lived away from Senegal for so long, and only joined the SFIO sixteen hours before the local party congress adopted him as candidate.[3] In short, he was parachuted into the constituency by Lamine-Guèye's personal influence. But there were good reasons for the choice. Electorally Senghor was valuable because he was himself a 'subject' by birth (he came from the fishing-village of Joal-la-Portugaise, south of Dakar) and because he was an ex-prisoner of war, which made him popular with an important group of voters – the 'anciens combattants'. On the parliamentary level he would be invaluable because of his unrivalled mastery of the French language, which would both be useful in itself and win the respect of metropolitan deputies. Both he and Lamine-Guèye were elected with overwhelming majorities.

*Ivory Coast:* Senegal was not the only territory which the elections found already in a ferment. The Ivory Coast was if anything more so, for its plantation economy was particularly sensitive to the fluctuations in prices and policies caused by the war. Until 1944, and especially under Vichy, the administration's policy favoured the big

---

[1] Decree of 30th May 1945. See Lamine-Guèye, *Itinéraire Africain* (Paris 1966).
[2] Morgenthau, op. cit., pp. 136–7.   [3] Ansprenger, op. cit., p. 154.

European plantations over the smaller but far more numerous African ones. From 1925 onwards special decrees regulated the canalisation of forced labour on to private plantations. At first both African and European planters profited from this, but from 1941, when the labour shortage became acute, the supply was reserved for Europeans; the latter moreover were paid much higher prices for their crops, as well as having priority rights to imported goods. Then, when AOF re-entered the war, there was a drive to increase production. Premiums were declared for all planters who had 25 or more contiguous hectares (about 60 acres) under cultivation. This neatly included all the European plantations, but only the 50 largest African ones. Besides, as 'subjects' the African planters were themseves liable to be drafted to forced labour; and many of their plantations were destroyed by 'sanitation' teams, allegedly because they were infected with plant disease but in fact because they were competing too successfully: for the number of African planters was increasing very rapidly, and so was their share of the market.

Potentially a safe bourgeois element in African society, the planters were driven to radicalism by government policy and European competition. Deprived of forced labour themselves, they began to reflect seriously on its iniquity as a system. In September 1944 they formed a union, the *Syndicat Agricole Africain*, which succeeded in winning the support of the new left-wing administrators appointed by the Provisional Government. Cars and petrol were allocated to its branches, and its members declared exempt from forced labour. Anyone could join who was cultivating two hectares of coffee or three of cocoa–and this meant some 20,000 people. Denouncing forced labour, the Syndicat's leaders managed to get workers for their own plantations by reaching agreements with the chiefs of the northern tribes from which most of the workers came. The chiefs agreed to send groups of volunteers for African plantations, on condition they were paid four times the rate paid by Europeans, and received a share of the crop as well. By these means some four or five thousand workers were secured for the harvest of 1944–5, and the Syndicat claimed that this proved forced labour was unnecessary. The European planters disagreed violently, and lobbied successfully in Paris for the replacement of Governor **Latrille,** who had helped the Syndicat, by the Comte **de Mauduit,** who shared their own views.[1]

Abidjan, capital of the Ivory Coast, had in 1939 been raised to the status of a '*commune mixte* of the second degree'; that is to say, it

[1] Morgenthau, op. cit., pp. 169–78.

was given a town council (*commission municipale*) elected on a limited frachise. Because of the war this reform had not been put into effect, and the first municipal elections were held on 26th August 1945–two months before the elections to the Constituent Assembly. The Syndicat, though not a political party, was now the most effective African organisation in the Ivory Coast; like the SFIO in Senegal it acted as a nucleus around which an African Bloc was formed. Its leader, **Félix Houphouët-Boigny,** persuaded the African voters in Abidjan to support a list of exclusively African candidates. The *commission municipale* had to be composed half of 'citizens' and half of 'subjects'; but this problem could be circumvented because Abidjan contained many immigrants from other territories, particularly from Senegal and Dahomey. The African Bloc formed a list of eight Ivoiriens, six Senegalese, two Guineans and two Dahomeyans; the Senegalese were citizens by birth, and three of the others were 'naturalised'. The European electors found it impossible to make up an alternative list, since there were no European 'subjects' and no African was prepared to stand against the Bloc. This situation exacerbated the mounting anger of the Europeans against African pretentions. They attempted, first to get the election postponed, then to secure mass abstention. The latter attempt was partly successful, for there was only a 37 per cent poll, but this did not invalidate the Bloc's victory.

At first the Bloc hoped to follow up its success with a similar walk-over in the second college election to the Constituent Assembly. But it proved impossible to agree on a candidate. The Abidjan intellectuals supported **Kouamé Binzème,** whom they considered one of 'les meilleurs enfants de la Côte d'Ivoire' because he practised law in Paris; whereas the Syndicat backed its own leader, Houphouët. Houphouët sent a messenger northward to enlist the support of the Moro Naba, king of the Mossi, who had co-operated with the Syndicat in recruiting volunteer labour for the plantations. But the Mossi had their own political aims; they did not enjoy being treated purely as a labour reserve for the south, and were therefore anxious for the reconstitution of the separate territory of Upper Volta, which had been abolished in 1932. To agitate for this they formed the *Union pour la Défense des Intérêts de la Haute Volta* (later known as the *Union Voltaïque*). They were encouraged by Governor Mauduit and some of his subordinates, who were hoping thus to defeat the Syndicat. It may have been administrative pressure which led the Moro Naba to withdraw his support from Houphouët and put up his own henchman, the Baloum Naba ('chief of the pages'), as candidate for the Constituent Assembly. Certainly his campaign received the administration's full support, despite his total ignorance of the French language. Only the strong organisation which the Syndicat had built up in the south, and the support of the Bobo tribe in the north, traditionally hostile to the Mossi, enabled Houphouët to win a slender majority.[1]

In the rest of AOF, and in AEF, the 1945 elections gave the first impulse to political activity, instead of acting as a vent for existing political agitation. In most territories, the lead given by chiefs and administrators was followed, simply because no other form of leadership was known. The idea of electoral campaigning, and *a fortiori* that of party organisation, took time to catch on.

*Guinea:* The case of Guinea is typical. Economically and educationally one of the most backward territories, in 1945 it was scarcely conscious of itself as a unit; its inhabitants still thought essentially in tribal and regional terms. For example, the Mandé-speaking peoples (mainly Malinké) of the south-east had more contact with their fellow-Mandé (mainly Bambara) down the Niger in the Soudan than with the Soussou of the coast of the Fulani of the Fouta Djallon plateau. The 1945 election was mainly a contest between Fula and Malinké tribal groups. But the Malinké vote split between two rival candidates, and this helped the Fula **Yacine Diallo** to win.[2]

*Soudan:* Similar conditions prevailed in the Soudan, a large, thinly populated territory lumped together in one constituency with the equally large and even less populous Niger. As in Guinea, the number of educated people was minute; but closer contacts with Senegal and better inter-regional communications made them slightly more aware of what was going on. There was an attempt to form an African Bloc, but it failed because there were too many would-be candidates. The eventual winner was Eboué's old protégé Fily-Dabo Sissoko, who like Senghor had been away from his territory for some time, but like Senghor gained prestige from the fact that he had already made a certain reputation as a writer. He was popular with the chiefs, especially among the pagan (animist) tribes. On the second ballot, opposition to him united behind **Mamadou Konaté,** a Moslem who had taught at the Ecole Normale William Ponty and

[1] F. J. Amon d'Aby, *La Côte d'Ivoire dans la cité africaine* (Paris 1951). Morgenthau, op. cit., pp. 179–80.  [2] Morgenthau, op. cit., pp. 220–3.

was much respected by the local intelligentsia. Even so, Sissoko won easily. He fought the election on a programme of social reform: equal rates of pay for white and black, emancipation of women, abolition of forced labour.[1]

*AEF:* In AEF the electorate was even less politically conscious than it was in Guinea. The dominant sentiment was pride in the successes of the Resistance and loyalty to General de Gaulle. This was especially true of Tchad, which more than any other colony was showered with accolades after the Liberation, both for having been the first to respond to de Gaulle's appeal, and as the military base from which Leclerc's desert campaign had been organised. It was therefore easy for Gaullist administrators, despite their ultra-conservative views on specifically African questions, to recruit African voters into a Gaullist party: the *Union Démocratique Tchadienne* (UDT). This party's candidates won both first- and second-college seats in the combined constituency of Tchad and Oubangui-Chari. Both candidates were Europeans and both had been officers in the Free French forces: Dr **René Malbrant** (a vet) and Colonel **Guy de Boissoudy.**

Gaullism was also strong in Moyen-Congo, especially in Brazzaville. Even among the ba-Kongo, whose sullenly anti-French feelings had been exacerbated by the death in prison of André Matsoua in 1942, de Gaulle was personally popular. 'Jesus Matsoua' was said to be his divine helper, and to have brought about both the military success of Free France and the reforms which followed the Brazzaville Conference. Electorally however the ba-Kongo were useless, as they either refused to vote or insisted on writing in Matsoua's name on the ballot paper. They left the electoral battle to be fought out between three other large ethnic groups: the Mbochi of northern Moyen-Congo (who also formed a large immigrant community in Brazzaville itself), the Fang of Gabon (which was joined with Moyen-Congo in a single constituency), and the ba-Vili of the coastal area around Pointe Noire (the territorial capital). It was the Vili candidate, **Jean-Félix Tchicaya,** who emerged victorious on the second ballot.[2]

*Dahomey:* In all non-Moslem territories missionary influence tended to be strong, since missions had usually been more active than the

[1] Ibid., pp. 271–4.
[2] Thompson and Adloff, *Emerging States* (op. cit.).

state in providing education. This was particularly true of Dahomey, where one missionary, Father **Aupiais,** had made a deep impression even on those Africans who remained animists. His profound sympathy for his African flock was based on years of anthropological research. Although it was now seventeen years since he had left Dahomey, Aupiais was elected as first-college deputy. (Dahomey was the one territory where 'naturalised' Africans–virtually all of whom were Catholic–formed a significant proportion of the tiny 'citizen' body.) It was also partly Aupiais's influence which enabled Apithy, who had been his pupil, to secure the second-college seat',[1] but Apithy had already established his own importance by his work on the Monnerville Commission, on whose proceedings he had sent reports to his friends in Dahomey, pointing out that the government had regrettably disregarded the findings of the majority of the commission.[2]

*The Mandated Territories:* Together with the 'subjects' of Dahomey voted the *administrés* of Togo–despite the fact that technically they did not have French nationality. 'The Constituent Assembly which was about to meet was so important that it was more or less legitimate for the mandates to be represented (especially when we remember that they were governed by French law).' (Devèze.) This seems to have been the official French view, but it was rejected by many Togolese *évolués*, including those who before the war had manifested their preference for French as against German rule. Now they were anxious to take advantage of the UN Charter, and to emphasise the distinction between themselves and the French 'subjects' of AOF. Especially the Ewe, the main coastal tribe, to which Sylvanus Olympio belonged, were hoping to be reunited with their compatriots in British Togoland and the Gold Coast. They saw no advantage in being integrated into the French Republic; indeed they sent petitions against French policy to the infant United Nations.[3]

There was a similar reaction in Cameroun. Enthusiasm for the idea of incorporation into AEF had vanished with the German threat which had originally provoked it; and a French proposal to form a *Union Camerounaise Française* (UNICAFRA), to carry on the work of the old JEUCAFRA, fell flat. Relations between Africans and Europeans were much strained by the economic situation; Cameroun's economy had developed rapidly under the stimulus of the war

[1] Thompson and Adloff, *French West Africa* (Stanford 1958).
[2] Apithy, op. cit.     [3] Cornevin, *Histoire du Togo*, op. cit.

effort, and Douala in particular had become a considerable industrial centre, with a relatively large number of African wage-labourers. Most of them were employed by European firms and worked very long hours for very low pay. As soon as trades unions were legalised in 1944, emissaries arrived from the French CGT (*Confédération Générale du Travail* – the largest, and by now mainly Communist-led, group of French trades unions) to help organise both African and European workers. The *Union des Syndicats Confédérés du Cameroun* (USCC) was founded in December 1944, and from then on strikes became frequent. The employers in their turn began to organise. They were further alarmed when, on 18th June 1945, the government published a 'native labour code', which was intended to give effect to the liberal principles enunciated at the Brazzaville Conference. The Douala Chamber of Commerce took the initiative in organising a meeting of settlers and businessmen from all over Afrique Noire and Madagascar. It was held in Douala in September 1945 and gave birth to a sinister organisation called the *Etats Généraux de la Colonisation Française*, one of whose principal objects was to oppose the abolition of forced labour. It condemned the Brazzaville policy as 'a mixture of fascism and demagogy'. These pronouncements enraged the workers in Douala, and a new wave of unofficial strikes, more violent than before, broke out on 24th September. Riots ensued, culminating in the murder (probably in self-defence) of the secretary of the Chamber of Commerce by a French CGT leader. Eight Africans were also killed.

It was in these very strained circumstances that the election campaign was conducted. The governor, rattled by his manifest failure to control the situation in September, tried to oppose the candidature of Prince **Alexandre Douala Manga Bell,** who was chief of the Douala tribe and a known opponent of forced labour. Some of his supporters were imprisoned – but this of course increased his popularity and he was elected on the second ballot. There was also a close contest for the first-college seat; the employers' candidate was eventually defeated by Dr **Louis-Paul Aujoulat,** a Catholic lay missionary who had worked mainly in the interior, where race relations had not deteriorated so much as they had in Douala.[1]

*The 'élus'*: So eventually eight negro Africans reached the Con-

[1] Mveng, op. cit. Also: Dr Aujoulat's private papers; *Le Monde*, 14–15th October 1945; *Marchés Coloniaux du Monde*, 8th December 1945; Ansprenger, op. cit., p. 193.

stituent Assembly: Lamine-Guèye, Senghor, Fily-Dabo Sissoko, Yacine Diallo, Houphouët-Boigny, Apithy, Douala, and Tchicaya. There was also one African mulatto: **Gabriel d'Arboussier,** a colonial administrator elected by the 'citizens' of Gabon and Moyen-Congo. These nine deputies did not all sit together, and though they could of course be distinguished from metropolitan Frenchmen by their colour, their appearance aroused less comment than that of their Algerian colleagues. For while the latter wore fezzes, or in one case full Bedouin-type robes, the black Africans were the soul of assimilated correctness in unadorned dark suits.[1] The franchise had been given to the traditional as well as the Europeanised élite, but it was essentially from the latter that the succesful candidates came; indeed even of the unsuccessful ones only the Baloum Naba had had no French education; and he is alleged to have advised people to vote against him for precisely that reason.[2] The choice fell on *évolués*, not necessarily because the voters admired or identified with them, but because they had special skills which were needed for this particular job. They seem to have been looked on less as legislators than as ambassadors–and there was no point in making someone ambassador to Paris unless he could speak French.

This criterion narrowed the field of selection, and it is scarcely surprising that three of the four non-Senegalese West African deputies had been educated at the Ecole Normale William Ponty, since as we have seen there was scarcely anywhere else where they could have been. Sissoko and Diallo had been trained there as teachers, while Houphouët had gone on to study medicine at Dakar and had become a 'médecin africain'–i.e. a doctor without full French qualifications.[3] Most of their defeated opponents were also Ponty men, and Lamine-Guèye himself had taught there for a time. Only he, Senghor and Apithy had had a university education. The even greater educational poverty of AEF was illustrated by the Africans' choice of a European to represent them in Tchad, and of Tchicaya, who had had only primary education and then been an orderly (*planton*) in the Public Works department, in Moyen-Congo. Prince Douala, deputy for Cameroun, was admittedly a very different case, a man of considerable European culture whose

[1] Gordon Wright, *The Reshaping of French Democracy* (London 1950), and Assemblée Nationale Constituante, *Notices et Portraits* (Paris 1946).

[2] Morgenthau, p. 179.

[3] It was France's policy to train African doctors to the point where they could be entrusted with the supervision of a dispensary, but no further–quantity rather than quality being the most immediate African need.

speeches tended to be liberally salted with quotations from Horace. But he was in a category entirely by himself: he had been educated at the court of Wilhelm II and had served as an officer in the *Reichswehr*. His father, Prince Rudolf Duala Manga, had been much cultivated by the Germans, but became suspect to them when he attempted to champion his people against the abuses of the administration. At the outbreak of the First World War he was suddenly arrested and summarily hanged on a charge (almost certainly false) of conspiring with the Allies. Alexander Duala was only sixteen when this happened. Later in the war he deserted from the German army and escaped to France, and after the war found his way back to Cameroun, where he was restored to a measure of authority by the French administration, and became a successful planter.[1]

Douala was not the only one of the new deputies who combined the advantages of a European education with those of high traditional status. Both Houphouët and Sissoko also came from chiefly families and held official posts as *chefs de canton*. This may have helped them to win votes from other chiefs, but not necessarily. The chiefs of the Fouta Djallon chose Yacine Diallo precisely because his low traditional status made him easier to control. In Houphouët's case it was the combination of chiefly status with plantation agriculture that counted; he was typical of numerous chiefs in the southern Ivory Coast who had ventured into coffee- and cocoa-growing. His education enabled him to speak for them to the French administration; he founded the *Syndicat* and led the attack on forced labour.

Sissoko, on the other hand, had made his name principally as an intellectual. He wrote poems and stories based on animist beliefs and legends, and was always ready to speak up for an indigenous African culture whose existence seemed implicitly denied by the assimilation policy. Both he and Senghor reacted strongly against European cultural arrogance. Senghor became the friend and follower of the West Indian poet **Aimé Césaire** (who arrived at the Constituent Assembly as Communist deputy from Martinique). They denounced the narrow rationalism of European culture and vaunted the spontaneity and intuitive genius of the negro. Césaire wrote:

> *Eia for those who have invented nothing*
> *for those who have explored nothing*
> *for those who have tamed nothing*

[1] Mveng, op. cit.

*but abandon themselves, possessed, to the essence of everything*
*not caring to tame, but playing the world's game*
*truly the world's elder sons*
*porous to all the world's breaths . . .*

*Listen to the white world*
*horribly tired from its enormous effort*
*its unwilling joints creaking beneath the hard stars*
*its steel blue stiffnesses piercing the mystic flesh*
*listen to its proditory triumphs trumpeting its defeats*
*listen to its wretched stumbling among pompous alibis*

*Pity on our conquerors omniscient and naïve!*[1]

Senghor was less contemptuous but equally firm. He wanted 'to assimilate, not be assimilated'.[2] If Africans could learn technology and rational processes from Europeans, there were at least equally important things that White must learn from Black. Only the negro could restore the values of instinct to a desiccated, over-calculating world.

*We must answer present at the World's rebirth*
*Like leaven which is necessary to white flour.*
*For who would teach rhythm to the defunct world of machines and*
  *guns?*
*Who would shout for joy to awaken the dead and the orphans at*
  *dawn?*
*Tell me, who would restore the memory of life to the man whose*
  *hopes are gutted?*
*They call us the men of cotton of coffee of oil.*
*They call us the men of death.*
*We are the men of the dance, whose feet draw strength as they*
  *strike the hard ground.*[3]

[1] From *Cahiers d'un retour au pays natal* (2nd ed., Paris 1956). The translation is my own.

[2] Subtitle of his essay, 'Vues sur l'Afrique noire' in R. Lemaignen, L. S. Senghor and Prince S. Youtévong, *La Communauté Impériale Française* (Paris 1945).

[3] From *Chants d'Ombre* (Paris 1945). Also my translation.

# Chapter 3

# *The First Constituent Assembly*

## A. General Composition. Party Affiliation of African Deputies

The Assembly which met in the Palais Bourbon on 6th November 1945 was dominated by three parties of almost equal strength. The Communists, who had greatly increased their strength during the Resistance, had 152 seats. They thus displaced the SFIO, which had 143, from its rôle as France's leading Marxist party. But both had to reckon with an entirely new party, the *Mouvement Républicain Populaire* (MRP), founded by a group of Catholic Resistance leaders who wanted to test the appeal of a left-wing social programme without traditional left-wing anticlericalism, and to fight Communism by imitating Communist party organisation. Their success came as a surprise even to themselves, for they swept straight in with 150 seats.

All these three parties were already represented in the Provisional Government, but not all of de Gaulle's ministers belonged to them. A number of his closest associates belonged to a non-party Resistance group – the *Union Démocratique et Sociale de la Résistance* (UDSR). Its 29 members included both the former Minister of Colonies, Giacobbi, and his successor, **Jacques Soustelle**, as well as **René Pleven**, Minister of Finance, who as commissioner for Colonies in the National Liberation Committee had presided over the Brazzaville Conference. The overseas Gaullists belonged to this group. It had no common ideology, and was held together only by hostility to Communism and unwillingness to be swallowed by either of the other monolithic parties.

Another Resistance group was the *Mouvement Unifié de la Résistance* (MUR). It was very small but of some importance because it provided a home for those who wanted to work with the Communists in the Assembly but were not members of the Party.

Next to the UDSR, and sandwiched awkwardly between Socialists and MRP, were the Radicals, once the dominant party of the Third Republic, now reduced by the Third Republic's disgrace to a mere 28

71

deputies. Further to the right was a chaos of 64 more or less Conservative deputies (to import a term from British politics). They gradually grouped themselves into loose blocs, of which the 'Peasants' and the 'Independent Republicans' were to be longest-lived; but they strongly resisted any attempt to subject them to party discipline. Beyond them again, the extreme right tip of the Assembly was the incongruous position chosen by the two deputies from Madagascar, who openly demanded independence for their country. Like the three Algerian parties, they held aloof from any metropolitan political allegiance.[1]

Not so the negro Africans. Lamine-Guèye did try to group them in a 'Bloc Africain', but he intended to affiliate it to the SFIO. The attempt failed, and while some of them did join the Socialist group (Lamine-Guèye himself, Senghor, Yacine Diallo, Apithy, Tchicaya), others were attracted elsewhere. Douala Manga Bell followed his European colleague, Aujoulat, into the MRP. Sissoko, Houphouët and d'Arboussier joined the MUR. That is to say, they allied with the Communists.

The Communist Party held that Africa was not yet ready for Communist organisation. The preliminary stage of 'bourgeois' revolution had to come first, and this would take the form of a 'national' revolution against imperialism. African nationalists, though they might well be bourgeois themselves (as Houphouët for example undoubtedly was), were nonetheless the natural allies of the French proletariat in its struggle against capitalism. This was why French Communists who went to Africa founded informal Study Groups rather than party cells, and tried to stimulate national consciousness rather than class consciousness, and this was why the Communist group in the Assembly did not try to recruit African deputies directly, but encouraged them to join the fellow-travellers in the MUR (which always voted with the Communists). It thus gained the votes of Sissoko and Houphouët, neither of whom was in any sense proletarian, and neither of whom was seriously interested in Marxist ideology, but both of whom had been befriended by Communist teachers and administrators in Africa. Houphouët especially owed much of his success in organising the *Syndicat Agricole* to the assitance of **Lambert,** a Communist who was head of Governor Latrille's *cabinet* – that is, his closest personal adviser.[2]

As in Africa, so in Paris, Africans found that Communists would

[1] Wright, op. cit.      [2] Morgenthau, op. cit., p. 177.

often give practical help where other politicians confined themselves to sonorous declarations of goodwill. Of the African deputies, only Senghor, Apithy and Lamine-Guèye had ever been in France before. The others arrived there for the first time just as winter was setting in. They found the country still suffering acutely from the effects of the war. Food and fuel were in short supply in Paris. It was difficult to find lodgings, and difficult to get transport to and from the Assembly. When lodgings were found they were usually inadequately heated even for Europeans, let alone new arrivals from tropical Africa. All these difficulties Communist deputies helped to solve or alleviate for their African colleagues; they even took them on sight-seeing excursions in the country, to show them a different France from the one they met in the Assembly. But they were helpful in the Assembly too, organising speaker's classes at which inexperienced deputies could learn how to present a report, how to criticise a text without missing the subtleties of punctuation, and so on.[1] More important still, they were ready to take up African grievances and press them during parliamentary debates and, unlike all the other parties, they were not afraid to proclaim the right of Africans to independence. Since they were the largest party in the house, and were represented in the government, they seemed highly desirable allies.[2]

To Houphouët, at any rate, the Communist Party seemed more attractive than either of the other big parties. The MRP had a local branch in the Ivory Coast which was allied with the Union Voltaïque (his opponents); while if he joined the SFIO he would inevitably fall under the shadow of Lamine-Guèye. He wanted to avoid this, not because he disliked Lamine-Guèye personally, but because he resented the privileged and dominant position of Senegal within AOF. To accept Senegalese leadership would be scarcely better than accepting colonial rule.[3]

So Houphouët joined the MUR. This brought him together with d'Arboussier, who also joined it, but perhaps for slightly different reasons. He was born in the Soudan, the son of a French administrator and an African woman. He had been educated by Catholic missionaries, then in France. After taking a law degree, he followed his father's career in the colonial service. But he was too conscious of his African inheritance to identify completely with his French colleagues. By the end of the war he had broken with his Catholic

---

[1] Apithy, reminiscences in conversation with the author.
[2] Morgenthau, op. cit., p. 85.
[3] Ansprenger, op. cit., pp. 124–5.

background and apparently accepted Marxist ideas. He made himself the champion of the alliance between the French proletariat and the 'national' democratic forces in Africa. He more than anyone seems to have convinced Houphouët that the alliance with the Communists was both natural and necessary.

## B. Colonial Reforms

Though the Assembly was constituent, it also had legislative powers. The colonial deputies were therefore able directly to propose and vote for some colonial reforms. They had many grievances to air and requests to make, but they found it difficult to capture the Assembly's attention. Inevitably there was a great backlog of legislative work on purely metropolitan affairs to get on with, besides the Constitution itself. It was difficult to obtain parliamentary time to discuss colonial questions, and whenever they did come up the house tended to be depressingly empty. This was a pattern that African deputies were to become all too familiar with over the next ten years. They found that to get things done it was usually more effective to approach the Minister of Colonies, either directly or through the Assembly's Colonial Commission, of which d'Arboussier was elected *rapporteur*–i.e. he wrote and read reports in the Commission's name, both to the Assembly itself and to the Constitutional Committee. The Colonial Commission had several other African members, and was chaired by a long-standing Afrophile–Marius Moutet.

Among many criticisms of the government's record in Africa, the most urgently pressed were those concerning forced labour and the *indigénat*. The former had still not been abolished, for the 'native labour code' of 18th June had not been enforced; and anyway this code was ambiguous on the subject. It asserted the freedom of labour, yet still assigned a rôle to the administration in the recruitment of workers, and in holding them to their contracts. The *indigénat* had not been abolished either, but the government seemed now to have realised that it was an intolerable anachronism. In August Giacobbi had issued a circular forbidding administrators to resort to it 'unless in exceptional cases'; this was not very helpful, since it left the individual administrator to decide what constituted an exceptional case, and the principal evil of the system was precisely that it placed the 'subject' at the administrator's mercy. Soustelle, who replaced Giacobbi in the new government which de Gaulle formed after the Assembly met, decided to go further. By a decree of 22nd December he formally abolished all provisions by which administrators could impose prison sentences and fines on individuals without the judgment of a court.[1]

Another measure taken by the de Gaulle government was the creation of an African currency: the franc CFA (*Colonies françaises d'Afrique*), worth 1.7–later 2–metropolitan francs. This was intended to protect Africa from some of the effects of the devaluation of the franc. 'This innovation', said Pleven, 'corresponds to our desire expressed at the Brazzaville Conference, to take fairly into account the interests of each of the territories which make up the French Union, and to respect their particular needs and local circumstances. It marks, on the monetary level, the end of the colonial pact'.[2] The economic interests of the colonies were no longer to be automatically subordinated to those of the metropole.

A month later, in January 1946, the Colonies themselves officially ceased to exist. De Gaulle, exasperated by differences of opinion between himself and the majority parties, resigned, and a new government came in, headed by the Socialist **Félix Gouin**. Marius Moutet became Minister of *la France d'Outre-Mer* ('Overseas France'), and this expression was used from then on in all titles or phrases where the word 'colonial' had previously figured. The Colonies became *Territories d'Outre-Mer* (T.O.M.), and the Assembly's Colonial Commission was now the *Commission des T.O.M.* Lamine-Guèye replaced Moutet as its chairman.

One of Moutet's first actions as Minister was to complete Soustelle's work of dismantling the *indigénat*. A decree of 20th February 1946 abolished 'administrative internment'–i.e. arbitrary house-arrest–and fines imposed collectively on communities. From now on colonial administrators would have no non-judicial sanctions with which to coerce the population.

At least, in theory. In practice, the administration proved very reluctant to accept this progressive impulse from above. In the Ivory Coast, Mauduit no sooner received news of Soustelle's decree than he re-enacted the principal *indigénat* provisions by an *arrêté* of his own. When this document was brought to Moutet's notice he promptly recalled Mauduit and sent Latrille back to the Ivory Coast.[3] But it

[1] Devèze, op. cit. Moutet's speech in the Assembly, 23rd March 1946.
[2] Debate in the Assembly, 26th December 1945.
[3] Moutet, loc. cit., 22nd March 1946.

was only one of many examples of colonial abuses which Lamine-Guèye and others were able to produce when at last d'Arboussier managed to force a full-dress debate on overseas affairs at the end of March.[1] Tactfully, the African speakers all proclaimed their admiration for France in general and Moutet in particular, and put as much of the blame as possible on Vichy. But they insisted that the spirit of Vichy lived on in the colonial administration, and some of Vichy's crimes had actually been surpassed since the Liberation—most glaringly, said Lamine-Guèye, in the provisions of the Native Penal Code of July 1944.

Perhaps the most impressive speech in the debate was Houphouët's long and passionate attack on forced labour. It was followed up by a bill formally abolishing forced labour in all the T.O.M., which was passed on 11th April and became known as the *Loi Houphouët-Boigny*. The news of its passage raised its author to semi-divine status throughout the Ivory Coast and beyond. Yet conceivably of even greater importance in the long run was the establishment (on 12th April) of FIDES: the Investment Fund for Economic and Social Development. This fund, financed from the metropolitan budget, was to make long-term loans for overseas development at a rate of one per cent. In accepting it, the Assembly showed that it recognised a debt of gratitude to the Empire (or rather, as everyone was now careful to call it, the Union) which could not be paid in words; it at last admitted the necessity of a coherent overseas development plan, the essential infrastructure for which could only be provided by a large initial public investment with no direct return. In the decade 1947–1957 Afrique Noire was to receive nearly 200,000 million francs CFA in credits from this source. Not all the money was wisely spent; but at least there was a capital expenditure on such things as education, health and communications on a scale incomparably greater than what had gone before. France spent 1·5 per cent of her national income during their period on aid to under-developed countries—and nearly all of it went to countries within the French Union. (The comparable figures are 0·6 per cent for Britain and 0·5 per cent for the U.S.A.)[2] Only if we keep this massive expenditure in mind can we understand the peculiarities of social and political development in French Africa during the same period.

[1] 20th to 23rd March 1946.     [2] Ansprenger, op. cit., p. 104.

## C. The Constitution of April 1946

The Constitution which the Assembly had met to produce was to be that not only of the French Republic, but of the new French Union as well. That was the whole point of having overseas representatives. Yet in determining the composition of the 42-man Committee which was to draft the Constitution, the Assembly only stipulated that the different Parties should be represented in proportion to their strength; and none of the parties particularly wanted to be represented by an African in a body which was to determine the new shape of democracy in metropolitan France. Only four overseas deputies became members of the Committee when it was first appointed, and only one of these was a non-European – **Paul Valentino** of Guadeloupe, nominated by the SFIO. In February 1946 he quarrelled with the party line over the question of local autonomy in the West Indies, and was replaced by Senghor, whose literary talents proved useful in drawing up the new Declaration of the Rights of Man.[1] It was Senghor who was given the task of reporting to the Assembly on the Constitutional proposals relating to the French Union. He did so on 11th April.

It had been intended, he explained, to have a special chapter in the Constitution dealing with the French Union. But on second thoughts the Committee had divided up the provisions of this chapter and grouped them under the sections dealing with the relevant institutions of the Republic. Why then was a special report on them submitted? Because this arrangement was in itself symbolic, indeed revolutionary. It showed that the former colonies were at last being treated on the same footing as the metropole. It continued the revolutionary tradition of emancipation and assimilation, and implicitly disowned the colonialist aberrations of Second Empire and Third Republic. But, said Senghor, the Committee realised that assimilation could no longer be considered an adequate solution to colonial problems. The slaves emancipated in 1794 and 1848 were already assimilated, at least to the extent that French civilisation was the only one available to them; whereas the masses who had just been liberated from forced labour and the *indigénat* had civilisations of their own which France had learnt to respect: 'the brilliant Arab civilisation which played such an important part in transmitting the heritage of Greece, then the mystic and metaphysical civilisation of India, the social humanism of China and Indo-China, the collectivist

[1] Wright, op. cit.

77

and artistic humanism of negro Africa'. These could not be forced into a Cartesian strait-jacket. They must be allowed to develop on their own lines, interacting with each other and with France, but not submerged by her. Was the Committee then suggesting a straight-forwardly federal solution? No, for a federation presupposed an approximate economic and technical equality between the federated states – something which was manifestly lacking in the French Union. No one solution would do for such a variety of problems. The system decided on was therefore a deliberate compromise: 'a system which will preserve not only the balance of the whole but also the individual and internal balances. This system is flexible. I could call it a transitional system; I prefer to call it a dynamic one which leaves the door open to the future, allowing for the greatest variety of adjustments and expansions, yet preserving the balance and harmony of the whole'.

The draft Constitution declared that all inhabitants of the French Union were citizens. It did not specify whether they were 'French citizens' or 'citizens of the French Union' – largely because no one was sure whether the inhabitants of the mandated territories could legally be made French citizens. 'We think', said Senghor, 'that that is a secondary question and we leave it to work itself out in practice'.

In fact the 'open door' policy was an undisguised compromise between assimilation and federalism. The T.O.M. were to be represented in the National Assembly of the Republic, but not in proportion to their population, and their representatives were not yet to be elected by universal suffrage. To compensate for these limitations, the local assemblies to be set up in each territory would have much greater powers than any local government body in France. The ambiguity of these provisions implied an eventual choice: 'the peoples of the Union will be able to develop freely; it will be possible for them, according to their wishes and their particular character, to take the road either towards assimilation and integration, or towards association and federation'.

The Constitution began with a new Declaration of Rights, which expressly extended to all the inhabitants of the Union the same political, economic and social rights as were enjoyed by metropolitan Frenchmen, including the rights of citizenship, without prejudice to the retention of 'personal status' in civil law; in criminal law, all the inhabitants of the same territory were to be on the same footing, whether they had formerly been 'citizens' or 'subjects'.[1]

The Constitution also recognised that the great danger for the T.O.M. lay in the difficulty of establishing effective parliamentary control over the colonial administration. It sought to overcome this difficulty, first by depriving the government of its right to legislate for the colonies by decree, and secondly by providing that the Minister of France d'Outre-Mer should have a resident Under-Secretary of State in each group of territories (e.g. one in AOF and one in AEF). Being a politician, directly responsible to the National Assembly, this official would–it was hoped–make real efforts to keep the career administrators in line. The colonial governors would thus be more effectively supervised from above; they would also be subject to some pressure from below, for each territory was to have a local assembly with power to vote the territorial budget and take decisions on many aspects of local administration. According to the Constitution these assemblies were to be elected by universal and direct suffrage, but the Law of 9th May regulating the details of their election specified that the electoral college should be the same as that for the National Assembly, as laid down in the electoral Law of 13 April. The latter certainly did not provide for universal suffrage, but it did provide for a much wider franchise than that of 1945. The African deputies admitted that it would be impossible to introduce full universal suffrage in practice until a census had been conducted–and the practical difficulties which this involved were considerable. Their most urgent demand was for the abolition of the double college, and this they succeeded in obtaining. The electoral law specified that Europeans and Africans should all vote on the same roll. There were also to be more overseas deputies than in the Constituent Assembly: each territory was to have one deputy for every 800,000 inhabitants (as against one to every 42,000 in metropolitan France). On this basis AOF would get 20 deputies, AEF 5, Cameroun 3 and Togo 1.

All these points were accepted more or less reluctantly by the MRP as well as the two Marxist parties. The only serious dispute came over the body to be known as the 'Higher Council of the French Union'. The Socialists and Communists, in voting for the creation of such a body, intended it to be merely an advisory assembly

---

[1] Moutet anticipated these provisions by a series of decrees; those of 13th March and 16th April extended full freedom of association to the T.O.M., that of 11th April freedom of assembly, and that of 30th April finally abolished 'native' criminal justice with its discriminatory penal code.

specialising in overseas affairs. The MRP and the Right wanted it to take part in the election of the President of the Republic, and in legislation. The point of this was not really to give more political weight to the T.O.M. (who were to have a larger representation in the Council than in the National Assembly) but to provide some constitutional limit to the power of the National Assembly. It was a matter of internal French politics in which the T.O.M. were only incidentally involved. The Left refused to let the Council be given any real power because they feared that it would inherit the reactionary rôle which the Senate had played in the Third Republic.[1]

There was a more genuine disagreement between Left and Right (that is, between Socialists and Communists on one side and MRP and the rest on the other) about overseas policy, namely the disagreement between federalists and assimilationists. Both sides eventually voted for the compromise embodied in the Constitution, but their conceptions of the future evolution of the French Union were very different. The interesting thing was that assimilation, which had formerly been thought of as a left-wing, Jacobin doctrine, had now been taken over by the Right, whereas the Left had lost confidence in it. The ideas of Lenin and Stalin on the one hand, of Gandhi and Senghor on the other, had convinced those who really wanted to extend liberty and equality to the non-white races that this could not be accomplished by simply treating them as Frenchmen. They should be equal, but they might also be different. They should be free, but free to accept or reject French civilisation – or to accept parts of it and reject others.

Both sides agreed that there should be a French Union, and that its disintegration should if possible be prevented. Everyone accepted this, including the Africans themselves, and even the Communists; they wanted to be citizens of a great power, and they felt that France with 110 million inhabitants would be a great power, whereas with 40 million she would not. They also believed that underdeveloped countries would be safer in association with a 'democratic' – i.e. partly socialist – power, than if they were left a helpless prey to Anglo-Saxon capitalism.[2] The disagreement was about methods. Could disintegration best be avoided by centralisation and the maintenance of metropolitan French authority – as the Right thought – or by decentralisation and an offer (which would be gratefully refused) of complete independence? The inclusion of the phrase 'a Union freely

[1] Wright, op. cit.   [2] Morgenthau, op. cit., pp. 25–7.

consented to' in Article 41 of the Constitution was a victory for the Left. The most eloquent exponent of the left-wing view was **Pierre Cot,** a pre-war Radical now in the process of becoming a fellow-traveller. (He joined the MUR group on 2nd April.) 'What we need', he declared in the March debate on overseas affairs, 'is to proclaim here and now a new policy which will be not only a policy for the individual but a policy for the nationalities [*Applause*] which we want to see gradually brought into the French Union. . . . Brazzaville has been overtaken by events. . . . From the political point of view it was an error, particularly on account of that first resolution which denied to the peoples living in the French Union any hope, even remote, in the direction of independence and liberty.' Brazzaville was now seen as the expression of a new form of colonialism, as reprehensible as the old one which it had itself condemned. Cot spoke of 'the right to independence'. But, he said, there might also be a 'duty not to use this right inopportunely'. He spoke of 'the road to independence–complete independence, as we all hope–within the framework of the French Union. . . . We understand what could be meant for us and for the world by a genuine association of all the peoples who believe in liberty, equality and fraternity. That is the true French Union. It must not be imposed on you, what am I saying? it must not even be proposed to you.' Such a union could only result from the spontaneous desire of its various members.[1]

Fourteen years later Africans were to be offered membership of a French Community almost identical with the French Union which Cot envisaged. By then they were divided and embittered and the proposal aroused little enthusiasm. But in 1946 Cot's speech made a highly favourable impression on the overseas deputies, and there can be little doubt that most if not all of them would have been glad to accept membership of a French Union so defined. Even Ho Chi Minh was at this time negotiating with Gouin's representatives, and had obtained recognition of the Republic of Viet-Nam as 'a free State with its own Government, its own Parliament, its own army and its own finances, forming part of the Indo-Chinese Federation and of the French Union'.[2] As for Afrique Noire, had its inhabitants been asked to give the 'free consent' of which the Constitution spoke, they would certainly have done so.

But African 'subjects' could not vote in the referendum on the Constitution. The Constituent Assembly drew its authority from a referendum in which only citizens had voted. According to the terms

[1] Debate of 23rd March 1946.　　[2] Devèze, op. cit.

of that referendum (devised by the de Gaulle government to prevent the Assembly's powers from being unlimited in time and scope) the new Constitution had to be submitted, within seven months of the Assembly's election, to the 'electoral body of French citizens'. Lamine-Guèye suggested that this should be taken to include all those who had been entitled to vote in the 1945 election. But legally this was inadmissible since the second-college voters would only become citizens by the terms of the Constitution itself. Therefore to allow them to vote in the referendum would be to prejudge the result. The irony of the situation was that no one was seriously afraid that the overseas voters might reject the Constitution; what they might do was to tip the balance in its favour, for the MRP had decided to oppose the Constitution on the grounds that it left too much power in the hands of a single Assembly. The MRP spokesman who was to present the full text of the Constitution to the house resigned at the last moment, and his task was taken over by Pierre Cot. It was Cot who suggested that the Assembly should anticipate the Constitution by an ordinary law, not subject to ratification by referendum, granting citizenship to all inhabitants of the T.O.M. and thus enabling them to vote. Lamine-Guèye quickly took up the suggestion and on 18th April brought in a bill of historic brevity: 'As from 1st June 1946, all inhabitants of the overseas territories (including Algeria) have the status of citizen in the same category as the French nationals of the metropole or of the overseas territories. Particular laws will establish the conditions in which they will exercise their rights as citizens.' This became the *Loi Lamine-Guèye* of 7th May 1946. But too late. The referendum was held on 5th May; the Assembly decided that the 'free consent' of the 'subjects' could best be established by a separate overseas referendum, which would be held two months after the first–if the result of the first was positive.[1]

But the result of the first was negative, by $10\frac{1}{2}$ million to $9\frac{1}{2}$ million votes.[2] France still had no constitution. Instead of 'subjects', she now had over 20 million black African citizens (not to mention Algerians, Malagasies, Polynesians, Indians and Oceanians). But her relationship with them remained undefined.

[1] Morgenthau, op. cit., p. 44. Devèze, op. cit.     [2] Wright, op. cit.

PART TWO

---

# The Cold War, 1946–1950

*Chapter 4*

---

# The Second Constituent Assembly

## A. Second Thoughts

The metropolitan electors who voted 'No' on 5th May did so primarily to avoid the creation of a single, all-powerful National Assembly, and to express their hostility to Communism. It can safely be assumed that few of them either knew or cared what the draft Constitution said about 'Overseas France'. It was the MRP's opposition which ensured the Constitution's defeat, and the MRP deputies had voted *for* its French Union provisions in the Assembly, even if they were a little uneasy about some of them. Their spokesman **Paul Viard,** replying to Senghor's report, emphasised the points it had in common with the MRP's original ideas, and personally claimed the credit for the introduction of Under-Secretaries of State resident overseas. Rather than repeat the arguments for a double college voting system which he had urged in the Committee (and which had been accepted for his native Algeria), he merely mentioned that he would have liked the powers of the local assemblies to be much wider; and he summed up: 'In general, the MRP gives its approval to the Constitution of the French Union, even if certain details call for adjustment or clarification'.[1]

The Gouin government therefore felt no inhibitions, immediately after the referendum, about issuing a statement 'that Sunday's vote cannot be interpreted as a disavowal of the position taken towards the overseas peoples'.[2] But it is significant that Moutet should have felt such a reassurance was necessary. To understand why, we need only look at the results of the referendum in overseas constituencies. In those where the natives were a majority of the voters – Senegal, French India, Réunion, the West Indies – the reply was a massive Yes.

[1] *Journal Officiel* (*Débats de l'Assemblée Nationale Constituante*), 11th April 1946.
[2] Morgenthau, op. cit., p. 44.

But in those where 'citizen' was still more or less synonymous with 'European', there was a majority of Noes.[1] The black 'citizens' of Senegal, for example, showed that they knew their deputy Lamine-Guèye had secured for his fellow-Africans the best offer they were likely to get–and certainly one far preferable to anything they had had before. The motives of the settler vote are harder to gauge. and may well have been mixed; many settlers no doubt shared the anti-Communist and pro-bicameral preoccupations of their metropolitan kith and kin;[2] but many also bitterly resented the off-hand revolution to which colonial society was being subjected by left-wing idealists and precocious native intellectuals. All the mechanisms which had kept the native in his place were being suddenly swept away, while the objections of those who had to deal with him directly were disregarded. How could you expect to install democracy overnight among populations who had no idea what it meant? Such were the complaints of the colonists. They did not of course deny that political and social evolution was desirable; but they claimed that Paris was trying to go too fast. A campaign against the Constitution was carried on by the magazine *Marchés Coloniaux du Monde*, organ of colonial business interests. Its editor derided the Constituents for wanting to give 'the same ballot-paper to the plate-lipped negress as to the Parisian working-woman, the same ballot-paper to the Soudanese witch-doctor as to Monsieur Joliot-Curie' (the famous nuclear chemist).[3]

On 2nd June a new Constituent Assembly was elected, with exactly the same franchise as the previous one. (The new electoral laws were automatically buried with the Constitution they had been intended to apply.) Many first-college electors showed their resentment of the first Assembly's proceedings by voting against their former deputies. Four first-college seats in Afrique Noire changed hands: all of them were won by local businessmen. D'Arboussier in Gabon-Moyen-Congo and **Reste** in the Ivory Coast (who had unexpectedly supported Houphouët's attack on forced labour) were both defeated, while the Resistance heroes who had carried Guinea and the Soudan in 1945 now stood down.[4]

---

[1] Wright, op. cit.      [2] Devèze, op. cit.
[3] *Marchés Coloniaux du Monde*, 4th May 1946, and passim.
[4] For election statistics see *Elections et referendums des 21 octobre 1945, 5 mai et 2 juin 1946* (ed. Le Monde, Paris 1946).
   For professions of deputies see *Assemblée Nationale Constituante, Notices et Portraits* (Paris 1946).

The African deputies, on the other hand, gained enormously in prestige from the first Assembly's work. They were no longer considered mere emissaries, but fêted as saviours of their people. Each was given the credit by his own territory for the abolition of forced labour: Senghor in Senegal, Apithy in Dahomey, Douala-Manga-Bell in Cameroun and, most justly, Houphouët in the Ivory Coast. All the second-college deputies were re-elected with overwhelming majorities–Apithy, for example, by 8,096 votes to 15, and Senghor with no opposition at all. In the Ivory Coast, Houphouët's picture was on sale everywhere, and he basked in the favour of the restored Governor Latrille. The Moro Naba decided not to oppose him this time; while to support him was formed the first independent African party to achieve electoral success in French Black Africa: the *Parti Démocratique de la Côte d'Ivoire* (PDCI). Its organisation was closely based on that of the Syndicat Agricole–which helped it to spread rapidly throughout the southern part of the territory–but its membership was by no means confined to the planters. Although Kouamé Binzème and two other candidates still insisted on standing against Houphouët, they won only a few hundred votes each, while he had 21,000.[1]

One might suppose that the situation which faced Houphouët and his colleagues when they returned to Paris was a relatively enviable one. They had received a clear mandate from their electors to consolidate gains already won, which had the support of all three of the major French parties and had been publicly guaranteed by the French government. But in fact these gains were in jeopardy, for the political climate in Paris was changing. In the new Assembly (which met on 11th June) the MRP was the largest single party, with 169 seats. Socialists and Communists no longer had an automatic majority whenever they voted together. To take account of this new political balance, the government was re-shuffled. It remained a three-party coalition, but **Georges Bidault** (MRP), the Minister of Foreign Affairs, replaced Gouin as prime minister. He was a fervent nationalist, who believed France's imperial power (i.e. her ability to

Reste's speech: *Journal Officiel* (*Débats*), 21st March 1946 (with Houphouët's interjection: 'You know that all those who sent you to sit in this Assembly were, and still are, firmly convinced that you would come here to support the opposite view. . . . I am very happy to see you support the view that I shall defend myself in a moment.').

[1] Morgenthau, op. cit., pp. 181–3.

control her empire) was vital to her international prestige and influence. Under his leadership, the MRP's attitude to colonial questions hardened.[1] At the same time, both MRP and Socialist groups in the Assembly were joined by new first-college deputies from Africa who set to work to persuade their colleagues that the French Union provisions of the April Constitution, so far from being non-controversial, were more muddled, less practical, and more drastically in need of revision than anything else in it.

Many deputies, especially in the MRP, began to feel that the French Union would fall to pieces before it had even been built if French governments did not take a firm line. In Madagascar, liberal reforms had been met with cries of 'A bas les Français' and a general strike. In Indo-China, French recognition of the Republic of Viet-Nam had failed to win over Ho Chi Minh's government, which was now noisily demanding that its authority be recognised in Cochin-China as well as Annam and Tongking.[2] Even in Algeria kindness did not seem to be paying dividends; an amnesty accorded to the nationalist leaders imprisoned in 1945 resulted in their winning 11 out of 13 second-college seats. Joined by the two Malagasies, these 'Friends of the Manifesto' constituted a colonial separatist bloc just big enough to help the Communists and Socialists outvote the MRP and the Right. Their leader **Ferhat Abbas** did not hesitate to exploit this excellent bargaining position, and got himself elected to the Constitutional Commission. Here too his vote could produce a deadlock on any issue where the MRP was opposed to the Left. His behaviour irritated many people, and especially of course the MRP. It seemed to provide an unpleasant foretaste of the possible effects of heavy overseas representation in the National Assembly, and increased the suspicion that in proposing this the Left was swayed by political self-interest.

On 16th June General de Gaulle broke his five-month silence with a great speech at Bayeux setting out his views on the constitutional problem. He made it clear that he regarded the structure of the French Union as crucial, and that he believed this structure should be federal.[3] This did not mean he was rallying to the views of Senghor and Pierre Cot. Far from it. His federalism was of the Brazzaville type; he seems to have shared the views of René Pleven, who in the first Assembly had criticised the 'Cot Constitution' both for failing to give the Union any effective federal institutions, and for enabling overseas deputies to sit in the National Assembly and thus

[1] Wright, op. cit.    [2] Devèze, op. cit.    [3] Wright, op. cit.

vote metropolitan taxes which their electors would not have to pay.[1] The federal and national legislatures should be distinct; but the executive should be both federal and national at once; it would thus – and this was de Gaulle's real preoccupation – avoid being the mere slave of the National Assembly. The corollary of this was that territories such as those of Afrique Noire, which were not yet states within the federation, would be governed by presidential decree.

The MRP took this speech as a rap over the knuckles for not giving the colonial question enough thought. Previously partisans of a quasi-assimilationist centralising policy, they now announced their conversion to 'progressive federalism'. For the next few months every party from extreme Left to extreme Right sought to demonstrate that its particular colonial policy was the most truly 'federal'. The Left wanted a federation of free and equal partners, each territory adhering voluntarily and defining its own status and relationship with France. The Right wanted a Federation with central organs strong enough both to prevent secession and to justify the exclusion of overseas deputies from the French National Assembly; and it wanted a federal citizenship distinct from that of France so that, for the time being at least, the same political rights would not have to be guaranteed in all the different territories. In the end the Right was constrained to accept a token overseas representation in the National Assembly, as the price of continued French supremacy,[2] and the Left was constrained to insist on such representation so that at least French supremacy would be palliated by overseas participation in the French state. Thus each side reverted to assimilation against its will, in order to please the other, and Africa became part of the Fourth Republic almost by mistake.

## B. The 'Intergroupe des Autochthones'

But this solution, or rather non-solution, was only reached after long debates, as heated as they were confused. The first move was made by the non-European deputies themselves. They knew which way the wind was blowing. They had read the attacks on the April constitution in *Marchés Coloniaux du Monde*. They knew that the *Etats Généraux de la Colonisation Française*, founded at Douala the year before, were about to hold a second and larger meeting, in Paris, to

[1] Journal Officiel (*Débats*) 11th April 1946.
[2] See Wright; the cry of 'Abbas go home' was soon dropped. It was too easy for Abbas to reply that he had much rather sit in a parliament in Algiers.

lobby in defence of settler interests—possibly even for a re-establishment of forced labour. They noted with alarm that the MRP withdrew its only African member, Douala-Manga-Bell, from the T.O.M. Commission, and replaced him with the new first-college deputy from the Soudan. They concluded that the presence of individual Africans scattered in the ranks of the governing parties might not be enough to avert disaster. On Lamine-Guèye's initative they formed an 'intergroup' of 'autochthonous' overseas deputies, thus breaking away from an existing overseas intergroup which had included both first- and second-college deputies. The new Intergroup was designed to co-ordinate the activity of all non-European deputies in defence of non-European interests, while allowing them to remain members of their various party groups. Its principal field of action was the T.O.M. Commission, and there it soon made an impact.

The MRP members of the Commission had succeeded in passing a motion to scrap the April texts on the French Union completely and start again by studying a new project. They then produced a project of their own, which established the President of the French Republic and the 'Assembly of the French Union' as central federal authorities, without specifying how they were to be elected. In reply, the Intergroup produced a set of six articles which took everyone by surprise. The first read as follows: 'France solemnly denounces systems of colonisation based on the annexation, conquest or domination of the overseas territories. She renounces all unilateral sovereignty over the colonised peoples. She recognises their freedom to govern themselves and conduct their own affairs in a democratic manner.'

After this dramatic opening, the draft went on to define the French Union as 'based on equality of rights and duties without distinction of race or religion'. Where the MRP project spoke of 'nations and peoples who pool their resources', the Intergroup's one read 'who freely agree to pool their resources'—and so on. It specified a time-limit of twenty years, by the end of which all the overseas peoples should be allowed to choose freely whether to remain linked with France, and if so by what sort of links. In the meantime, the Constitution of the French Union should not be decided by the present Constituent Assembly at all; the Constitutions of the individual territories should be worked out by local assemblies, and then that of the Union by an Assembly representing the Union as a whole in proportion to population. (As Lamine-Guèye put it, 'you can't federate something until it exists'.) Until the Union Constitution should be voted, the territories represented in the present Constituent Assembly should continue to be so in the French National Assembly. Finally, the use of war or force against the freedom of any of the peoples of the Union was formally forsworn.

This project was opposed by the MRP but nonetheless secured a narrow majority in the T.O.M. Commission. On 24th July it appeared before the Constitutional Commission. Here it was supported by Ferhat Abbas, Pierre Cot and the Communists, and also, a little more cautiously, by the Socialists. Aujoulat, representing the minority of the T.O.M. Commission, explained the MRP's objections to it. The strongest of these was that it involved delaying the solution of a problem which was becoming every day more urgent. 'The colonial territories have the right to know, as soon as possible, the context in which they will be called upon to live.' Aujoulat was supported by **Jean-Jacques Juglas,** an MRP deputy who was one of the government's representatives in the negotiations with Ho Chi Minh which were then in progress at Fontainbleau. He asked how he could be expected to propose membership of the French Union to the Viet-Nam delegates, if the constitution of the French Union was not yet defined. But this argument failed to convince the 'autochthones': they knew that the Viet-Nam government would gladly accept membership of a community which did not yet exist, for it would then be able to negotiate about that community's constitution from a position of *de facto* independence. In fact, it was precisely this development that Bidault's government was determined to avoid; it wanted a ready-made French Union constitution which would give it a legal right to restore French authority in Indo-China.

Up to this point it had been accepted doctrine that the government should not intervene in the discussion of the Constitution. But Bidault and his colleagues felt that their task of holding the French Union together would become impossible if the Union constitution were left undefined much longer. A minister of state, **Alexandre Varenne,** was deputed to inform the Constitutional Commission of the government's views. A motion was put to the Commission, tending 'to include in the Constitution, here and now, the permanent organs of the French Union'. This motion would have been blocked if all the Commission's members had been present at the time of the vote for exactly half of them (including the Socialists) were committed to support the Intergroup's proposal that the Union constitution should be left to a Union Assembly to work out. But it happened that two of the Communist members were out of the room; so the motion passed by 21 votes to 19.

The Commission therefore proceeded to consider an eight-article 'Charter of the French Union' which had been drawn up by an interministerial committee of civil servants under Varenne's chairmanship. These proposals resembled those of the MRP, except that they made the 'Assembly of the French Union' a purely consultative body, and added to it a 'High Council of the Union' in which would sit representatives of the governments of the 'associated states' (i.e. Viet-Nam and the former protectorates – Laos, Cambodia, Tunisia and Morocco) alongside a French government delegation, the whole to be presided over by the President of the French Republic.

During the discussion of this 'Charter', the Left managed to insert into it a number of the Intergroup's proposals – notably the phrase about 'freely agreeing', and the promise of an eventual choice of status for each territory (although the twenty-year deadline disappeared). The Loi Lamine-Guèye, conferring citizenship on all inhabitants of the T.O.M., was explicitly confirmed; and a watered-down version of the article denouncing oppressive colonialism was inserted into the preamble. It was specified that the local assemblies overseas should be elected by universal and direct suffrage. Next, Varenne's articles defining the organic institutions of the Union, and laying down that the President of the Republic was automatically President of the Union, were thrown out, and replaced by an article which simply stated: 'The status of each territory, federation or group of territories, will be established by the local assemblies and by Parliament.' This amounted to a reversal of the vote by which the Commission had agreed to define the Union constitution unilaterally, and thus placed the Commission in direct conflict with the government. Reluctantly the MRP representative, **Paul Coste-Floret,** who was to present the draft Constitution to the Assembly, accepted this decision; he agreed that in his report he would leave the question of the Union constitution open, in the hope that a federal solution would eventually emerge as the different territories developed. Senghor secured the insertion of an assurance that in the meantime the T.O.M. would continue to be represented in the French Parliament.[1]

[1] Devèze, op. cit., and *Séances de la Commission Constitutionnelle* (Paris 1947).

## C. The Etats-Généraux

The result of these concessions was to make Coste-Floret's report—or rather the section of it which concerned the French Union—a hopelessly confused compromise which scarcely satisfied anyone, and least of all the government. But it was not until the end of August that this section of the report came up for discussion in the Assembly. Meanwhile, from 30th July to 24th August, the long-awaited Congress of the *Etats-Généraux de la Colonisation Française* took place. It was dominated by the European planters and employers of the Ivory Coast and Cameroun. These men lost little time in producing their own set of resolutions for the French Union, intended as a counterblast to those of the Intergroup. They protested against any attempt to dismantle 'the admirable work accomplished by the Third Republic in all the territories of the Empire, and to abdicate a sovereignty which is still necessary, in their own interests, for populations who still look to France for the order and tranquillity that are indispensable to their evolution towards freedom and independence'. A truly 'federal' solution, they thought, would involve the retention of the double electoral college for all overseas elections, with 'at least equal representation of the two colleges' both in local assemblies and in the 'Assembly of the French Union'. At this price, overseas representation in the French parliament could safely be abolished. French citizenship proper should be kept clearly distinct from that of the Union, and made available only to those individual natives 'who are able to grasp its moral, social and political significance'.[1] As for forced labour, its abolition was accepted, but this did not mean that the native could be allowed to slack. Every able-bodied man between the ages of 18 and 55 should be able to prove that he had done at least 240 days' work in the year, and defaulters should be set to work by the administration.[2] All this, of course, in the interests of progress.

The direct influence of this Congress has probably been exaggerated. Even the new first-college deputies did not automatically follow this extreme settler line. For example, **Jean-Baptiste Ferracci,** first-college deputy from Guinea, was present at the Congress;[3] but this did not prevent him from supporting African demands for full French citizenship and a single electoral college when they were debated in the Assembly.[4] Nonetheless, the meeting enraged all

---

[1] Quoted in Devèze, op. cit.      [2] Morgenthau, op. cit., p. 47.
[3] Ibid., p. 46.      [4] Journal Officiel (*Débats*), 18th September 1946.

educated Africans, and rightly or wrongly they held it largely responsible for their failure to secure such favourable terms from the second Constituent Assembly as they had from the first. Whether the influence of European settlers (other than those in Algeria) was really very great either in the Assembly or in the government may well be doubted. Probably they gained some sympathy from non-Communist deputies as a result of the wrath and vituperation heaped upon them by the Communist press. At all events, the *Etats-Généraux* did help to draw attention to the fact that the white minority problem was not confined to Algeria; and this may have made some moderates more willing to reconsider the arguments for and against the double college.

### D. The Battle with the Government

During August the negotiations at Fontainebleau made little progress. Semi-anarchy persisted both in Vietnam and in Madagascar. There were nationalist demonstrations in Tunisia. The government's anxiety about colonial affairs increased. MRP and Socialist ministers were irritated by the Communists' vociferous support of Ho Chi Minh and their irresponsible demands for inflationary wage increases; they felt less and less confident of the loyalty of their Communist colleagues. The MRP especially resented the Communists' behaviour, and especially the fact that Communists persisted in violently attacking the Constitutional draft although the latter now contained very large concessions to their views–and this in spite of their defeat in the referendum of 5th May.[1] In these circumstances it was unfortunate for the African deputies that the Communists were their most loyal and outspoken allies.

It was on 27th August that the debate in the Assembly first touched the Commission's proposals for the French Union, grouped together as Title VIII of Coste-Floret's constitutional draft. **Edouard Herriot,** the elderly Radical leader, turned to this section of the draft with evident distaste. He objected to its apparent repudiation of the Third Republic's colonial achievement. He still belonged in spirit to the Third Republic himself, and was far from ashamed to recall the exploits of its great colonial servants: the politician Jules Ferry, the soldier Gallieni and the explorer Brazza. Moreover, he was unhappy about the indiscriminate extension of French citizenship. 'How many overseas French citizens will there be?' he asked.

[1] Wright, op. cit.

'More than there are metropolitan ones. Does the Commission want France to become a colony of her former colonies?'[1] The remark was to be much quoted, for it neatly expresses the dilemma of the Jacobin tradition, the assimilationist's fear that he himself might be assimilated.

Herriot certainly did not resolve this dilemma; but he had no difficulty in showing that Coste-Floret's Title VIII would not resolve it either, for it simply did not make sense as it stood. It asserted the existence of the French Union, but failed to provide any institutions which could make it a visible reality. (It did not even include the Intergroup's original proposal for a French Union Constituent Assembly.) This objection was urgently backed up by Moutet, speaking for the government, which, he said, 'cannot accept texts that tend to damage the sovereignty of our country'. Moutet made it clear that it was above all the Vietnam situation which made precision and speed essential: 'when we insist on respect for the agreement of 6th March, viz. the incorporation of Viet-Nam into the French Union, we must be able to specify what will be the respective rights of Viet-Nam and of the Union.'[2] After his intervention the Assembly agreed to postpone discussion of the French Union until it had dealt with the rest of the Constitution, so that the Commission could hear evidence from the government and then revise Title VIII.[3]

Accordingly, on 11th September Varenne and Moutet appeared in person before the Commission with a new text which had the formal approval of the Cabinet. This time there were 23 articles. The following were the most important points:

(a) The Union was now defined as consisting of the French Republic on the one hand and the Associated States on the other. The T.O.M. were explicitly included *within* the French Republic.

(b) The government again insisted on the creation of a 'High Council of the French Union', which, Moutet explained, was intended as an embryo federal government.

(c) The 'Assembly of the French Union' was to include separate representation for 'persons of French status established in the different parts of the Union'; this could only mean—as Pierre Cot was quick to point out—that the elections for this Assembly would be held in double college; and Moutet hedged rather than give a definite guarantee that the single college would be maintained for

[1] *Journal Officiel* (*Débats*), 27th August 1946.    [2] Ibid.    [3] Wright, op. cit.

local and National Assembly elections. In fact the contrary seemed to be implied in Article 19, which said that the elective Assemblies in each territory 'must assure the representation of all parts of the population which have a distinct status'.

(d) The composition and powers of these assemblies were left 'to be decided by a law which will be the organic statute of the territory'.

(e) It was reaffirmed that colonial governors were responsible to the government of the Republic.

(f) The T.O.M. were to be represented in the National Assembly 'in conditions fixed by law'.

(g) Union citizenship was to be distinct from French citizenship, and the latter available only to individuals fulfilling certain legal requirements. This was precisely the castration of the Loi Lamine-Guèye which the Etats-Généraux had asked for.

In short, this text allowed the benefits of a federal Union only to the 'Associated States'. For the T.O.M. it proposed a highly centralised, even authoritarian, system which approximated more closely to the *status quo* than to any of the other constitutional proposals so far produced. Small wonder that the Left and the Africans were unwilling to swallow it. The MRP, however, was ready to accept it as a basis for discussion, and the Socialists reluctantly agreed to this, impressed by the fact that it had the unanimous authority of a government which included both Socialists and Communists. On 12th September the Commission went through the first seven articles and accepted them with only minor changes, except that the provision to reserve some seats in the Assembly of the French Union for the white minority overseas was cut out. Even this change was opposed by the MRP, who announced their intention of demanding its reversal when the draft came before the Assembly.

At the Commission's next session, on the 17th, the remainder of the government text was approved only after considerable amendment. The Commission insisted on specifying that the territorial assemblies overseas would be elected by universal suffrage, and that their function would be to 'administer and manage' the interests of their respective territories. In particular, they would have to be consulted before Parliament could finally pass each territory's 'statute'. As for the colonial governor, instead of being 'trustee of the powers of the Republic' and 'Head of the administration of the territory', he became merely 'a delegate responsible for the interests of the French

Union'. The Loi Lamine-Guèye was reaffirmed in the sense that its author had intended it (assuring the inhabitants of the T.O.M. of the rights and freedom of *French* citizens, without prejudice to their personal status); and the 'anti-colonial' paragraph in the Preamble was retained, with the addition of the Intergroup's 'liberal' definition of the Union, now omitted from Title VIII.

But the MRP did just succeed in keeping in the clause assuring representation in the territorial assemblies of 'parts of the population which have distinct status'. This was universally taken as implying the re-establishment of the double college for these assemblies, and moreover it effectively reversed the MRP's defeat on the question of the Assembly of the French Union, since it was the territorial assemblies who were to elect the overseas representatives in the latter.[1] At all events, the issue of the single college now became the crucial one for the African deputies; they determined to rescue that even if all else were lost. In the debate in the Assembly on 18th September they rose one after another to plead with desperate eloquence that France should keep her word, and not continue to treat her erstwhile subjects as merely second-class citizens. Leaving Pierre Cot to make the case for keeping the door open to greater autonomy, the Africans themselves concentrated on demanding their equal rights as Frenchmen. Senghor, Lamine-Guèye, Diallo and Sissoko all made extravagant statements of their loyalty to France and their sense of identity as Frenchmen. Again and again they appealed to the African war record as evidence that they were 'as French, as Republican, as anyone else'. Even Sissoko, a long-standing opponent of assimilation, who described himself as an 'extreme African traditionalist', nonetheless declared his goal to be 'pure and simple integration into the French nation', and spoke of 'our deep conviction which makes us want to remain French until the end of time'. African demands were now reduced to two: full French citizenship, which was promised by the Commission's new text but opposed by the Government and the Radicals, and the single college, which was rejected by the Commission but supported by a Socialist amendment. Only the MRP supported the Commission's text as it stood.[2]

Next morning the government made yet another attempt to browbeat the Commission. Moutet and Varenne reappeared before it, this time with a new text for the Preamble. The main purpose of this

[1] *Séances de la Commission Constitutionnelle* (Paris 1947).
[2] Journal Officiel (*Débats*), 18th September 1946.

was to eliminate all words and phrases which might suggest that the overseas peoples had the right to refuse co-operation, or to become independent. Thus such words as 'accept' and 'co-ordinate' disappeared; 'their respective civilisations' became simply 'their civilisation'—and so on. Even the word 'democratic' was rigorously suppressed. Once again the Commission took account of the government's views but refused to treat them as sacrosanct. A compromise text was adopted which made only slight concessions to Moutet's amendment, but was by now very much gentler than the Intergroup's resounding original.[1]

In the afternoon, the debate in the Assembly continued, with further passionate pleas for the single college from Houphouët and Tchicaya. Half way through it came an announcement that the government had put down a 'Bill relating to the French Union', and in the evening Bidault himself came into the Commission to issue what amounted to an ultimatum. The Commission must accept this bill, he said, without adding to it; the utmost change he would admit was that some provisions might be dropped from the Constitution as such, and left for definition by an 'organic law'. In particular, he insisted absolutely on the retention of the double college, the distinct French Union citizenship, and the government's control over the colonial administration. 'Delegate' was not an adequate word to describe a colonial governor, and the government could not accept such a diminution of French sovereignty. If the Commission would not satisfy him on these points, Bidault said, he would regretfully have to push the matter to a showdown before the Assembly, and if defeated there he would resign.

The Commission was duly overawed by this display of presidential rage. Next morning, after a further audition of Moutet and Varenne to clarify certain points, it accepted the government text for Title VIII more or less as it stood, ignoring bitter protests from Abbas and Senghor (as well as Houphouët and Lamine-Guèye who were present as substitutes for other members of their groups).[2] The Intergroup met hurriedly and decided to play its last card. When the debate on Title VIII opened in the Assembly that afternoon, all the non-European deputies (including those from the West Indies, now fully integrated departments of the French Republic) got up and left the chamber. They all signed a letter resigning their seats: not only the Africans and Malagasies and Aimé Césaire but even such

[1] *Séances de la Commission Constitutionnelle* (Paris 1947).
[2] Ibid.

eminently assimilated figures as Gaston Monnerville and Felix Eboué's widow[1] who was deputy for Guadeloupe. ' "That's it", we said. "We cannot be second-class Frenchmen. Either we are French-men in all respects [*à part entière*] or the whole thing is of no interest to us." ' **Vincent Auriol**, president of the Assembly, declared himself incompetent to receive such a letter, and referred its authors to the government. Bidault, with Moutet and Coste-Floret, received a delegation consisting of Lamine-Guèye, Monnerville, Houphouët, Césaire and Ferhat Abbas. He tried at first to browbeat them by suggesting that resignation in these circumstances was tantamount to an attack on France herself. 'We said: "No, *monsieur le Président*, there is no question of an attack on France, direct or indirect. The question is, are we Frenchmen like any other Frenchmen, or not?– that's all. For example, why don't you declare that because there are so many Corsicans in Paris, therefore *they* must have a deputy of their own–and so on? Why is it only we who are subjected to special treatment? It's *you* who say that we are not Frenchmen like other Frenchmen; *we* had believed that we *were*. But that's the way it is, there's no point in our staying here. Of course you can issue decrees and order us about. We don't dispute that; but if you want to get us this way we say: 'No thank you . . . *c'est fini*!' " '[2]

Bidault realised that this collective resignation must be averted, for if confirmed it would do more harm than anything to the Union. After long and hard bargaining, therefore, he made two concessions: first, he allowed Article 80 of the Constitution to confirm explicitly that the inhabitants of the T.O.M. were 'citizens, on the same basis as French nationals' (using the same words as the Loi Lamine-Guèye). Secondly, he allowed the overseas electoral system to be dropped from the Constitution and left to an organic law. Thus even if the double college were retained for the time being, it would not have the unalterable character of a constitutional principle.

On these terms the Intergroup deputies reluctantly agreed to resume their seats and vote for the Constitution. Their final battle against the double-college system came during the debate on the

---

[1] Eboué himself had died a few months after the Brazzaville Conference.

[2] Tape-recorded statement made by Lamine-Guèye in 1959 to Dr Franz Ansprenger and quoted by him (in German) in *Politik im schwarzen Afrika*, op. cit., pp. 72–3. Dr Ansprenger kindly allowed me to reproduce this, but was unable to give me the original French version. The above is therefore a second-remove version of what President Lamine-Guèye actually said, and therefore probably only a very rough translation.

electoral law. The Commission still favoured the single college for elections to the National Assembly, and Lamine-Guèye succeeded in getting the government to accept this as far as AOF and Togo were concerned. But in return the government insisted that the Commission give way (i.e. retain the double college) for AEF, Cameroun and Madagascar. When the law was debated by the Assembly on 4th October, Tchicaya actually obtained a vote by show of hands extending the single college to AEF and Cameroun. But Moutet immediately intervened to demand a second reading, and the Commission's report was re-adopted against its own wishes. Finally, the government refused to pass a law organising the overseas local assemblies before the Constituent Assembly broke up; instead it obtained power to organise them provisionally by decree, until a law should be passed by the new National Assembly. This meant that in practice they would be elected by double college throughout Afrique Noire (except in Senegal, where a single-college assembly had already been instituted by a decree of February 1946).

## E. The Constitution of October 1946: Africa within the Fourth Republic

The Constitution produced by the second Constituent Assembly was accepted without enthusiasm, by a disillusioned electorate. (The majority in favour on 13th October was as narrow as the majority against had been on 5th May, while one third of the electorate abstained.) It had the half-hearted support of all three government parties, but was opposed by General de Gaulle, who thought that it still left the National Assembly far too strong and the executive far too weak. Overseas, the result was much the same as in May. The settlers voted 'No', partly because many of them were Gaullists, partly because they still considered the colonial provisions too liberal. The coloured citizens voted 'Yes', fearing that any further revision would bring new triumphs to the Reaction.[1]

Under this unloved Constitution, France and French Africa were to live for the next twelve years. Nominally they belonged to a 'French Union', which was but a pale shadow of the federally organised empire envisaged by the Brazzaville Conference. 'President of the French Union' was simply an extra title for the President of the French Republic. The 'High Council of the French Union' (Moutet's 'embryo government') which was to unite delegates from the ex-

[1] Wright, Devèze, Morgenthau (p. 54).

ecutives of France, Viet-Nam, Laos, Cambodia, Morocco and Tunisia, did not even meet till 1950. And the Assembly of the French Union, far from being the federal parliament originally called for at Brazzaville, had purely advisory functions. It was to vegetate outside the main political arena, at Versailles, and the French Parliament in Paris usually ignored its proposals. Its main value to Africa was to be as a training-ground for junior politicians.

To negro Africans, the institutions of the French Republic were of far greater importance than those of the Union. AOF, AEF, Somaliland and Madagascar were *Territoires d'Outre-Mer*, formally included within the Republic itself. Togo and Cameroun were protected from this fate by their special position in international law; they were given the special title of 'Associated Territories'. But in practice they were treated in exactly the same way as the T.O.M. Only their Governors were disguised under the title 'High Commissioner of the Republic', and their local assemblies were called 'Representative Assembly', whereas those of the T.O.M. were called 'General Council' in order to sustain the pretence that they were ordinary local government bodies like the General Councils of Departments in metropolitan France.

The T.O.M. and 'Associated Territories' were represented in both houses of the French Parliament, the National Assembly and the 'Council of the Republic' (an emasculated version of the old Senate). Deputies to the National Assembly were elected directly, as they had been to the Constituent Assemblies. The franchise for these elections was wider than that used for the Constituent Assemblies,[1] but, as defined by the electoral law of 5th October, was narrower than that prescribed by the abortive one of 13th April: the categories entitled to vote still only contained 3½ per cent of the total population in AOF, 2¾ per cent in AEF, 1½ per cent in Cameroun and 1 per cent in Togo.[2] The total number of deputies allotted to Afrique Noire was 24 (as against 30 in the April law). Of these, two represented the Europeans (or, more strictly, the *citoyens de statut français*— i.e. those subject to French civil law) of AEF and one those of

[1] Law of 5th October 1946; the vote was given to all former members of co-operatives and unions, all regular wage-earners in establishments recognised by law, all ex-servicemen, and all who owned legally registered property or held hunting- or driving-licences. The ex-servicemen tended to be the largest category of voters. But the electorate remained a predominantly urban one, although the towns contained only a tiny minority of the African population.

[2] Calculated from the same sources as Table I above.

Cameroun. The remainder were elected mainly by Africans (*citoyens de statut local*), and were divided as follows:

| | |
|---|---|
| AOF | 13 |
| AEF | 4 |
| Cameroun | 2 |
| Togo | 1 |
| (Somaliland | 1) |

Africa was rather more generously represented in the Council of the Republic. This had 315 members (as against the National Assembly's 618), yet of these AOF had 19, AEF eight, Cameroun three and Togo two. But they were elected, not directly, but by the 'General Councils' and 'Representative Assemblies', and, like those assemblies themselves, on a double-college system. This enabled the settlers of AOF to retain some official voice in Parliament. The Council of the Republic could not veto legislation, but it did provide considerable opportunities for filibuster, and these were to be used.

The local assemblies themselves were provisionally instituted by decrees issued on 25th October. The proportion of first- and second-college 'councillors' which they were to contain varied from territory to territory, but in most cases the first college secured two fifths; there would therefore be a narrow African majority. But the powers of these assemblies were severely restricted. Although they were to vote the territorial budgets, there was a long list of categories of expenditure which they could not refuse. They therefore had little hope of gaining control of the administration by the power of the purse.

Even from an assimilationist point of view the Constitution left much to be desired. Unlike the April draft, it confirmed the pre-war system by which the French Council of Ministers could legislate (within fairly wide limits) for the colonies by decree; the only difference was that it now had to ask (but not necessarily accept) the opinion of the French Union Assembly before doing so. Similarly the resident under-secretaries overseas, responsible to Parliament, who had seemed such a hopeful feature of the April Constitution, had vanished without trace in the October one. In practice the over-worked National Assembly was to find that it could leave colonial problems to be dealt with by the executive—unless and until they erupted in actual violence. And since the governments of the Fourth Republic were as short-lived as those of the Third, the colonial administration remained almost as inadequately supervised as it had been before the war. Once again the officials of the *Rue Oudinot* (the address, and *sobriquet*, of the Ministry of France d'Outre-Mer) and the career administrators overseas were to have a practically free hand.

## The Federations of AOF and AEF

The law organising the local assemblies overseas was not passed during the lifetime of the first legislature of the Fourth Republic, and consequently they lived out their first five-year mandate under the 'provisional' régime of October 1946. For AOF and AEF this was supplemented by a law passed in virtue of Article 78 of the Constitution, which declared: 'In groups of territories, the management of common interests is entrusted to an Assembly consisting of members elected by the territorial Assemblies. Its composition and its powers are fixed by law.' Accordingly, the law of 29th August 1947 created two Great Councils, one at Dakar and one at Brazzaville, which were to vote the federal budgets of AOF and AEF respectively, and to advise the Governors-General (now rechristened 'High Commissioner'). As the federal budgets were considerably larger than those of the individual territories, these assemblies were to take on a certain importance. They also provided a meeting-point for political leaders from different African territories. Each territorial General Council elected five 'Great Councillors' from among its own members, by proportional representation. (The same system was used for the election of the 'Councillors of the French Union' who sat in the Assembly at Versailles.) The Great Councils met only for a few weeks each year, yet an imposing palace was built for the AOF one at Dakar–out of FIDES credits. This of course increased its self-importance. But its moral authority was less than that of the territorial assemblies from which it emanated, for the system of indirect election made it remote from the population. For many territories Dakar and Brazzaville were also physically remote, and were resented as power-centres at least as much as Paris itself. This tension between federal and territorial interests, which was to become much more important in the period after 1956, was aggravated by the organisation of the federal budgets. Their revenue came principally from the proceeds of indirect taxes, and it considerably exceeded their expenditure. The surplus, known as *ristournes*, was dealt out in the form of subsidies to the territorial governments. According to the law of 1947, each territory should have received an amount proportional to the revenue derived from it—i.e. the richest territories would get most. In fact the Great Councils tended to redistribute the *ristournes* so that the territories whose need was greatest got the largest share. For example, relatively wealthy territories such as Senegal and the Ivory Coast normally drew only 35 per cent or at most 50 per cent of their government income from this source, while some of the poorer territories depended on it for as much as 90 per cent of theirs. The Senegalese, traditionally resentful of this system, now came gradually to accept it—partly because they gained some economic benefit from the presence of the federal Government-General in their territory. But the Ivory Coast, which was only now becoming the richest territory in AOF, resented it more and more. The Ivoirien Great Councillors demanded the application of the 1947 law, but they were always defeated on this point (since the poorer territories were in the majority). As a result, hostility to the over-centralised federations, commonly expressed in most parts of AOF and AEF, became particularly intense in the Ivory Coast.[1]

[1] For this section see the excellent article by Elliot Berg: 'The Economic Base of Political Choice in French West Africa', *American Political Science Review*, June 1960.

*Chapter 5*

# The Bamako Congress

The strength of the reaction against colonial liberalism during the second Constituent Assembly, and especially the desertion of the African cause by the SFIO and the MRP, made a deep impression on the African deputies. It was deeply shocking to them to see a white-haired man like Moutet apparently going back on his pledged word, and even deliberately misleading them about the government's intentions–for in traditional African society respect for old men is one of the most carefully cultivated instincts.[1] The experience did not turn them against the French Union as such, but it convinced them that if Africa was to have a fair deal within it, Africans must rely on each other rather than on French political parties. The partial success of the Intergroup showed the way. Houphouët persuaded Lamine-Guèye that it should be turned into a permanent alliance or *rassemblement* of all African political movements. Lamine-Guèye himself had no intention of breaking with the SFIO, but he too was anxious to bring about African political unity. In September 1946, while the battle over the Constitution was still raging, a manifesto was sent out to political leaders or potential leaders all over Afrique Noire, summoning them to a *Rassemblement* at Bamako. It was signed by Houphouët, Lamine-Guèye, Tchicaya, Apithy, Sissoko, Diallo and d'Arboussier.[2] Senghor was absent at the moment of its composition but gave his support as soon as he heard of it. It was decided to hold the Congress as soon as possible after the dissolution of the Constituent Assembly. Eventually the opening session was fixed for 18th October.[3]

Invitations were sent to all French political parties, but whereas the Communists eagerly offered any assistance they could give, all other parties remained coldly aloof. They were not at all anxious

[1] Apithy, in a conversation with the author.
[2] Text in *Le RDA dans la lutte anti-impérialiste* (undated RDA pamphlet published in Paris about the end of 1948).
[3] Ibid.

to encourage what they assumed would be a Black African nationalist movement, taking its cue from those in Vietnam and Madagascar. This assumption was scarcely justified by the terms of the manifesto, whose signatories rejected 'the "autonomist" sentiment founded on a utopian view of African realities' and 'solemnly proclaimed' their adhesion to the French Union, but it was of course strengthened by the very fact of Communist support. Once Moutet realised that there was no hope of the projected 'Rassemblement Africain' merely becoming a satellite of the SFIO (as Lamine-Guèye would probably have liked), he did everything in his power to sabotage the Congress. He sent telegrams to his subordinates in Africa instructing them to discourage people from going to it, and suggesting that this might be achieved by playing up the known differences of opinion between the signatories of the manifesto. He used both his personal influence and the authority of the Socialist party to dissuade the African Socialists–Lamine-Guèye, Senghor and Yacine Diallo–from attending.[1] In so doing he undoubtedly helped to ensure that the new African party would be *more* radical and *more* pro-Communist (if not more nationalist) than it would otherwise have been. As Houph- ouët himself later pointed out: 'If Lamine-Guèye had gone to Bamako, the socialist deputies there would have been more numerous than those of us who were affiliated to the MUR. In view of his age, in view of his record as a militant, and in view of his culture, I don't think we could have failed to ask Lamine-Guèye to be president of the R.D.A. The presidency was clearly his by right, just as here in Paris we had recognised him as president in the intergroup of overseas deputies.'[2] As it was, it was inevitable that d'Arboussier– and through him the PCF–would set the ideological tone.

Moutet also succeeded, indirectly, in preventing Tchicaya from going to Bamako. Not that Tchicaya felt any loyalty to the SFIO. On the contrary, he had already, during the second Constituent Assembly, transferred from the Socialist group to the MUR. But the AEF administration interpreted Moutet's instructions with such enthusiasm that it confiscated the money which had been collected to pay the travelling expenses of delegates to the Congress. So Tchicaya was forced to stay at home. Nonetheless, 800 delegates, mostly from West Africa but including some from Tchad and Cameroun, had reached Bamako by the 18th October.[3] The fact is

[1] Ibid. and Morgenthau, pp. 88–9.
[2] Evidence to the commission on Ivory Coast incidents, 1950.
[3] RDA pamphlet, op. cit.

striking evidence of the rapid growth of political consciousness in West Africa since the 1945 elections. In all territories except Mauritania political parties had now formed or were in the process of forming; and to those who were building them at grass-roots level the September manifesto made more sense than the subsequent misgivings of some of those who had signed it. African unity was more important to them than the Cold War, or Moutet's personal views.

Apithy, Houphouët and d'Arboussier made the journey from Dakar to Bamako aboard what had formerly been Hermann Goering's personal aeroplane, put at their disposal by the Communist Minister of Aviation. Sissoko had arrived ahead of them, and they found him haranguing a wildly enthusiastic crowd, partly in French and partly in Bambara.[1] The crowd had come to hear their deputy open the Congress to which he was to act as host. But Sissoko announced dramatically that he refused to do so; he denounced the Congress as 'a political swindle for the Communists' benefit' (without mentioning that he himself was affiliated to a group which regularly voted with the Communists in the Assembly), and even denied having signed the manifesto in the first place. He declared he would not attend the Congress, since he did not wish to become 'a prisoner of the Communists'.[2] Clearly someone had been getting at him during the month since he had signed the manifesto – for there is little doubt that he had signed it in fact.

In consternation, the newly arrived deputies quickly demanded permission to speak. They rightly suspected that Sissoko's sudden change of front was partly the result of rivalry between himself and other Soudanese leaders. His supporters had lately formed a Soudanese Progressive Party (PSP), but had still not won over the Moslem intellectuals in Bamako. Two rival parties had been formed: a 'Soudan Democratic Party' based on the Communist Study Group, and a 'Soudanese Bloc'. The leaders of the latter were Mamadou Konaté, who had stood against Sissoko in the elections to both Constituent Assemblies, and **Jean Silvandre,** a West Indian Socialist who had contested the first-college seat both times (and the second time had almost won it).[3] Sissoko seems to have feared that if the Congress were a success, and a new African movement were formed,

---

[1] Apithy, as above.    [2] Ernest Milcent, *L'AOF entre en scène* (Paris 1958).
[3] Morgenthau, p. 275. *Elections et referendums des 21 octobre 1945, 5 mai et 2 juin 1946* (published by Le Monde, Paris 1946).

either Konaté or the Communists would take it over and he would be pushed into the background. But to the deputies from other territories it was of course intolerable that the Congress should be wrecked by conflicts of this sort. Apithy begged the Soudanese to forget their quarrels of *amour-propre* in the interests of African unity. He reminded them that the Congress had been summoned as an answer to the Etats-Généraux: if Africans did not stand together they would fall a helpless prey to the settler lobby.[1] D'Arboussier spoke in much the same sense, and finally Houphouët leapt to the microphone and urged the crowd to disregard what Sissoko had said, since he had clearly fallen victim to the pressures of 'la réaction' and of the Minister of France d'Outre-Mer.[2]

In private, Apithy implored Sissoko to reconsider his decision. In this he was seconded by Sissoko's own supporters, the leaders of the PSP, who brought such moral pressure to bear on their deputy that finally he gave in. At four o'clock in the afternoon the Congress was at last officially opened in front of a crowd that still numbered some 8,000 people. But Sissoko insisted on declaring that he had accepted the presidency 'against his will and under pressure from the electors'.[3] According to one account, his speech began:

'If I have agreed to preside over the first session of your congress . . .' Everyone shouted: 'You must say "*our* congress".' He replied: 'No, it is yours, because it is a communist manœuvre. I am French and a traditionalist, I don't want to be a communist.'[4]

During the night there were further attempts to persuade Sissoko to change his attitude. It was pointed out that some delegates had come in lorries all the way from Tchad, and that they had not come for the unedifying spectacle of internal Soudanese dissensions.[5] Again Sissoko reluctantly gave in. Next day both he and Konaté accepted a motion urging them to be reconciled, and all three Soudanese parties were merged in a 'Union Soudanaise' (US), nominally led by d'Arboussier.[6]

## Foundation of the RDA

The Congress now turned its attention to the problem of metropolitan French politics. Houphouët wanted the new *Rassemblement*

---

[1] Apithy, as above.     [2] Milcent, op. cit.     [3] Ibid.
[4] Evidence of Dignan Bailly, Ivory Coast Socialist leader, to the commission of inquiry on incidents in the Ivory Coast, 1950.
[5] Apithy.     [6] Milcent, op. cit.

to form a distinct parliamentary group, which would affiliate to the 'democratic worker parties'[1]–by which he clearly meant the Communists and the MUR. Apithy opposed this, feeling that it would be a pity to force the African Socialists to choose between an African group and their French Socialist friends. He felt that people like Lamine-Guèye were useful to the African cause inside the SFIO; they could exert some influence on its policy, and their presence in it helped to reassure French doubts about African loyalty. (Not that he personally had any objections to joining a separate African group; he was thoroughly disillusioned by the Socialists' failure to support his proposal that the 'statute' of each overseas territory should be worked out by its local assembly, and he was embarrassed by a vote which had been cast in his name–and in his absence–by the Socialist group, against subsidies to Catholic schools, and which was now held against him by many of his Catholic constituents.)[2] In the end the question was left open. In the final Resolution[3] of the Congress, the *Rassemblement* merely undertook 'in the name of its future parliamentary representatives to maintain in Parliament the union sealed at Bamako and to achieve the grouping which will be most effective in the struggle against the colonialist reaction.'

The congress was firmly opposed to any call for complete independence, and at once rejected a suggestion that it should appeal to the United Nations for support.[4] It pronounced 'formally in favour of a freely consented union founded on equality of rights and duties'. Apithy even heard himself denounced by d'Arboussier as an 'autonomist', because of his insistence on decentralisation.[5] But since d'Arboussier himself produced a report advocating revision of the Constitution, so as to include a sovereign assembly in each territory, with a government responsible to it,[6] the disagreement was clearly more verbal than real. At all events, the Congress agreed to adopt the total abolition of the double college as its immediate goal. Beyond that, the Resolution expressed its aims only in the most general terms, none of which can at all easily be interpreted as

[1] Ibid.    [2] Apithy.    [3] As printed in the 1948 pamphlet.    [4] Milcent, op. cit.
[5] Apithy. In the second Constituent Assembly he had declared: 'Our ideal is not to sit on the banks of the Seine nor to impose ourselves in what are essentially metropolitan affairs, but to regulate the affairs of our own country on the banks of the Congo or of the Niger, free to discuss with the people of France matters interesting the *ensemble* which we form with them.' (Journal Officiel (*Débats*), 18th September 1946. Translated by Michael Crowder and quoted by him in his excellent article, 'Independence as a goal in French West African politics' in *French-Speaking Africa*, ed. William H. Lewis, New York 1965.)    [6] Milcent, op. cit.

'separatist' or anti-French. (Yet these epithets were commonly applied to the Congress by its opponents.) Indeed, the purpose of the *Rassemblement* is made to seem essentially defensive: 'to do away with a typical instrument of the trusts'–i.e. the double college; 'to triumph over the reaction'; to defeat 'the repeated efforts of the colonialist reaction to reduce African representation' by 'securing the election to Parliament of the greatest possible number of democratic or progressive candidates'.

This terminology was visibly Communist-inspired. So indeed was the word 'rassemblement' itself, and the doctrine which it implied. The *Rassemblement Démocratique Africain* (RDA) was not, in the Marxist sense, a political party (although the Congress did 'express a desire for the formation of an African democratic party'). It was intended to be a broad alliance of parties and groups whose ultimate class interests might well be in conflict, but whose immediate interests brought them together with the French proletariat in the struggle against capitalism and imperialism. Therefore, instead of insisting on doctrinal purity, as a Communist Party would have done, it should permit all ideologies to co-exist within it, and unite all the political movements within any given territory. A 'Committee of Co-ordination' was appointed, which was to 'undertake all such action as is necessary to bring about the union of political parties within each territory and to prepare their fusion into a single African movement'. Houphouët was chairman of the Committee; Sissoko, Apithy, Tchicaya, d'Arboussier and Konaté were vice-chairmen. Its immediate task was to try and achieve a single list of African candidates in each territory for the forthcoming National Assembly elections. It was also instructed to prepare a set of statutes for the RDA and submit them to a second Congress, to be held within six months.[1]

The Congress wound up with another public meeting, still under the presidency of Fily-Dabo Sissoko. Houphouët made a speech stressing the 'indefectible attachment of the African populations to republican and democratic France', and the proceedings ended with Konaté and Sissoko leading the 'Marseillaise' in slightly awkward unison.[2]

[1] Ibid.    [2] Ibid.

Chapter 6

# The First Year of the Fourth Republic
# (November 1946–November 1947)

## A. The Election of November 1946

The National Assembly elections were held on 10th November–too soon to give the RDA much chance of achieving a united African front. In the Soudan the brittle unity achieved during the Congress broke at once. Sissoko refused to fight the election on the same ticket as d'Arboussier. He left the Union Soudanaise and reconstituted the PSP, this time in alliance with Jean Silvandre. Of three parliamentary seats now allotted to the Soudan, the PSP won two and the US–RDA one (by proportional representation).[1] This result had the unfortunate effect of projecting internal Soudanese rivalries into the National Assembly; Sissoko and Silvandre joined the Socialist group, while Konaté, who had headed the RDA list, joined the MUR. This confirmed the impression that the RDA was a pro-Communist party and opposed to the Socialists, and this impression was further reinforced when Apithy resigned from the Socialist group. None of the African Socialists joined the RDA, and in the end all the RDA deputies affiliated to the MUR. Thus Moutet's anti-Communist machinations resulted in a reinforcement of the Communist bloc!

There were ten RDA Deputies altogether, three of whom represented the Ivory Coast. Of these, only Houphouët came from the Ivory Coast proper. His colleagues were both natives of Upper Volta. One, Ouëzzin Coulibaly, represented the Bobo tribe whose support had helped Houphouët to win in 1945. (We have already noticed him (p. 44) as a professor at the Ecole Normale William Ponty, where he had been a colleague of Mamadou Konaté: in

[1] Morgenthau, p. 276. US support came mainly from the towns, whereas Sissoko won overwhelmingly in rural areas where virtually all voters were chiefs or influenced by chiefs. (See J. Delval, 'Le RDA au Soudan Français' in L'Afrique et l'Asie, no. 6, 1951.)

111

1937 the two of them together had organised the first African teachers' union.)[1] The other, **Kaboret Zinda,** was a chemist from Ouagadougou,[2] the Moro Naba's capital, and himself the son of a Mossi chief. His presence on the ticket secured the support of the Moro Naba and other Mossi chiefs. He became the youngest member of the National Assembly (twenty-five a week after the election).

The other RDA deputies were: Apithy (Dahomey), Tchicaya (Moyen-Congo), Konaté (Soudan), **Hamani Diori** (Niger), **Gabriel Lisette** (Tchad), **Martin Aku** (Togo), and **Mamba Sano** (Guinea). In Guinea, as in the Soudan, the vote split fairly evenly between RDA and Socialists (one seat falling to each); and, as in the Soudan, the conflict was much less ideological than regional. The 'Socialist' Yacine Diallo was supported by the chiefs of the Fouta Djallon, and opposed by a so-called 'Socialist Party of Guinea', which supported Mamba Sano! (The reason for this was that Sano, who was essentially a Malinké candidate, had made an electoral alliance with the handful of 'Socialist' Fula intellectuals who had previously supported Diallo but now considered him too subservient to the chiefs.)[3]

The Socialist group in the new Assembly could eventually count six deputies from AOF–Lamine-Guèye, Senghor, Sissoko, Silvandre, Yacine Diallo and **Horma ould Babana** (Mauritania)–one from AEF (**Jean-Hilaire Aubame,** Gabon) and one from Cameroun (**Jules Ninine**). Cameroun was the only black African territory to be divided into two separate constituencies; Ninine sat for the predominantly Moslem, dynastically ruled and still quite un-westernised North (which in all these respects closely resembles its neighbour, Northern Nigeria). Like Lisette across the border in Tchad, Ninine was a negro administrator of West Indian origins.

The MRP had Douala-Manga-Bell (southern Cameroun), the Abbé **Barthélémy Boganda** (Oubangui-Chari), and, in the first college, Dr Aujoulat (Cameroun). All of these represented predominantly Catholic electorates. Somaliland was represented by a European, **Martine,** who joined the MUR (but was not a member of the RDA). Finally, the UDSR had the two first-college deputies from AEF, Dr Malbrant and Dr **Bayrou**–both vets, both ex-Free French officers, both Gaullists, and soon to be notorious as the twin spokesmen of colonial conservatism.

Such was the 'African' composition of the new National Assembly. Its general composition was as follows:

[1] Morgenthau, p. 22.      [2] Ibid., p. 183.      [3] Ibid., p. 97.

| | |
|---|---|
| Communists (and MUR) | 168 |
| Socialists | 105 |
| MRP | 167 |
| Radicals and UDSR (in alliance) | 70 |
| Various right-wing groups | 71 |

This election result produced a prolonged cabinet crisis. Communists and MRP had both apparently won, and each wanted a chance to govern the country without the other, while the Socialists, who had lost, nonetheless irritatingly held the balance between them. For a month Bidault was left in office simply because there was no agreement as to who should succeed him.

## B. The Togo Problem and the UN Trusteeship Agreements (December 1946)

During this time the first session of the UN General Assembly was held at Lake Success, N.Y. On the agenda were the 'Trusteeship' agreements which were to replace the former League of Nations Mandates. France and Britain had already worked out a form of agreement for Togo and Cameroun at a conference in London in January 1946. The French government had then received sharp protests from Apithy, Aujoulat and Douala-Manga-Bell, the elected representatives of the territories in question, because they had not been consulted. Bidault as foreign secretary was forced to apologise for this piece of tactlessness, and Moutet succeeded in convincing the deputies that the agreements were in the best interests of the African population. Douala-Manga-Bell claimed that some of Cameroun's inhabitants thought the word 'trusteeship' meant that France was selling them down the river into the hands of Anglo-American 'trusts'–particularly as the news came immediately after that of the resignation of their hero, General de Gaulle. This statement was received with incredulity by the Constituent Assembly.[1] In any case, opposition did not come only from those who were afraid of being abandoned by France. There were also men, both in Togo and in Cameroun, who hoped that trusteeship, as defined by the UN Charter, would mean the end of French rule and a swift transition to independence.

In Togo the problem was complicated by the movement for Ewe reunification. There were more Ewe living under British rule than

[1] Journal Officiel (*Débats*), 20th March 1946.

under French (515,000 to 435,000 in 1948–51). At first, therefore, the Ewe hoped for the reunification of former German Togo, under British trusteeship. In January 1946 **Daniel Chapman**, an English-speaking Ewe professor at Achimota College (Gold Çoast), sent a telegram to the UN Secretariat demanding that all Ewe territory be placed under British trusteeship. Meanwhile the Ewe in French Togo, led by Sylvanus Olympio, were protesting against France's tendency to treat Togo as if it were part of AOF. Since commercially Olympio represented the (British) United Africa Company, it was easy for the French to leap to the conclusion that politically he represented some kind of Anglo-Saxon plot to seize French Togo. Governor **Noutary** took steps to prevent him from founding a political party. But the Ewe neatly turned his flank by staging a take-over of the *Comité d'Unité Togolaise* (CUT), a body which had been founded under government auspices in 1941 to promote con-tacts between northern and southern tribes within French Togo, but which now began to campaign for the reunion of French and British zones. With the 78-year-old **Augustino de Souza** as president, and Olympio as vice-president, it at once opened negotiations with Ewe organisations in British territory. On 9th June 1946 an All Ewe Conference was founded in Accra, with Daniel Chapman in the chair.

Meanwhile the French government rapidly withdrew all official support from the CUT and encouraged opposition to it, both among the northern chiefs (who quickly withdrew from the CUT, not being anxious either to submit to Ewe domination, or to be cut off from the sea by the creation of an Ewe state) and among the coastal oligarchy itself. On 9th April 1946 a pro-French 'Togolese Progress Party' (PTP) was founded. Both its leaders were related to their opponent Sylvanus Olympio: Dr **Pedro Olympio** was his cousin, and **Nicolas Grunitzky** his brother-in-law. But these manoeuvres took time to bear fruit. At first the CUT carried all before it. While the All Ewe Conference petitioned the UN to create a national Ewe state under unified (i.e. probably British) trusteeship, the CUT sent delegates to the Bamako Congress and affiliated to the RDA. In the National Assembly election its candidate, Dr Aku, easily defeated Grunitzky, and when the Togo Representative Assembly was elected on 8th December, the PTP did not even bother to compete; the CUT won 15 out of 24 second-college seats, the remainder going to representatives of the Northern chiefs. Sylvanus Olympio became President of the Assembly.

If the British government had really been behind the pan-Ewe movement, the latter might well have secured a favourable hearing at the UN, and the French would have been gravely embarrassed. But in reality the British were scarcely if at all less hostile than the French to the idea of a pan-Ewe state, for such a state would have included not only the 139,000 Ewe of British Togoland but, much more important, the 376,000 Ewe of the Gold Coast. I.e. it involved, not merely a reversal of the partition of 1919, but the loss of a sizeable slice of an old-established British colony. Temporary British trusteeship over an Ewe state would not compensate for the fragmentation of the Gold Coast. On the contrary, the British hoped to preserve the integrity of the unit which they had created out of the Gold Coast and British Togoland together. They were therefore opposed to the reunification of former German Togo, and fully prepared to co-operate with the French in playing down the Ewe problem. The two colonial powers supported each other, and succeeded in defeating the anti-colonial amendments proposed by India and the Soviet bloc. France had some difficulty in convincing the Assembly that, if she wanted to be allowed to continue to treat her Trust territories as an 'integral part of her national territory', and if she had already admitted them to the French Union, this was more in their own interests than in hers. But in the end she succeeded in getting the text she had submitted approved. Some floating votes may have been won by the presence, as a member of the French delegation, of Douala-Manga-Bell–who made a short speech favourably contrasting the work of the French in Cameroun with that of their predecessors, his father's murderers.

The agreements were finally ratified by the General Assembly on 13th December, in the form proposed by the tutelary powers–which amounted to a continuation for the time being of the former mandates, with certain modifications. France now promised 'to take such measures as shall be necessary in order to guarantee participation of the local populations in the administration of the territory by the development of democratic representative bodies, and to proceed, when the time comes, to such consultations as may be appropriate in order to allow these populations to pronounce freely on their political régime and attain the ends defined by Article 76.'[1] She

[1] The basic objectives of the trusteeship system, as stated by Article 76 of the UN Charter, are:

(a) to further international peace and security;

(b) to promote political, economic, social and educational advancement of the inhabitants of the trust territories and their *progressive development towards self-government or independence* as may be appropriate to the particular cir-

was to make annual reports to the UN, which would be examined by the General Assembly and by the Trusteeship Council. More important, these bodies could arrange periodical visits of inspection and receive petitions directly from the inhabitants. In these circumstances it seemed unlikely that the granting of independence, or at best the soliciting of 'free consent' to membership of the French Union, could be postponed for ever. But at least it had been avoided for the immediate future. As for the Ewe, the only concession to them was the creation of a Permanent Consultative Commission to make minor adjustments to the frontier between the two zones and advise on matters of common interest. This Commission was to include two representatives of the native population on each side.[1]

## C. The Governments of Léon Blum and Paul Ramadier

The ratification of the Trusteeship Agreements was the last achievement of Bidault's government. On 16th December the parliamentary deadlock was temporarily solved by the formation of an all-Socialist cabinet led by the semi-invalid Léon Blum. The departure of Communists and MRP from the government left numerous vacancies to be filled by loyal but hitherto unrewarded Socialists. One of these was Lamine-Guèye, who became under-secretary of state in the prime minister's office—the first African since Blaise Diagne to sit in the French cabinet.

The next step in putting the Constitution into action was the election of the Council of the Republic, which was held in December 1946 in metropolitan France, and in January 1947 overseas. The result in Afrique Noire was noticeably different from the result of the National Assembly election, not only because of the double college, but also because the system of indirect election facilitated backstairs manoeuvre and administrative pressure. Under Moutet's patronage

---

cumstances of each territory and the *freely expressed wishes* of the peoples concerned, and as may be provided by the terms of each trusteeship agreement;

(c) to encourage respect for human rights and for fundamental freedoms for all without distinction as to race, sex, language, or religion, and to encourage recognition of the interdependence of the peoples of the world;

(d) to ensure equal treatment in social, economic and commercial matters for all Members of the United Nations and also equal treatment for the latter in the administration of justice, without prejudice to the attainment of the foregoing objectives. . . . (my italics).

[1] For the Ewe problem, see Ansprenger, pp. 209–10, and Cornevin, *Histoire du Togo* (2nd ed., Paris 1962).

Aujoulat's and Douala-Manga-Bell's speeches at the UN are on a gramophone record issued by the *Archives Sonorés de la Fondation Um.*

the Socialists won themselves a reputation for electoral machinations overseas which was to stay with them for a long time. As a result the SFIO could claim 12 out of 20 second-college senators from Afrique Noire (including Moutet himself for the Soudan!), and four out of 12 first-college senators.[1] The remainder were distributed as follows:

*First College:*
| | | |
|---|---|---|
| Radicals and UDSR | 5 | |
| Right-wing | 2 | |
| MRP | 1 | (a 'naturalised' African from Dahomey) |

*Second College:*
| | | |
|---|---|---|
| RDA | 7 | |
| Gaullist | 1 | **(Béchir Sow,** Tchad) |

National Assembly and Council of the Republic met in joint session and elected Vincent Auriol (SFIO) first President of the Fourth Republic. Léon Blum resigned as prime minister and a reluctant coalition of Communists, Socialists, MRP and Radicals took office under the right-wing Socialist **Paul Ramadier.**

The events of 1947 increased rather than dispelled the new Republic's difficulties. Already in December 1946 a full-scale war had begun in Indo-China which was to last seven and a half years.[2] Next, in March 1947, a revolt broke out in Madagascar. Thousands of people (but few Frenchmen) were massacred by nationalist rebels belonging mainly to the old ruling tribe of the island, the Hovas. As so often, the government's belated reaction was more violent and terrible than the original revolt. While peasants were killed or driven from their holdings in the Malagasy forests, the three Malagasy deputies in Paris (whose followers had unleashed the rebellion) were deprived of their parliamentary immunity and arrested–despite vigorous protests from their African colleagues, many of whom broke party discipline to vote against the measure.[3]

At the same time the Republic was more seriously threatened from inside France. On the Right, the Gaullists formed their *Rassemblement du Peuple Français* (RPF) to agitate for Constitutional Revision and the return of the General to power– a programme that smacked of Boulangism or even Bonapartism, and attracted many followers who had been far from Gaullist during the war. On the Left, the

[1] This accounts for nearly half of the SFIO's total of 37 senators. See Wright, op. cit., Morgenthau, p. 76, and *Tableaux des élections au Conseil de la République de 1946 à 1955* (Paris 1955).

[2] Some would say it is still going on.

[3] Journal Officiel (*Débats*), 1st August 1947–*scrutins* 220 and 221.

Communists behaved less and less like supporters of a coalition government, and more and more like agitators hoping to start a revolution. They refused to accept the restrictive wages policy which all other parties agreed was necessary to curb inflation, and they openly supported the rebels in both Indo-China and Madagascar. Eventually, in May 1947, even the Communist ministers voted against the government to which they belonged—whereupon Ramadier had them bundled out of office by presidential decree. The Party went out into an opposition from which it has not yet returned.

From then on French internal politics became part of the Cold War. Denounced at the inaugural meeting of the Cominform for 'opportunism, legalitarianism and parliamentary illusions', the PCF leaders returned to France chastened and armed with a programme of revolutionary action whose principal feature was the use of large-scale and violent strikes as a political weapon;[1] and they had no hesitation about throwing their African allies into the forefront of the battle. When a general 'insurrectional' strike against the government was called by the CGT in October 1947, the African unions affiliated to the CGT were ordered to take part. For five months the railwaymen on the Dakar-Bamako line were out on strike—yet there was no immediate interest of theirs at stake. Not surprisingly the AOF railwaymen's union subsequently broke with the CGT.[2] But many other African unions continued to belong to it; and in Parliament the RDA remained in alliance with the PCF. The RDA deputies continued to benefit from Communist advice and instruction in the day to day work of the Assembly. They continued to be grateful for Communist support for their demands. They continued to admire the selflessness with which Communist parliamentarians handed in their salary and their petrol coupons to the Party office. They remained friendly with individual Communist deputies, especially Aimé Césaire.[3] And they still believed d'Arboussier (who came to Versailles as Councillor of the French Union for the Ivory Coast) when he told them that African interests were indissolubly linked with those of the French proletariat. But the price which they, and their African supporters, paid for the Communist alliance was high. For it earned them the implacable and uncomprehending hostility of the parties which remained in the government, and therefore controlled the colonial administration.

[1] Philip Williams, *Crisis and Compromise* (London 1964), p. 74 and note.
[2] Ansprenger, p. 85.
[3] Apithy, in conversation with the author.

In the municipal elections of October 1947 the Gaullists won control of the thirteen biggest cities in France. It looked like a popular vote of no confidence in the régime, and de Gaulle did not hesitate to demand the immediate dissolution of Parliament, while his followers in the Assembly tried to paralyse the government by voting systematically with the Communists. The latter meanwhile launched their great series of quasi-revolutionary strikes. Ramadier's government tottered; in November he was finally overthrown by his own party, which hoped to check the drift to the Right. In this it failed, for Blum was unable to form another government without support from the Radicals or groups further Right. In the end it was **Robert Schuman** (MRP) who headed the reshuffled coalition, and Moutet was replaced at the Ministry of France d'Outre-Mer by Paul Coste-Floret, one of the most determinedly anti-Communist members of the MRP. An era of 'tough' colonial policy was beginning.

# Chapter 7

# The Coste-Floret Era and the Origins of the IOM (1947–1949)

## A. Some Events in Africa, 1947–1948

### (i) *The Failure of Socialism in Senegal*

In the 'Four Communes'[1] of Senegal the result of the municipal elections of October 1947 was the exact opposite of what it was in France. The RPF came bottom of the poll, while the Socialists won an overwhelming victory. Lamine-Guèye was triumphantly re-elected mayor of Dakar with 26,400 out of 34,000 votes. The RDA list, which came second, had less than 2,000.[2] The Socialists also dominated the Senegal General Council, whose 50 members had been elected (at the end of 1946) on a single list entitled *Bloc d'Union Socialiste et Républicaine*. Only one of them, the European **Guy Etcheverry,** later joined the *Union Démocratique Sénégalaise* (UDS) which was founded as the Senegal section of the RDA. He was the owner of a pro-Communist Resistance newspaper in Dakar, *Réveil*, which he made the RDA's official organ. It was convenient for the RDA to have a base in the federal capital of AOF, and it gained some following there among intellectuals and trade unionists but failed to touch the mass of the population.[3]

The real tension in Senegalese politics lay within the SFIO, between former 'citizens' and former 'subjects'. Lamine-Guèye had the unconditional loyalty of the former, but no real contact with the latter. Although the 'subjects' were now citizens thanks to Lamine-Guèye's law, many of them remained profoundly discontented. The price of groundnuts was beginning to fall, and for most Senegalese

---

[1] Actually there were now only three, since Gorée had been incorporated into Dakar.

[2] Ansprenger, p. 154.

[3] Ibid., p. 128. Morgenthau, pp. 141, 144, 408–9.

farmers the groundnut crop is the only source of cash income. Lamine-Guèye appeared unconcerned about this situation. Worse, he managed to antagonise **Ibrahima Seydou Ndaw,** the head of the Native Traders' Union in Sine-Saloum (the area round Kaolack, which is the most important groundnut-producing region). Ndaw was an important figure not only in the groundnut industry but also in the popular Tidjaniya Moslem sect. His electoral influence was great, and he had helped Senghor to win the elections of 1945 and 1946. Yet Lamine-Guèye allowed his newspaper *l'AOF* to become a platform for attacks on Ndaw by one of his local enemies, **Djim Momar Guèye,** a low-caste member of the rival Mouride sect. This was doubly tactless because Djim Momar Guèye was a personal opponent of Senghor's and had started a local political party of his own. Nonetheless Lamine-Guèye insisted on his adoption as an SFIO candidate for the French Union Assembly, in preference to Senghor's protégé Mamadou Dia, apparently because Mamadou Dia had spoken out of turn in criticising SFIO policy.

Senghor was riled by this, and also by being left to explain to the SFIO in Paris why he and Lamine-Guèye had voted against the party line on the arrest of the Malagasy deputies–while Lamine-Guèye himself went off to Mecca in the hope of strengthening his prestige with the Moslem electorate. (Senghor himself was of course unable to play this particular card, being Catholic.) Lamine-Guèye's prestige needed strengthening, for he had failed to persuade his friend Moutet to increase the powers of the Senegal General Council at the expense of those of the AOF Great Council, even though the General Council had daringly backed its demand by holding up the ordinary territorial budget for six months. In the autumn of 1947 Senghor felt strong enough to attack Lamine-Guèye openly at the party congress in Kaolack. Only the delegates from the Four Communes supported Lamine-Guèye, and the executive's report was rejected. The great grievance of the 'subjects' was that they were excluded from participation in running the party's affairs, leadership being monopolised by Lamine-Guèye's 'citizen' cronies.

From this time onwards Senghor must have had it in mind to break with the SFIO. He began to build a personal following among those who opposed Lamine-Guèye–a minority in the General Council, which did not include more than 15 'subjects', but a majority among the rural voters. From 11th February 1948 he published his own paper in Dakar, *Condition Humaine*, which rapidly became a rebel voice within the party. It concentrated on local grievances, and

121

defended the CGT railway strike–clearly angling for trade union support. Gradually the Senghorites became identifiable as a distinct group in the General Council, while in Paris Senghor himself took less and less notice of party discipline. In the summer of 1948 he was dropped from the executive committee of the French SFIO, on which he had sat since 1945.[1]

## (ii) *Ivory Coast and Upper Volta*: *the Administration versus the RDA*

Immediately after the Bamako Congress, Houphouët's *Parti Démocratique de la Côte d'Ivoire* (PDCI) persuaded its former opponents, the *Progressistes* led by Kouamé Binzème, to join the RDA and support the PDCI candidates for the National Assembly. A joint list of candidates was put up for the Ivory Coast General Council, and won all the second-college seats. But the alliance was short-lived. The Progressistes had links with the MRP, and disliked the RDA's Communist connections. They were angry when Houphouët refused to nominate Binzème for a seat in the Council of the Republic, and felt that they had simply been taken over by the PDCI.[2]

In the spring of 1947 the settlers again succeeded in getting the pro-RDA Governor Latrille recalled–this time for good. From then on the administration encouraged opposition to the RDA. It was with official blessing that the Progressistes seceded from the RDA in May 1947. More serious, the administration succeeded in breaking the alliance between Houphouët and the Mossi chiefs. Early in 1947 the latter repudiated their RDA deputy Kaboret Zinda and denounced the RDA itself (possibly in return for a government promise to reconstitute Upper Volta as a separate territory). Kaboret fought back with a violent speech in Ouagadougou denouncing the chiefs' dependence on the administration. They walked out of the meeting. On 24th May, Kaboret died suddenly in Abidjan. Many believed that he was poisoned. His seat in the National Assembly was left vacant, but in the General Council he was replaced by **Nazi Boni,** an opponent of the RDA.[3]

The settlers were delighted at the growing identification of the RDA with Communism, since it tended to convert the French government to their own view that Houphouët and his friends were

---

[1] Morgenthau, pp. 139–45.
[2] F. Amon d'Aby, *La Côte d'Ivoire dans la citè africaine* (Paris 1951).
[3] Morgenthau, p. 183. Ansprenger, p. 132.

a pack of agitators financed by Moscow. This view was widely held also in the colonial administration, especially among Gaullists, who were increasingly obsessed by the Cold War, or rather by the possibility of a hot one. 'If there is a war in which France is involved on the American side against Russia,' asked Governor **Louveau** of the Soudan, 'what will be the attitude of the Africans controlled for the most part by the RDA?' Houphouët replied: 'we should do exactly the same as the people of France'.[1] But since by the 'people of France' he was assumed to mean the Communist workers, this reply was not entirely reassuring.

Minister Coste-Floret, for one, was convinced of the RDA's disloyalty. **Orselli,** who was appointed Governor of the Ivory Coast in February 1948, later said that his brief instructions from the Minister 'can be summarised as follows: "You are going there to suppress the RDA" '. But Orselli was not a career administrator. He was an ex-Free French airforce officer whom de Gaulle had made governor of New Caledonia against his own wishes. In the Ivory Coast he kept an open mind, and soon found himself in conflict with the settlers as well as many of his own subordinates. He was infuriated to find that **Laurent Péchoux,** the head of the civil service, who had been acting as interim governor, had spread rumours that he, Orselli, was a Communist–while others took it for granted that he was RPF. In fact he regarded himself as non-political, but was horrified by the violently racist attitude of many European residents. He found Houphouët remarkably reasonable in comparison, and began to hope that he would be able to co-operate with the RDA majority in the General Council. At the same time **Paul Béchard,** a Socialist deputy who had been made High Commissioner for AOF, seems also to have hoped for an understanding with the RDA. In June 1948 he visited the Ivory Coast, and to the scandal of the settlers both he and Orselli accepted an invitation to lunch with Houphouët in his home village of Yamoussoukro. Béchard even suggested that if the RDA would co-operate with the government, he might persuade Lamine-Guèye to leave the SFIO and join it. Houphouët was pleased, but cautious. He suspected a Socialist plot to seize control of his movement–and just at this time an event occurred which threw grave doubt on Béchard's good faith.[2]

[1] Houphouët's evidence to the commission on incidents in the Ivory Coast, 1950.
[2] Orselli and Houphouët to the same commission. (Its report is printed as annexe no. 11348 (séance du 2–11–1950) in *Assemblée Nationale, Ière legislature*, Impressions 127, 1946–51.)

The territory of Upper Volta had been reconstituted in March 1948, and in June the elections were held for its first General Council. The RDA was defeated – and this defeat was blatantly stage-managed by the Governor, **Mouragues**, apparently with Béchard's connivance. At very least it showed that even if Béchard himself was genuinely prepared to trust the RDA, he would have great difficulty in imposing this policy either on his subordinates or on the government. Mouragues was a self-proclaimed MRP man, and had been a close collaborator of Coste-Floret's in the Rue Oudinot. He was sent out to Upper Volta in great haste when it was learned that the RDA had done better than expected on the first ballot, and there was no doubt what he had been sent to do. RDA meetings were banned, chiefs intimidated, voters disqualified, and so on. Probably the results were falsified as well. In any case the Union Voltaïque won a comfortable majority in the General Council, and all three of the seats allotted to Upper Volta in the National Assembly.[1]

Even in the Ivory Coast itself, when by-elections were held to fill the seats in the General Council vacated by the representatives of Upper Volta, official backing was given to a Progressiste list (which, however, the PDCI easily defeated). In these circumstances the RDA leaders were naturally anxious to see concrete evidence of Béchard's and Orselli's good will before falling over themselves to accept their overtures. When the General Council met in July, they continued to oppose the government. Orselli blamed this on **Robert Léon,** one of the few settlers who supported the RDA, and who apparently acted as unofficial liaison officer between the PDCI and the French Communist Party. Léon's return from Paris coincided with a sudden stiffening of the PDCI's attitude. Orselli believed that he was an *agent provocateur* used by the settlers to discredit the RDA by pushing it into extreme positions and strengthening its ties with the Communists.[2] If so, the Communists themselves played into his hands. **Raymond Barbé,** their chief spokesman in the Assembly of the French Union, sent a circular to Communist militants in Africa urging them to keep a tight hold on the RDA and not to let it develop any 'Titoist' deviations. The time had come for 'mass action against reaction' in Africa.[3] In October 1948 he followed this up with a personal visit to Abidjan.

All this was fuel to the flames of settler propaganda. Since the lunch party at Yamoussoukro the settlers were determined to get rid

[1] Ouëzzin Coulibaly in the National Assembly, 22nd March 1949.
[2] Orselli, evidence as above.     [3] Morgenthau, p. 187. Ansprenger, p. 86.

of Orselli. He was denounced in *Climats* (a Paris colonialist weekly) and lobbied against by individuals in the Rue Oudinot. It was the same treatment which had got rid of Latrille. The case against Orselli was strong; he had not suppressed the RDA as instructed, nor had he succeeded in winning it over. He had merely enraged the European population without doing anything to prevent the Communist rebellion which they claimed was imminent. In October 1948 he was recalled. His anxious warnings that continued repression would soon lead to bloodshed were ignored. Coste-Floret would not even grant him an interview.[1]

### (iii) *Cameroun: The Birth of the UPC*

Among the unofficial delegates at the Bamako Congress was a young trade unionist from Cameroun, **Ruben Um Nyobé,** one of the secretaries of the CGT-affiliated *Union des Syndicats Confédérés du Cameroun* (USCC). He was thirty-three years old at the time, already well grounded in Communist trade union organisations—in fact it was a training course in Dakar that had brought him to West Africa.[2] Back in Cameroun, he set to work to found a local section of the RDA. A preliminary attempt, the *Rassemblement Camerounais* (RACAM) quickly petered out in 1947.[3] But it was followed in April 1948 by the *Union des Populations Camerounaises* (UPC) which was to have a much longer history. Initially based on the CGT trades unions, its organisation spread rapidly into the country-side of southern Cameroun, especially the province of Sanaga-Maritime just inland from Douala (Um Nyobé's own homeland), and the Bamiléké province which boardered on the British zone. French Communist advisers helped set up workers' committees and village committees, and parallel movements for youth and women. Communist influence was undoubtedly stronger in the UPC than in any other section of the RDA.[4]

Yet the most important items in the UPC programme were not specifically Communist; nor were they shared by other RDA sections (except in Togo): namely, national independence within a fixed time limit, and reunion of the French and British zones. Both these demands sprung from Cameroun's special position as a Trust territory, and the right of petition to the United Nations provided the

---

[1] Orselli, as above.     [2] Ansprenger, p. 193.
[3] Engelbert Mveng, *Histoire du Cameroun*, op. cit.
[4] Ibid. and Ansprenger, pp. 193–5.

UPC (like the CUT in Togo) with an international platform which contributed greatly to its prestige.

Needless to say the UPC was regarded with intense hostility by the European employers in Douala. Like their colleagues in the Ivory Coast, they concealed racist feelings under a parade of anti-Communism, and so succeeded in bringing the administration on to their side. As in AOF the administration responded by encouraging African opposition to the RDA, both Socialist and Catholic. The leading Socialist (so-called) was the wealthy businessman Paul Soppo-Priso, who had led the pro-French JEUCAFRA before the war, had virtuously refused an invitation to the Bamako Congress,[1] and was now one of Cameroun's five representatives in the Assembly of the French Union. But he had a reputation for feathering his own nest, and was distrusted by the deputy Prince Douala-Manga-Bell.[2] Douala-Manga-Bell, who retained an enormous popularity in most parts of southern Cameroun, was an individualist who refused to integrate into any local political party, whether pro-Communist or pro-Government (though he belonged to the MRP group in the National Assembly). As a result, the most effective opposition to the UPC was the Catholic trade union movement organised in and around Yaoundé, the capital of the territory, by the first-college deputy, Dr Aujoulat.[3]

## B. The Indépendants d'Outre-Mer

Aujoulat was anxious to halt the spread of Marxism and 'separatism' in Africa. But he was convinced it would not be done by force, and could not be done at all unless a genuine policy of colonial reform was introduced. Consequently he felt less and less at home within the MRP as it drifted slowly further Right. He realised that his hope of winning Africans over was weakened by the fact that he belonged to the same party as Coste-Floret and **de Chevigné** (the 'pacifier' of Madagascar).[4] He was frustrated by the failure of successive governments to take overseas problems seriously. They devalued the franc in the interests of metropolitan France, then forgot their promises of compensation to the T.O.M. There was even talk of suppressing FIDES as part of an economic retrenchment programme.[5]

[1] So he told Dr Ansprenger in 1959 (p. 193).
[2] Report of conversation with Prince Douala in Dr Aujoulat's private papers.    [3] Ansprenger, p. 193.    [4] Milcent, *L'AOF entre en scène*, op. cit.
[5] Aujoulat's speech in the National Assembly, 10th September 1948 (as quoted in *Afrique Nouvelle*, 19th September 1948).

Almost the only colonial reform adopted in the first two years of the legislature was the extension of the vote to all who could prove literacy in French or Arabic (Law of 12th August 1947). Yet the need for reform was indisputable. The 'native labour code' of 18th June 1945 had still not been enforced. In any case it was outdated since the abolition of forced labour and the extension of French citizenship to African natives. Moutet had tried to replace it by a general Overseas Labour Code which put all workers overseas, whether European or native, on the same footing, and gave them substantially the same rights as workers in France. This code was promulgated by a decree of 17th October 1947. But a month later Moutet was out of office. The *Comité de l'Empire Français*–the colonial employers' pressure-group, which had sponsored the Paris meeting of the Etats-Généraux de la Colonisation the year before– succeeded in persuading Coste-Floret that the Labour Code was an over-hasty measure which should not have been issued by simple ministerial decree without waiting for the opinion of the newly-elected Assembly of the French Union, and which in any case needed extensive revision. On 11th January 1948 the *Journal Official* published a new decree, implausibly backdated to 25th November 1947 (Coste-Floret's first day in office!), repealing that of 17th October. The backdating was necessary because the time limit allowed by the Constitution for the government to legislate by decree on this subject had expired on 27th November. From now on the Labour Code could only be put into force by a law. The officials in the Rue Oudinot were therefore instructed to redraft it in the form of a parliamentary bill. The effect of this was to postpone action almost indefinitely. Meanwhile the African worker was left without minimum wage or maximum working week, usually also without pension, paid holiday or family allowance; women and often children worked in the same conditions as men; and forced labour often persisted in thinly disguised forms, benefiting from the failure of the Loi Houphouët-Boigny to give it a precise definition.[1]

Meanwhile, war dragged on in Indo-China. Sometimes negotiations were started, but no significant concessions were ever offered until it was too late. As for the much-vaunted French Union, would it ever be a reality? The status of the local assemblies was still only provisional; the Assembly of the Union sat unnoticed in Versailles;

---

[1] Ansprenger, pp. 236–7. V. Thompson and R. Adloff, *French West Africa* (Stanford 1958). Milcent, op. cit. P. F. Gonidec and M. Kirsch, *Le Droit du Travail des T.O.M.* (Paris 1958).

and the High Council had never even met. The UN General Assembly was to hold its autumn session of 1948 in Paris. A fine gesture, but what was France to say in defence of her colonial policy? Did she even have a policy to defend?[1]

Aujoulat was not the only overseas deputy to ask himself these questions, nor to be embarrassed by his own party. Senghor was equally disenchanted with the SFIO, and Apithy was increasingly unhappy in the RDA. He was under strong pressure from his Catholic electors to break with the Communists, and he began to feel that the RDA would have much more hope of achieving its aims if it did so. Early in 1948 he had talks with Aujoulat and Senghor,[2] and the three found themselves in agreement that an African group in Parliament could be useful, if it preserved its independence from other groups and used its voting-strength to force overseas issues on the attention of governments which might need its support. The RDA had forfeited its bargaining potential by giving unconditional support to the one party which all other politicians were determined to keep out of office.

Apithy tried first to persuade his colleagues in the RDA to change their tactics. He stressed especially the difficulties which the Communist alliance was creating for the RDA in Catholic constituencies. This point was all too effectively illustrated by the RDA's defeat in Upper Volta, where the church joined the administration in an anti-Communist crusade and the Bishop of Ouagadougou sent out a pastoral letter warning his flock that Catholicism and Communism were incompatible.[3] It seems that just after this, and after his meeting with Béchard, Houphouët wrote from the Ivory Coast to the RDA deputies in Paris, putting much the same arguments as Apithy in favour of breaking with the Communists. But d'Arboussier suppressed this letter, and succeeded in persuading the deputies to reject Apithy's suggestion and stay loyal to their Communist friends.[4]

Apithy now decided that, since the RDA as a whole was not willing to break with the Communists, he would try and form a new parliamentary group which would be anti-Communist but open to

[1] Aujoulat's speech, 10th September 1948.
[2] Milcent, op. cit.
[3] Morgenthau, p. 198.
[4] Apithy, in conversation with the author. It seems that Houphouët himself referred to this episode at the time of his breach with d'Arboussier in 1950. (See Senator Raphael Saller's reports on his conversations with Houphouët at this time, typed and apparently circulated to the IOM parliamentary group. Dr Aujoulat has copies. Also private letters from Saller to Aujoulat, July to August 1950.)

both RDA and non-RDA deputies who wished to join it. He gained the support of Aku, RDA deputy for Togo, of Martine, deputy for Somaliland, who belonged to the MUR but shared Apithy's reasons for wanting to leave it, of the three new deputies from Upper Volta (Nazi Boni, **Henri Guissou** and **Mamadou Ouëdraogo**), and of one deputy from Algeria. These seven formed, at the beginning of September 1948, the *groupe des Indépendants d'Outre-Mer* (IOM).[1]

The new group found itself unexpectedly plunged straight into the limelight owing to the parliamentary situation of the moment. Schuman's government had fallen in July. That of his successor **André Marie** (Radical) lasted only till the end of August. Both governments were thrown out by the Socialists for being too right-wing. On 31st August, Schuman was narrowly re-elected on the understanding that he would permit a swing to the left in social and economic policy (himself retaining the Ministry of Foreign Affairs which he had taken over from Bidault in July). Accordingly he appointed, for the first time since 1946, a Socialist Minister of Finance (**Christian Pineau**). This incensed many of the big business Radicals and Conservatives who were now a normal ingredient of the majority.[2] Schuman knew that when his cabinet met the Assembly on 7th September there would be a close vote. It was at this moment that the IOM group came into existence.

Immediately, Schuman's supporters descended on Apithy, urging him to vote for the government. They even suggested he was morally bound to do so, because one of the Socialists who had been given a junior portfolio was an African. This was tactless of them. In the first place, the African in question was Fily-Dabo Sissoko, whose performance at the Bamako Congress and after had distinguished him more for his subservience to a Socialist Minister of France d'Outre-Mer than for his loyalty to the African cause. In the second place, the appointment he had been given was an under-secretaryship of state for Commerce and Industry. Sissoko knew nothing about either commerce or industry: he was a teacher and man of letters. As Apithy said, there might have been some sense in it if he had been put in the ministry of Education, or that of France d'Outre-Mer. As it was, it was difficult to resist the impression that Schuman was pandering to African parliamentary pretensions with his tongue in his cheek. Certainly such an appointment could not be taken as

[1] Apithy, in conversation with the author. *Afrique Nouvelle*, 19th September 1948.
[2] Williams, *Crisis and Compromise* (op. cit.), pp. 34–5 and 36n.

evidence that the government would now pay more attention to the needs of the T.O.M.

In the debate on the composition of the cabinet, Apithy put a number of questions to the prime minister about his future overseas policy. To his fury, his was the only speech which Schuman failed to answer in his closing statement–either because he was afraid of frightening away more right-wing votes if he made specific promises of colonial reform, or simply because the need to placate other and more powerful interests pushed it out of his mind. Apithy, Aku, Martine and their Algerian colleague **Laribi** met hurriedly to decide how to vote. The three Voltaic deputies were away, but the group was authorised to cast their votes for them. The four agreed that in the circumstances it was impossible to vote for the government. They considered abstaining, but this seemed pointless. Apithy and Aku were anxious to refute the label of 'gouvernementaux' which had already been bestowed on them by the pro-Communist members of the RDA. They decided to cast the group's seven votes against the government.[1]

Schuman was defeated by six votes. The IOM tactics had succeeded so embarrassingly well that they appeared to have made themselves –like the Irish Nationalists in nineteenth-century Britain–the arbiters of metropolitan politics. Although a group of seven was not large enough to be represented on the Assembly's Commissions, or to be automatically consulted by the President of the Republic before a new government could be formed (the minimum was 14), it is hardly surprising that the next prime minister–**Henri Queuille** (Radical)–took the trouble to see Apithy before the Assembly voted on his investiture, and to mention overseas affairs in his investiture speech. Even so, his promises were disappointingly unspecific.[2] Only two of the IOM voted for him. The remaining five abstained, which was equivalent to voting against (since to be invested a prospective prime minister had to have an absolute majority of votes in his favour).[3]

Meanwhile Senghor prepared for his final breach with the SFIO. The moment came at the end of September when the party voted against a proposal to suspend proceedings against the arrested Malagasy deputies. Lamine-Guèye and Silvandre only made a token protest against this, by temporarily resigning from the Socialist group in the Assembly. Senghor resigned from the party altogether.[4]

---

[1] Apithy, as above.
[2] *Afrique Nouvelle*, loc. cit.
[3] Williams, op. cit., pp. 498–9.
[4] *Afrique Nouvelle*, 3rd October 1948.

On 27th September he sent an open letter to **Guy Mollet,** General Secretary of the SFIO, explaining his reasons for doing so.[1] These were twofold: on the one hand, the SFIO in Senegal had become 'an organisation whose object is to establish the personal power of Lamine-Guèye'; on the other, the SFIO in France only defended its own metropolitan electoral interests and ignored overseas problems. He announced to the press that he would join the IOM.[2] He did so on 16th November.[3] By the end of the year the group had also gained the adherence of Mamba Sano (ex-RDA, Guinea), **Georges Condat** (a new deputy from Niger),[4] Aubame (ex-SFIO, Gabon), and Aujoulat (ex-MRP, first college, Cameroun). When the bureau of the group was renewed in January 1949, Aujoulat was elected president of it instead of Apithy.[5] From then on the group normally voted with the MRP–which, so far from resenting Aujoulat's resignation, gave him every encouragement in his new rôle as an African leader.[6] Although Coste-Floret did not allow the IOM to dictate his African policy, he encouraged it as an instrument of MRP interests against both Communists and Socialists. A majority of its members were Catholic, and nearly all of them were supported by the missions and administration in their territories.[7] The three Voltaic deputies owed their election directly to the MRP, and were embarrassed to find their votes had been cast against Schuman on 7th September. It was hoped that under Aujoulat's leadership such an event would not recur. Apithy understandably resented this take-over bid.[8] But Aujoulat did not intend to let the IOM be unconditionally attached to the MRP, as the RDA was to the Communists. It was to remain an independent group, as its name implied, and its voting power could be used to increase his own standing with the MRP leaders, and so to attract their attention to African problems.

[1] Ansprenger, p. 155.
[2] *Afrique Nouvelle*, loc. cit.
[3] Morgenthau, p. 145.
[4] Niger had been allotted a second seat at the time of the reconstitution of Upper Volta.
[5] *Assemblée Nationale, Liste Par Groupes* (1949).
[6] Apithy, as above.
[7] In Senegal, Senghor had the support of the missions but the senior administrators, led by Governor-General Béchard and Governor Wiltord, supported the SFIO.
[8] By his own account (conversation with the author, May 1967).

## C. The Bloc Démocratique Sénégalais

Senghor's first victory over Lamine-Guèye in the Assembly was to gain parliamentary approval for an electoral law providing for the use of proportional representation in the election of overseas representatives in the Council of the Republic–which was renewed in November 1948. This enabled the minority in the Senegal General Council (18 out of 50) which supported Senghor to elect Mamadou Dia to one of the seats.[1]

This minority took the name of the *Bloc Démocratique Sénégalais* (BDS). Some thought that it would seek an alliance with the RDA. But as long as the RDA itself remained allied with the Communists, such an alliance would have defeated its purpose. Senghor was not only a Catholic but an instinctive moderate; and he realised that the young intellectuals who represented the RDA in Senegal were no more in contact with the rural masses than Lamine-Guèye himself. The leaders who could swing votes in the countryside were those whose position depended on the existing social structure: Moslem *marabouts*, groundnut-traders, traditional chiefs. These three categories overlapped to a very large extent, and none of them were likely to be attracted by the Marxist theorising and violent speeches of the RDA. These groups Senghor set out to court. He announced, a little startlingly, that 'the maintenance of traditional chiefs is in conformity with the spirit of scientific socialism', and urged that they be given higher salaries and greater security of status. He promised democratically run co-operatives to market groundnuts and so cut out the middlemen from the towns (many of whom were prominent Socialists). And he appealed to the two great Moslem fraternities, the Tijaniyya and the Mourides.[2]

### *The Tijaniyya*

The former, probably comprising about half the total population of Senegal, owed its strength in West Africa to the crusades of the great nineteenth-century warrior **El-Hadj Omar Tall** and his disciples. El-Hadj Omar himself was a Toucouleur from the Senegal River region who had built himself a vast, if ephemeral, empire on the upper and middle Niger. (He was killed in battle in 1863 or 1864.)[3] One of his descendants, **Seydou Nourou Tall,** was still a powerful

---

[1] Morgenthau, p. 145.     [2] Ibid., pp. 144–9.
[3] See E. Mage, *Du Sénégal au Niger* (Paris 1867).

figure on the river, and his adhesion to the BDS gave it an air of respectability. But more important was the support of Ibrahima Seydou Ndaw of Kaolack, for he brought with him many Tijani Moslems from Senegal's most populous and prosperous area, the Sine-Saloum,[1] evangelised in the 1860s by El Hadj Omar's disciple **Ma Bâ.**[2]

The pilgrimage centre for many Tijani was Tivaouane, near Thiès, and here too there was an important dynasty of *marabouts*, the Sy. Headship of the family was disputed between two brothers, one of whom, **Ababacar Sy,** turned to the BDS for support. This gave Senghor an approach to Lamine-Guèye's urban electorate, for the Sy had been associated with the pre-war deputy Galandou Diouf, and had many followers among the workers. The most prominent of these was **Abbas Gueye,** leader of the Senegal CGT.[3]

## The Mourides

The Mouride sect was smaller than the Tijaniyya, but more central-ised and more disciplined; it was particularly strong among the Wolofs, economically and educationally Senegal's most advanced tribe. It had been founded in the late nineteenth century by a native Senegalese, **Cheikh Ahmadou Bamba,** and it had played a part in stimulating Senegalese economic growth somewhat similar to that which Max Weber attributed to Protestantism in Europe. For the peculiarity of Ahmadou Bamba's teaching was his insistence on work. Salvation was indirectly related to the size of the ground-nut crop– provided that the proceedings were devoted to religious purposes, i.e. to maintaining the *marabouts* who prayed for the faithful while the faithful were working. As a result the Mouride leaders grew enormously wealthy, and had an exceptionally well-organised and devoted congregation. Ahmadou Bamba died in 1927, and over his tomb at Touba an enormous mosque was slowly raised by manual labour. Each year it is visited by hundreds of thousands of pilgrims. Another 'Protestant' characteristic of the Mourides is their habit of conducting religious rites in their native tongue (Wolof).

At the time when the BDS was founded, the succession to Cheikh Ahmadou Bamba was in dispute. As with the Sy, this gave the new

[1] Morgenthau, pp. 143, 147.
[2] See J. D. Hargreaves, *Prelude to the Partition of West Africa* (London 1963).
[3] Morgenthau, p. 148.

political party an opening. **Falilou Mbacké,** the established Mouride Kkalifa, decided to ally with the BDS against his young rival **Cheikh Mbacké,** who continued to support Lamine-Guèye. Falilou's prestige both increased, and was increased by, that of the BDS. He was followed by other Mourides, and by **Ibrahima Sarr,** the leader of the railway workers who had left the CGT after the failure of the railway strike (and who were grateful to Senghor for supporting them while the strike was in progress).[1]

The BDS wooed all these Moslem groups by seeing that they were represented on its central and local committees, and by taking up Moslem demands for subsidies to mosques, Koranic schools and pilgrimages, and for the teaching of Arabic in state schools.[2] It also took trouble to investigate local economic and social grievances, and established links with ethnic and regional associations whose demands had been ignored by the SFIO. Its greatest success was with the groundnut farmers round Kaolack, but it also gained support from various groups within the Four Communes: the fishermen of Saint-Louis, the Dakar taxi-drivers, the considerable Guinean immigrant community, even in some areas caste-groups such as the 'jewellers' or the young 'griots' (bards whose function was to sing the praises of a chief and his ancestors).[3]

### 'Négritude' and 'African Socialism'

Just as these 'professional' castes, traditionally looked down on in African society, were now reacting and asserting their self-respect, so Senghor inspired young intellectuals to react against assimilation and proclaim the virtues of the African personality – or 'négritude', to use the word which he has made famous throughout the world. Quite deliberately Senghor stressed the word 'nègre', previously used as an insulting name (cf. 'nigger') by white racists. He accepted the implication that negroes were fundamentally different from whites, but insisted that this was because they had something positive to contribute: a civilisation, a way of life, even a method of reasoning. 'Negro reasoning does not detract from the things it contemplates,

---

[1] Ibid., pp. 148–9.
[2] Mamadou Dia, who had become Senghor's right-hand man, was noted both for his Moslem piety and for his eloquence in Wolof. This compensated for the fact that Senghor himself was a Catholic and not very fluent in Wolof (ibid., p. 148). Senghor came from the Serère tribe, which had only been partly Islamised by Ma Bâ.
[3] Morganthau, pp. 146–51.

it does not mould them into two rigid schemes, thereby ignoring their very essence; it flows through the veins of things to arrive at the living heart of reality. The reasoning of the white man is analytical by utilisation, that of the Negro intuitive by participation.'[1]

With such statements as this, Senghor provided a quasi-philosophical rationalisation of what was essentially a literary movement. Started by Aimé Césaire, it had found expression in Senghor's own poems, and more recently in a bi-monthly magazine, *Présence Africaine*, founded in Paris in 1947 by another Senegalese, **Alioune Diop.** Now in the BDS Senghor strove to give it a political form as well. In leaving the SFIO, he explained, he did not abandon socialism, he merely assumed the leadership of the 'revolutionary socialists' as against the 'nepotist-socialists'. His newspaper, *Condition Humaine*, described itself as being 'in the service of the Social Revolution', but added the significant qualification, 'Revolution, but not Revolt'.[2] What distinguished Senghor's socialism from that of Guy Mollet was certainly not any greater degree of violence. It was rather that he sought to rewrite socialist dogma in a specifically African form. Marx was to be respected, but he could not be supposed to have written the whole truth about Africa, since Africa was completely unknown to him. Unknown to Marx, Africa already had its own form of socialism: the collective life of the village. No African in a traditional society could become rich by himself. He must share his success with the community to which he owed it. Private property in Africa was a less absolute concept than in capitalist Europe. Land at least was always communal and could be alienated only by consent of the community as a whole. Decisions were taken collectively. There was no need of majority-rule democracy, for in a village society, as in Rousseau's city-state, the general will could be discovered directly and adhered to fully and willingly by all.

The African road to socialism, therefore, lay through a re-discovery and adaptation of traditional African institutions. It could not be through a Marxist class struggle, for the class situation as described by Marx did not obtain in Africa. The wage-earning proletariat was itself a privileged group in a society where the mass of independent peasants had an average income of £14 a year. So, instead of destroying one another, the different African social groups should avail themselves of their natural African talent for overcoming differences

[1] M. Crowder, *Senegal* (London 1967), p. 56, quoting L. S. Senghor, 'L'Esthétique négro-africaine' in *Diogène*, 16th October 1956.
[2] Ansprenger, p. 164.

and acting in common. They should work together to achieve freedom and development for all.[1]

Of course that is a telescoped, and perhaps a distorted, account of Senghor's political thought, and of course Senghor himself has a somewhat idealised view of traditional African society. But there was an element of truth in it, and above all there was an ideal which appealed to a generation that was tired of learning everything from Europe. Now Africa was going to teach Europe something for a change, and Senghor, the man who had assimilated European culture but not been assimilated by it, was going to be Africa's mouthpiece. This belief helps to explain his overwhelming popularity in Senegal, among people who can have had no idea what 'socialism' or 'assimilation' meant. His intellectualism was a political asset even with his utterly non-intellectual supporters, once he had convinced them that he intended to use it in the interests of African society. To European journalists and diplomats Senghor often seems conceited and touchy. But to the Senegalese peasants in 1948 he seemed approachable, even down-to-earth. He tramped the country districts dressed in khaki (a certain vote-catcher with the war veterans), while Lamine-Guèye stayed in Dakar and wore a dark suit.[2] He built, with Mamadou Dia's help, a party to which all were encouraged to belong, whether or not they had yet been given the right to vote. He accepted support wherever it was offered, whether from ex-RDA intellectuals who responded to the ideal of *négritude*, or from European Gaullists who wanted to break the SFIO. The Socialists affected contempt for this motley opposition, and boasted openly of Lamine-Guèye's close friendship with the High Commissioner and the Governor. It was suspected that Governor **Wiltord** would try and rig elections against the BDS, as Mouragues had apparently done against the BDA. But if he did try, he failed. Even before its founding congress in April 1949, the BDS had won a by-election for the General Council. It would not be long before 'Senghor' and 'Senegal' were thought of as political synonyms.[3]

[1] Crowder, op. cit., pp. 60–1.   [2] Morgenthau, p. 138.
[3] Ansprenger, pp. 164–5.

Chapter 8

# The RDA, 1947–1950.
## Voyage au Bout de la Nuit

### A. General Situation at the end of 1948

On 2nd October 1948 the RDA Committee of Co-ordination met in Dakar. A long report was read by d'Arboussier, who since January 1947 had held general responsibility for the movement's organisation.

Although the Bamako Resolution had called for a second congress within six months to approve the statutes of the movement,[1] no such congress had been held. In practice the Co-ordination Committee had become the governing body of the party–for a political party the RDA now was even if it refused to call itself that. If there were any doubt of this it was dispelled by the action taken at this Committee meeting, when Apithy and Aku were expelled from the RDA because they had joined the IOM (thus joining forces with parties opposing the RDA in Niger and Upper Volta) and because they had refused to bind themselves in advance to accept the decisions of the next RDA Congress.[2] This action also confirmed the principle that RDA deputies were subordinate to the Co-ordination Committee, a principle laid down in the statutes as drawn up by that Committee at Abidjan in April 1947; executive power was vested in the parliamentary group in Paris, but between Congresses the Co-ordination Committee assumed the rôle of *organisme supérieur*. It included, besides the parliamentary representatives, and the *bureau* elected in full congress, a delegate from the steering committee of each territorial section.[3]

According to the statutes, the territorial sections were subordinate to the inter-territorial movement. But this principle was difficult to apply in practice. The exclusion of Apithy and Aku from the move-

[1] Milcent, op. cit.      [2] Ansprenger, p. 129.
[3] See *Le RDA dans la lutte anti-impérialiste* (pamphlet already cited), which also contains the text of d'Arboussier's report, and photographs of the RDA leaders at the time.

ment did not result in their expulsion from their local parties, but in the secession of their local parties from the RDA. As a result the RDA disappeared altogether from Togolese politics, while in Dahomey it was left with only a handful of talented individual adherents.

Nonetheless, as d'Arboussier surveyed the progress made in the two years since the Bamako Congress, he was able to feel a certain satisfaction. The movement claimed 'nearly a million members and several million sympathisers'. Admittedly, no other section was comparable in strength to 'that of the Ivory Coast which is incarnate in the strong personality of our president FÉLIX HOUPHOUËT-BOIGNY, and which has the whole country behind it'. Nonetheless there were active sections in six out of eight territories in AOF (seven if Dahomey is included), in three out of four territories in AEF, and in Cameroun.

## Moyen-Congo

After the PDCI, the most securely entrenched RDA section at this time was Tchicaya's *Parti Progressiste Congolais* (PPC), which was comfortably in control of the Moyen-Congo General Council. Although its mass support was confined to the Vili tribe, it had also won the backing of many influential traditional chiefs, and even of a few big trading firms. Above all, it benefited from a less hostile administration than other sections had to cope with—especially since the arrival in Brazzaville of a new High Commissioner for AEF, **Bernard Cornut-Gentille,** with whom Tchicaya was on reasonably good terms. Tchicaya wisely confined his support of Communism to Paris, and avoided any verbal attacks on General de Gaulle. He thus avoided the fate of Raymond Barbé, who when he visited AEF in the autumn of 1948 was almost lynched, both in Brazzaville and in Pointe-Noire, because he was ill-advised enough to denounce de Gaulle and the Gaullist first-college deputy, Maurice Bayrou, who had led many Congolese soldiers on the glorious march across the Sahara.[1]

## Oubangui-Chari

In Oubangui-Chari the General Council was controlled by a party called the *Union Oubanguienne*, founded by the half-caste **Antoine**

[1] V. Thompson and R. Adloff, *The Emerging States of French Equatorial Africa*, op. cit.

**Darlan,** who had lately affiliated it to the RDA. This party claimed 18 regional branches, more than 20,000 members, and funds of one million francs. It had an extensive social programme which included the building of schools, dispensaries, workers' canteens and even two brick factories, and for which it voted itself a subsidy of 300,000 francs on the territorial budget. To the fury of the first-college members, the majority in the General Council sent out missions to investigate conditions in different parts of the territory and check administrative abuses. These missions were also useful, of course, for party propaganda. All this provoked furious opposition from the administration, which was almost uniformly Gaullist. At first sight the situation was similar to that in the Ivory Coast, but in the event the Union Oubanguienne proved far less able to resist administrative repression than the PDCI. Darlan was an arrogant leader who antagonised his own followers by extremist outbursts. His organisation was much less solid than it looked, and he entirely lacked Houphouët's charisma. The man who inspired popular devotion in Oubangui-Chari was the deputy, Father Boganda – and he held aloof both from Darlan and from the RDA.[1]

*Tchad*

In Tchad an RDA section had been organised immediately after the Bamako Congress by Gabriel Lisette, a negro administrator from Guadeloupe. Lisette was twenty-seven years old when he defeated his fellow Free French officer, de Boissoudy, in the November 1946 election. He owed his success partly to the fact that the electorate was twice as large as that which had voted for the Constituent Assemblies. The enfranchisement of wage-earners, trade union members and driving-licence holders brought in many semi-*évolués*, mainly in Fort-Lamy (the capital) and the south-west of the territory, who liked the RDA's radical tone. Lisette's popularity, and the strength of his party, were always greatest in the southern, non-Moslem areas, whose negro inhabitants profited from French education and institutions to escape from the servile rôle to which earlier African history had condemned them. The Moslem chiefs, especially the nomads of the north, tended to despise Lisette and support the Gaullist administration. In the General Council, Lisette's *Parti Progressiste Tchadien* (PPT) won only three seats. The remaining 27 (10 first- and 17 second-college) went to members of the Gaullist

---

[1] Ibid.

UDT (*Union Démocratique Tchadienne*)–Europeans, chiefs, sultans and notables. The PPT's protests against the frequent dismissals and transfers of civil servants who supported it were regularly ignored, and in 1947 the Council actually voted in favour of maintaining the double college–the African members modestly admitting their own political inexperience. In 1948 even the few chiefs who had supported the PPT resigned from it and formed an 'Independent Socialist Party', affiliated to the French SFIO. Their leader was **Ahmet Koulamallah,** a merchant of noble Arab descent who was the local head of the Tijaniyya sect.[1]

The policy of using Moslem Emirs to maintain Europeans control, which Lord Lugard had inaugurated in Northern Nigeria, was copied by the French in the neighbouring areas of Northern Cameroun, Tchad and Niger. When the RDA appeared in Tchad and Niger after 1946, it was natural for French administrators to rely on the Moslem chiefs to oppose it, and to help them organise the semblance of political parties. In Tchad they simply recruited them into their own Gaullist party, the UDT. This was easy because Tchad had already been organised as a Gaullist stronghold ('the turntable of Resistance') during the war.


## Niger

In Niger a slightly different tactic was used. The Emirs were encouraged to form an anti-RDA party of their own: the *Union Nigérienne des Indépendants et Sympathisants* (UNIS). This group included a comfortable majority of the General Council and was led by a member of one of the most important chiefly families, Prince **Issoufou Seydou Djermakoye,** who was twenty-seven years old at the time of his election to the Assembly of the French Union in 1947. UNIS was formed in 1948 when an extra seat was given to Niger in the National Assembly. With the help of Governor **Toby** (whose rôle was that played by Mouragues in Upper Volta) it defeated the RDA in the by-election. Georges Condat, the new deputy, was a half-caste teacher from Maradi (a Hausa town just across the border from Katsina in Northern Nigeria). The Emirs–like most other chiefs–preferred to support a 'tame' *évolué* rather than stoop to fight an election campaign themselves. As for the RDA, it was forced on to the defensive, but it still had a number of representatives in the French assemblies: Hamani Diori in the National Assembly,

[1] Ibid.

**Boubou Hama** in the Assembly of the French Union, and the trade unionist **Bakary Djibo** (nominated by the CGT) on the 'Economic and Social Council' (a post which did not confer parliamentary immunity, but did bring a salary and a car–rare advantages in such an impoverished territory). All three of these leaders were old boys of the Ecole Normale William Ponty.[1]

## Upper Volta

The reasons for the RDA's failure in Upper Volta have already been mentioned. In the east it was totally excluded after the death of Kaboret Zinda in 1947. The Mossi chiefs were hostile to it, and they had complete control over their subjects. In the western, non-Mossi area (round Bobo-Dioulasso), there was a strong RDA section led by **Ali Barraud** and **Djibril Vinama.** Only violent repression (and probably falsification of results) accounted for its defeat by Nazi Boni.[2]

In the Soudan too the RDA was subject to administrative persecution. French Communist teachers and civil servants who had helped oganise the Union Soudanaise (US-RDA) lost their jobs. Many of the US-RDA leaders themselves were also government employees, and found themselves fircd, demoted, barred from promotion, or transferred to areas where they were useless to the party. **Modibo Keita,** secretary to deputy Konaté, was even arrested in the streets of Paris. Meanwhile all possible advantages were accorded to the Progressive Party (PSP) of Fily-Dabo Sissoko, which benefited from the support of nearly all official chiefs (those who backed the US-RDA were quickly dismissed), and was therefore able to put both administrative and judicial pressure on recalcitrant electors. Yet the US-RDA was often able to turn its misfortunes to account, building up victimised leaders as martyrs and fostering a strong *esprit de corps* among its militants. It retained a strong base among the educated and semi-educated population in the towns, and especially in the Bambara areas of the south, bordering on Guinea and Upper Volta.[3]

In Senegal the success of the BDS put an end to RDA hopes of capturing the rural masses. But there was a strong RDA nucleus

[1] Morgenthau, pp. 317, 406. Ansprenger p. 282 (and 'Personenverzeichnis' at end).

[2] See Ouezzin Coulibaly's speech in the National Assembly, 22nd March 1949.

[3] Morgenthau, pp. 289–90. Delval, art. cit.

among Senegal's relatively numerous educated urban population, especially among its younger members, and this was supported by some – but not all – of the CGT trade unionists. Some of the RDA's most important individual leaders were normally resident in Dakar: d'Arboussier, Guy Etcheverry (whose newspaper *Réveil* was now subtitled *La Voix du RDA*), **Doudou Guèye** (a Senegalese doctor who had worked in the Ivory Coast, and now acted as the RDA's permanent delegate in Dakar), and **Abdoulaye Guèye** (Senegalese trade unionist, one of the most rigidly pro-Communist leaders of the CGT).[1]

Finally, in Guinea there was a small RDA section, the *Parti Démocratique de la Guinée* (PDG), which d'Arboussier had helped to found in 1947. But so far it included only a few intellectuals and trade unionists. Mamba Sano's defection deprived it of any wide popular support.[2]

### Arguments for the Communist Alliance

It was apparent to many people outside, and some inside the RDA, that most of its difficulties stemmed from its involvement with the Communist Party. D'Arboussier was the chief apologist of this involvement, and he devoted the greater part of his report to a vindication of it. First, he dismissed ideological scruples by pointing out that no RDA member was asked to join the Communist Party, or to accept its ideology. The RDA, by reason of its nature as a *Rassemblement* – a broad mass movement 'which must be at once the expression of the mass and the mass itself' – could not expect to impose a single ideology on all its members. It could not be *anti-*Communist, but nor could it be anti-Christian, anti-animist or anti-Moslem. It must include in its ranks everyone, whatever his ideological standpoint, who accepted its primary objective, namely: 'emancipation of the various African countries from the colonial yoke by the assertion of their political, economic, social and cultural individuality and by freely consented membership in a union of nations and peoples founded on equality of right and duties'.

What united the RDA with the French Communist Party, d'Arboussier went on to say, was not a common ideology but a common interest, and above all a common enemy. He does not seem to have seen that this doctrine was itself part of Communist ideology. He thought – and he convinced his hearers – that the community of

[1] Ansprenger, p. 128.  [2] Ibid., pp. 127–8, 133.

interests was an empirically established fact. Anti-Communism in France coincided with action against the RDA in Africa. So far from showing that the RDA's alliance with Communism was unwise, this proved it was necessary. Only the triumph of Communism in France would initiate a really liberal French policy in Africa. The only time when real colonial reforms had been achieved was 1944–6, when the PCF had been most influential. Then, as the Communists were edged out of power, the colonial reaction had gathered strength. 'The PCF is the only party which has never betrayed the fundamental interests of the colonial masses. . . .'

It was wrong, d'Arboussier insisted, to suppose that the administration only opposed the RDA because the RDA was *apparenté* to the Communist groups in Parliament. The *apparentement* was a recent phenomenon, whereas colonial oppression had been going on since before living memory. No one should suppose that it would miraculously cease if the RDA allied with the Socialists or the MRP. Why had Senghor left the SFIO, if Socialist support was so valuable?[1] Konaté and his friends had been allied with the Socialists before the RDA was formed, at a time when Sissoko was still a friend of the Communists. Yet even then Sissoko had been favoured by French administrators in the Soudan and the radicals had been persecuted. 'Our militants are *not* persecuted because of our *apparentement*, but because of the RDA's fundamental position of struggle against colonialism. . . . Either we remain *apparentés*, but in fact abandon the struggle, in which case all persecution will stop, but we shall have betrayed our ideal and the African masses; or we give up our *apparentement*, thereby losing its advantages, but remain faithful to our militant line, in which case the persecution will continue.' At the same time d'Arboussier indignantly rejected the notion that the RDA had become a mere tool of the Communists. So far from meekly accepting instructions, he said, the RDA leaders formulated their own demands on African policy and the Communists took them up.

These arguments convinced the Committee. It was decided to maintain the *apparentement*, and one of the fundamental principles of the RDA's action was declared to be 'the alliance of the African democratic forces with the democratic and progressive forces of the entire world, and above all with those of the French people in their common fight against imperialism.'

[1] Senghor had not yet joined the IOM; the RDA leaders may still have been hoping he would join them.

*The Treichville Congress, January 1949*

The Committee also decided that the general line of the movement should now be ratified by a second general congress. The first idea was to hold this at Bobo-Dioulasso, centre of the non-Mossi region of Upper Volta. This would have helped raise the morale of the RDA militants in the area where they had been most blatantly persecuted and misrepresented during the recent elections. Not surprisingly, Governor Mouragues was having none of this. He categorically forbade it. The Congress was held instead at Treichville, across the lagoon from Abidjan, from 1st to 5th January 1949. Only 167 delegates were present, but there was a strong contingent of French Communist politicians and journalists.[1] They set the tone for the African speakers, one of whom declared: 'We must move boldly in the direction of those masters of proletarian thought who are in the vanguard of progressive humanity. We must move boldly towards Marx, Engels, Lenin, towards Stalin who is in the present day their inspired continuator. Stalin, the indisputable authority on the problems of nationality and the colonial questions which are precisely our problems and our questions. . . .' The political resolution adopted by the Congress was in a similar vein: 'The Congress welcomes the powerful upsurge of the democratic forces in the world and affirms its confidence in their certain victory over the forces of imperialism. . . . It expresses its faith in the alliance of the peoples of Afrique Noire with the great people of France, which, led by its working class and its Communist Party, is struggling with courage and confidence for its national independence against American imperialism.'

Houphouët was confirmed in the office of President of the movement, with Konaté, Tchicaya, Doudou Guèye and Um Nyobé as vice-presidents. D'Arboussier was given the new and important office of Political General Secretary. Needless to say the *apparentement* was approved. Yet it should not be supposed that d'Arboussier's arguments had penetrated the mass of RDA militants. In most cases they accepted the policy because their local leaders did, rather than from conviction. In fact, only a month after the Congress, the Ivory Coast territorial steering committee actually passed a motion asking that the *apparentement* be dropped.[2]

[1] Ansprenger, p. 128.      [2] Milcent, op. cit.

## B. The 'Incidents' in the Ivory Coast, 1949–1950

It was in the Ivory Coast that the final trial of strength between the administration and the RDA was held. Governor Orselli, who was recalled in October 1948, had predicted the clash. Péchoux, who succeeded him–and who was already regarded by the RDA as an arch-reactionary[1]–did not intend to avoid it. Nor, to judge by the language of the Treichville Congress, did the leaders of the RDA.

The Ivory Coast administration perfected a technique often used by colonial rulers when in difficulties. They encouraged African opponents of the RDA to provoke incidents, which were then used to justify direct action against the RDA by police (or, in extreme cases, troops).[2] Incidents were easy to provoke because in most parts of the territory the population was devoted to Houphouët and could be relied on to behave badly if he were insulted or his authority threatened. The administration's dislike of Houphouët stemmed partly from a suspicion that he controlled the territory more effectively than it did. The PDCI-RDA had developed its own judicial system, which settled many disputes between Africans before they got to the official courts. It even had its own law-enforcement officers, armed with symbolic wooden weapons, who styled themselves *la police du député* (as opposed to the official *police du gouverneur*). In some areas a PDCI party card was more essential than an official identity card. A customer could even be asked to show it before a market-woman would sell him anything. In short, a totalitarian society was growing up under the nose of an authoritarian government–which helped the latter to pose as a champion of the individual.[3]

As often happens, the individuals who first challenged the mass movement were drop-outs from its own bandwagon, nursing a wounded *amour-propre*. **Etienne Djaument** had been Houphouët's leading backer in 1945, and in return Houphouët had backed him for Senator in January 1947. But when the Council of the Republic was re-elected in November 1948 Houphouët dropped Djaument in favour of a member of his own Baule tribe, **Victor Biaka Boda.**

---

[1] Houphouët's evidence in Annexe 11348 (op. cit.). But interestingly enough Robert Léon, the RDA's leading European supporter in the Ivory Coast, told the Commission that he (Léon) had lobbied *in favour* of Péchoux's appointment, thinking he would be a good governor. If Houphouët was telling the truth, this seems to support Orselli's contention that Léon was an *agent provocateur* (see above, p. 124).

[2] Morgenthau, p. 198.          [3] Ansprenger, pp. 131–2.

Consequently Djaument left the PDCI, and with official encouragement founded a new opposition party, the *Bloc Démocratique Eburnéen* (30th January 1949). At the inaugural meeting in Treichville he denounced Houphouët (who was present), but would not allow him to reply. Thereupon the predominantly RDA audience drowned Djaument's own speech with boos, catcalls and hisses. The meeting was adjourned till 6th February. On the latter date Houphouët himself was out of town, but his supporters rioted and attacked the homes of some of their principal opponents, as well as the headquarters of the Progressiste party. One man was killed, four seriously injured, and forty-six arrests were made. The Ivory Coast 'incidents' had begun.

Three days later the government took occasion to arrest eight PDCI leaders. Almost the only members of the steering committee left at large were those protected by parliamentary immunity (deputies, senators, and councillors of the French Union). Further small incidents occurred in the Baule area round Dimbokro, and the administration began a campaign against the RDA throughout the Territory. Charges were brought against the Syndicat Agricole Africain, and against the local RDA paper *Le Démocrate*. There were wholesale sackings of RDA sympathisers in the civil service, and several hundred pro-RDA village chiefs were de-stooled.[1] One village whose chief refused to pay taxes to an anti-RDA superior was attacked and occupied by troops. Four people, including the chief, were killed, and all the villagers either fled or were arrested. This episode was reported in *Réveil* (20th June 1949) by Doudou Guèye, who had gone on a tour of the Ivory Coast as a kind of war correspondent. According to him 'five weaponless people were summarily shot, including . . . a small child on its mother's back. After the shooting the village was regularly plundered, and the *chef de canton* had it burned down'. The paper was prosecuted for 'publishing false information'–but saved by the fact that Etcheverry had prudently handed over its editorship to d'Arboussier, who was covered by parliamentary immunity. (This did not protect Doudou Guèye himself. His case came up a year later, when he was sentenced to three months' imprisonment.)[2]

The RDA tried to fight back by refusing to vote the budget in the Ivory Coast General Council. Péchoux immediately prorogued the session. By the time the Council reassembled he had managed to convert the RCA's 29 to 16 majority into a minority of 15 to 30.

[1] Morgenthau, pp. 188–91.    [2] Ansprenger, p. 136 and n.

This was done by a mixture of threats, arrests and bribery.[1] Yet another anti-RDA party was formed—the *Entente des Indépendents de la Côte d'Ivoire*, composed mainly of northern Moslem chiefs whom the administration had won over.[2]

The struggle came to a climax in December 1949 and January 1950. Incidents occurred all over the territory, usually starting with quarrels provoked by the RDA's opponents, which the administration then used as a pretext for arresting local RDA leaders. This usually led to popular demonstrations, and these in turn were dispersed by force.

In the gaol at Grand Bassam the eight leaders who had been imprisoned on 9th February went on hunger strike from 12th to 27th December 1949. Simultaneously there was a boycott of European goods, and during Christmas week there were demonstrations outside the prison. On 2nd January an African died after being interrogated by the police. On the 5th the demonstrations culminated in a mass march on the prison by women. According to *Climats* they lay down on the pavement and undressed, before being dispersed with firehoses. Next, the servants went on strike in European houses, and there was a four-day boycott of the railways. Meanwhile the government tried desperately to reassert its authority, even resorting to an announcement in the newspapers that the paramount chief of the Baule had resigned from the RDA. In fact he had refused to do so, despite considerable inducements, and made a personal trip to Abidjan to say so.

On 19th January twelve houses were pillaged at Affère. On the 21st and 22nd three people were killed at Bouaflé. On the 23rd there were incidents near Yamoussoukro, Houphouët's home village, and on the 24th a warrant was issued for the arrest of Houphouët himself. On the 27th the *substitut du procureur* arrived with troops at Houphouët's plantation and made two attempts to put the warrant into effect. But Houphouët insisted on his parliamentary immunity, and the troops withdrew. It was just as well, for crowds had gathered from all over the region to protect him, and he was only just able to restrain them from violence.

The following night a weird and still unexplained event occurred. Senator Biaka Boda disappeared, never to be seen again. Europeans gleefully put it about that he had been 'eaten by his constituents'. More probably he was the victim of over-zealous interrogation by

---

[1] Morgenthau, p. 191. Ansprenger, p. 135.
[2] Morgenthau, p. 188.

agents of the local chief, newly installed in office thanks to his opposition to the RDA.[1]

The worst of all the incidents took place on 30th January at Dimbokro, where thirteen Africans were shot by troops. The French government was now badly rattled, and on 1st February a decree was issued banning all RDA meetings throughout Africa.[2]

## C. Towards a Change of Course

Neither the government nor the RDA was really gaining from the struggle. Nor for that matter were the settlers. The authority of both government and party was rapidly collapsing, and the Ivory Coast was slipping into an anarchy which would be detrimental not only to its public order but to its economy as well.[3] The RDA was particularly embarrassed because, for all the strident vocabulary of 'struggle' which it had borrowed from the Communists, it had conspicuously failed in action. By and large the leaders were remarkably successful in restraining their followers from violence. (For example, not a single European was attacked throughout the incidents, although many of them lived on isolated plantations which would have been easy targets,[4] and many had predicted a massacre when trying to discredit the RDA.[5] It seems not even to have occurred to Houphouët and Coulibaly to start a war of independence or a Mau-Mau-type uprising. They continued to protest their loyalty to the French Union and to assert that it was not they, but the colonialists, who were really anti-French. Indeed their main preoccupation seems to have been to save the Ivory Coast from the fate of Madagascar.)[6] But on the other hand the attempts at non-violent resistance were not very effective. Nor was French Communist support. The PCF provided cheap legal aid for RDA political prisoners; but otherwise its contribution mainly took the form of shrill propaganda,[7] whose only effect was to make most non-Communist Frenchmen assume that RDA complaints against the administration must be wildly distorted and exaggerated.[8]

[1] Ibid., pp. 194–8. Milcent, op. cit.    [2] Milcent, op. cit.
[3] Morgenthau, p. 199.    [4] RDA electoral manifesto, 1951.
[5] Orselli's evidence in Annexe 11348.
[6] See for example the debates in the National Assembly on 22nd March 1949 and in February 1950.
[7] Morgenthau, p. 93.
[8] This probably explains the apparent callousness with which normally conscientious deputies ignored RDA evidence of electoral malpractices in Africa. See below.

## The Failure of the Communists

The Communist alliance would only really become valuable if and when the Communists gained power in France. But there was still no immediate prospect of this happening. The successive 'revolutionary' strikes failed to achieve their political ends, but slowly eroded the workers' loyalty to the CGT. When prime minister Queuille in his turn (after record tenure of over a year) fell a victim to the Socialists' frustration in October 1949, the CGT staged a new political strike against the nomination of **Jules Moch,** the Socialist Minister of the Interior whose tough methods had broken their previous strikes, to head the next government. The strike was a flop. Most workers stayed at their jobs, and Communist hatred won Moch unexpected support elsewhere in the Assembly—so that his investiture actually passed by one vote.[1]

## The Minor Successes of the IOM

This razor-edge majority confirmed the king-making reputation of the IOM, without whose votes (14 of them now)[2] Moch would not have made it. He had been obliged to earn their votes, not merely with a policy statement, but with the promise of a portfolio. In the event he was unable to form a cabinet—the Communists were by no means his only enemies.[3] But Aujoulat saw to it that the MRP's recapture of the prime ministership, which was the eventual result of the crisis, did not involve any loss of ground by the IOM. In the new cabinet formed by George Bidault he, Aujoulat, figured as Under-Secretary (later Secretary) of State in the Ministry of France d'Outre-Mer; and the Minister was no longer Coste-Floret but **Jean Letourneau,** also an MRP man but one whose principal interests were in Indo-China and who held less dogmatic views on African policy.[4]

Aujoulat's work was mainly concerned with social and cultural

---

[1] Williams, op. cit., pp. 37 and 74.

[2] Eleven from Afrique Noire, two Algerians and an Indian. This strength made the IOM a full parliamentary group with representation on commissions.

[3] Moch's 'unforgivable clarity' (Williams, p. 92) made him unpopular both with the MRP and with many of his fellow-socialists. He was also believed by many Africans to be responsible for the SFIO's backsliding on colonial policy in 1946. He was alleged to have said that he 'did not want to be the equal of the grandsons of Makoko' (the tribal chief with whom Brazza had signed the Congo protectorate treaty in 1880).

[4] Milcent, op. cit.

problems, and his special preoccupation was the snail-like progress of the Overseas Labour Code. Hitherto the government had shown little sense of urgency about it. Twice it had ignored demands from the Assembly of the French Union that Moutet's decree be provisionally enforced until a law could be passed. Not until five months after the decree's repeal did a government bill even appear on the table of the National Assembly (5th May 1948). Then, when the French Union Assembly had already debated and accepted most of this, it was replaced by a second bill (20th August 1948), which did not reach the French Union Assembly until February 1949. Then it was long and thoroughly discussed and amended. The amended version was adopted in March–only to be shelved when on 13th April the government produced a third bill which took account of some but not all of the French Union Assembly's amendments. This in its turn had to plod through that Assembly. Then, in 1950, it was examined by the Economic Council. Not until November 1950 did it begin its first reading in the National Assembly, where it was allotted one session a week, on Saturday mornings–when most metropolitan deputies had left for their constituencies.[1]

All this was frustrating for Aujoulat, but gave him plenty of work to do, and at least there still seemed to be some hope that the Code would actually be law by the end of the legislature (due to expire in November 1951). Meanwhile, in April 1950, he had the more immediate satisfaction of seeing a decree issued which set up an 'Institute of Higher Studies' at Dakar. For the first time some French-speaking Africans would be able to obtain Higher Education on African soil. It was the first step towards the creation of an African university–a plan discussed since 1944 but not finally implemented till 1957.[2]

## Second Loi Lamine-Guèye

Another measure of reform, and one of considerable importance to many politically conscious Africans, was introduced by Lamine-Guèye in January 1950; a bill providing for equality–in pay, recruitment, and promotion–of African and European civil servants overseas. Although this was opposed by some first-college deputies

---

[1] Gonidec and Kirsch, op. cit. The Saturday morning sessions are remembered by M. Max Jalade, a parliamentary journalist who specialised in African affairs, as being more like meetings of a club for overseas deputies than of the full National Assembly.

[2] Ansprenger, p. 112.

150

and senators, it did not offer such extensive opportunities for filibuster as did the Labour Code. It went through Parliament in just under six months and became, on 30th June, the *deuxième Loi Lamine-Guèye*.[1] Present-day African ministers, who find their budgets eaten up by a disproportionately expensive civil service, must often have regretted this essentially assimilationist reform. But in 1950 very few French-speaking Africans were thinking in terms of independence, and least of all Lamine-Guèye. The important thing was that a blow had been struck for what Senghor called 'the mystique of equality'.

These gains may seem insignificant when measured against the magnitude of African problems, or even against the ground lost in 1946. Yet they compare favourably with the parliamentary achievements of the RDA. Clearly African problems were not going, in the foreseeable future, to get the attention they needed from an Assembly preoccupied with the problem of holding together a non-Communist and non-Gaullist majority in an atmosphere of continuous crisis over wages policy, the war in Indo-China, the Atlantic Pact, and then the Korean War. For the time being Afrique Noire would continue to be governed mainly from the Rue Oudinot, and if Africans were to have any say in the matter it was there that they must make themselves heard. Lamine-Guèye had achieved this to some extent by personal influence within the SFIO–at least he had got some friendly Socialist administrators sent out to West Africa (friendly to him, that is). Now Aujoulat appeared to be doing better by means of pressure–a mixture of personal prestige and parliamentary blackmail–on the MRP.

## The Failure of the RDA

No such avenue of pressure was open to Houphouët, so long as he was yoked to the Communists. Indeed, after 1948 he seems practically to have given up speaking in the National Assembly, realising no doubt that his speeches had little effect. When RDA deputies did speak, they did so to a half-empty and cynical house, receiving only automatic Communist applause. In March 1949, for example, Ouëzzin Coulibaly delivered a long and detailed indictment of administrative interference in the Upper Volta elections the year before. It was brushed aside with a mixture of contempt and incredulity by the MRP (and indeed by Aujoulat), and the Assembly

[1] I am told, however, that it took a long time to be fully applied.

validated the election of three deputies whose value was not that they genuinely represented the population of Upper Volta,[1] but that they reinforced the parliamentary majority. It was a discouraging but all too typical result. Small wonder that RDA deputies came less and less frequently to Parliament–especially as their presence was often necessary in their constituencies to prevent the population from responding to official provocation and starting another Madagascar.[2]

At some time in the spring of 1950 Houphouët must have realised that another Madagascar was what the Communists really wanted, a stick which they could beat the government with, without endangering their own rank and file. The RDA was playing Uriah the Hittite to Stalin's King David. What could it hope to gain? If it resorted to violent rebellion, as the Communists perhaps hoped, the result would be bloody repression. If on the other hand it remained in an attitude of virtuous but passive protest, the loyalty of its educated adherents would continue to be eroded by alternate threats and bribes, and finally even its stalwart peasant supporters were bound to lose confidence in it. Some sort of compromise began to seem essential.

### Attitude of the Government

Fortunately the government was beginning to think so too. It was certainly not anxious to have another Madagascar on its hands, still less another Vietnam. The Vietnamese experience was gradually teaching it that, the further repression went, the more moderates would rally to extremist leadership. There were indications that this could happen in Africa too. The banning of the projected RDA congress at Bobo-Dioulasso at the end of 1948 had drawn protests even from Senghor's *Condition Humaine*.[3] Now, in February 1950, Senghor (who had taken over from Aujoulat as group president of the IOM) joined with the RDA deputies in demanding that a Parliamentary Commission of Inquiry be sent to investigate the Incidents in the Ivory Coast. Another IOM deputy, Henri Guissou of Upper Volta, said (referring to the massacre at Dimbokro): 'It is

[1] Coulibaly admitted that if the election had been fairly conducted the Union Voltaïque would still have won two seats, because of the strength of the Mossi vote, but the RDA would certainly have got one.
[2] Debate of 22nd March 1949. Speeches by Coulibaly and Konaté.
[3] Ansprenger, p. 133.

no longer the moment to insult each other when fifteen inhabitants of the Ivory Coast have just been buried. For us Africans there is a simple but tragic question to be answered. Twice we have been ready to die for France. For whom are these men dying now?'[1]

The Assembly was disturbed by the course events were taking. It was no longer ready to accept official explanations entirely without questioning, and eventually a Commission of Inquiry was sent. Meanwhile Minister Letourneau went on a personal tour of AOF. What he saw seems to have convinced him that it would be unwise to outlaw the RDA altogether. On 24th March he admitted, in reply to an enquiry from Konaté, that no action had been taken to implement the decree of 1st February. The authorities had been instructed to allow RDA meetings within the normal limits of the law.[2]

## Elimination of d'Arboussier

For the time being Houphouët continued to act with the Communists. Early in April he attended the Twelfth National Congress of the PCF, bringing the fraternal greetings of the African peoples and assuring Maurice Thorez (the PCF's leader) of Africans' affectionate sympathy and gratitude. But probably he was already contemplating a change of course. Certainly the question was discussed at a meeting of the RDA parliamentary group on 23rd June.[3] The deputies were agreed that it was necessary, but d'Arboussier was predictably opposed. He more than anyone was the architect of the alliance, and he had devoted a great deal of time and energy to working out its theoretical basis. As recently as December 1949 he had been calling on RDA militants 'to find the most effective means of struggle, avoiding the traps of the enemy but seeking out his vulnerable points in order to strike them more and more vigorous blows.'[4] The language was perhaps used figuratively. But it would be embarrassing for its author to come to terms with 'the enemy' so soon (and difficult to convince 'the enemy' of his good faith even if he tried to do so).

The deputies therefore decided that d'Arboussier must go. On 7th July Houphouët persuaded him to write a letter to the Co-ordination Committee, asking to be relieved of his functions as

[1] Journal Officiel, *Débats de l'Assemblée Nationale*, February 1950.
[2] Milcent, op. cit.
[3] Ansprenger, p. 138.
[4] Milcent, op. cit.

153

General Secretary. He seems to have understood that this was a temporary move, designed to disguise but not to abolish his influence in the movement, and to facilitate a *rapprochement* with the IOM. Probably he must have guessed, if he was not told, that it would be the prelude to an announcement that the *apparentement* was at an end. But if so, he probably thought that this announcement would merely be a feint for the benefit of the colonialists, and that in reality the alliance would persist.[1]

### Negotiations

Meanwhile, during June, Houphouët made tentative and secret approaches both to the government and to the IOM. Senator **Raphaël Saller** (IOM, Guinea–first college) told him that an RDA-IOM alliance was possible if the RDA disaffiliated from the Communists, and if it repudiated its attacks on local organisations which supported IOM deputies, especially in Guinea and Niger. He also put him in touch with Vincent Auriol, President of the Republic, who was anxious to arrange a reconciliation between the RDA and the government. At the same time High Commissioner Béchard renewed his efforts to get the RDA to join up with the African Socialists.[2]

While these negotiations were going on, the government fell. The Socialists voted Bidault out of office on 24th June, Queuille back in on the 30th and out again because they disliked his cabinet (which included Coste-Floret as Minister of France d'Outre-Mer) on 2nd July. This time they were helped by the left wing of MRP. The pendulum swung a little way back to the left, and the Socialists returned to office (which they had left half way through the Bidault government) in a cabinet headed by René Pleven, leader of the UDSR.[3] During this crisis the leader of the MRP, François de Menthon, went so far as to say that 'the IOM had the key of the situation in their hands'.[4] This was perhaps an exaggeration. The IOM dared not sell their votes too dearly, for fear of uniting the majority against them as Abbas had done in the second Constituent Assembly. But the remark shows that their 'Irish Nationalist' tactics were having their effect. Some members of the group felt, after

---

[1] Ibid.
[2] Duplicated report from Saller to IOM parliamentary group, among Dr Aujoulat's papers.
[3] Williams, p. 37.       [4] Saller, as above.

Pleven's cabinet was formed, that they had been wrong not to hold out for more than one Secretaryship of State, particularly since Aujoulat now had to accept a Socialist colleague in the Ministry of France d'Outre-Mer, and the new Minister was the anti-clerical **François Mitterrand** (UDSR), who was friendly to the SFIO. There seemed to be a grave danger that the next National Assembly elections, at any rate in AOF, would be rigged in the Socialists' favour.[1]

Negotiations between IOM and RDA were therefore renewed with redoubled enthusiasm. It was arranged for Houphouët to have a personal audience with the President of the Republic, after which High Commissioner Béchard was instructed by telegram to 'change his policy towards the RDA'. Béchard was angry at having failed to win over the RDA himself, and alarmed at the possibility of an IOM-RDA anti-Socialist front. He sent one of his Socialist aides, **Jean Ramadier** (son of the ex-prime minister), to warn everyone in Paris against being taken in by Houphouët's apparent change of heart, which he now suggested was only a feint inspired by the Communists. But the IOM leaders, who detested Béchard, refused to be put off. Negotiations continued, and on 9th August a secret conditional agreement was signed. According to this, 'The RDA *élus*[2] will resume their autonomy in order to constitute, with the IOM, a parliamentary formation independent of the metropolitan political parties and groups; the existing political and ethnic organisations will retain their autonomy, but, making a clean sweep of the past, they will unite their efforts for the defence of African interests within the French Union . . .

'The details of the final agreement must ensure the consolidation and development of the political positions of the organisations represented by the signatories in the Territories whose *élus* they are.'

The IOM interpreted this as meaning that the RDA would no longer oppose the local parties of IOM deputies, but would support them against the SFIO and/or MRP. On this basis, the RDA would back IOM candidates in Guinea, Dahomey, Togo, Senegal, Upper Volta, Cameroun and possibly Oubangui-Chari, but would be left a clear field in the territories where it was still holding its own—

---

[1] Ibid.
[2] This term could include members of local assemblies in Africa. But in the context it seems only to concern members of the parliamentary assemblies in France–the National Assembly, the Council of the Republic, and the Assembly of the French Union. The RDA was *apparenté* to the MUR in the first and directly to the Communist groups in the other two.

Soudan, Ivory Coast, Tchad and Moyen-Congo. The only difficult case would be Niger, which at the moment had one IOM deputy and one RDA. Probably the answer would be to maintain this *status quo*.

This agreement was conditional on ratification by the local organisations on both sides. A final settlement was put off until after the parliamentary recess, and above all until the RDA had formally disaffiliated from the Communists.[1] On 19th October the following communiqué was published:

The RDA *élus* in the different metropolitan assemblies, realising that the higher interests of Africa can only be effectively defended by joint action of all the *élus* of the T.O.M. on the basis of a specific programme, have decided to disaffiliate themselves permanently, as from 17th October 1950, from the metropolitan parliamentary groups to which they belonged until that date.

It was, to say the least, doubtful whether they had the right to take such a decision without the authority of the Co-ordination Committee, to which they were nominally subordinate. D'Arboussier refused to sign the communiqué. But his protests were ignored, and no meeting of the Co-ordination Committee was summoned. Houphouët played his hand adroitly, for he knew that so sharp a change of policy was bound to provoke dissension within the party. He succeeded in postponing public discussion until the new policy could be seen to pay dividends. *Réveil*, which would normally have been the forum for such discussion, abruptly ceased publication.[2]

Negotiations with the IOM were resumed, this time on a more official basis. But they soon ran into difficulties. The IOM were prepared to accept joint action in Parliament, but some of their local sections, especially those of Upper Volta and Niger, refused to merge with the RDA sections in a pre-election year. They owed their existence mainly to the administration's anti-RDA policy, and they feared that if they now joined the RDA either they would lose administrative support, or the RDA would simply swallow them up, or both. The RDA on its side was not specially keen to come to the aid of those who had deserted it, or benefited from its misfortunes, in 1948. The RDA deputies refused to join the IOM group unless

[1] All the above information comes from letters and reports by Saller in Dr Aujoulat's papers.

[2] D'Arboussier had become editor (see above, p. 146) but Etcheverry was still owner and he supported Houphouët. Financially the paper depended on the support of the PDCI (Ivory Coast RDA), which was solid behind Houphouët.

there was a merger at territorial level as well.[1] Understandably, they resented the patronising tone adopted by Senghor, who benignly announced: 'It is our duty to help the RDA change its policy in the interests of France . . . We want to try, in the interests of Africa and of France, to bring the RDA back to a more objective view of reality. . . .'[2] By the end of November the negotiations had reached deadlock. The best that could be hoped for was a revival of the Intergroup of 1946–with Lamine-Guèye as president once again.

Meanwhile Houphouët negotiated separately with Mitterrand, the Minister of France d'Outre-Mer. Mitterrand belonged to the left wing within the UDSR, whose relative importance had been increased when the group as a whole was diminished by the departure of its Gaullist members to join the RPF. He was on bad terms with the group leader (and now prime minister), Pleven, whose conservative and pro-Catholic tendencies he disliked. But both he and Pleven were anxious to reinforce the majority, and since the colonial reactionaries had deserted them for RPF, they were not averse to courting African votes by a slightly more liberal colonial policy. There was also the possibility that if the RDA deputies did not join the IOM they might be persuaded to affiliate to the UDSR. If Mitterrand could achieve this result he would strengthen both the group itself (now dangerously near the minimum of fourteen needed to secure representation on Commissions) and his own position within it.[3]

Mitterrand promised Houphouët that if the RDA would support the government, he would use his influence to make things easier for it in Africa. At first, after disaffiliating from the Communists, the RDA deputies took to abstaining in National Assembly votes. D'Arboussier alleged that on the first occasion when this happened– a vote on Vietnam–he heard Mitterrand ask Houphouët 'in a sarcastic and threatening tone', 'Is this how you show your loyalty to the government?' D'Arboussier said that he then realised for the first time that agreements were being made behind his back.[4] However that may be, the RDA deputies continued to abstain for a time. But when negotiations with the IOM broke down, they seem to have decided that Mitterrand was their most promising ally. On 1st December, in a confidence debate, Tchicaya announced that the

---

[1] Minutes of IOM Parliamentary group, in Aujoulat's papers.
[2] Milcent, op. cit.
[3] Morgenthau, p. 101. Williams, p. 176.
[4] 'Lettre Ouverte à Félix Houphouët-Boigny' in *L'AOF*, 6th July 1952.

RDA would vote for the government–for the first time since the Communists left office in 1947. In reply, Pleven thanked the group for its *ralliement à la thèse nationale*.[1] For the first time in its life, the RDA was officially respectable.

[1] Milcent, op. cit.

## PART THREE

The Hungry Sheep Look Up
and Are Not Fed

## Chapter 9

# The Elections of 1951 and 1952. Eclipse of the RDA

## A. Houphouët and Mitterrand in Alliance

The RDA had started on a new chapter in its history. In the long run its new policy was to prove much more profitable than the old, and to make it, in 1958, the governing party in five of the eight territories in AOF and three of the four in AEF. But it took six years for the investment to pay off. At the end of 1950 the movement's situation appeared pathetic. The much-trumpeted struggle of the African masses against the anti-democratic colonist reaction seemed to have ended in sackcloth and ashes at Canossa. Houphouët was suing for peace from a government which he had many times denounced, seeking an alliance with rivals he had derided, and adopting a policy which he had hitherto rejected. He was violently attacked from the Left both within the movement and outside it. D'Arboussier repeatedly called for a meeting of the Co-ordination Committee which Houphouët dared not summon, and distributed copies of his protest to all RDA territorial sections.[1] The French Communists reviled him as an 'accomplice' of 'the slave-traders, the purveyors of prisoners who might call themselves Pleven, Queuille, René Mayer, Péchoux, Béchard and Co.' Even the Communist lawyers defending RDA political prisoners in the Ivory Coast deliberately misadvised their clients in order to keep them in prison longer[2].

But if there were new enemies on the Left, there were still plenty of old ones on the Right. Many Frenchmen and some Africans were at first incredulous at the sudden change in policy. They found it difficult to accept protestations of loyalty from men who had so long been the faithful allies of the Communists; they could not help suspecting that it was not d'Arboussier but Pleven and Mitterrand who had been duped. Others, who were opposed to the RDA not

[1] D'Arboussier, 'Lettre Ouverte . . .', op. cit.    [2] Morgenthau, p. 200.

161

because it was pro-Communist but because it favoured democracy and social reform in Africa, were furious to find the anti-Communist platform pulled from under their feet. Neither the settlers nor the colonial administration believed that Houphouët had changed from ape to angel overnight just because a weak government had thanked him for his vote.[1]

Thus at the beginning of 1951 Houphouët and Mitterrand found themselves as it were back to back, fighting off attacks from both political extremes. Mitterrand used his authority to make reluctant colonial governors co-operate with a three-man mission, composed of Konaté, Ouezzin Coulibaly and Hamani Diori, which Houphouët sent on tour to explain his change of policy to the various territorial sections.[2] This proved surprisingly successful. In most areas the RDA militants were not interested in ideology. They had accepted the Communist alliance out of loyalty to their leaders. The same motive led them to accept its rupture. Only in Senegal, where the RDA was a party of the intellectuals rather than the masses, and in Cameroun, where it had been built mainly upon Communist trades unions, did the territorial sections accept d'Arboussier's line.[3] Elsewhere the personal prestige of Houphouët and his fellow-deputies proved decisive.

On 5th February 1951 Mitterrand opened the new harbour at Abidjan, built out of FIDES funds. To the horror and indignation of local white opinion, Houphouët appeared beside him on the platform, along with Governor Péchoux. Mitterrand was inundated with letters from settlers and petitions from government-appointed chiefs appealing for the suppression of the RDA and an assurance that Péchoux would not be recalled. Fortunately he was able to keep his head. He was determined to avoid repeating in Afrique Noire the mistakes his predecessors had made in Indo-China. If a further lesson was needed it came in this very month of February 1951 and only a few hundred miles from Abidjan; the Gold Coast elections were overwhelmingly won by the nationalist Convention People's Party (CPP). The British governor released its leader from the prison where he had spent the last two years and asked him to form a government. The man in question was **Kwame Nkrumah,** a member of the same racial group as Houphouët. For the next six years the

---

[1] See for example the remarks of Senator Marc Rucart, *Paris-Dakar*, 26th October 1950 and *Afrique Nouvelle*, 26th January 1952. Several others are quoted by Mitterrand in *Presence française et abandon* (Paris 1957).

[2] Mitterrand, ibid., p. 187.       [3] D'Arboussier, op. cit.

Gold Coast's steady progress towards independence was eagerly studied by French-speaking Africans. Most of them continued to believe that progress within the French Union was preferable, but the visible presence of the alternative could not fail to affect them emotionally. Perceptive Frenchmen like Mitterrand realised this, and realised that the prestige of such fundamentally moderate and pro-French leaders as Houphouët needed to be fostered rather than destroyed if French presence in Africa was to be maintained.[1]

More immediately, Mitterrand was anxious to draw Houphouët into the UDSR, whose numbers now fell to 13. (At which point only the gallant gesture of the Minister of Finance, hitherto Independent, in having himself put down as UDSR, saved the group from officially ceasing to exist.) Pleven was replaced by Queuille as prime minister at the beginning of March, but otherwise the cabinet was unchanged. The UDSR ministers remained in office, but if they did not have a full group behind them they were in danger of being left out of future cabinets.[2]

## B. The Electoral Law of 1951

The burning political question of the moment was the forthcoming general election; the government was anxious both to bring forward the date from October to June and to modify the electoral system. The object in each case was to minimise the damage which the republican majority would suffer from the double onslaught of Communists and RPF. The African deputies were generally hostile to the June election, which removed any hope of seeing the Overseas Labour Code become law before the end of the First Legislature, and left little time for any extension of the African franchise to be put into effect. They were indifferent to the mode of election to be used in metropolitan France. But the hope of achieving significant improvements in the electoral system for Africa persuaded them to support the government, which in return helped to push through a special overseas electoral law. This, in the form passed by the National Assembly on 24th April, would have extended the single college for National Assembly elections to AEF and Cameroun, as well as increasing the number of overseas deputies and giving the vote to all heads of households who paid the minimum tax, and all mothers of two children 'living or dead for France'. Some provision

[1] Mitterrand, op. cit., passim.
[2] Morgenthau, p. 101. Williams, pp. 38 and 176.

was also included to prevent the more flagrant local abuses such as withholding voting cards from known opponents of the administration, and registering non-existent pro-government voters. As Senghor said, 'it would be no use extending the franchise if the local administration continued to practise an anachronistic electoral Malthusianism'. He claimed that Governor Faidherbe, who had left Senegal in 1866, still voted regularly at Saint-Louis, and usually three or four times. Significantly, he held up British proceedings in the Gold Coast as an example to be emulated; the use of a virtually universal suffrage there gave the lie to ostensibly practical objections to the extension of the franchise in French Africa. 'Certainly out of 38 seats, 35 were won by the party most hostile to Britain, but the English prefer to negotiate with authentic representatives of the population . . . France can and must do better.'[1]

The Africans concentrated their arguments, both for the abolition of the double college and for the increase in the number of seats, on the necessity of treating all Frenchmen equally, whatever their colour. Thus, as in 1946, they tried to turn the assimilationists' flank by demanding that assimilation be made a reality. Once again the first-college deputies had to fall back on a rejection of assimilation without finding any alternative theory to justify the empire's existence. They merely pointed out that if the T.O.M. were really to be represented equally, in proportion to their population, with metropolitan France, either the Assembly would have to be increased to the impossibly large total of 1,040 members, or, if it remained at its present strength of 620, only 319 of these would come from France and the rest from overseas. No one was prepared to advocate this step (least of all the Africans, whose principal concern was to make demands moderate enough to have a chance of being accepted), but nor did anyone produce an alternative formula for making former 'subjects' into genuinely equal French citizens. The cry for autonomy had been, for the time being, successfully muffled by anti-Communist propaganda; it had become almost *de rigueur* for African politicians to begin their speeches with a heated disclaimer of all 'separatist' ideas.[2]

On 30th April the Assembly adopted the Overseas Labour Code. But everyone knew that the Council of the Republic would hold it up until well after the June election. There was a danger that the

[1] Journal Officiel (*Débats*), 24th April 1951, 3rd session.
[2] Ibid., especially speeches of Lamine-Guèye ('Whatever our birthplace, whatever our colour, all of us here defend the interests of France.') and Duveau (who produced the arithmetical argument).

same fate might befall the Overseas Electoral Law, which would thus be rendered inoperative. As in 1946 the prospect of losing ground already gained drew the African deputies together, and the revived Intergroup began to squeeze the government for all it was worth. On 1st May Mitterrand recalled Governor Péchoux from the Ivory Coast.[1] This was not enough to convince the African deputies of the government's good faith. The memory of Moutet's rôle in 1946 undermined African faith in a 'liberal' minister of France d'Outre-Mer when confronted with an issue of positive political reform. Africans feared that the government, having hammered through its electoral law for metropolitan France, would gladly see the overseas one buried by the Council of the Republic. On 11th May Lamine-Guèye, as leader of the Intergroup, attempted to tie the government's hands by a motion which would prevent Parliament from dissolving until the overseas electoral law had been passed. Queuille, the arch-conciliator, was anxious to avoid a head-on clash with the Council of the Republic, anxious also to hold the African deputies in his majority. He promised to exert all his personal influence to get the overseas electoral law debated in time by the Council of the Republic (which had already sat on it for nearly three weeks), and implored Lamine-Guèye to withdraw his motion. Lamine-Guèye refused, and Queuille was forced to ask for a vote of confidence against him.[2] He got it, but the members of the Intergroup voted against the government, while Aujoulat threatened resignation from it.[3]

But Queuille kept his promise. The Council of the Republic did debate the overseas electoral law, which came back to the Assembly on 22nd May—now less than a month before the elections were due. It came back, however, in a much changed form. The double college had been restored for AEF and Cameroun. The number of seats (fixed by the Assembly, as in the abortive law of April 1946, at one per 800,000 population) had been altered to the disadvantage of several border-line cases. And the enfranchisement of African mothers had been dropped. Normally these amendments could have been overridden by the Assembly. But the Council of the Republic had used its unusually strong bargaining position for blackmail; the government had only been able to get the law through at all by promising that the amendments would be respected. Reluctantly

[1] Morgenthau, p. 101.
[2] Journal Officiel (*Débats*), 10th and 11th May, 1951.
[3] Morgenthau, p. 102.

the Assembly accepted this engagement. Only by insisting on giving the vote to mothers of two children 'living or dead for France' did it flout both government and second chamber (Mitterrand protesting vainly that the new voters could not now be registered in time for the elections).[1]

The law thus passed gave the vote for the first time to a significant number of African women; and for the first time it shifted the balance of the African electorate from the towns to the countryside.[2] Something of its immediate effect can be seen from a comparison of Tables I and II (pages 58 and 168–9). The African electorate was no longer quite such a risibly small fraction of the total population as it had been in 1945. It varied from 3 per cent in Togo to 33 per cent in Senegal, the overall average being 17 per cent. On the other hand, a comparison of the number of registered voters in June 1951 with that at the next general election in January 1956, which was held under the same electoral law,[3] shows the immediate effect was by no means the whole story. For the 1956 total is nearly double that of 1951. Hundreds of thousands of Africans, who were legally entitled to vote in 1951, did not get themselves registered in time for the elections. This was by no means always through their own fault. The whole complex machinery of colonial administration was geared to secure the defeat of the RDA (and in Togo of the CUT), and neither Mitterrand's vigorous instructions nor the eleventh-hour electoral law could set it automatically in reverse. In the Ivory Coast especially it would have been necessary to sack virtually every administrator and de-stool every chief in order to secure a genuinely free election. This explains why the Ivory Coast, in spite of being by now the most economically advanced territory in all Afrique Noire, still had only 9 per cent of its population registered as voters in 1956, while Mauritania, the most isolated and backward, already had as much as 26 per cent. The fact was that in the Ivory Coast it was impossible for any new voter to get his name on the roll, except in the few regions where chiefs opposed to the RDA could be relied on to bring out a tribal vote; whereas in Mauritania the administrators counted on the new voters (many of whom were registered even without being qualified under the new law, but nearly all of whom were docile followers of the chiefs) to defeat Horma ould Babana, whom

[1] Journal Officiel (*Débats*), 22nd May 1951, 3rd session.
[2] Law of 23rd May 1951 (Journal Officiel, Recueil des Lois, 1951, p. 229). See Ansprenger, p. 100.
[3] Supplemented by that of 6th February 1952 which gave the vote to heads of households even if they did not pay tax.

they regarded as a dangerous radical. One president of a Mauritanian polling station was said to have declared: 'had a dog come before me with a voter's card, I would have made him vote.'[1] The RDA claimed that in the Ivory Coast the electorate only increased by 1 per cent as a result of the electoral law, while in the Soudan (where the swing from town to country voters was likely to favour the SFIO against the RDA) it was as much as 479 per cent.[2] The corollary of this was that between 1951 and 1956 (by which time the electoral rolls were more or less in order) the increase was only 15 per cent in the Soudan, but 371 per cent in the Ivory Coast, 545 per cent in Togo, and 634 per cent in Niger (another territory where RDA strength was carefully held under in 1951).[3]

Not only were new RDA voters unable to register. Many who had previously been inscribed were struck off the roll. This practice was so common that in 1952, when a law was passed regulating the election of the new territorial assemblies, a special provision had to be inserted declaring that anyone who had been so struck off was still entitled to vote unless he had been found guilty of a crime whose legal penalty included disfranchisement.[4] Nor was everyone whose name was on the roll by any means certain to obtain his voter's card. Sometimes all the cards were dealt out to known opponents of the RDA who in turn distributed them to their friends – or used them to vote more than once themselves. All these methods had been used in the Upper Volta elections of 1948. Now they were applied all over Afrique Noire; and as in 1948 administrators took care to restrict all RDA activities as far as possible, while giving every possible help to their opponents. Often RDA respresentatives were excluded from the polls, potential RDA voters were intimidated, and the ballot papers of anti-RDA parties were distributed in advance to the illiterate population. In Tchad and Oubangui-Chari the administration worked all out to secure an RPF victory, playing on the still-strong reverence of many Africans for General de Gaulle. At Bangui, capital of Oubangui-Chari, it was alleged that the head of the governor's military establishment had distributed uniforms to African veterans, saying that they had been sent by General de Gaulle, who asked them to vote for the RPF candidate.[5]

---

[1] Morgenthau, p. 103.       [2] Ibid., p. 201.       [3] See Table II.
[4] Law of 6th February 1952, clause 2.
[5] Morgenthau, pp. 201–2. Thompson and Adloff, *Emerging States* . . . , (op. cit.)

TABLE II

The Franchise, June 1951

| Territory | A. Estimated Pop.* in thousands (1949) | B. Registered Voters, in thousands 1951 (1956) | B as % of A (approx) | Increase in registered voters 1951–1956 | No. of deputies | Actual vote in thous. |
|---|---|---|---|---|---|---|
| SENEGAL | 1,992 | 665 (835) | 33 | 26% | 2 | 316 |
| MAURITANIA | 518 | 136 (218) | 26 | 60% | 1 | 52 |
| SOUDAN | 3,164 | 917 (1,058) | 29 | 15% | 4 | 320 |
| GUINEA | 2,180 | 394 (975) | 18 | 147% | 3 | 224 |
| IVORY COAST | 2,066 | 189 (890) | 9 | 371% | 2 | 111 |
| DAHOMEY | 1,505 | 333 (385) | 22 | 16% | 2 | 147 |
| NIGER | 2,029 | 95 (697) | 5 | 634% | 2 | 57 |
| UPPER VOLTA | 3,070 | 334 (978) | 11 | 193% | 4 | 251 |
| AOF Total | 16,524 | 3,063 (6,036) | 19 | 98% | 20 | 1,479 |
| TOGO | 982 | 32¼ (213) | 3 | 545% | 1 | 27 |
| CAMEROUN | 3,006 | 517 (844) | 17 | 63% | 3+1† | 289 |

| | | | | | | |
|---|---|---|---|---|---|---|
| GABON | 409 | 75† (126) | 18 | 68% | 1} +1† | 32† |
| MOYEN-CONGO | 684 | 124† (240) | 18 | 94% | 1} | 56† |
| OUBANGUI-CHARI | 1,072 | 113† (274) | 11 | 142% | 1} +1† | 69† |
| TCHAD | 2,241 | 253† (555) | 11 | 119% | 2} | 168† |
| AEF Total | 4,408 | 565 (1,195) | 13 | 112% | 5+2† | 325 |
| AFRIQUE NOIRE (exc. Somaliland) Total | 24,920 | 4,117 (8,288) | 17 | 98% | 29+3† | 2,120 |

*Source:* Annuaire Statistique de l'Union Française (Outre-Mer) 1939–1949 (Paris, 1951)

*Source:* F. Ansprenger. Politik im schwarzen Afrika (Köln & Opladen, 1961)

† First College

169

*Notes*

\* These population figures were the latest available at the time the electoral law was framed. In most cases they are probably underestimates. A telegram from Dakar gave a higher figure for Senegal, based on an unofficial estimate made in 1950. On this basis the government was willing to give Senegal an extra deputy. But this was rejected by the Council of the Republic, which also deprived the Ivory Coast and Niger of one deputy each. (Both just qualified for three if their population were calculated to the nearest 800,000.) Tchad would have had three deputies, and Cameroun four, if the single college had been accepted.

† I have divided the first-college voters somewhat arbitrarily between the different territories in AEF. Gabon and Moyen-Congo had 9,400 registered first-college voters between them, Oubangui-Chari and Tchad 4,500.

## C. The Election Result

This tactic seems to have been inadequate, for in Oubangui-Chari the RPF candidate was not elected. The Abbé Boganda (recently unfrocked for having married his French secretary in Paris) triumphantly retained his seat. This was a defeat for the administration, which had arrested Boganda during the campaign and had him condemned to 45 days' imprisonment,[1] but not a victory for the RDA. For Boganda, though he had left the Catholic fold of the MRP,[2] still held aloof from West African political groups. Instead, he formed his own *Mouvement d'Evolution Sociale en Afrique Noire* (MESAN) which rapidly eclipsed the Union Oubanguienne (RDA) of Antoine Darlan.[3]

In Tchad the manoeuvres of the Gaullist administrators (who already securely controlled the General Council) were more successful. Lisette was defeated and both second-college seats went to members of the Gaullist UDT—former Senator Béchir Sow and **Sou Quatre.** Bayrou and Malbrant held both the AEF first-college seats for RPF, while that of Cameroun, formerly Aujoulat's, now fell to the Gaullist **Molinatti.** Unlike Bayrou and Malbrant, Aujoulat had lately been supporting African demands for the suppression of the double college,[4] and was able to transfer from a European to an African electorate: he won the third second-college seat which was now allotted to Cameroun, and founded a new African party, the *Bloc Démocratique Camerounais* (BDC) as an attempted counterweight to Um Nyobé's UPC.[5]

In West Africa the RPF won two seats, in the two territories where administrative influence was most blatant: **Sidi el Mokhtar,** candidate of the pro-French nomadic chiefs, was elected in Mauritania, and in the Ivory Coast, although Houphouët still scraped home, the other seat went by proportional representation to **Sékou Sanogo,** who represented the northern Moslem chiefs. These results neatly bring out the paradoxical situation of Franco-African politics at this time. In Paris, the UDSR was one of the governing parties, and in particular that of the minister of France d'Outre-Mer, while

---

[1] Ansprenger, p. 185.

[2] In the new National Assembly he joined the right-wing 'Peasant' group.

[3] Thompson and Adloff, op. cit.

[4] The MRP, including even Coste-Floret, had changed its mind on this point since 1946, partly owing to pressure from the IOM (see references in the debates of April and May 1951, and MRP documents among the Aujoulat papers).　　　　　[5] Ansprenger, p. 197.

the RPF was regarded as an almost treasonable opposition and a blatantly partial electoral law was introduced in order to defeat it.[1] Yet in Africa the representatives of the French government, who officially took their orders from the minister of France d'Outre-Mer, deliberately engineered the election of RPF candidates against opponents like Coulibaly, who as a member of the RDA now voted for the government and was in close contact with the UDSR, and Horma ould Babana, who had even been formally *apparenté* to the UDSR since 1948.[2] It was an absurd situation, all too typical of the Fourth Republic.

Only in Niger did the UDSR benefit from the RDA's downfall. Here the successful candidates were Condat and **Zodi Ikhia,** both of whom joined the UDSR group in the National Assembly.[3] The IOM emerged from the elections as the dominant African party. They lost a seat to RPF in Somaliland, and Aujoulat's first college seat in Cameroun; but won the new seats created in Cameroun, Dahomey, and Upper Volta (which last now had four IOM deputies altogether). They held their ground in Guinea and Gabon, and effectively also in Togo, for though in the election there Aku was defeated, the new deputy, Grunitzky, joined the IOM when he arrived in Paris. The IOM also gained a seat in Senegal, for Lamine-Guèye was spectacularly defeated by Senghor's trade unionist associate Abbas Guèye. Here the administration was accused of working against the Socialists (whereas in the Soudan it clearly favoured them against the RDA). The Socialist Governor Wiltord had been replaced in September 1950, and a month before the election High Commissioner Béchard was also recalled after misguidedly turning against the influential Pères Blancs (missionaries, and publishers of the Dakar weekly *Afrique Nouvelle*) the weapons of press control intended for the RDA. The anti-clerical Socialist trio of Béchard, Wiltord and Lamine-Guèye was swept away by a more powerful alliance between French Catholic opinion (especially in the MRP) and Senghor's BDS.[4] Lamine-Guèye's defeat was a

[1] Williams, pp. 312–14.

[2] A. Blanchet, *L'Itinéraire des partis africains depuis Bamako* (Paris 1958), pp. 18–19.

[3] UNIS, to which both belonged, broke off its connection with the IOM at the time of the negotiations between IOM and RDA. Condat remained in the UDSR group after the RDA joined it in 1952, but left UNIS to form an ephemeral local party of his own. Zodi Ikhia, who remained in UNIS locally, transferred to the IOM group in parliament. (Minutes of IOM group meetings in 1950 among Dr Aujoulat's papers. Morgenthau, pp. 104 and 422.)

[4] Morgenthau, p. 97. *Afrique Nouvelle*, passim.

severe blow for the SFIO both in France and Africa. But the Socialists held their other four African seats, and won two new ones in Guinea and the Soudan. In the Soudan they now held three seats out of four, but proportional representation enabled Konaté to hang on to the remaining one. He, Houphouët and Tchicaya were now the only three RDA deputies left.

Such an election result might well seem to put d'Arboussier in the right. What had the RDA gained by supporting a government which either could not or would not control its 'colonialist' servants, and joining a 'third force' which was officially opposed to Gaullism but in practice seemed to play into its hands? Queuille's electoral machinations had succeeded in reducing the Communists from 177 deputies to 101, but they had not prevented the RPF leaping from 23 to 121; and the net result was a National Assembly in which the centre of gravity was further to the right and Socialists as well as Communists were pushed out of the governing majority. On 10th August Pleven formed a new government and for the first time since the war the Rue Oudinot was given to a Conservative (**Louis Jacquinot**); Mitterrand, whom Pleven detested, was kept out of office altogether.[1]

## D. Houphouët Joins the UDSR

But Houphouët did not despair. The UDSR was still in power, and was still in grave danger of falling below minimum strength. There was still no coherent majority in the Assembly, and therefore for the foreseeable future there would continue to be ministerial crises in which African votes would matter. The essential thing was to establish influence with the executive and work to change the administrative climate in Africa. Then there would be some hope of future elections giving a fairer result. Meanwhile, the RDA would need plenty of time to put its house in order.

In fact, despite ill feeling over the elections, the tension in West Africa was gradually relaxing. A hopeful sign was the promotion from AEF to AOF of the conciliatory High Commissioner Bernard Cornut-Gentille, which occurred in September. On 6th October Houphouët made an important speech in Abidjan, appealing for unity and peace. Instead of complaining about the way the election had been conducted, he congratulated his fellow citizens on the fact that in the Ivory Coast it had been managed without serious

[1] Williams, Appendix III.

violence. He explained at some length the circumstances which had led him to ally with the Communist Party, and those which had led him to break with it. He reiterated that the class struggle was irrelevant to Africa, and that what mattered was that all, former friends and former opponents alike, should now work together in unity for the development of the Ivory Coast. This speech was favourably reported in the settler paper *La Côte d'Ivoire*, which itself sought and printed a long interview with Houphouët. Already the atmosphere in Abidjan was much less tense than it had been at the time of Mitterrand's visit eight months earlier.[1]

By December Houphouët and Etcheverry felt secure enough to bring out a new RDA newspaper in Dakar, *Afrique Noire*, which publicly defended their new political line. On 7th January 1952 Pleven's second government fell. Next day the three RDA deputies formally affiliated to the UDSR.[2] From now on about half the UDSR's members were overseas deputies, with the result that its colonial policies were suspect to many metropolitan Frenchmen, and neither Mitterrand nor any other member of the group was ever again allowed to occupy the Rue Oudinot. None the less Mitterrand was brought back into the government (as Minister of State for North African affairs) by the next prime minister, **Edgar Faure** (Radical), who otherwise kept Pleven's cabinet unchanged.[3]

### E. The Electoral Law of 1952

Faure's government lasted only just over a month (20th January to 29th February), but it did see the passage of an electoral law for the African territorial assemblies. These were still functioning under the 'provisional' régime of 1946. Now at last their existence was recognised by law and they were officially entitled 'Territorial Assemblies'. African deputies were anxious to increase their powers as well, but once again were defeated by the time factor. The electoral law had to be rushed through because the assemblies were already due to be re-elected. It therefore left the question of their powers to be settled by a second law, which was supposed to be promulgated before 31st July. But in fact this second law failed to materialise, and the new assemblies were left with the same restricted powers as

---

[1] Ansprenger, p. 141. See *La Côte d'Ivoire*, 27th October 1951.
[2] *Afrique Nouvelle*, 19th January 1952.
[3] Williams, loc. cit.

the old. They were also still elected on the double college system—though Togo as well as Senegal was now excepted from this.[1]

### Pinay Government

Faure's government was thrown out by the Right. **Antoine Pinay,** a Conservative, was nominated to succeed him and to the general surprise succeeded in winning the House's confidence. The main reason for this was that 27 Gaullists broke party discipline and voted for him. At the same time it was noticeable that he had only 11 votes to spare, and 21 of them were from African constituencies. In other words, the majority now depended on the fact that all African representatives except Gaullists and Socialists had adopted a policy of always voting for prime ministers or potential prime ministers unless there was a good reason not to.[2] This policy could be justified on two levels. In the first place, Africans were anxious to contribute to political stability in France both for her own sake and because they knew that continual ministerial crises were bound to delay colonial reform. Secondly, they preferred to earn the gratitude of whoever was in power rather than make enemies by precipitating or prolonging crises. In this instance they were rewarded by the appointment of a relatively liberal MRP man, **Pierre Pflimlin,** as minister of France d'Outre-Mer.

### F. Elections of 30th March 1952

The new Territorial Assemblies were elected on 30th March. By and large the results followed the pattern of the National Assembly elections the year before; Tchicaya's PPC won 17 out of 24 second-college seats in Moyen-Congo, Konaté's US 13 out of 40 in the Soudan; everywhere else the RDA was virtually annihilated, except in the Ivory Coast. There the effects of Houphouët's conciliatory policy were already apparent. Both settlers and administration were coming to accept the PDCI as part of a new order with which they would have to make terms. Houphouët was anxious to establish himself as leader of the territory as a whole. Against the wishes of many PDCI militants he insisted on including some Europeans, and

[1] See law of 6th February 1952 and preceding debates in the National Assembly.
[2] Phillipe Guillemin, 'Les élus d'Afrique noire à l'Assemblée Nationale sous la IVe République' in *Revue Française de Science Politique*, 1958.

even some former RDA members who had deserted during the repression and now rejoined, in the RDA-sponsored list of candidates. On this basis the RDA was able to claim 28 out of 32 second-college members in the new assembly,[1] including four Europeans and five 'ex-RDA-RDA'. Conversely, at least three of the eighteen first-college seats went to Africans.[2]

In Oubangui-Chari, where the former assembly had been dominated by the RDA, the election of the new one confirmed its eclipse. Seventeen out of 26 second-college seats went to Boganda's MESAN and the remainder to Independents. Antoine Darlan, the former RDA leader, was forced to accept a back seat on Boganda's bandwagon. Like Houphouët, Boganda was now evolving into a new type of 'respectable' African leader, critical but co-operative, whose mass following made him less dependent on the administration than the administration was on him. He showed no interest in joining the interterritorial RDA, for he had no need of its support. He was already the unquestioned leader of his territory.[3]

In Tchad the elections were a victory for the administration rather than a conclusive defeat for the RDA. The Gaullists won 24 out of 30 second-college seats, as well as all 15 first-college ones, but Lisette increased his following in the assembly from three to six. In many areas the Gaullist victory was regarded as spurious; and in the Logone region in the south, where RDA support was strong, resentment at the official results erupted in violence. The Governor sent troops to restore order; 14 Africans were killed and another 18 wounded.[4]

In Niger the RDA débâcle was total. All the second-college seats were won by UNIS, the party of Djermakoye, Condat and Zodi Ikhia. Bakary Djibo's pro-Communist splinter-group, the *Union Démocratique Nigérienne* (UDN), which styled itself 'de tendance RDA', was no more successful than the official, pro-Houphouët, RDA list of Hamani Diori and Boubou Hama.[5] Other territories in

---

[1] And notably to defeat deputy Sékou Sanogo in his own home constituency.

[2] Morgenthau, pp. 204–5, 402. *Afrique Nouvelle*, April 1952.

[3] Thompson and Adloff, op. cit.

[4] *Afrique Nouvelle*, April 1952.

[5] The split in the Niger RDA was regional as well as ideological. Djibo's support came mainly from the south-eastern Hausa-speaking area which had close ties with Northern Nigeria; Diori's came from the Songhay-inhabited Niger valley in the south-west. The chiefs and the desert nomads of the north at first opposed both these parties, later held the balance between them (see Morgenthau, pp. 317–18).

which the RDA was unrepresented on the new Territorial Assembly were: Mauritania, Senegal, Togo, Dahomey, Cameroun and Gabon. Of these, only Senegal and Cameroun now had properly organised RDA sections–UDS and UPC respectively–and these were the two sections that had declared for d'Arboussier rather than Houphouët. If anything, therefore, the results strengthened Houphouët's position within the movement.

In Guinea, the RDA was still an insignificant minority. In Upper Volta, it appeared to have been totally eclipsed. Yet five years later it was to control both these territories as well as Tchad, Ivory Coast and Soudan. The RDA leaders had good reasons not to despair, but they had a hard task in front of them. It was a task to be accomplished on two levels. On the one hand they had to work, both in Paris and in Africa, towards an understanding with the administration which would permit them to mobilise their support at the polls. On the other they had to build up that support among the rural masses who now had the vote for the first time, and who till now had been accustomed to look for leadership only to the chiefs, and hence to the administration on which the chiefs depended. Their degree of success in this task was to vary from territory to territory according to circumstances, and according to the different methods and personalities of the individual leaders involved.

For the RDA, then, 30th March 1952 was not a turning-point but merely a milestone on a long uphill road. For the RPF, it was a resounding victory. They swept the first college throughout AEF and wiped out the first-college Socialists in Guinea and the Soudan. More surprisingly, they won six second-college seats in Upper Volta, where they now formed the main opposition to the Union Voltaïque. Their leader here was a European officer, **Michel Dorange,** who had formed an alliance with the Yatenga Naba, the chief of a large sub-group within the Mossi tribe. Dorange and his supporters, whose main stronghold was Ouahigouya, the Yatenga Naba's capital, challenged the despotic power of the Moro Naba, and indeed the feudal privileges of the Mossi chiefs in general. So, by yet another of the local paradoxes of Franco-African politics, the RPF became the party of radicalism in eastern Upper Volta, and Dorange was to succeed where Kaboret Zinda had failed.[1]

For the Socialists the results were disastrous everywhere. Not only

[1] See above, p. 122. *Afrique Nouvelle*, April 1952. Morgenthau, p. 319. Ansprenger, p. 181.

did they vanish almost completely from the first college; they also lost ground in the second to their African opponents: to the RDA in the Soudan, to various small groups in Guinea, and most dramatically (though not unexpectedly) to the BDS in Senegal, which won all constituencies except Saint-Louis and Dakar–and even in Dakar Lamine-Guèye was accused of using his position as mayor to rig the election in his own favour. Only in the north of Moyen-Congo, where the Mbochi tribe returned six Socialists led by **Jacques Opangault,** and in the Ivory Coast, where some Socialists were included in Houphouët's list, did the SFIO manage to hold its ground. Its collapse in AOF was triumphantly pointed out by *Afrique Nouvelle* (the Dakar missionary paper), which saw it as the inevitable and overdue consequence of High Commissioner Béchard's departure.[1] In this sense 1952 *was* a turning-point. These elections were the first to be held when the SFIO was out of office in France, and under a mainly non-Socialist administration in Africa. From then on, governing parties in France did not try to recruit members in Africa. Instead, they sought for allies among indigenous African parties.

## G. The Failure of d'Arboussier

A strange example of this was the first session of the Territorial Assembly in the Soudan, where the RDA minority voted with the RPF in order to prevent Fily-Dabo Sissoko from being elected president.[2] This unholy alliance was maintained at the end of April when the newly elected Assemblies in their turn elected the Great Councils of AOF and AEF. It gave further substance to the violent criticisms of d'Arboussier, who on 25th April again demanded a meeting of the RDA Co-ordination Committee, this time publicly. On 12th June **Temoko Diarra,** RDA spokesman in the Assembly of the French Union (of which d'Arboussier was one of the vice-presidents), pointed out that he had resigned as General Secretary of the RDA on 7th July 1950, and no longer had any authority to speak for the movement. D'Arboussier replied by resorting to the 'enemy' press. On 6th July Lamine-Guèye's paper *l'AOF* published an 'Open Letter to Félix Houphouët-Boigny', in which d'Arboussier set out at great length his arguments against the RDA's new line, and challenged the authority of the parliamentary group to impose such a change of policy without reference to the Co-ordina-

[1] Loc. cit. See above, p. 171.     [2] *Afrique Nouvelle.*

tion Committee. He also claimed that his resignation had been only a temporary tactical move, and that he now had both the right and the duty to resume his post. The parliamentary group was un-chastened by these admonitions, and proceeded to presume even further on its own authority by formally expelling d'Arboussier from the movement (12th July). The official party paper *Afrique Noire* indulged in weekly vilification of the former General Secretary, the highpoint being Houphouët's own *Réponse à d'Arboussier* in the issue of 24th July. To d'Arboussier's ideological tirade and comradely use of the second person singular, Houphouët replied with cool, slightly mocking rationality and a polite *vous*. Perhaps unfairly, he compared the failure of the RDA before 1950 with the success of Kwame Nkrumah since 1951: 'Did Kwame refuse to collaborate with the Conservatives who replaced Labour in power? He raised no battle cry against the British in Malaya, the Atlantic Pact, English constituencies or German rearmament. Kwame acts. He has his feet on the ground. He does not dream.'

The steering committees of the Senegal and Cameroun RDA sections continued to support d'Arboussier, but he entirely failed to achieve the mass repudiation of Houphouët by RDA militants which he evidently hoped for. Certainly the younger and more radical RDA leaders, such as Modibo Keita in the Soudan and **Sékou Touré** in Guinea, sympathised to some extent with his misgivings. But only Bakary Djibo of Niger felt strongly enough about it to be willing to split his territorial party. In October the Union Soudanaise held a territorial congress which endorsed the Houphouët line, and Modibo Keita without demur allowed himself to be elected its General Secretary.[1] By the time that d'Arboussier's 'Second Open Letter' appeared on 4th November his cause was already lost. It was even longer than the first, and *l'AOF* never bothered to print the end of it.[2]

[1] Ansprenger, p. 142.
[2] At least, I searched through several months of issues following the one in which the first half appeared, and could not find the promised conclusion.

## Chapter 10

# Colonial Reforms of the Second Legislature

### A. The Overseas Labour Code and Trade Union Development

Small wonder if, on 4th November 1952, the internal divisions of the RDA seemed unimportant. The day before, workers throughout West Africa had gone on strike.[1] The long struggle for the passage of the Overseas Labour Code was at last reaching its climax.

The struggle for the Labour Code is closely linked with the development of African trade unions. Overseas trade unions gained new status and security from section II of the Code, which gave them practically the same rights as their counterparts in metropolitan France, and liberated them completely from control by the administration.[2] More important, industrial action by the trade unions helped to force the Code through a reluctant or apathetic parliament, and subsequently to ensure its effective enforcement by the colonial governors. The experience of the struggle reinforced the unity of African workers, and made them more aware of their particular interests as Africans. Its successful outcome greatly increased the strength and prestige of the unions. Also, because the struggle was carried on simultaneously in Parliament and in African offices and factories, it brought parliamentarians and trade unionists into alliance, and strengthened the orientation of the African labour movement towards political goals.

In this respect, however, it merely reinforced a tendency which was already apparent, and which resulted from an extension to Africa of the union structure of France itself. In Britain and America trade unions are normally organised within a single industry, the entire labour force of which the relevant union will aim to control. Political alliances come later. But in France trade unions are much more closely tied to different political tendencies, and usually

---

[1] Morgenthau, p. 228.    [2] Ansprenger, p. 238.

compete with each other for the allegiance of the same workers. In postwar France there were three main groups of unions, each of which could claim adherents in every important branch of industry: the Communist-dominated CGT, the Socialist FO (Force Ouvrière, which split off from the CGT in 1948), and the Catholic CFTC (Confédération Française des Travailleurs Chrétiens), which was closely linked to the MRP. All of these tried to recruit members among African workers. The CGT was most successful, largely because it was first in the field. It had already established a bridgehead in West Africa in the days of the Popular Front, and its militants were active in all the larger French African towns immediately after the general legalisation of African trade unions in 1944. Though very few African workers were actually Communist, most remained loyal to the CGT even after its split in 1948. FO failed to take root in Africa, being regarded as a movement for European workers, and often as a tool of the administration, which too conspicuously encouraged it. The CFTC did rather better, especially of course in territories such as Dahomey and Cameroun where missionary influence was strong, but also at first in others such as Guinea where, although Christians were a tiny minority, so were urban workers, and the two often coincided.

Thus even more clearly than the political parties, the African trade unions at first followed the pattern of metropolitan French politics. Only gradually did the emerging differences between French and African political interests bring about a corresponding regroupment of African labour. The first important break was the secession of the Senegal and Soudan railwaymen from the CGT after the failure of their strike in March 1948. Another came in 1952 with the formation in the Ivory Coast of a *Union des Syndicats Autonomes* which had the blessing of the now anti-Communist PDCI. But this was as yet untypical. The CGT remained easily the most important group of African unions and continued to increase its strength both absolutely and in proportion to its rivals. Membership of it was far from incompatible with loyalty to the Houphouëtist RDA. On the contrary, in Guinea the CGT leaders formed the central core of the RDA section, and even in the Ivory Coast CGT members continued to outnumber those of the autonomous unions.[1]

Like the parliamentarians, African trade union leaders were in competition with each other on the local level, but found themselves united in a common exasperation at the apathetic attitude of most

[1] Ansprenger, Table 5.

French politicians to African problems. When the Labour Code was discussed in the National Assembly at the end of the First Legislature, there were at one point only eight deputies present. None the less it was passed, on 30th April 1951, by 463 votes to 110 (the opposition consisting principally of Radicals and RPF, the two parties in which white settler influence was strong). But after the election, events resumed their old unhurried pace. Not until 18th December was a report on the bill laid before the Council of the Republic, which then proceeded, from 22nd December to 6th February 1952, to a lengthy discussion of the Code.[1] Numerous amendments were adopted, nearly all of a reactionary tenor. Many of them were proposed by **Luc Durand-Reville** (Radical), the ultra-reactionary first-college Senator from Gabon.[2]

It was now up to the new National Assembly, either to accept the Council of the Republic's *avis*, or to overrule it and order the promulgation of the Code as passed by its predecessor. Either way a further full-dress debate was necessary. But the Assembly's agenda was crowded. It had just passed the electoral law for the Territorial Assemblies and was not in a hurry to find more time for the discussion of overseas affairs. It was bad enough to have a war on in Vietnam and a desperately tense political situation in Tunisia at a time when most deputies were preoccupied either by the problem of the European Defence Community, or by taxation in France (the issue which brought down Faure's government on 29th February), or by the agitation and strikes which followed the arrest of the Communist parliamentary leader Jacques Duclos, or by all of these things at once, without having to worry about such an apparently minor problem as overseas labour conditions. Consequently nothing happened.

It was this intolerable situation which began to draw African trade unionists together–as similar situations had periodically brought African parliamentarians together since 1946. Significantly the initiative came from Guinea, hitherto one of the most backward territories but now entering on a phase of rapid economic and industrial development, and where at this time the CGT (led by Sékou Touré) and CFTC (led by the European **Antoine Lawrence** and the Catholic African **David Soumah**) were of roughly equal strength.[3] At the Guinean workers' request all French-African unions held a joint conference at Dakar from 6th to 8th October

---

[1] Gonidec and Kirsch, *Droit du Travail des T.O.M.*, op. cit.
[2] Morgenthau, p. 58.     [3] Ansprenger, Table 5.

1952. Soumah reported on the content of the Labour Code, Sékou Touré on the methods needed to secure its passage.[1] Resolutions were adopted calling for 'vigorous and unified action of all African trade unions, which alone can defeat the forces opposed to the implementation of the Labour Code'.[2] From this conference stemmed the AOF general strike of 3rd November, which in its turn helped to impart a sense of urgency to the National Assembly. On 6th and 22nd November the Code went through its last ordeal by hot air. With the support of Minister Pflimlin the African deputies succeeded in demolishing most of Durand-Reville's amendments, stoutly defended though these were by the Radicals **Caillavet** and **Devinat**.[3]

The final wrangle centred on Article 237, which empowered Governors to institute compulsory family allowance systems, after consultation of the Territorial Assemblies and the local *commissions consultatives du travail*. This would extend to the children of workers in private firms benefits already accorded to those of public employees by the second Loi Lamine-Guèye–the difference of course being that it was not the state but the private employer who would foot the bill. The clause was bitterly opposed and finally passed by 320 votes to 269 only after the Socialists and IOM had threatened to vote against the entire Code if it were not included.[4]

The Code finally passed with 345 votes in favour, the Radicals and Conservatives abstaining. It became the law of 15th December 1952, published in the *Journal Officiel* of 16th December and promulgated in all the African territories by the end of January 1953. Besides confirming and clarifying the abolition of forced labour, and guaranteeing the rights of trades unions, it protected the worker against sudden dismissal, prescribed equal pay for those doing the same job under the same conditions with the same qualifications, instituted a 40-hour working week with one full day of rest and paid annual holiday–and so on. In brief, it gave the overseas worker the same (or in some cases better) legal protection against exploitation as workers in France already had. This could not of

[1] Touré, although only thirty years old, was already a veteran trade unionist. He had formed Guinea's first trade union (for post-office workers) in 1945, and attended a CGT Congress in Paris in March 1946, after which he is said to have studied for a short time in Prague. His activities cost him his own post-office job, and even earned him (in 1947) a short spell in prison. (Jean Lacoutre, *Cinq Hommes et la France* (Paris 1961), p. 329.)

[2] *Le Proletaire* (Dakar CGT paper), October 1952.

[3] Gonidec and Kirsch, op. cit.        [4] Ansprenger, p. 239–40.

course put an end to the difference in standards of living between France and Africa. But it did institute an equality of legal rights. It was thus a logical application of the principle enunciated by the first Loi Lamine-Guèye, and has been called 'the last monument of the assimilation policy'.[1]

Even after the Code became law the employers and administration were unwilling to accept its implications. The working week had been shortened from 48 to 40 hours, but the minimum hourly wage did not automatically increase by a corresponding 20 per cent. It was left to the government to fix it, and the increase was not forthcoming. Again the unions had to act. Again the Guinean leaders took the initiative, summoning a second inter-union conference which met in Bamako in March 1953. Strikes occurred all over AOF throughout 1953. The most famous was the joint CGT-CFTC strike in Guinea, which lasted from 21st September to 25th November. Two days after it ended, the AOF administration granted the 20 per cent increase.[2]

There remained the question of family allowances. Governors were under strong pressure from employers not to introduce them, on the grounds that polygamous families would place an impossibly heavy burden on the firms and bring about a final breakdown of the flimsy colonial economy. (This had been said about every colonial reform from the abolition of slavery to the Labour Code itself.) The employers artfully suggested that a state-financed social security programme would be more to the point. Not until 1955 was this red-herring finally disposed of, and even then it took thunder from the Rue Oudinot and threat of a further strike from the unions to frighten the governors into action. As from 1st January 1956 an employer had to pay a monthly allowance for every child between one and fourteen years old whose father worked for him at least 18 days or 120 hours per month—whether the marriage was polygamous or not. The allowance was paid directly to the child's mother, who also received special grants before, and at the time of, birth. The system was modelled exactly on that of France herself. Only the sums involved were smaller.[3]

## B. Décret Jacquinot

One other social reform of this period should be mentioned, although

---

[1] Ibid., p. 236.    [2] *Afrique Noire*, 24th–30th November 1953.
[3] Ansprenger, p. 240.

it attracted much less attention than the Labour Code: the 'Jacquinot Decree' (named after the minister who issued it) of 1951.[1] This protected African girls from being married without their consent, and limited the bride-price which their families could ask for them. The extent to which this decree was publicised and applied varied, of course, according to the enthusiasm and energy of individual administrators. But it had the keen support of the missions, and was soon much invoked by young educated or semi-educated bachelors who wanted to marry but were unable to meet the exorbitant demands of their prospective in-laws. It could not emancipate African womanhood overnight—a task that may take at least another two generations yet. But it was an important step in that direction.[2]

### C. FIDES Programme

Meanwhile French economic aid to Africa, channelled through FIDES, continued and increased. In 1953 the first ten-year development plan, which had concentrated on building up the economic infrastructure (docks, roads, airports, etc.) and 'social investments' (e.g. schools and hospitals), was replaced by a second, more short-term plan, which gave greater emphasis to industrial and agricultural development and therefore had a more direct effect on productivity.[3]

### D. Chiefs

Reforms of a more specifically political nature had to wait. One such was the projected reorganisation of the African chiefs, canvassed in the National Assembly since 1947. In this case the reason for delay was not simply inertia, nor government hostility, but a profound confusion about the aims of reform. Before 1956 almost everybody accepted in principle that chiefs should have an improved status, both economically and socially. They should be less like junior officials, and more genuinely the leaders of their people. This policy was inherited from Eboué, who was claimed as a hero by both Right and Left. It appealed to many administrators because the chiefs constituted an element of stability in African society, and were usually pro-French; therefore they might be built into a useful counterweight to the new educated élite. But it appealed also to

[1] Mveng, *Histoire du Cameroun*, op. cit.    [2] *Afrique Nouvelle*, 1952.
[3] Ansprenger, pp. 104–5.

many of this new élite itself, because it emphasised the value of a typically African institution, and thus protected Africans against an extreme assimilation policy. There was of course a contradiction between these two points of view, stemming from internal contradictions within each of them. Administrators wanted to strengthen the chiefs' standing with their subjects, while retaining the principal factor which had undermined that standing, namely their docile attitude to colonial rule. African politicians wanted to revive a traditional African institution by introducing into it a notion that was typically European, namely elections. To put it even more bluntly, political parties wanted strong chiefs elected on a party ticket, while administrators wanted strong chiefs appointed and controlled by the administration. In these circumstances it is hardly surprising that periodic appeals from Territorial Assemblies and from the chiefs themselves for higher pay and other privileges got no definite answer from Paris. From 1948 until his death in 1954 Yacine Diallo worked on the text of a bill which would at least have defined the status of chiefs more clearly, and given some satisfaction to his aristocratic backers in the Fouta Djallon. After his death Senghor took it over, and some chiefs began to be worried at the prospect of reorganisation by the new-style African politicians. The Fulani of Guinea and the Soudan took the lead during 1955 and 1956 in organising a kind of chiefs' trade union.[1] But in the event the Diallo-Senghor bill never reached the statute book. Autonomy came first, and France left her former servants to the mercy of the new leaders.

## E. Municipal Reform

Another bill prepared by Yacine Diallo before his death was the Municipal Law for the T.O.M., and with this he had greater posthumous success. This law beat even the Labour Code's record for the length of time it took to get through Parliament. Initiated by the French Union Assembly on 16th November 1948, it finally passed the National Assembly seven years later to the day. Its object was to increase the number of fully self-governing municipalities overseas, and to allow them to elect their town councils in single college with fully universal suffrage. In one respect this simply repaired an obvious gap in the 1946 Constitution, which had provided for overseas representation in the French parliament, and for

[1] Ibid., pp. 120–1.

185

territorial assemblies, but no democratic organisation below that. (This contrasted strongly with the British policy of building democracy in Africa from the communal level upwards. Some Africans suspected that the omission was deliberate, and that France's real object in inviting them to Paris was to postpone their attainment of political maturity at home.)

On the other hand, the bill was bound to meet with violent opposition from the representatives of European settlers, since if it went through it would introduce a working example of single-college, universal-suffrage democracy into every Black African territory. (At least the capital city in each was earmarked for full communal status.) Once this was done, it could hardly be long before all the Territorial Assemblies were elected on the same system. So Bayrou and Malbrant in the National Assembly, and their allies in the Council of the Republic, deployed all their talents for filibuster to block the bill. It did not pass its first reading in the National Assembly until 13th August 1954, some four months after Diallo's death (although in the final vote it had 433 deputies in its favour, including Communists, Socialists, MRP and UDSR, and only 62 against). Then, in the Council of the Republic, a coalition of Gaullists, Conservatives and Radicals (led of course by the first-college Senators) succeeded in getting an alternative bill adopted which would have created no new full communes but, instead, 114 *communes de moyen exercise*.[1] These might eventually be raised to full communal status, but only with the assent of two thirds of the Territorial Assembly–which meant that in most territories the first-college assemblymen would have a veto.[2]

The National Assembly was not prepared to accept this high-handed treatment of its work. But a constitutional reform passed at the end of 1954 made it no longer possible for the Council's *avis* to be simply overruled. Instead there was a system known as the *navette*, by which bills could be shuttled to and fro between the two houses until an agreed compromise was reached. A time-limit of 100 days ensured that legislation which the Assembly considered urgent could in fact be got through quicker than before. But if on any given reading the Assembly exceeded its time, the Council automatically acquired the right to do the same.[3] This meant of course that the scope for delay on low-priority matters such as colonial reform was increased. In the case of the Municipal Law

---

[1] See note at the end of the chapter.    [2] Ansprenger, p. 242.
[3] Williams, p. 284.

the *navette* went on for nearly a year before the Council gave in on 15th November 1955, and AOF at last gained its 26 new full communes (in addition to the existing ones in Senegal). AEF got six, and Cameroun three.[1]

*Note on the different sorts of commune in Overseas France:*
'Mixed communes' dated from 1912, and consisted of a 'municipal commission' and an 'administrator-mayor'. The latter was always nominated by the governor of the territory, and so at first was the municipal commission. But after 1920 it could be partly elected, either on a restricted suffrage (in mixed communes 'of the second degree'), or even in theory by universal suffrage (mixed communes 'of the third degree').[2]

*Communes de moyen exercise* were introduced by a decree of 26th November 1947, and were intended as a transitional stage, lasting five years, between the third degree and full communal status. The Mayor was still a government-appointed civil servant, but the town council became a fully elective body, and was able to vote a larger expenditure. According to the decree it should have been elected in single college.[3] But the Council of the Republic provided for double-college elections in the new *communes de moyen exercise* which it proposed to create. Before 1956, no *commune de moyen exercise* in Afrique Noire had yet been allowed to graduate to full communal status.[4]

[1] Ansprenger, loc. cit.      [2] Amon d'Aby, *La Côte d'Ivoire* . . . , (op. cit.).
[3] Thompson and Adloff, *French West Africa* (op. cit.).
[4] Ansprenger, loc. cit., and Kenneth Robinson, 'Local Government in French Tropical Africa' in *Journal of African Administration*, October 1956.

# Chapter 11

# The African Parties in 1953

## A. The IOM and the Congress of Bobo-Dioulasso

The largest group of African parliamentarians during this legislature was the IOM. By 1953, when Béchir Sow had come over from the Gaullists, Douala-Manga-Bell from the MRP, and Zodi Ikhia from the UDSR, the IOM group in the National Assembly included 14 representatives of Black African constituencies – and this despite the defection of its founder Apithy.[1] It was not by any means an exclusively Catholic group. It hardly could be, since its strongest local base was Senegal, and it included representatives of other predominantly Moslem areas such as Tchad (Béchir Sow), Niger (Zodi Ikhia), Guinea (Mamba Sano), and northern Dahomey (**Hubert Maga**). But the most prominent individual IOM deputies – Aujoulat, Senghor and Dr **Joseph Conombo** (founder and leader of the Union Voltaïque) – were all Catholics with missionary backing at home and friends in the left wing of MRP in Paris. The IOM remained in loose alliance with the MRP. Like the RDA, they normally voted for the government, and were careful to assert their independence as a group. But on issues where the governing parties were divided, especially if these had no direct bearing on African problems, they would vote with the MRP, while the RDA voted with the UDSR – in so far as the UDSR voted together at all, for its discipline was loose in the extreme.[2]

An important item in the MRP programme at this time was the drive for European unity. Robert Schuman had inaugurated the

[1] Apithy joined the right-wing 'Independent Republican' group (RI). This had two advantages:

(a) Right-wing groups did not attempt to enforce strict voting discipline on their members.

(b) The RI were ignorant of African affairs and tended to seek advice from RPF deputies before voting on them. Apithy was able to explain to them the other side of the case.

[2] See Williams (op. cit.), Appendix IVa, p. 499.

Coal and Steel Community in 1950, and MRP leaders were now agitating in favour of the projected European Defence Community (to which Gaullists and Communists were both bitterly opposed) and of an eventual political union. Senghor associated himself with these demands, insisting that Africa should find its place in a united Europe, or rather, as he called it, 'Eurafrique'. He was a member of the French delegation to the *ad hoc* assembly at Strasbourg which was working out the terms of union. On 9th January 1953 he assured this assembly that he was 'impassioned by the Eurafrican idea', and pleaded eloquently and successfully for the participation of the French T.O.M. both in the eventual community itself and in the various meetings which would be necessary to devise the form of its institutions. This speech was the high point of the honeymoon between the IOM and the French government. Senghor's pro-French declarations won him the warm support of other members of the French delegation, including MM. Paul Reynaud (Conservative), Teitgen and de Menthon (MRP), Debray (RPF), and Laffargue (Radical).[1]

But his speech also included a prophetic warning: 'Africa has caught the mystique of equality in co-operation. If you refuse to satisfy it, men of goodwill such as ourselves will tomorrow, in twenty years' time, be seen by the younger generation as collaborators. That generation will have the mystique of independence in secession . . . the future belongs to the independence of peoples.' Bold words, which showed the IOM expected something from French governments in return for their votes, and that they were aware their own electorate would not let them remain docile indefinitely.[2]

Even while Senghor was speaking in Strasbourg, the bonds of mutual confidence were being badly frayed in Paris. The Pinay government had fallen on 23rd December,[3] and on 8th January the Radical **René Mayer** became prime minister. He was a member of both the big business and the Algerian settler lobbies. None the less he accepted the IOM's programme, and received their votes in the Assembly. It was assumed that Aujoulat would continue as Secretary of State for France d'Outre-Mer, as in the previous seven cabinets. But Mayer decided to simplify the difficult task of satisfying all his

---

[1] *L'Eveil du Bénin*, 15th January 1953.

[2] Text reproduced ibid.

[3] By bringing down a government which had just pushed through the Overseas Labour Code, the MRP lost the allegiance of its only remaining African deputy, Douala-Manga-Bell. He joined the IOM. (*Le Cameroun de Demain*.)

various supporters (who included 'Europeans' and 'anti-Europeans', as well as Africans and settlers) by splitting Aujoulat's post in two. Jacquinot, who returned as Minister, was thus to be assisted by two Secretaries of State: Aujoulat for the application of the Labour Code, and Caillavet for everything else. This announcement incensed the IOM, for Caillavet had been the leading Radical opponent of the Labour Code at its last reading in the National Assembly, less than two months before. It was easy to guess what his general policy would be in dealing with overseas affairs. The Group therefore instructed Aujoulat to refuse the offer, which he did. The IOM left the government, though they remained in the majority. Senghor issued a communiqué expressing the Group's intention 'to show an active vigilance proportionate to the unfailing loyalty with which for more than three years it has supported the seven governments to which it has belonged.'[1]

### Foundation of the 'Mouvement des IOM'

From the point of view of public relations, it was a convenient moment for the IOM to leave the government. They could now claim the credit, both for achievement in office (the Labour Code), and for knowing when to refuse office rather than sacrifice the interests of their electors. Also, they had lately decided to link their various territorial parties in an interterritorial Movement which could compete with the RDA. The founding Congress for this Movement was held at Bobo-Dioulasso in February 1953. Freed from responsibility for government policy, the speakers at this Congress were free to take a fiercely anti-colonialist tone.

The purpose of the Congress was not only to found a Movement, but to provide a coherent statement of realistic political goals for the French Union. Some of the delegates, such as Dr **Emile Derlin Zinsou,** Councillor of the French Union for Dahomey, had been present at the Bamako Congress in 1946, and now saw their chance to recreate the sense of unity and hope which they had felt at that time. It was in this spirit that *Condition Humaine* summoned its readers to a 'rendez-vous des audacieux'.[2]

The 'audacieux' who actually arrived at Bobo-Dioulasso on 12th February were a heterogeneous bunch. They ranged from genuine popular leaders like Senghor to administration stooges like Sékou

[1] *L'Afrique Nouvelle*, January 1953.
[2] Article by Joseph Mbaye, February 1953.

Sanogo.[1] They included an ex-colonial governor (Raphaël Saller), an ex-minister (Aujoulat) and leaders of both Catholic and Marxist trade unions (Antoine Lawrence and Abbas Guèye). Among the parties represented were:

> the Bloc Démocratique Sénégalais (Senghor)
> the Bloc Démocratique Camerounais (Aujoulat)
> the Union Voltaïque (Conombo)
> the Mouvement Démocratique Dahoméen (Hubert Maga)
> the Union Progressiste Dahoméenne (Zinsou)

and the Union Nigérienne des Indépendants et Sympathisants (Zodi Ikhia).

Notable features were the predominance of West as against Equatorial Africans (even stronger than in the RDA), the fact that many delegates either had no real party organisation in their home territories or were the heads of opposing regional factions (e.g. Zinsou and Maga in Dahomey, Conombo and Nazi Boni in Upper Volta – contrast the RDA's insistence on only one section in each territory), and the dominant rôle of a few outstanding individuals. Five main personalities dominated the debates. Of these two were Europeans (Aujoulat and Saller), two were Senegalese (Senghor and Mamadou Dia), and the other (Zinsou) was a *citoyen de statut français* with a first-college seat in the Dahomey Territorial Assembly. In these circumstances it is perhaps not surprising that the *Mouvement des Indépendants d'Outre-Mer* never became an interterritorial mass party comparable to the RDA – despite valiant efforts by Manadou Dia, who was elected its General Secretary.[2]

## Federalism

But nor is it surprising that the Congress did make a distinctive contribution to the ideology of Franco-African politics. In essence this was no more than a reopening of the debate of 1946 and a re-statement of the 'federalist' theses which had then been in vogue. But that in itself was a necessary, and to some Frenchmen an embarrassing reminder that the French Union provisions of the

---

[1] Sékou Sanogo was not in fact a member of IOM. He had been elected on an RPF ticket, and later became *apparenté* MRP. He attended the congress as an observer.

[2] Report by Alioune-Badara Mbengue in *L'Eveil du Bénin*, 15th February–1st March 1953. Mamadou Dia had already displayed considerable organising talent as General Secretary of the BDS. (Ansprenger, p. 165.)

Constitution had been worked out in excessive haste under pressure of events, and had more to do with the immediate needs of government policy at that time than with any clear set of principles. The French Union as defined in the 1946 Constitution had been designed mainly for Indo-China. Yet in Indo-China by 1953 it had already broken down. Ho Chi Minh's republic had still not been brought to heel, and even the supposedly pro-French governments of the Emperor Bao Dai and the Kings of Cambodia and Laos were escaping more and more from French control. Meanwhile the T.O.M., which were still anxious to participate in the French Union, remained strait-jacketed inside the 'one and indivisible' French Republic.

The IOM therefore demanded that the projected revision of the Constitution, which was now grinding its way through Parliament, should not be limited to such essentially mechanical problems as the relations between the two Chambers and the procedure for voting confidence in the government, but 'should also cover Title VIII, which concerns the French Union, and should move in the direction of an active federalism'.[1] At the Congress only Raphaël Saller opposed this idea. He clung to an assimilationist outlook, and demanded that any revision should be left for the next generation to decide.[2] But Aujoulat and Senghor carried the Congress with them in condemning assimilation as insufficiently flexible, and at the same time rejecting the formula of 'associated States or territories' as liable to lead to secession. 'We are in favour of maintaining the Republic', said Senghor, 'but a Republic one and indivisible'. He deliberately chose an expression which directly challenged the Jacobin tradition. He insisted that a Federal Republic was not the first step towards independence, but the only alternative to it. In his view it was a preferable alternative, for African states would continue to need protection, 'and that protection can only come from the great Lady called France'. Not that he expected such a Federation to come into existence overnight. 'We still have much to learn', he admitted. 'It will take many years to achieve a solid structure for our house.'

Both Senghor and Aujoulat angrily rejected any suggestion of United Nations interference in the internal affairs of the French Union, and Senghor refused to be tempted by the glittering prospect of independence. 'We consider ourselves better off than our comrades

[1] Text of Resolutions in Mbengue, op. cit.
[2] See *Marchés Coloniaux du Monde*, 21st and 28th February 1953.

in Gold Coast, in Liberia or in British Gambia.'[1] In the words of the Congress's political resolution: 'the temptation of narrow nationalisms represents a serious danger in a world where independence may be no more than an illusion. The overseas peoples prefer "liberties" to "liberty", and attach less importance to the independence of their countries than to the material independence of each of their fellow-citizens.'[2]

All agreed that integration into the existing French Republic remained the best solution for the time being, provided only that some measures of 'decentralisation and deconcentration' were introduced. The exact nature of these was not specified in the Resolution, but Aujoulat suggested some which would have involved a fairly radical revision of the Constitution: a delegation of powers from the National Assembly to the local assemblies overseas, and to the Assembly of the French Union, so that the French parliament in Paris would henceforth be concerned only with metropolitan affairs, while the Assembly at Versailles became virtually a distinct Federal legislature, as the Brazzaville Conference had originally envisaged.[3] Senghor, for his part, wanted to revise the wording of Title VIII in such a way that the T.O.M., instead of being offered a vague possibility of either departmental or associated status, would get a firm promise of eventual recognition as 'integrated States within a federal French Republic'.[4]

All this may seem harmless enough, not only in the light of what has happened since, but even when read against the background of the debates of 1946. Yet in 1953 it caused considerable alarm among the Radicals and Conservatives who dominated the French parliament. The bogy of Stalinist 'separatism' still haunted the thinking of many Frenchmen on colonial problems, and the 'audacieux' of Bobo-Dioulasso now experienced a milder version of the reflex which had outlawed the RDA in the late 1940s. To call the 1946 Constitution in question on such a point as the relation between France and the T.O.M. smelt of treason to republicans who for six years had had to defend that Constitution tooth and nail against both Stalinist revolutionaries and Gaullist 'revisionists'. Worse, to suggest that the Republic was divisible seemed to imply that it could

[1] *Bulletin des Affaires Economiques et Politiques de L'Union Française*, February 1953.
[2] Mbengue, op. cit. The last sentence is a quotation from a speech which Senghor had made at Strasbourg in 1950.
[3] See *Bulletin des Affaires . . .* , February 1953.
[4] *Marchés Coloniaux . . .* , 28th February 1953.

break up into its component parts–something which republicans had been struggling to avoid ever since 1793.

## Horizontalism

Further fears were aroused by garbled versions of a speech in which Zinsou had urged the necessity of 'horizontal' co-operation, between adjacent African territories both inside and outside the Republic, as well as 'vertical' co-operation between the different territories and France. Such a suggestion was no more than common sense from a spokesman for Dahomey, which was a thin sliver of AOF stretching down to the coast between Togo and Nigeria. The Dahomeyan ports were part of an old economic and cultural entity known as the Slave Coast, extending along the shores of the Bight of Benin roughly from the mouths of the Volta to those of the Niger. Zinsou himself, who came from the eighteenth-century slaving port of Ouidah (Whydah) had a good deal more in common with the urbanised, semi-Europeanised inhabitants of Accra, Lomé and Lagos than he did with the Moslem tribesmen of northern Dahomey. In deliberate evocation of this common African heritage he called his newspaper *L'Eveil du Bénin*–the awakening of Benin. The name denoted both the geographical fact of the common coastline, and the civilisation, centring on Benin City in Western Nigeria,[1] which in the sixteenth century had produced some of Africa's finest works of art.

All Zinsou wanted was to keep the door open for cultural and economic contacts. He objected, reasonably enough, to the absurdities of a colonial system in which, for example, a telephone call from Porto Novo to Lagos (a distance of some fifty miles) had to be put through Paris and London. He obtained the inclusion, in the Congress's Resolution, of a clause which read: 'The assertion of an indispensable "vertical solidarity" between Africa and France does not eliminate the need for economic and cultural interpenetration and for exchanges of every sort between territories in the same continent.'[2] Unfortunately this was a point on which, as Olympio had found out in 1946,[3] French opinion was particularly sensitive. The French empire had been built largely upon the Anglophobia of the late nineteenth century, and almost the only consistent theme in French colonial policy since then had been the determination to keep out Anglo-Saxon meddlers. Now, in the 1950s, the approaching

[1] Later capital of the Mid-Western Region.    [2] Mbengue, op. cit.
[3] See above, p. 114.

194

independence of the Gold Coast and Nigeria made contacts between these territories and the French T.O.M. seem particularly undesirable. It was widely believed in French right-wing circles that what Zinsou really wanted was not a federal French Republic at all but an independent African federation.[1] An idea took root in France, which was to grow stronger over the next seven years, that all attempts by different African territories to establish direct links with each other were fundamentally anti-French. By the end of the decade it was almost true.

*Federalism Expounded*

Senghor did not allow himself to be bullied into dropping his federalist ideas. Nor did he accept the reproach that he was anti-French. He set out to allay the suspicions of the colonial business community by writing an article for *Marchés Coloniaux du Monde* in which he explained what he meant by a Federal Republic, and why he wanted one. This was his analysis of the future options of the T.O.M.:

'Departmentalisation' leads to the suicide of the native soul and of native civilisation, because it implies a sterilising assimilation. . . . Moreover, it is hypocritical, because impossible. To take but one example, it would logically have to bring with it *the presence of three hundred autochthonous deputies in the National Assembly*. On the other hand, some distinguished persons look forward to the integration of the T.O.M. in the Republic 'one and indivisible', combined with decentralisation. But if this decentralisation is real, it will amount to a *de facto* federation . . . . As for the *Associated State*, the experience of Indo-China has shown that it is subject to a centrifugal current which leads to secession. . . . *It is because we want to stay within the French community*—but in our own district, with our own church and our own school—*that we prefer, as the final goal of our evolution, not the status of Associated State but that of Integrated State within the French Republic.*
We know that the French Federal Republic will not come into being overnight. We know that a modern federation presupposes . . . the existence, in each State, of a sufficient number of educated men and technicians. In the case of the French Federation, *I do not think it can be brought about in less than twenty years.*
But people's minds must be prepared for it . . .[2]

[1] See *Marchés Coloniaux* . . . , 21st February 1953 (and Senghor's *mise au point* the following week). Also letter from Georges Riond (RI spokesman in the Assembly of the French Union) to *L'Eveil du Bénin*, 1st May 1953.
[2] *Marchés Coloniaux* . . ., 4th April 1953. Senghor's own italics throughout.

In the immediate future, Senghor suggested three main forms that this preparation should take; first, the revision of the Constitution to include the 'integrated State' formula, second, an increase in the powers of the local assemblies, and third the institution of local *executive councils*. These councils were to be partly nominated by the Governor or High Commissioner, and partly elected by the local assemblies. Their members were not, to start with, to have individual ministerial portfolios. 'It is still a question of apprenticeship.' Indeed it was, for such councils could scarcely have had more than an advisory rôle. Four years later Senghor was to dismiss an offer of much more real autonomy than this as 'toys and lollipops'. It is interesting to see how cautious were his demands in 1953. It is also interesting to notice that he took it for granted that AOF and AEF would have one executive council each, at the level of the federal Government-General, rather than one in each territory. Evidently he was already a 'federalist' in that sense as well.

In 1953, these still seemed to be points of detail. Senghor's main concern was to defend the *principle* of the 'divisible' republic: 'what is important for us, and for France, is not indivisibility but *indissolubility*, and the latter we fully accept.' In practice, he argued, the Republic was not only divisible, but already divided by the 1946 Constitution, since the non-European territories were not represented in proportion to their population, since French law was not automatically applicable to them, and since it was constitutionally possible for them to reach the status of Associated State, in which case they would be outside the Republic. Was federalism really such a revolutionary idea? In its favour Senghor was able to quote the positions taken up in 1946, not only by Lamine-Guèye, not only by the MRP, but also by Radicals, Conservatives, and the Gaullist **René Capitant**. If it was now branded as dangerous and disloyal, this was due, not to any change in its character, but to the success of reactionary propaganda. '*At the present time we are witnessing a reawakening of colonialism or even of racism*. For, in the view of certain politicians, all the IOM are "niggers", including Aujoulat, Lenormand and Borrey.'[1]

Senghor's federalist ideas were not taken up by the government, which continued to drift slowly to the right. Consequently the IOM became readier to vote against it, irrespective of the MRP's attitude.

[1] Maurice Lenormand was IOM deputy for New Caledonia. Dr Borrey was IOM councillor of the French Union for Niger. Both, like Aujoulat, were white.

They provided 12 of the votes which brought down René Mayer on 21st May. During the five-week ministerial crisis which followed they voted regularly in favour of each of the candidates proposed: the Conservative **Reynaud,** the left-wing Radical **Mendès-France,** Bidault of the MRP, the right-wing Radical Marie (though here five of them followed the MRP in abstaining), and finally the Conservative **Laniel,** who was at last able to form a government.[1] For the first time since 1946 the cabinet now included Gaullists, for de Gaulle in disillusionment had disbanded the RPF and his followers in the Assembly became simply another right-centre group, the Social Republicans (RS).[2] The centre of gravity of the majority thus moved yet further to the Right. This result did not please the IOM, who began to vote almost regularly with the opposition. They did so as early as 10th July, when Laniel obtained the special financial powers which had been refused to Mayer. They voted against the constitutional amendment on 23rd July (because nothing had been done to extend it to Title VIII). They voted against the government in an important division on social policy on 9th October.[3] And on 27th October they abstained in a vote of confidence on the government's Indo-China policy.[4] The worsening military situation in Vietnam was gradually making the failure of this policy apparent, and it was more and more difficult for African deputies to support a government which was now incontrovertibly fighting a full-scale war against a colonial people.

## B. The RDA

Such was also the feeling of the RDA deputies, who in this division actually voted against the government (as did Mitterrand, while Pleven's wing of the UDSR voted for).[5] Up to now the RDA had followed the UDSR in voting fairly regularly for each successive government, and in ministerial crises their policy had been the same as that of the IOM (except that they had refused to vote for Bidault on 10th June).[6] But whereas the IOM was essentially a parliamentary

[1] Williams, Appendix IVa.   [2] Ibid., p. 136.

[3] Williams, Appendix IVa.

[4] Guillemin, 'Les Elus d'Afrique Noire . . .' (op. cit.). Division list in *Journal Officiel.*

[5] Ibid. Pleven was Minister of Defence. Mitterrand had resigned from the government on 2nd September as a protest against the deposition of the Sultan of Morocco.

[6] Williams, Appendix IVa. Guillemin, op. cit.

group which failed to achieve an effective grass-roots organisation, the RDA was under-represented in Parliament and concentrated its attention more on events in Africa than on those in Paris. During 1953 it made progress in Tchad, in the Ivory Coast, and above all in Guinea.

(i) In Tchad ill-feeling persisted about the RPF victory in the 1952 elections and the repression which had followed it. RDA spokesmen raised the subject in the National Assembly in February, and in the French Union Assembly in March, but failed to get a commission of inquiry appointed. Meanwhile, however, the disintegration of the RPF in France was paralleled by that of its satellite, the UDT, in Tchad. While deputy Béchir Sow joined the IOM in Paris and formed a short-lived local party of his own (*Union de la Défense des Intérêts Tchadiens*), six European members of the Territorial Assembly broke with the administration and went into opposition, some calling themselves UDSR and others Independent. Of the latter the most prominent was **André Kieffer,** spokesman of the cotton-growers, who became noted for his frequent denunciations of the administration and of the remaining Gaullist majority, now re-baptised as *Action Sociale Tchadienne* (AST). In 1953 a new party appeared, the *Union Démocratique Indépendante du Tchad* (UDIT), led by the misleadingly named Moslem **Jean-Baptiste** and affiliated (rather oddly) with the Radical party in France. The key figure in this group, which was soon joined by Kieffer and by some of the UDSR, was **Jacques Rogué,** himself a former governor of Tchad (1944–9), but now at odds both with his successor **Colombani,** and with the AST. In October 1953 he stood against the AST candidate, **Laurin,** for membership of the Assembly of the French Union. This presented the PPT-RDA with an awkward choice. Should it vote for Laurin, an arch-conservative, or for Rogué, who as governor had not been soft on it (one of its leaders, **François Tombalbaye,** had been dismissed under his régime from a civil service job), who had subsequently been governor of Mauritania during the notorious election of 1951 (which he was generally credited with having rigged),[1] and whose victory might help to build up UDIT as a rival opposition party? Lisette and Tombalbaye decided to vote for Laurin. This decision provoked a second rupture between Lisette and the Arab leader Koulamallah, who had joined forces for the 1952 elections. Koulamallah re-formed his Independent Socialist Party (PSIT). The PPT-RDA group in the Territorial Assembly was reduced to four,

[1] Morgenthau, pp. 102–3.

and its vote was not sufficient to keep Rogué out. At the same time the party was threatened with a further split, when two of its members, objecting to Lisette's support of Houphouët against d'Arboussier, seceded and formed a 'Communist' Party. But none of these developments made any difference to the hold which the PPT-RDA had on the southern part of the territory, whereas the attacks made by ex-Gaullists such as Kieffer, Béchir Sow and **Ahmed Kotoko** on the political pressures and electoral frauds used by the administration tended to vindicate the PPT's complaints. It would be difficult to use the same techniques against the PPT in future elections.[1]

(ii) In the Ivory Coast the PDCI-RDA was now virtually in power, and 1953 brought a final settlement of its various quarrels with the administration. **Jean-Baptiste Mockey,** one of the PDCI leaders imprisoned after the riot of February 1949, was at last brought to trial–and acquitted. Most of his fellow accused were given suspended sentences.[2] The original charges of 'rebellion' and 'complicity in rebellion' were dropped. So was the prosecution of Ouezzin Coulibaly in connection with his newspaper *Le Démocrate*. Coulibaly was no longer deputy, and had therefore lost his parliamentary immunity. But he regained it when the new Territorial Assembly elected him to the Council of the Republic.[3]

(iii) It was in Guinea that 1953 was really a turning-point both for the RDA and for the whole history of the territory. For it was in that year that Guinea began to feel the effects of a minor industrial revolution which it had been undergoing since the war. Large-scale production of iron, bauxite and diamonds had been got going just in time to profit from the rise in world prices generated by the Korean War. This in turn made possible the installation of secondary industries. Even agricultural production began to rise. Guinea overtook Dahomey and became the third richest territory in AOF (after the Ivory Coast and Senegal). This rapid development brought with it an increase in the industrial labour force, and therefore in the importance of the trades unions. The CGT leader, Sékou Touré, also became the dominant figure in the *Parti Démocratique de la Guinée* (PDG-RDA), and the prestige which he won through his trade union activities in the series of battles over the Labour Code rebounded to the RDA's advantage. Touré had already stood for the National Assembly on an RDA ticket in 1951, but at that time had been very much an outsider. There may have been official

[1] Thompson and Adloff, *Emerging States* . . . (op. cit.). Ansprenger, p. 183.
[2] Ansprenger, p. 143.  [3] Morgenthau, pp. 203 and 205.

pressure against him, but it was hardly necessary. By early 1953, however, after the inter-trade-union conference at Dakar and the subsequent general strike had helped to secure the passage of the Labour Code, he was a figure of inter-territorial importance,[1] and potentially the greatest danger to Houphouët's position within the RDA. For his membership of the CGT brought him into close and continuous contact with French Communists.[2] His situation was analogous to that of Bakary Djibo who had split the party in Niger. But he valued African unity above loyalty to any European organisation or ideology, and he knew that the CGT in Guinea would soon be able to stand on its own feet without French Communist support. In May 1953 he made a final agreement with Houphouët, promising to break with the French CGT as soon as possible.[3] In August he won a by-election to the Guinea Territorial Assembly at Beyla, in the Upper Guinea region inhabited by his Malinké kinsfolk. Among the defeated candidates was deputy Mamba Sano, hitherto the most successful Malinké politician. Touré thus showed that he was able to appeal to the rural tribesmen of the hinterland[4] as well as to the workers in and around Conakry. In the Territorial Assembly he became the leader of the tiny RDA group and made frequent and vigorous attacks on the established ethnic and regional party leaders.[5] Then the great strike of 21st September to 25th November, culminating in the concession of the 20 per cent increase in hourly wages, made him a hero throughout AOF. For there was no doubt that his personal energy and determination were the crucial factors in keeping the strike going for so long.[6] Although it was called jointly by CGT and CFTC, the CGT took all the credit for it and vastly increased its membership in Guinea as a result, leaping from 2,600 in 1953 to 10,700 in 1954 and 39,000 in 1955 (when the CFTC only had 2,000).[7] The PDG-RDA grew at least equally fast, and Touré, as leader of both union and party, soon had most of the population behind him.[8]

[1] Morgenthau, pp. 226–9. See above, pp. 181–2.
[2] And not only French. He had been with d'Arboussier at the Warsaw Peace Conference in November 1950–just *after* the RDA broke with the Communists in Parliament. (Lacouture, *Cinq Hommes et la France*, p. 329.)
[3] Ansprenger, p. 142–3.
[4] He was helped by being descended from Samory Touré, the great Malinké warrior who fought against French expansion from 1882 to 1898.
[5] Morgenthau, p. 232.      [6] Ibid., p. 229.      [7] Ansprenger, Table 5.
[8] Morgenthau, pp. 229–30.

# Chapter 12

# The Mendès-France Government and its Aftermath, 1954–1955

## A. 'PMF' in Power

On 7th May 1954 the French camp at Dien Bien Phu surrendered; on 8th May the Geneva Conference began; on 12th June Laniel's government was defeated on a vote of confidence; and on 18th June Pierre Mendès-France was elected prime minister after promising to resign if he did not make peace within a month.

'PMF' was the first, and indeed the only, Fourth Republic prime minister whom African deputies supported with enthusiasm as well as calculation. He alone showed a genuine interest in reaching an understanding with the overseas peoples on their own terms. He made peace in Vietnam as he had promised; and in Tunisia, where the settler lobby had succeeded in imposing a repressive policy since 1951, he started negotiations with a view to granting full internal autonomy, and allowed **Habib Bourguiba's** hitherto outlawed Néo-Destour party to come to power. It was on this policy that his government was overthrown in February 1955.

His cabinet was oddly composed. It was supported by Socialists, Radicals, UDSR, IOM, Gaullists and, at first, Communists. It was opposed by most Conservatives and the MRP. (Gaullists liked Mendès, and the MRP disliked him, principally because he refused to commit himself to the European Defence Community.) But the Socialists refused to join the government, the Communists were not asked, and the prime minister insisted on choosing his ministers as individuals rather than as representatives of their groups. On this basis he assembled a team of Radicals, Gaullists, UDSR, Conservatives, IOM, and a few individual MRP deputies who joined it at the price of expulsion from their party. Of the IOM, Aujoulat was Minister of Health (later transferred to Labour), and Conombo Secretary of State (under Mitterrand) for the Interior. More important for Africa was the appointment of **Robert Buron** (ex-MRP) as Minister of France d'Outre-Mer.

Buron was the most liberal politician to hold that office since Mitterrand. He was determined both to complete the 'integration' of the RDA–still regarded by many politicians and administrators as *un méchant parti*–and to prepare a *transformation des structures* which would give a measure of autonomy to the T.O.M. Ninine dubbed him *le Ministre Tornado* because he replaced all the heads of department (*directeurs*) in the Rue Oudinot within a few weeks of his arrival there. He also recalled some of the more notoriously 'tough' colonial governors, notably Péchoux of Togo (formerly of the Ivory Coast) and Toby of Niger. The new governor of Niger was Jean Ramadier, this time promoted not for his Socialist pedigree but because he shared Buron's own views on the necessity for 'progressive decolonisation'. Another typical Buron appointment was Governor **Sanmarco** of Oubangui-Chari, chosen because he had been the first administrator to invite Monsieur and Madame Boganda to his house. Buron's policy was to deal with genuine popular leaders (*interlocuteurs valables*) rather than cultivate a series of African Bao Dais. 'France', he said, 'has no need for Yes-men.'[1] But as far as large-scale political reform was concerned, he did not enjoy full freedom of action. Mendès-France was stretching the tolerance of his Gaullist allies over Tunisia and Indo-China. He did not want to risk a head-on clash with them over Afrique Noire. Therefore he instructed Buron to keep the explosive constitutional questions in the background, and concentrate on administrative reform for the time being.[2]

Buron obeyed. But there was one territory whose consitutional problems could not be shelved, for their solution did not depend on France alone. That territory was Togo.

## B. Window-dressing in Togo

Since Nkrumah came to power in the Gold Coast in February 1951, it had been official British policy to support his demand for the integration of British Togoland with the Gold Coast in a single independent state. This put an end to any hopes or fears that Britain might sponsor a united Ewe state, or even a reunification of former German Togo. Instead, she was committed to cajoling the Ewe of British Togoland into accepting the domination of the Gold Coast CPP (Convention People's Party). France was thus given a splendid

[1] 'La France n'a pas besoin de Béni-Oui-Ouis.'
[2] Buron, in conversation with the author, May 1967.

opportunity to turn the tables on Britain, and demonstrate that her half of Togo was getting a better deal.

From then on, Togo became the 'shop-window' of the French Union. Its local government was partly democratised by the institution of *conseils de circonscription*, elected by indirect universal suffrage, with advisory powers on local budgets, taxation and public works. By the electoral law of February 1952, Togo became the only black African territory besides Senegal with a single-college Territorial Assembly. In the 1951 and 1952 elections the administration was able to secure the defeat of the Ewe nationalist CUT by an alliance of Grunitzky's Progress Party (PTP) and the *Union des Chefs et des Populations du Nord* (UCPN). Grunitzky replaced Aku in the National Assembly, and **Derman Ayéva,** leader of the UCPN, replaced Sylvanus Olympio as president of the Territorial Assembly.[1] With these pro-French leaders safely installed in office, Pflimlin began working on a bill which would give Togo limited autonomy; and in 1953–4 Jacquinot carried on with it, being ready to swallow his conservative scruples in the interests of scoring off the British.

Buron at once saw that Togo could be the thin end of a reforming wedge. What was done there to embarrass Britain and impress the United Nations could soon be made a precedent for similar reforms in the T.O.M.[2] He therefore decided to press ahead with the Togo project as quickly as possible. If Parliament tried to slow things down, he could stress the importance of not letting the French timetable fall behind the British. On 23rd June 1954, when Mendès-France had been prime minister for just four days, the British government presented a memorandum to the UN Trusteeship Council, stating that in its view the objectives of Trusteeship in British Togoland had now been attained, and suggesting that the time had come for the UN itself to ascertain the wishes of the population concerning the territory's future status. Clearly France too would soon have to give an account of her stewardship.

Such was the background of the Togo Statute which Buron piloted through the National Assembly, and which eventually became law on 16th April 1955. By it, Togo acquired a 'council of government', presided over by the *Commissaire de la République* (i.e. governor) and partly selected by him, but five of its nine members being elected by the Territorial Assembly.[3] This council was more like a permanent commission of inquiry than a cabinet, for its members lacked real

[1] Cornevin, *Le Togo, nation pilote* and *Histoire du Togo* (op. cit.).
[2] Buron, as above.      [3] Cornevin, *Le Togo, nation pilote.*

executive, as the Assembly did real legislative, power.[1] But the formula, already briefly applied to the tiny French colonies in India before their cession to the Indian Union in 1954,[2] went further than anything yet tried in Afrique Noire. At the same time the *conseils de circonscription* were promoted from being merely advisory bodies to ones with the actual disposal of local budgets.[3]

Although Buron took trouble to cultivate the opposition as well as the pro-French parties in Togo (making friends with Sylvanus Olympio and even secretly subsidising a CUT newspaper out of government funds!),[4] he was out of office by the time the Statute came into force, and it was Grunitzky and the PTP who reaped the immediate benefit of it. The CUT and its independent youth movement, JUVENTO, had now switched the main emphasis of their programme from pan-Eweism to Togolese nationalism. Since 1951 they had been petitioning the UN to end French Trusteeship and give Togo full independence (*Ablodé*). Consequently they rejected the 1955 Statute as totally inadequate, and boycotted the elections to the new Territorial Assembly, which were held on 12th June. In spite of this there was an 80 per cent poll, and an overwhelming victory for the pro-French parties. The UCPN won 92 per cent of the votes in the north, and the PTP 95 per cent in the south.[5]

From the French point of view this result was literally too good to be true. Grunitzky appeared the hero of the hour, and although his party had demanded full autonomy and the end of Trusteeship, it also favoured continued membership of the French Union, and was prepared to accept the Statute as an interim measure. It was too good to be true, because some administrators had been far from scrupulous about the methods they used to achieve it. Even so respectable a source as *Afrique Nouvelle*, the Dakar missionary paper, denounced the practices by which known PTP supporters in Lomé were enabled to vote twenty or more times each, while their opponents were prevented from obtaining voters' cards.[6] It was the same technique which had defeated the RDA in 1951 and 1952. But, like the RDA, the CUT was buried rather than dead.

On 4th July 1955 the new Territorial Assembly gave resounding support to Grunitzky's policy, calling for full internal autonomy but 'categorically rejecting any form of reunification [sc. with

---

[1] See F. Borella, *L'Evolution politique et juridique de l'Union Française depuis 1946* (Paris 1958).
[2] Cornevin, *Histoire du Togo*.      [3] Id., *Le Togo, nation pilote*.
[4] Buron, as above. See also his book *Carnets Politiques de la Guerre d'Algérie*.
[5] Ansprenger, pp. 211–12.      [6] *Afrique Nouvelle*, 21st June 1955.

British Togoland] which would result in a loosening of its [French Togo's] ties with France', and asserting its intention to remain 'within the French system', represented in the French parliament. But JUVENTO sent an able advocate, Maître **Anani Santos,** to put the other side of the case at the UN. In August and September a UN mission toured Togo, collecting some 200,000 petitions and noting that public opinion remained divided. On its advice the General Assembly decided, in December 1955, not to end Trusteeship in either half of Togo without holding a plebiscite beforehand.[1]

## C. The Guinea By-election

The Togo Statute was one problem which Buron had to deal with as soon as he arrived in office. Another was the by-election in Guinea to fill the National Assembly vacancy left by Yacine Diallo. Diallo had died on 14th April 1954, and the election was held on 26th June. Inevitably it was the occasion for a trial of strength between Sékou Touré, whose attacks on the luxurious style in which deputies lived had almost literally hounded Diallo into the grave,[2] and the various ethnic and regional groups whose rivalries had previously dominated Guinean politics. These groups now drew together in a new party, the *Bloc Africain de Guinée* (BAG). Their candidate was **Barry Diawadou,** a Fula 'Socialist' of chiefly birth, who had stood down in favour of Yacine Diallo in 1945, then run against him in 1946 and 1951 as number two on Mamba Sano's ticket. Like almost all other Guinean politicians except Sékou Touré, he was a graduate of the Ecole Normale William Ponty. Now, in 1954, he was supported by the same traditionalist elements that had hitherto backed Yacine Diallo, while some of his own former supporters repudiated him and founded *Démocratie Socialiste de Guinée* (DSG), which ran a third candidate, Barry Ibrahima, generally known as **Barry III.** Barry III denounced the quasi-feudal Fulani chiefs of the Fouta Djallon, who had been Yacine Diallo's principal backers and were now Diawadou's; but he was supported by the French SFIO, to which Yacine Diallo had belonged. Diawadou was supported by the Gaullists, and by the administration.

The official result was:

---

[1] *Le Togo, nation pilote* and Ansprenger, p. 213.
[2] He was still denouncing Diallo on this point in the Territorial Assembly only two days before his death. (Morgenthau, p. 232, quoting minutes of the ordinary session March-April 1954.)

| Diawadou | 147,701 votes |
| Touré | 85,906 ,, |
| Barry III | 7,995 ,, |

The PDG-RDA refused to accept this. The campaign had been marked by enthusiastic demonstrations in favour of Touré in virtually every region of Guinea except the Fouta-Djallon. No regional breakdown of the voting figures was available, and it seemed more than possible that they had been doctored by the administration before publication. Moreover it was known that only in the Fouta had large numbers of voters been registered since 1951, whereas in areas where the PDG was known to be strong many had been struck off the roll. Voting-cards were irregularly distributed by *chefs de canton* who openly favoured Diawadou (one of them was even his father!), PDG ballot papers were often not dealt out, PDG representatives were chased away from the polling stations, and so on. These methods discredited Diawadou's victory, and many Guineans spoke of Touré as 'the real deputy'. Even the French SFIO, whose annual congress occurred a week after the election, condemned 'the interference of the administration' and demanded the recall of Governor **Parisot** and one of his subordinates, who was said to have gone round from *cercle* to *cercle* informing the chiefs that Parisot wanted Diawadou to be elected. RDA and UDSR deputies announced their intention of voting against validation of the results in the Assembly.

But when the vote came up six months later (21st January 1955), few French politicians felt strongly enough about it to challenge the findings of the relevant committee, which were favourable to Diawadou. It was always embarrassing to unseat a deputy once he had been around the Palais Bourbon for a month or two and been addressed as 'mon cher collègue'. Besides, Diawadou had joined the Social Republican (Gaullist) group,[1] and was therefore a member of that section of Mendès-France's now precarious majority which he was most anxious to placate. In voting against the committee's findings, the three RDA deputies found themselves alone with the Communists–it was almost like old times. The Socialist group abstained.

So the affair of the Guinea by-election blew over in Paris. But it was certainly not forgotten in Guinea. The distinction which many people drew between the 'real' and the 'official' deputy was not

[1] Assemblée Nationale, *Notices et Portraits*, 1955.

calculated to spread belief in parliamentary democracy. As had happened in the Ivory Coast before 1950, the RDA party institutions gradually became more important than those of the state. But the PDG in Guinea was better organised than the PDCI in the Ivory Coast, and it did not have so fierce or so single-minded a repression to contend with. Consequently its unity, and its opportunity to unify the territory, were preserved. There was admittedly a series of incidents between PDG partisans and those of Diawadou's BAG, both before and after his election was validated. But they were less serious than the Ivory Coast incidents of 1949–50, and the French government no longer assumed the RDA was in the wrong. Buron himself toured Guinea in October 1954, promising honest elections in future, and going out of his way to show courtesy to Touré and the PDG.[1]

### D. Origins of the Loi-Cadre

On 26th December 1954, in a debate on the overseas budget, Senghor congratulated Buron on having introduced 'a new style' into overseas administration. But despite Buron's determination to see for himself that his orders were carried out ('My office will be an aeroplane', he had declared expansively), this new style took time to filter down to the subordinate ranks of the colonial service—as the Togo election of 1955 was to show. In any case, the changes which Senghor and his colleagues wanted were not merely a question of style. They were waiting for the *transformation des structures* which would give Africans a chance to govern themselves and prepare the Federal Republic which Senghor still hoped for. On this point Buron was unable to give them satisfaction. He assured the Assembly that his subordinates had prepared measures of 'decentralisation and deconcentration' for Cameroun, AEF and AOF, but the details that he gave concerned only the decentralisation of the federal services within the two African federations. Nothing was said about 'councils of government' even of the Togo type, let alone genuine elected executives.[2] Doubtless this was not for lack of good will on Buron's part. By his own account,[3] he had already worked out the principles of the Loi-Cadre of 1956. But the government dared not own up to such principles in 1954–5. Both Buron and the African deputies

[1] Morgenthau, pp. 106–7, 240–3.
[2] *Journal Officiel, Assemblée Nationale (Débats),* 16th December 1954.
[3] Conversation of May 1967, already cited.

were prisoners of the conservative majority with which they were obliged to work.

## E. Decline and Fall

Mendès-France earned the implacable hatred of the MRP by allowing the Assembly to veto the European Defence Community on 30th August. (That was also the end of the projected political union, and *a fortiori* of 'Eurafrica'.) He alienated the Communists, and some of his right-wing supporters, by forcing the Assembly to accept German rearmament on 12th October. He annoyed many right-wing Radicals and nearly all Conservatives by his liberal policy in North Africa, where the Algerian war broke out on 1st November. By January 1955 he was so anxious to placate the Gaullists that he actually offered the Ministry of France d'Outre-Mer to Maurice Bayrou.[1] (Buron was promoted to the Ministry of Finance as part of a general reshuffle.) Fortunately Bayrou refused, and it was Jean-Jacques Juglas, another MRP rebel, who took the post for the few days that the government had left. A few days later Jacques Soustelle was appointed Governor-General of Algeria. This pleased most of the Gaullists, but angered the settler lobby, which regarded Soustelle as a liberal. On 5th February the government was defeated on its North African policy by a combination of opponents who agreed with it (MRP, Communists) and supporters who didn't (Conservatives, Radicals and a few Gaullists). Among deputies from Afrique Noire only Apithy, who belonged to the (Conservative) Independent Republican group, voted against the government.[2]

### 'L'Affaire Pineau'

Mendès-France's fall inaugurated the first ministerial crisis under the new rules instituted by the Constitutional amendment at the end of 1954. A prospective prime minister had now to form a cabinet before the Assembly could vote on his investiture. Pinay (Conservative) and Pflimlin (MRP) having both failed to do so, it was not until 18th February that a candidate appeared before the Assembly, and then for the first time since 1951 it was a Socialist, Christian

[1] *Paris-Dakar*, 20th January 1955.
[2] See division list in Journal Officiel. Boganda also belonged to a Conservative group (the Peasants) but he did not vote. Malbrant (RS) abstained. Otherwise all the Afrique Noire deputies, first college included, voted for the government.

Pineau. He proposed a 'European' cabinet, based on the old left-centre coalition of the previous legislature–Socialists, Radicals, MRP, UDSR. **Gaston Defferre** (Socialist) was billed for Minister of France d'Outre-Mer, and Fily-Dabo Sissoko was to be Secretary of State for Industry (as in the abortive Schuman cabinet of September 1948).

Pineau offered the IOM two Secretaryships of State, and asked them to name their own candidates. Instead of asking him to keep the two ministers chosen by Mendès-France (Aujoulat and Conombo), the IOM group decided to propose its two presidents: Saller in the Council of the Republic and Senghor in the National Assembly. At this point Pineau backpedalled rapidly. Senghor had never yet been a minister, and a Socialist premier could hardly make him one without provoking a grave crisis in the African branch of the SFIO. Senghor was a renegade Socialist himself. He had first double-crossed and then defeated Lamine-Guèye. From a Socialist point of view he was the arch-villain of African politics. Deeply embarrassed, Pineau apologised to the IOM but regretted he was unable to offer Senghor a portfolio. The IOM rose up in righteous indignation at this 'ban pronounced on one of two men whom all Black Africa esteems and respects', and announced their intention of voting against the prime minister designate–the only time they ever did so in all the countless ministerial crises of the Fourth Republic.[1] The RDA also voted against him, for once in opposition to both Pleven and Mitterrand. Here too a local opposition–between Konaté and Sissoko–was the deciding factor. The RDA were afraid that under a Socialist Minister of France d'Outre-Mer there would be a new spate of Socialist governors–and that would mean Socialist elections. They would have preferred to see Juglas retained in office. He had a good record of interest in overseas affairs as president of the T.O.M. commission, and could not be suspected of playing party politics in Africa since he had just been expelled from his party.[2]

So on this occasion the SFIO paid the price of its former follies in Africa. Apart from his fellow-Socialists (who now numbered five), the only black Africans who voted for Pineau were Sékou Sanogo (now affiliated to the MRP), and Barry Diawadou (Gaullist)–the two West Africans who most blatantly owed their seats to administrative support. Pineau was defeated principally by a combination of

---

[1] In 1948 they had voted against Schuman's cabinet, not his investiture. (See above, pp. 129–30.)
[2] Reports in *Paris-Dakar* and *Afrique Nouvelle*, February 1955.

Conservatives, Gaullists and Communists. But once again those representing Afrique Noire were enough to have turned the scale if they had voted differently.[1] The point aroused comment, particularly because of the apparent *rapprochement* between RDA and IOM.

### Second Edgar Faure Government

After Pineau's failure the Socialists remained in opposition. The Right-Centre coalition (Radicals, Conservatives, Gaullists, MRP, UDSR) was revived under Edgar Faure, a flexible Radical who since his short-lived prime ministership of 1952 had been Minister of Finance under both Laniel and Mendès-France. The IOM agreed to support him when he assured them that this time Senghor would not be left out. Once again Africans compromised rather than risk the odium of prolonging a crisis; all of them except the Socialists voted for Faure, even though he gave them no definite promise to abolish the double college. (Pineau's failure to do this had been their principal pretext for voting against him.) Both Gaullists and RDA reluctantly accepted the appointment of an orthodox MRP man as Minister of France d'Outre-Mer. A general election was due in 1956, and they feared a return to the Coste-Floret tactics. But at least they had to admit that the personal integrity of the new minister, **Pierre-Henri Teitgen,** was above suspicion. The Gaullists were reassured by the appointment of Bayrou as Teitgen's Secretary of State, but this was scarcely a consolation for the Africans. Senghor's post, as Secretary of State to the Prime Minister, with special responsibility for scientific research, was more flattering than useful to Africa. He was unlikely to have a great deal of influence on the general policy of a government so conservative that Mendès-France and Mitterrand had refused to vote for it.[2]

### F. Bandung

During the spring of 1955 the pace of events seemed to quicken in French Africa. The war spread rapidly in Algeria, where a state of emergency was declared on 1st April. This gave a new sense of urgency to colonial problems in general and African ones in particular. French liberals and African federalists repeated that Afrique Noire was now the only area where France could still make a success

---

[1] Guillemin, *Les Elus d'Afrique Noire* . . . (op. cit.).
[2] See division lists for 23rd February 1953.

of her overseas policy, if she did not leave it too late as she had done elsewhere. Proposals to revise Title VIII of the Constitution were now becoming respectable. Even if nothing was actually done about them, they were discussed at length in the Assembly of the French Union, and this time there were fewer and fainter cries of 'separatism' or 'sedition'.[1]

On 18th April (two days after the Togo Statute had become law), the great Afro-Asian Conference opened at Bandung. Four sub-Saharan African states were represented: two that were independent already (Ethiopia and Liberia) and two that soon would be (the Gold Coast and the Anglo-Egyptian Sudan). France forbade the representation of Tunisia, Algeria and Morocco, but an unofficial 'North African Delegation', representing the nationalist parties of all three countries, was present. French policy in North Africa was unanimously condemned, and a more general resolution condemned 'colonialism in all its forms' and called for independence for all peoples under foreign domination. French statesmen expressed their indignation at this 'flagrant violation of the United Nations charter which forbids foreign interference in a country's internal affairs' (since Algeria was theoretically part of France).[2] But many of them also realized that the Bandung manifesto would have an inevitable psychological appeal to all colonised peoples. If France was to provide an acceptable alternative to independence, she must do so soon. The bonds of the French Union would have to be loosened – for Africans would leave it rather than suffocate. The first institutions to recognise this formally were the Catholic trade unions. At the CFTC General Congress in May 1955, it was decided that African unions should no longer be expected to adhere to the CFTC as such. Instead they could belong to a more loosely-constructed *Conseil des Organisations Syndicales de l' Union Française* (COSUF), in which the CFTC would only be *primus inter pares*.[3]

[1] See Ansprenger, p. 254.
[2] *Paris-Dakar*, 19th April 1955 and days immediately following.
[3] Ansprenger, p. 222.

## Chapter 13

# Towards Rebellion in Cameroun

But it is not for this event that May 1955 is remembered in Africa. On 22nd May violence broke out in Cameroun. An armed struggle began between the UPC and the administration which is still smouldering in 1967.[1]

## A. Development of the UPC

The dominant facts of Cameroun policies between 1950 and 1955 were the growing strength of the UPC in organisation and publicity, and its failure to register this strength in terms of votes. In the 1951 elections Douala-Manga-Bell (MRP) and Ninine (SFIO) retained their seats on the coast and in the north respectively, while Aujoulat (IOM), transferring from first to second college, won the new constituency in the centre–the area round Yaoundé. The UPC, defeated, then produced a new programme of action, whose main points were a complete overhaul of party organisation and an intensive press campaign through the party newspaper *La Voix du Cameroun*.[2]

The UPC also retained and developed the theme of reunification with the British Cameroons as a principal item in its programme. In December 1951 Um Nyobé led a group of 26 delegates to a 'Kamerun United National Congress' at Kumba in the British zone. The adoption of the German spelling 'Kamerun', which later became a UPC trademark, was meant to symbolise the national unity of the

[1] See *Le Monde*, 28th and 29th May 1967.

[2] The press had a more important political role in Cameroun than in most other territories, because of the activities of the missions in providing primary education. By 1958 it had 47·7% of its school-age population in private schools and a further 22·2% in state ones. The global figure of 69·9% was comparable only with those for neighbouring Gabon (66·8%) and Moyen-Congo (72·1%). No other territory was higher than 38·2% (Togo). These figures do not include Moslem Koranic schools. (See Direction de l'Enseignement et de la Jeunesse du Ministère de la France d'Outre-Mer, Bulletin No. 10, December 1958.)

former German colony. But neither reorganisation nor propaganda succeeded in winning the UPC a single seat in the Territorial Assembly (known as ATCAM, to distinguish it from the former Representative Assembly, ARCAM) elected on 30th March 1952. Electoral success went mainly to the Catholics (*Bloc Démocratique Camerounais*–BDC) in the south, and entirely to the Moslem chiefs and their protégés in the north. The two combined to elect Aujoulat, leader of the BDC and Secretary of State for France d'Outre-Mer, as president of the new Assembly. The UPC militants, like those of other RDA sections, were convinced they had been cheated. In the Moungo region (north of Douala) violence flared up on 27th May similar to–though less serious than–that which occurred in April in Tchad.[1] One man was killed and several wounded.[2]

But although the UPC shared the sufferings of other RDA sections, its reaction to them was different. While Houphouët worked for an understanding with the government to ensure fairer elections in future, Um Nyobé and his friends began to lose faith in elections as such. They were cut off from the interterritorial RDA by this outlook, by their support of d'Arboussier in his quarrel with Houphouët (like Bakary Djibo they were closely associated with the CGT), and above all by their open demands for independence, which like JUVENTO in Togo they based on the Trusteeship clauses of the UN Charter. Despite protests from ATCAM, Um Nyobé travelled to New York in 1952 and put his case before the Trusteeship Council. His appearances became an annual feature of UN proceedings: each time he came with a petition demanding independence and reunification. He claimed that while Camerounians respected and valued French culture they had no desire to remain politically within the French Union, even if granted autonomy.[3] Neither the Trusteeship Council nor the UN mission which visited Cameroun in 1952 were convinced that Um Nyobé represented the mass of Cameroun's population, as he claimed to do. But the very fact of his appearance at the UN, skilfully publicised by the UPC, helped to increase his prestige at home.

The UPC held a Congress in December 1952. **Félix-Roland Moumié** was elected President, while Um Nyobé remained General Secretary. Moumié was untypical of UPC leaders in that he came from the Moslem north (although admittedly the area immediately adjacent to the Bamiléké region), and was a graduate of the Ecole Ponty.

[1] See above p., 175.    [2] *Le Cameroun de Demain*, June 1952.
[3] Mveng, *Histoire du Cameroun* (op. cit.).

Like Houphouët he was a *médecin africain*. But he was twenty years younger than Houphouët, and very different from him in political attitudes. Isolated among his own people, the Bamoun (whose feudal ruler, Sultan **Seidou Njimoluh Njoya**, easily defeated him in the 1952 elections), Moumié became within the UPC the leading proponent of violence and extreme policies, and the rigidest supporter of Communism.[1]

## B. ATCAM: the Socialists versus the BDC

The UPC's drift to the left, coinciding as it did with a rapid increase in its membership (from about 30,000 at the end of 1952 to about 100,000 at the beginning of 1955),[2] naturally alarmed the more moderate politicians. But they were not united among themselves, and their pragmatic doubts about the value of independence unless preceded by economic development, or of reunification unless preceded by unity within French Cameroun, were less politically infectious than the more positive slogans of Um Nyobé and Moumié.

At first it seemed that Aujoulat's BDC was best placed to compete with the UPC. It benefited from the considerable personal prestige of its founder, from the support of the Catholic Church (the UPC's most feared and hated enemy), and after the Bobo-Dioulasso Congress from its affiliation to an interterritorial movement with considerable parliamentary influence–the IOM. In April 1953, when Aujoulat returned from Paris to address the first BDC party congress at Yaoundé (the centre both of his constituency and of his political influence), his position seemed uniquely strong for a European in African politics. Representing, since 1951, a purely African electorate, he had continued to be forced into the French cabinet by the votes of other Africans. As a minister he had pushed through the long hoped-for Labour Code, and then resigned in protest against the reactionary colleagues with whom he was expected to work. Subsequently he had been one of the dominating figures of a Congress which had founded a new African political movement and boldly indicated the lines of future political development. If he now rejected the goal of independence for Cameroun,[3] this was because he believed in an alternative and no less ambitious vision: the federal French Republic.

Yet Aujoulat was now at the zenith of his political career. The

---

[1] Ansprenger, p. 197.  [2] Ibid., p. 195.
[3] *Le Cameroun de Demain*, April 1953.

214

time when a European, however liberal, could dominate political life among Africans, even Africans of moderate views, was not to last much longer. Those who wanted an alternative leader to Um Nyobé realised that he must be someone whose election handouts would not have to claim, as Aujoulat's had done in 1951, that 'This saviour's skin may be white, but he is blacker of heart than the black man himself.' As for the other deputies, Prince Douala still disdained to organise his following into a political party, and Ninine might have a black skin but was otherwise just as much an alien as Aujoulat–he came from Guadeloupe. In any case, he was more interested in French parliamentary business than in Cameroun's local politics.[1] Neither Ninine nor Douala was a member of ATCAM.[2]

Within ATCAM, Aujoulat's leading opponent was Paul Soppo Priso, the *Socialiste milliardaire*.[3] The High Commissioner, **J. L. Soucadaux,** was also a Socialist, and therefore preferred to encourage Socialist rather than Catholic opposition to the UPC. In January 1953 a *Union Sociale Camerounaise* (USC) was founded as an affiliate of the SFIO. Its leader was **Charles Okala,**[4] a portly Socialist who enjoyed some popularity in the Mbam region (north of Yaoundé), but in the 1962 election had been defeated by the BDC. He was believed[5] to have been involved in some shady deals with Soppo Priso during the previous Assembly (ARCAM), which had elected him a Senator. In that capacity he had been a member of the French delegation to the UN in 1952, and answered Um Nyobé's petition by declaring that to talk of independence for Cameroun was 'pure Utopia'.[6]

With Soucadaux's help the Socialist group in ATCAM grew at the expense of the BDC, and by April 1954 the latter was in a minority. Soppo Priso replaced Aujoulat as president. The bitterness between the two groups was similar to that between Lamine-Guèye and Senghor in Senegal, but in Cameroun it was the Socialists who gained from the Catholics instead of the other way round. **André-Marie Mboida**, a former theology student who had been elected both

[1] He was the only deputy from Afrique Noire to bring in bills which had no special relevance to overseas affairs (Guillemin, op. cit.).

[2] List of members in *Le Cameroun de Demain*, April 1952.

[3] Buron, conversation cited in Chapter 12.

[4] Mveng, op. cit. For Okala's figure, see any photograph. He was later famous for having one of the best wine-cellars in tropical Africa.

[5] See notes and letters among Dr Aujoulat's papers.

[6] Ansprenger, p. 197.

to ATCAM and to the Assembly of the French Union on a BDC ticket, suddenly turned against Aujoulat and allied with Soppo Priso.

## C. Roland Pré

In November 1954 Buron transferred Soucadaux to Madagascar, and replaced him with **Roland Pré,** an experienced administrator who had made a liberal reputation as governor successively of Gabon, Guinea, Upper Volta and Somaliland. No doubt Buron hoped that by appointing a new man with no party connections he could gain the confidence of the authentic popular leaders in Cameroun, as he was trying to do elsewhere. But in Cameroun it was not so easy. No one party could claim convincingly to represent the whole population. The UPC had most prestige in the south, but was unrepresented in ATCAM. It organised increasingly frequent strikes, and distributed violent propaganda not only against the employers but also against the Church and the Catholic trade unions.[1] When Roland Pré arrived in January 1955 he established contact with Um Nyobé's secretary, **Théodore Mayi Matip.**[2] But a new series of strikes and disturbances soon convinced him that indulgence to the UPC would be a mistake. A big strike at Dizangué (mouth of the river Sanaga) occurred within a few days of his arrival. This and other incidents may have been deliberately provoked by anti-UPC employers and administrators who wanted to prove their point. But the UPC was also encouraged in its hostility to Pré by the refusal of the majority in ATCAM to co-operate with him. Soppo Priso and the Socialists resented the removal of their friend Soucadaux. Both they and Mbida denounced Pré as a creature of Aujoulat's. (Although Aujoulat denied having solicited his appointment, he could not deny that he was a member of the cabinet which had approved it.)[3]

Less than two months after his arrival, Pré decided to take a tough line with the UPC. On 19th February he issued an order permitting the use of troops to disperse unruly crowds, and a few days later he announced his intention of 'crushing Communist activity'.[4] He began by transferring those UPC leaders who were employed by the

[1] Mveng, op. cit. Ansprenger, pp. 194–5, 198–9.      [2] Buron, as above.
[3] Buron, Mveng, *Le Cameroun de Demain* and Aujoulat's letter to his constituents, January 1955.
[4] *Afrique Nouvelle*, 8th March 1955.

administration to posts in Yaoundé and Douala where he thought he could keep an eye on them. This move backfired, as one of the leaders in question was Moumié, who was thus enabled to take his place on the UPC political bureau and to make fiery speeches to the militants, both in the capital and in the insanitary industrial suburbs of Douala where the UPC's trade union base was strongest.[1]

## D. The Riots of May 1955

During April there were further strikes in Douala and demonstrations at Yaoundé and in the Bamiléké region. The Catholic bishops of Cameroun issued a joint pastoral letter condemning the UPC, and Moumié retaliated with a remarkable circular entitled 'Religion or Colonialism', in which he asserted that Christ himself was a nationalist and that the priests by supporting colonialism were betraying his cause.[2]

The UPC leaders were apparently frustrated by the relatively small numbers which they could muster for their strikes and demonstrations. They may have feared that Um Nyobé's failure to obtain UN intervention would result in a decline of his popular following. If so, they must have been further alarmed by the arrival of Félix-Tchicaya and Ouezzin Coulibaly, who tried to start an 'orthodox' (i.e. pro-Houphouët) RDA section. It may have been this that made them decide to resort to violence before it was too late. One of the targets of the violence in Douala when it came was a meeting of the anti-Communist 'National front' which Coulibaly had organised.

But it is not certain that there was any decision at all. Although there were riots more or less simultaneously in Douala, Yaoundé and the Moungo region between 22nd and 27th May, they do not seem to have been particularly well co-ordinated. 'The fools!', a French Communist is said to have exclaimed, 'they behaved like children – They hurled themselves into the fight three months too soon, without preparing for it.'[3] Pré later said he believed Um Nyobé, who was away in Nigeria at the time, had advised against violence, and that Moumié was the ringleader.[4] At all events, 26 people were killed (three Europeans, one gendarme and 22 African civilians) and more than a hundred injured. Of course these events had no remotely comparable effect to the Algerian war. But they did make clear to some Frenchmen that movements of the Algerian

[1] Ansprenger, p. 200.  [2] Ibid., pp. 198–9.
[3] Typed reports in Aujoulat papers.  [4] *Afrique Nouvelle*, 19th July 1955.

217

type might occur in tropical Africa too. It was even said that the UPC was inspired partly by the Viet Minh, whose organisation it was thought to have copied. Um Nyobé became known as *le Ho Chi Minh camerounais*.[1]

To Camerounian students in Paris it was self-evident that the UPC was blameless, the victim first of provocation, then of repression by the administration.[2] To administrators on the spot it was equally obvious that the UPC was responsible and must be suppressed. On 13th July it was banned, along with its women's and youth organisations. The leaders of the USCC-CGT were arrested. In August the political leaders–Moumié, with the Bamiléké **Ernest Ouandié** and **Abel Kingué**–fled across the border to join Um Nyobé in the British zone. Um Nyobé later returned to head a revolutionary maquis in the Sanaga-Maritime region. The others constituted a kind of government in exile.

The legal opposition–Soppo Priso and Mbida–redoubled their denunciations of Pré and Aujoulat, whom they insisted on lumping together. Yet Aujoulat had grave doubts about the wisdom of Pré's policy, and the BDC now called for autonomy and a 'realistic Cameroun nationalism'.[3] Mbida went one better and took up a barely disguised racism. He announced his intention of standing against Aujoulat at the general election, and his supporters campaigned with the slogan '*A bas les blancs négricides*'.[4]

[1] Aujoulat papers. *Afrique Française*, May-June 1956. *Témoignage Chretien*, 1st February 1957.
[2] Typed manifesto, and letter from Aujoulat to a correspondent in Cameroun.
[3] *Afrique Nouvelle*, 14th June 1955.
[4] Open letter to Mbida written by a supporter of Aujoulat's while interned under Mbida's government in 1957 (Aujoulat papers).

# Chapter 14

# 1955 (A Pre-election Year)

## A. The RDA Co-ordination Committee at Conakry

The May riots in Cameroun achieved one thing at least. They prevented the formation of an 'orthodox' Cameroun section of the RDA. Tchicaya and Coulibaly returned empty-handed. But this failure could not efface the success with which Houphouët reimposed his authority on the movement elsewhere. Even in Senegal, where the majority of the UDS-RDA still supported d'Arboussier, there was an important minority, led by Doudou Guèye and Guy Etcheverry, which accepted the orthodox line. By 1955 Houphouët at last felt secure enough to summon the Co-ordination Committee, which had now been dormant for nearly seven years. It met on 8th July, at Conakry.

The choice of place was significant. It indicated a shift in the centre of gravity of the movement. Sékou Touré was now a leader second in importance only to Houphouët himself, although still not a member of any metropolitan French assembly. Many Frenchmen, especially in the Guinea administration, suspected him of Communist sympathies, and doubted the sincerity of his acceptance of the Houphouët line. Certainly there were profound differences of outlook between the two men, and these were to be increasingly apparent. But Communism was not directly relevant to them. Both regarded Communism as essentially a French ideology, and while Houphouët was uninterested in ideology, Touré was uninterested in things French. These attitudes, which were to force them apart in the years that followed, tended to bring them together in 1955. Houphouët was anxious to exonerate the PDG from the suspicion of Communism, and so to help it towards the electoral success which had been denied it in 1954. On his instructions Ouezzin Coulibaly had been in Guinea for much of the year since the by-election, working to improve relations between the PDG and the administration. Now the arrival of the entire 'orthodox' RDA leadership in Conakry

219

provided a spectacular demonstration that it considered the PDG fully respectable.[1]

Unanimously the Committee resolved that the UPC could no longer be considered a section of the RDA–though without specifically condemning it. On the other hand it 'definitely excluded' the UDS, thus clearing the way for a new RDA section in Senegal.[2] It also reaffirmed that Hamani Diori's party was the authentic RDA section of Niger, thus unequivocally disavowing Bakary Djibo. Apart from these inevitable mopping-up operations, the meeting was notable principally for its extremely moderate and pragmatic tone, which made the strongest possible contrast with d'Arboussier's great ideological *tour d'horizon* in 1948. On the constitutional problem, Houphouët was content to echo vaguely the views expressed by the IOM at Bobo-Dioulasso two years before: true independence only possible in the context of 'organised interdependence', assimilation and association both bankrupt formulae, future Franco-African relations would be of a federal type. But, he insisted, the constitutional question was not the fundamental one, and the revision of Title VIII was not the essential point. 'We rely less on institutions than on the spirit which animates them.' What really mattered was the improvement of the ordinary African's standard of living.[3]

We may wonder whether Sékou Touré made mental reservations as he listened to Houphouët's report. If so, they remained mental. At this time the unity of the movement was more important to him than specific political ideas. The demonstration worked. From now on the RDA's respectability was no longer questioned, in Guinea or elsewhere. Houphouët's long and careful efforts to restore confidence had paid off.

## B. The End of a Legislature

*Algeria*

The RDA deputies could afford to be away from Paris on 9th July, when the National Assembly voted on the agreements giving

[1] Morgenthau, p. 241.

[2] Within a month one had been set up–the *Mouvement Populaire Sénégalais* (MPS). Leader: Doudou Guèye. (*Afrique Nouvelle*, 15th August 1955.)

[3] 'Les travaux de la deuxième session du Comité de Co-ordination du RDA, Conakry 8–11 juillet 1955.' (Special edition of *Afrique Noire*.)

autonomy to Tunisia. The policy which five months earlier had brought down Mendès-France's government was now endorsed with only 44 votes against and 32 abstentions.[1] Belatedly, the majority parties had accepted the inevitable. But it was to be a long time before they could bring themselves to adopt the same attitude to Algeria. Many deputies persisted in asserting that whereas the Moroccan and Tunisian problems were 'political', the Algerian one was exclusively 'social'. Faure's government had little policy beyond the strengthening of military and police powers to deal with terrorism–and even this it was half-hearted about. It had embarrassedly to disavow an article by Senghor in which, in accordance with his federalist views, he had advocated internal autonomy for Algeria. As a minister, Senghor had to vote for the government on 29th July when it brought in a bill to prolong the Algerian state of emergency beyond the original six-month time limit. But Aujoulat and Zodi Ikhia voted against the bill, as did the RDA, while the rest of the IOM abstained.[2]

*Constitutional Revision?*

Senghor remained in the government, suppressing his disapproval of its Algerian policy, principally because he still hoped to achieve a 'federalist' revision of the Constitution. In February the IOM had tabled a bill which proposed to increase the powers of the Assembly of the French Union, as the first step towards making it a federal parliament. So far this had not been discussed. But on 24th May the National Assembly passed a resolution declaring that Title VIII of the Constitution was *révisable*, and on 19th July this was accepted by the Council of the Republic.[3] Meanwhile a government committee of experts, chaired by Senghor, was already at work on the problem. At the end of July it reported to the prime minister, insisting on the necessity of creating *states* overseas–'not states in the international, but in the federal sense, with both executive and legislative power in those matters which fall within their autonomy. . . .'[4] But on this subject as on others the government was reluctant to take any bold

[1] Williams. Appendix IVb, p. 500.
[2] Journal Officiel Assemblée Nationale (*Débats*), July 1955.
[3] A. Coret, 'Le problème de la révision du Titre VIII durant les deux premières années de la troisième legislature', in *Revue Politique et Juridique de l'Union Française*, 1958, vol. 3.
[4] Text in Senghor, 'Pour une République fédérale', *Politique Etrangère*, 1956, vol. 2.

initiative. It was paralysed by a conservative majority, and by the approach of a general election.

## Morocco

On 20th August the situation in North Africa got still worse. There were massacres not only in Algeria but also in Morocco, where European sabotage had wrecked the liberal policy of the French Resident. He resigned, but the French government was unable to reimpose its authority. Power slipped rapidly into the hands of the nationalist *Istiqlal* (Independence) party. Soon Faure and his foreign minister, Pinay, decided that there was nothing for it but to grant Morocco 'independence in interdependence' and restore the Sultan **Mohammed Ben Youssef** who had been deposed in 1953. This decision lost them the support of the Gaullists, whose general policy at this time was to discredit the régime by joining each government when it was formed and leaving it when it was in difficulties.[1] Faure had to dismiss the Gaullist ministers (including Bayrou) at the beginning of October after they had approached the President of the Republic with suggestions of a 'government of national union'.[2] From now on Faure's was virtually a minority government, relying on left-wing support for its Moroccan policy and right-wing support for most of its others.

## The Electoral Law

Faure wanted to hold elections as soon as possible, in the hope that a clear majority would emerge which could take firm decisions about Algeria.[3] No one was against early elections as such, but most deputies, especially on the Left, felt that it was essential first to amend the electoral law so as to remove at any rate the more flagrant anomalies of the system used in 1951. Africans of course were particularly anxious to secure electoral reform since this would almost certainly involve an increase in the number of overseas deputies, the introduction of universal suffrage, and the abolition of the double college in AEF and Cameroun. Faure did not openly oppose electoral reform, but he refused to delay the elections to make time for it, reckoning that if no law were passed within the

[1] Williams, p. 136.  [2] *Paris-Dakar*, October 1955.
[3] Williams, p. 47.

time limit he set, the 1951 system would have to be used again, and this would probably benefit his conservative coalition.[1]

During November Faure's own electoral law was discussed. It was opposed by Mendès-France and most of the Left because it did not satisfy their demand for the restoration of the pre-war system of single-member constituencies. At first it was also received coolly by the African deputies, for it extended the single college only to Cameroun and not to AEF. On hearing this, the AEF Great Council in Brazzaville went on strike and refused to vote the federal budget – until a telegram arrived from Minister Teitgen promising that the government would not oppose an amendment proposed by the T.O.M. Commission, which extended both single-college and universal suffrage to Africa as a whole. This amendment was adopted by the National Assembly on the same day (18th November) that the Municipal Reform Bill at last became law. 'Death of the Double College', headlined *Afrique Nouvelle* triumphantly. The same clause of the electoral law provided that each territory should now have one deputy for every 700,000 inhabitants (Conombo had proposed one for every 500,000).

On this basis AOF would have 27 deputies instead of 20,

|  |  |  |  |
|---|---|---|---|
| Togo | 2 | instead of | 1, |
| AEF | 9 single-college | instead of | 6 second and 2 first, |
| and Cameroun | 4 single-college | instead of | 3 second and 1 first. |

Cameroun also became, like other territories, a single constituency.[2] This was an amendment carried by Aujoulat, who was anxious to reinforce the unity of Cameroun (and stood a better chance of being elected on a list with Africans than by himself), and opposed by Ninine and the Socialists, who insisted on the special character of northern Cameroun (because they expected to win it).[3]

But the new electoral law never came into force. On 29th November Faure was defeated on a vote of confidence and seized the opportunity to dissolve the Assembly. The general election, fixed for 2nd January 1956, would have to be held under the law of 1951. It was a bitter disappointment for Africans, especially in AEF.

[1] Ibid., pp. 47 and 315.
[2] *Afrique Nouvelle*, 22nd November 1955.
[3] Journal Officiel Assemblée Nationale (*Débats*), 18th November 1955.

## C. The End of an Era?

Even so, everyone knew that the new legislature was likely to bring a new phase of Franco-African relations. The *status quo* now had few open defenders, and the sense of urgency imparted by the Algerian war showed signs of overcoming the normal parliamentary inertia. On the African side too attitudes were changing. African deputies like Apithy and Senghor frequently emphasised that they expected to be succeeded by a younger generation less patient than themselves. This younger generation existed already. It was less excited by the old slogan of 'a thousand million Frenchmen' and the memory of Eboué than by the idea of independence. It looked less to Paris for inspiration than to Bandung and Accra. More and more Africans were coming to regard participation in French organisations as a hindrance rather than a privilege, and to want African organisations of their own. The youth leaders of Senegal took the initiative: they seceded from the *Conseil de la Jeunesse de l'Union Française* and started a *Conseil Fédéral de la Jeunesse de L'AOF,* which held its founding congress in July 1955.[1] The trade unions were soon to follow suit. Sékou Touré had promised Houphouët he would break with the French CGT. At the Conakry meeting he repeated the promise, and suggested the creation of an autonomous West African trade union movement. The suggestion was taken up by the CGT of Senegal and Mauritania, which decided at its annual congress in November 1955 to disaffiliate from the French CGT and become the 'CGTA'.[2] Meanwhile the Christian trade unions prepared to take up the freedom offered them by the CFTC. The first autonomous group (*Confédération Camerounaise des Syndicats Croyants*) was formed in Cameroun on 18th December.[3]

From now on it would be very difficult to interest African voters in any idea or institution that was not specifically African.

[1] Ansprenger, p. 227.    [2] *Paris-Dakar*, November 1955.
[3] Ansprenger, p. 225.

# PART FOUR

---

## 'Toys and Lollipops'
### January 1956–September 1958

*Chapter 15*

# The 1956 Election

## A. The Results in Africa

It is generally agreed that the elections of 2nd January 1956 were free from any large-scale administrative interference. Their results therefore give us a fairly reliable indication of party strengths in the different African territories at this time. The following is a brief summary, giving in capitals the names of deputies elected or re-elected on 2nd January.

The RDA was now the largest African party, with nine deputies. These included the three who had sat in the previous Assembly— HOUPHOUËT (Ivory Coast), KONATÉ (Soudan), TCHICAYA (Moyen-Congo); three who had sat in the 1946 Assembly but had been defeated in 1961—COULIBALY (Ivory Coast), HAMANI DIORI (Niger) and LISETTE (Tchad); and three newcomers—Modibo KEITA (Soudan), SÉKOU TOURÉ and **DIALLO SAIFOULAYE** (both Guinea). Konaté died in May 1956 and was replaced by **Bocoum Baréma**, also RDA. The RDA now formed more than half the UDSR group, whose name was consequently changed to UDSR-RDA. GEORGES CONDAT (Niger) remained a member of this group although elected on an anti-RDA list.

The IOM, which had had 14 deputies from Afrique Noire in 1955, now had only seven. Béchir Sow (Tchad), Mamba Sano (Guinea), Zodi Ikhia (Niger), and Aujoulat (central Cameroun) were all defeated. Abbas Guèye (Senegal) was dropped by his local party, the BDS, in favour of MAMADOU DIA. Mamadou Ouedraogo (Upper Volta) did not stand for re-election. Those who survived from the previous legislature were AUBAME (Gabon), MAGA (Dahomey), NAZI BONI (Upper Volta), SENGHOR (Senegal), DOUALA MANGA BELL (coastal Cameroun) and GRUNITZKY (Togo).

CONOMBO and GUISSOU (both Upper Volta) were re-elected on a list called *de tendance IOM* but left the IOM group in the Assembly. The old Union Voltaïque had now split into two regional parties:

the *Mouvement Populaire d'Evolution Africaine* (MPEA,) a western, non-Mossi party led by Nazi Boni, and the *Parti Social d'Education des Masses Africaines* (PSEMA), centred on Ouagadougou. Nazi Boni remained in the IOM while Guissou and Conombo, the leaders of PSEMA, manoeuvred towards an alliance with the RDA.

The Gaullists (RS–formerly RPF) had had seven deputies from Afrique Noire in 1955–three first-college, one second and three mixed. In the new Assembly they had six (three, one and two). In the first college, BAYROU and MALBRANT (both AEF) were re-elected, while Molinatti (Cameroun) was defeated by another Gaullist, **PLANTIER.**[1] In the second college Sou Quatre (Tchad) was replaced by **ARABI EL-GONI**, who had strong support in the Moslem north–whereas LISETTE won overwhelmingly in the animist and Christian south. In Somaliland (single college), **Magendie** was replaced by **MAHAMOUD HARBI**, both RS. In Mauritania SIDI EL-MOKHTAR, till now RS, was re-elected with Gaullist support but then transferred to the MRP, which was thus compensated for the defeat of Sékou Sanago (Ivory Coast), who had been *apparenté* to it in the later years of the outgoing legislature. In Guinea BARRY DIAWADOU, formerly RS, fought the election at the head of a BAG list styled '*de tendance IOM*', on which Mamba Sano took second place. It was therefore he and not Sano who secured the one seat which did not fall to the PDG-RDA. But in the new Assembly he joined Edgar Faure's wing of the Radicals, now known as *Rassemblement des Gauches Républicaines* (RGR).[2] The Gaullists made up for this defection by winning a seat in Upper Volta which went to **GÉRARD KANGO OUÉDRAOGO**, a Mossi aristocrat but an opponent of Conombo and the Moro Naba. Michel Dorange, who had made RPF the party of radicalism among the Mossi,[3] took second place on the list. Its 120,000 votes (against 272,000 for Conombo, 103,000 for Nazi Boni and 75,000 for the RDA) were not enough to win it more than one seat, but showed that the former Union Voltaïque leaders were rapidly losing ground among the Mossi, as well as having lost the west.

[1] In fact neither Molinatti nor Plantier was the official RS candidate in the election. Both ran as independents. (*Afrique Nouvelle*, January 1956.)

[2] Faure and his supporters were expelled from the Radical Party by the Mendèsist majority after the dissolution of Parliament in December 1955. The RGR was originally the name of the combined Radical-UDSR groups in the Council of the Republic and the Assembly of the French Union, and of the combined lists in elections. Now it became a separate Radical right-wing splinter-party. (Williams, pp. 176–8.)

[3] See above, p. 173.

## The Results in Africa

The SFIO dropped from five Afrique Noire deputies to four. SISSOKO and **Hammadoun Dicko** held two seats out of four in the Soudan, but this time the third as well as the fourth went to the RDA.[1] **Liurette**, former Socialist deputy for Guinea, did not run for re-election. Barry III, who did run as a Socialist in Guinea after refusing a place on the RDA ticket, was easily defeated.[2]

NININE (Northern Cameroun) was re-elected, although closely pressed by **Ahmadou Ahidjo**, a Moslem with aristocratic connections who was a member of the BDC (pro-Aujoulat) group in ATCAM and sat in the Assembly of the French Union. Aujoulat himself was overwhelmingly defeated in central Cameroun by MBIDA, who was supported by the 'Socialist' Soppo Priso–although opposed by the 'Socialist' Okala–and joined the Socialist group in the new National Assembly. Since Mbida and most of his supporters were fervent Catholics, while the SFIO was an openly anti-clerical party, this choice of group was gleefully publicised by Aujoulat's supporters.[3]

Finally, the two African deputies who had belonged to Conservative groups in the old Assembly–APITHY ('Independent Republican', Dahomey) and BOGANDA '(Independent Peasant' Oubangui-Chari) – were both re-elected, and both joined the new united Conservative group (*Indépendants et Paysans d'Action Sociale* –IPAS).

Nine seats changed hands as a result of these elections in Afrique Noire, and the RDA completely turned the tables on the IOM and Socialists in AOF. Yet the campaign, voting and announcement of results all took place in comparative calm, except in one territory: Moyen-Congo.

---

[1] The former Socialist deputy Jean Silvandre split off from Sissoko's PSP and ran at the head of a separate list, which won only 16,000 votes. (Sissoko's list had 158,000 and the RDA 213,000.)

[2] The votes in Guinea were distributed as follows:
PDG-RDA (Touré): 339,176
BAG-IOM (Diawadou): 147,107
DSG-SFIO (Barry III): 55,193.
It is worth noting that Diawadou's total vote is only 600 lower than when he defeated Touré in the 1954 by-election. Yet Touré's is up by over 250,000 and Barry III's by nearly 50,000. This shows how successful the administration had been in keeping unwanted voters away from the polls in 1954.

[3] See *Le Cameroun de Demain*, February 1956.

## B. The Rise of Fulbert Youlou

Tchicaya had never succeeded in extending his personal influence much beyond the Vili tribe who lived round the territorial capital, Pointe Noire. Up to now his chief rival had been the Socialist Jacques Opangault, whose supporters were Mbochi living in the north of the territory and in Poto-Poto, a suburb of Brazzaville. Tchicaya was more active in the affairs of the interterritorial RDA than in representing the local interests of Moyen-Congo. No doubt resentment of this fact, and the last-minute disappointment about the abolition of the double college in AEF, helped to exasperate the voters and stimulate desire for a change. But the essential political divisions were tribal. Tchicaya had only escaped a challenge from the Brazzaville population for so long because of the uncompromisingly anti-political attitude of its most numerous and most enterprising ethnic group, the ba-Lari (ba-Kongo), who refused to vote for anyone but their dead Messiah, André Matsoua. This situation was changed almost by accident in 1955 when **Fulbert Youlou,** a little-known parish priest who fancied himself as an intellectual, wrote a brief life of Matsoua in the form of a panegyrical tract. Suddenly–and no one knows quite why–Youlou was accepted by the majority of the ba-Lari as Matsoua's heir. He decided to cash in on this by standing for deputy. At once the mutual jealousy between the ba-Lari and other tribes was transformed into intense political hostility. Forseeing the likely results, Youlou's bishop forbade him to stand, and, when he ignored this, forebade the faithful to vote for him. In vain: Youlou stood. The ba-Lari whipped themselves into a fury of political enthusiasm, and on election day they joined forces with the Mbochi in physical attacks both on the ba-Téké (an ethnic minority in Brazzaville which supported Tchicaya) and on those of their own fellow-tribesmen who stuck to an 'orthodox' Matsouanism and refused to vote for Youlou. At least one person was killed and 46 injured.

In the circumstances, the result of the poll could hardly have been more unfortunate: Tchicaya had 46,000 votes, Opangault 43,000 and Youlou 41,000. Both the Mbochi and the ba-Lari at once demanded a new election, and sent a joint complaint to Paris alleging electoral malpractices. Youlou was sent to protest in person, his fare being paid by public subscription. His failure to get the election annulled did not damage his popularity. Nor did his rapidly acquired reputation for dubious financial practices. Provided by his doting supporters with a car, chauffeur and monthly stipend to keep him in full-time politics, he soon became the Adam Clayton Powell of Equatorial Africa.[1]

## C. The Results in France

In France the 1956 election brought a swing back to the Left. This resulted more from the weird workings of the electoral system than from a preference clearly expressed by the electorate. In terms of votes the Gaullists lost heavily and the MRP slightly. The supporters of **Pierre Poujade,** an extreme right-wing agitator, won 13 per cent of the votes, those of Mendès-France 10 per cent, and the Conservatives increased their share. But the main effect of Poujade's success was to give the Communists 52 extra seats and the Conservatives 40 fewer! The Socialists, who lost eight seats, nonetheless found themselves back in power, for they held the balance of the new majority. The left-centre coalition (Socialists, Radicals, UDSR) was revived without the MRP and with the addition of a few left-wing Gaullists. Guy Mollet, the Socialist leader, became prime minister.[2]

This result was a defeat for the outgoing government of Edgar Faure, and a victory for the 'Republican Front' led by Mendès-France, Mitterrand, Mollet and the left-wing Gaullist **Jacques Chaban-Delmas.** As in Africa, so in France, the IOM were on the losing and the RDA on the winning side. Senghor had fought the election as a member of Faure's government, and partly on its record. (He claimed that it had paid more attention to overseas affairs than any previous one, and even attributed this to the prime minister's personal initiative.)[3] After the election the IOM no longer had the minimum of 14 deputies necessary for an independent group. They were therefore obliged to affiliate formally with the MRP, alongside which they went into semi-opposition. Meanwhile the RDA became a party of government. Houphouët was appointed a *Ministre-délégué* in the prime minister's office,[4] and Mamadou Konaté spent the last months of his life as a vice-president of the National Assembly.[5] One of the new Assembly's first laws 27th)

[1] See Thompson and Adloff, *Emerging States* . . . (op. cit.).
[2] Williams, pp. 48–9 and Appendices III and IVb.
[3] *Afrique Nouvelle*, December 1955.
[4] But Mollet did not forget the Africans in his own party; he gave an Under-Secretaryship to Hammadoun Dicko.
[5] After his death he was replaced by Modibo Keita, who also replaced him as the leader of the Soudan RDA.

March 1956) was an amnesty for all RDA supporters who were still in prison and/or deprived of their political rights.[1]

Paradoxically, the RDA's participation in a left-wing government reinforced its movement to the Right, whereas the IOM's involvement in the fall of a right-wing government pushed it further to the Left. Since the Bobo-Dioulasso Congress the IOM had taken the lead in agitating for political and constitutional reform, while Houphouët devoted his speeches mainly to the themes of economic development and the 'Franco-African-Community'. This reversal of rôles became particularly noticeable during the election campaign. Several IOM leaders tried to strengthen their precarious position by means of fiery denunciations of colonialism and demands for autonomy and a federal constitution, while RDA leaders were anxious to demonstrate their respectability in order to protect their supporters from renewed maltreatment by the administration.[2] Then, after the election, the RDA became directly associated with French policy in Africa, owing to Houphouët's presence in the cabinet. Eventually this situation was to create an intolerable strain within the RDA, as its more radical members began to challenge Houphouët's position and leadership. But these tensions did not come into the open until the summer of 1957, after local executive councils had come into existence in Africa. Until then, the RDA territorial leaders were glad to shelter under Houphouët's umbrella while consolidating their local positions. Meanwhile the IOM benefited from the freedom of opposition and adopted a critical attitude to the government's policy.

[1] Morgenthau, pp. 109–10.
[2] Ibid., p. 108 (where, however, the author hints that the RDA leaders' speeches in vernacular languages were less moderate than those in French. Certainly I have heard this said about both Sékou Touré and Modibo Keita at later dates).

# Chapter 16

# The Loi-Cadre

## A. Gaston Defferre

In Mollet's cabinet, as in the abortive Pineau cabinet of the previous year, the Minister of France d'Outre-Mer was Gaston Defferre. He was the first Socialist to hold this office since Moutet. This fact was not in itself particularly important. What was important was that he had positive ideas on colonial policy, and above all that the new Assembly, unlike the old one, was prepared to accept large-scale and swift colonial reform. Defferre was appalled by the bloodshed in Algeria, convinced that it could have been avoided if a more enlightened policy had been applied in time, and determined to avoid a similar catastrophe in Afrique Noire. He may have seen already that independence was the manifest destiny of the African territories. If so, he must also have seen that this destiny could and should be realised without war or even bitterness between France and the Africans, and without real damage to France's interests. At the same time, there were several reasons why the word '*indépendance*' could not at this stage be pronounced. In the first place, most sections of French public opinion were not ready for it. In the second place some African politicians–and mostly notably Houphouët himself–were actually hostile to it. And thirdly it would be difficult to promise independence explicitly without naming a date, and so giving encouragement to those Africans who would inevitably want to go too far and too fast, thereby undermining the position of the moderate, pro-French leaders who were now in power.

Short of independence, Defferre believed it was essential to undertake some large measure of reform which would convince Africans of France's benevolent and democratic intentions, and thus dissuade them from taking up arms against French rule. His first action, on taking office at the beginning of February 1956, was to ask the officials in the Rue Oudinot to suggest such a reform. Their first reply was a project for the abolition of the double college and the introduction of universal suffrage. But Defferre and his advisers

233

realised that this reform, the final goal of the old assimilation policy, was now too long overdue to produce the desired effect. The 'mystique of equality' was already being replaced by the 'mystique of independence'. At very least the T.O.M. must now be given a status equivalent to that which Togo had been granted the year before.

The chief difficulty for Defferre was that he wanted both to do something important and to do it quickly. Up till then colonial reforms of any importance (such as the Labour Code and the Municipal Reform Bill) had only passed after long years of debate. The Togo Statute was an exception, but this had been possible only because of the sense of urgency created by what was happening on the British side and because Togo was formally outside the Republic, and therefore its constitutional development could not be held to damage the Republic's indivisibility. Defferre had a strong sense of urgency about the colonial problem in general, and he was able to communicate it to an Assembly which had been elected to take firm decisions about Algeria, and which had made up its mind for the time being to accept leadership from the Left. This sense of urgency enabled the Assembly to turn a blind eye to the constitutional problems involved in what Defferre proposed, and so permitted him to disguise a measure which was essentially political and even constitutional (or rather *un*-constitutional, as the Constitution stood) as a purely administrative reform.

## B. The Constitutional Problem

Mollet's government took office on 1st February. On the 29th of the same month Defferre deposited his bill with the National Assembly. As might be expected, the text was extremely brief. It had been drafted by **Gaston Espinasse**,[1] a thirty-two-year-old Socialist whom Defferre had recruited into his *cabinet* from the secretariat of the Assembly of the French Union. It was the product of consultation with the permanent officials in the Rue Oudinot, and also with the African deputies – especially of course with Houphouët, whose signature is to be found beneath the final text of the law alongside those of

[1] I was told this by M. Fernand Wibaux, who was Defferre's *chef de cabinet*, and later French ambassador in Mali. He put me in touch with M. Epinasse himself, and between them they kindly supplied me with most of the details which I reproduce here about Defferre's motives and the difficulties which he encountered. (A minister's *cabinet* in France is the private office of personal assistants which he brings with him into his department.)

**Coty** (President of the Republic), Mollet, Mitterrand (Minister of Justice) and Defferre himself. It took the form of a *loi-cadre*-a 'framework law'-enabling the government to take action by decree. By this means Defferre intended to avoid seeing his policy immobilised by endless parliamentary wrangling over details, as had happened to previous colonial reforms.

The preamble of the bill announced that 'in order to associate the overseas poulations more closely with the management of their own interests, measures of administrative decentralisation and deconcentration will be introduced within the framework of the territories, groups of territories, and central services, controlled by the Ministry of France d'Outre-Mer.' By this formula the bill was disguised as the result of the plans for decentralisation which Buron had begun and which had been further eleborated by Teitgen during 1955. But the disguise was transparent, for the contents of the bill were apparently inspired partly by the report which Senghor had submitted to Faure in July 1955, tending to the revision of Title VIII of the Constitution. Defferre knew that such revision was being considered, and would go on being considered. He was not prepared to wait for the result before embarking on his reforms. Some deputies objected to this attitude. Defferre sidestepped their objection by adding a face-saving phrase to his preamble: 'Without prejudice to the expected reform of Title VIII of the Constitution . . .' He did not explain how such reform could fail to be prejudiced by a measure which set up councils of government, at least partly elective, in the different overseas territories, and thus endowed the territories with a political personality which once given could hardly be taken back. Nor did he explain how the measure could be reconciled with Articles 74 and 75 of the Constitution as it stood. Article 74 said:

The status and internal organisation of each overseas territory or of each group of territories are determined by the law, after consultation with the Assembly of the French Union and of the territorial Assemblies.

And Article 75:

The respective statuses of the members of the Republic and of the French Union are liable to evolve.

    Statutory amendments and the passage from one category to another . . . can only be brought about by a law voted by Parliament, following consultation of the territorial Assemblies and of the Assembly of the French Union.

In short, whether Defferre was trying to 'determine' the status and internal organisation of the T.O.M., or whether he was treating it as already determined (although formally it never had been) and trying to amend it, he was constitutionally obliged to consult the Territorial Assemblies. This his timetable did not permit. Also, the use of the word 'each' in the Constitution presumably meant that there should be a separate law for each territory or group of territories, whereas Defferre was proposing a blanket law followed by a series of decrees. These decrees were admittedly subject to parliamentary approval, but they did not have to be formally passed like laws; either chamber could be assumed to have adopted the government's text if it failed to give an opinion within a time limit.

Fortunately, however, France had no court competent to pronounce laws unconstitutional, and if Parliament chose to ignore constitutional difficulties this merely provided fodder for learned articles in juridical reviews. In this instance it did so choose (and such articles in due course appeared).[1]

## C. Balkanisation

The government was allowed until 1st March 1957 to produce its decrees.[2] The decentralisation which these were to introduce was of two main sorts: on the one hand a devolution of administrative services from the federal Governments-General of AOF and AEF to the governments of the individual territories, and on the other a devolution of legislative power from the Paris parliament to elected African authorities. The latter was the more controversial of the two, and was to some extent pushed through under cover of the former. At a casual reading the text gives the impression that the powers acquired by the Territorial Assemblies are purely regulatory, i.e. concern the application of law rather than the making of it. But the borderline is hard to draw, and a clause not included in the original text, but resulting from a private member's amendment artfully inspired by Defferre's *cabinet*, empowered them to '*reprendre les dispositions législatives existantes*'. This harmless-sounding phrase could be interpreted as giving them *carte blanche* to adopt, revise

[1] See, among others, the article by A. Coret, already cited, in *Révue Juridique et Politique de l'Union Française*, 3, 1958, pp. 452–94.
[2] Clause 7. For the text of the law, and the decrees that followed it, see 'Réformes outre-Mer, Loi No. 56–619 du 23 juin 1956 et décrêts d'application. (Ed. mise au jour au 11 sept. 1957)', Paris 1957.

and reject, according to their fancy, all French law relating to the matters within their competence.

The list of these matters was to be considerably lengthened, for the Territorial Assemblies were henceforth to be entitled to deliberate on many topics which had hitherto been the preserve of the federal Great Councils. The government was empowered to 'modify the rôle and powers of the Governments-General in order to transform them into organs of co-ordination. . . .' I.e. there would no longer be a federal authority at Dakar or Brazzaville, but merely a meeting-point for co-operation between the different territorial governments, and a channel of communication between them and Paris. All government services overseas were divided into *services d'état*, which were the responsibility of the French Republic as a whole, and administered by the territorial Governors on instructions from Paris, and *services territoriaux*, paid for out of the territorial budgets, and therefore subject to the territorial assemblies which voted those budgets. Each territory was to have its own executive council, whose composition was not yet specified. Probably it was intended that it should be partly nominated by the governor, partly elected by the assembly–on the model of the Togo Statute, and of the programme which Senghor had been propounding since 1953.

Where the law departed from Senghor's ideas was in proposing to dismantle the federal Governments-General, and to install executive councils in the individual territories rather than at the level of the federal group.[1] The motives for this decision have been much discussed. Clearly it fits in with the general, decentralising, purpose of the bill. But some of its effects ran counter to this: many of the services hitherto administered from Dakar and Brazzaville were now classified as *services d'état*, and therefore would–in theory, at least–be run directly from Paris, because either by nature or by expense they were too big to be taken on by the individual territories. A more genuine decentralisation would have been achieved if elected or partly-elected executives had been set up at both the group and the territorial levels. Defferre rejected this solution as unnecessarily cumbersome and expensive. The choice therefore lay between two executives and twelve. Two would have been cheaper, but would have given fewer Africans the chance to participate directly in

[1] What Senghor had suggested in 1955 was that AOF should be divided into two groups of territories, each with its own executive. This interesting proposal seems to have been forgotten, or dropped. (See André Blanchet, *L'Itinéraire des partis africains depuis Bamako*, Paris 1958.)

democratic government, and would not have satisfied the many Africans for whom Dakar and Brazzaville were scarcely less remote than Paris.

Among those pressing for Defferre's ear, **Paul Chauvet,** High Commissioner in AEF, was in favour of a federal executive at Brazzaville, whereas his colleague Bernard Cornut-Gentille of AOF was against having one at Dakar.[1] But none was more insistently 'territorialist' than Houphouët, who thought first and foremost as an inhabitant of the Ivory Coast. For him, Senghor's desire to maintain the federal structure of AOF was an intolerable example of Senegalese arrogance. For half a century the Ivory Coast had endured the spectacle of Senegalese political and cultural superiority. Yet because of the *ristournes* system,[2] its own, more recently acquired, economic superiority had served only to make it a 'milch cow' for the poorer territories of AOF. To Houphouët, as to most Ivoiriens, the AOF federation was simply a particularly unpleasant example of over-centralised French colonial rule. An AOF federal executive would be neither truly African nor truly democratic. Only a territorial executive would enable Africans to feel that they were governing themselves. Such was Houphouët's view, and probably his advice did more than anyone else's to make up Defferre's mind. He was after all the leader of the largest African party, and Defferre's main purpose was to meet African aspirations at least half way. It would have been peculiarly embarrassing for him if Houphouët had resigned from the cabinet in protest against his decision.

Another virtue of the 'territorial' solution, from the French point of view, was that it avoided giving the Africans everything at once. The territorial executives could cut their teeth on the less important services, while the more important ones, classified as *services d'état*, were kept fully under French control, at least for the time being. A federal executive might or might not come later–if the Africans wanted it.

Senghor attacked this policy as an attempt to 'balkanise' Africa, viz. to keep the embryonic African states weak by keeping them small and divided, and therefore dependent on France. 'During the parliamentary debates . . . M. Senghor was the only person who pointed out publicly that the division of AEF and especially of AOF, a massive bloc whose political weight was embarrassing, into enfeebled Territories more or less hostile to each other, was not without

[1] 'Africanus', *L'Afrique noire devant l'indépendance* (Paris 1958).
[2] See above, pp. 103–4.

an ulterior motive among certain members of the Government and of Parliament, who disliked any implied possibility of independence.'[1]

Personally I am reluctant to believe that this motive really influenced the policy of either Defferre himself or any of his close collaborators. Two of them to whom I have spoken both assured me that they regarded the subsequent 'balkanisation' of West Africa as disastrous, particularly from the economic point of view. They pointed out that events have since shown that individual territories are if anything more likely than large federations to demand independence, since their governments almost inevitably try to outbid each other politically in order not to lose face with their subjects. (This is true, but would not necessarily have been foreseen in 1956.) One also suggested that in fact a single federal government would have been weaker and easier to resist than eight territorial ones, if only because it would have been less unified and less securely in control of its subjects. Even if AOF had become independent as a federation, would its subsequent history have been any happier than that of Nigeria? In short, the federal solution was economically desirable, from both the French and the African points of view, but politically it was impossible for France to impose it on Africans who did not want it, any more than Britain had been able to in Central Africa, or any more than the French West Africans who did want it were able to impose it on those who didn't in 1958 and 1959.

As arguments against having executives only at Dakar and Brazzaville, without anything in the individual territories, these are convincing enough. If Defferre had attempted that solution, he would certainly have met with more, not less, African opposition. Perhaps he was wrong not to set up federal and territorial executives at once. If the RDA as well as the IOM had insisted on it, perhaps he would have. But Houphouët was against it, and the other RDA leaders did not want to rock the boat at this stage. They preferred to concentrate for the time being on demanding that the territorial executive councils be made fully elective and given real executive powers. Although as early as March 1956 Senghor put down a bill calling for federal councils of government at Dakar and Brazzaville, and though this demand was echoed by the Great Council of AOF on 28th June[2] (five days after the Loi-Cadre was promulgated), it was not until a year later, when the territorial executives had already

[1] 'Africanus' op. cit. This work is a vigorously critical account of the Loi-Cadre, published anonymously by a senior French administrator in AEF.
[2] *Paris-Dakar*, 29th June 1956.

been set up, that agitation for a federal executive developed within the RDA.

Besides the political and administrative measures, a further series of decrees was envisaged which would tend to raise the standard of living in the T.O.M. and to favour their economic development. These were less controversial than those affecting the political status of the territories, and did not require parliamentary approval. They actually came into force as early as November 1956.[1]

The second chapter of the Loi-Cadre dealt with Togo and Cameroun. Togo was promised a new status, closer to full autonomy, which was to replace UN trusteeship, and which would be submitted to the population by referendum (thus satisfying the requirements of both Grunitzky and the UN General Assembly). For Cameroun there was a more vague indication of 'institutional reforms', including a division into provinces, each of which was to have its provincial assembly and council. The powers and composition of these bodies were not specified.

Finally, besides being a framework for decrees to come, the Loi-Cadre itself introduced universal suffrage and the single college for all future elections overseas.[2] Tabled in the National Assembly on 29th February, it had the approval of the Assembly of the French Union on 13th March, had its first reading in the National Assembly on 22nd March, passed the Council of the Republic (with minor amendments) on 12th June, finally passed the National Assembly on 20th June, and became the Law of 23rd June 1956, generally known as the Loi-Cadre Defferre, or simply the Loi-Cadre.

[1] Decrees 56–1131 to 56–1145 (13th November 1956).
[2] Titre III, clauses 10 and 12.

# Chapter 17

## New Statutes for Togo and Cameroun

### A. The Second Togo Statute and the Grunitzky Government

Once again it was the Togolese timetable that was forcing the pace. Already on 9th May 1956 the plebiscite was held in British Togoland. The population was asked to pronounce itself for or against uniting with the Gold Coast in the independent state of Ghana, which was to come into being the following year. In the south, where the Ewe were in the majority, 55,000 voted *no* and only 44,000 *yes*. But the British had persuaded the UN to treat the territory as a single unit, so that the Ewe's views were easily smothered by the overwhelming pro-Ghana majority in the north. British Togoland as a whole was declared to have said *yes*.[1]

Defferre and Grunitzky lost no time in preparing an equally satisfying conclusion to French Trusteeship. A new statute for French Togo was drafted in Paris, and submitted to the Territorial Assembly in Lomé. Under it Togo was to be an 'autonomous territory'. This did not satisfy the Assembly, which insisted on changing the name to 'autonomous republic'. Otherwise it accepted with only minor amendments the form of limited autonomy which was offered, but was careful to keep the door open for further constitutional evolution in the near future. The French also gave a promise that Togo would remain eligible for FIDES credits. On these conditions the Territorial Assembly unanimously accepted the Statute (14th August), and it came into force by a decree of the French Council of Ministers dated 24th August. On 30th August the Autonomous Republic of Togo was formally proclaimed, and on 10th September Grunitzky became its first prime minister. On the 18th his government was invested by the Assembly which had elected him. Parliamentary democracy had made its début in Afrique Noire. On the same day the new Republic acquired a national flag.[2]

[1] See H. Didier, 'Les plébiscites togolais' in *Nouvelle Revue française d'Outre-Mer*, December 1956.

[2] Cornevin, *Le Togo, nation pilote* (op. cit.).

It remained only to ratify these proceedings by a referendum, which was held on 28th October. Since the choice was between acceptance of the new Statute and retention of the old Trusteeship, the issue could not be seriously in doubt. The CUT urged its followers to abstain. In Lomé and one or two other southern areas a majority of voters did so, but only 35·3 per cent over the south as a whole, and in the north the poll was nearly 88 per cent. Of those who did vote, 94 per cent voted *yes*. Jubilantly the French and Togolese governments made a joint report to the UN, asking it to end Trusteeship. But unlike that in British Togoland, the referendum had been carried out without UN supervision. The General Assembly decided to send a final fact-finding mission to Togo before it recognised Grunitzky's demand as representing the wishes of the Togolese people. This mission arrived in June 1957.[1]

## B. The Cameroun Statute and the Mbida Government

### 'National Union'

Defferre knew that Cameroun would present him with problems far more difficult than those of Togo. Governor Pré himself admitted that the banning of the UPC had left a dangerous 'political vacuum' in Cameroun.[2] He had been sent out in 1954 to try and reach an understanding with the UPC, but by now he was identified with a repressive policy towards it. In April 1956 he was recalled. The UPC at once claimed this as a victory.[3]

In his place Defferre sent out **Pierre Messmer,** the director of his *cabinet*. Messmer had been Governor of the Ivory Coast from 1954 to 1956 and had a good record of co-operation with the RDA. He hoped at first that the same policy would succeed with the UPC. The repression was relaxed, and there was talk of a general amnesty. In June, Soppo Priso formed a 'National Union' which demanded such an amnesty and a reversal of the ban on the UPC. He rejected the Loi-Cadre in advance, and insisted that France accept the principle of complete independence. At the same time he condemned the use of violence for political ends. Clearly he hoped to win back the UPC militants to legal political activity. Messmer encouraged him, and at first it looked as if he was succeeding. The 'Upécistes'

---

[1] Ansprenger, p. 214.    [2] *Afrique Nouvelle*, 19th July 1955.
[3] Typed report in Aujoulat papers.

joined the National Union *en masse*, and two of the main legal parties of southern Cameroun also affiliated to it: the BDC (Aujoulat's supporters) and the USC (the Socialists led by Charles Okala).

But Mbida, who had hitherto been Soppo Priso's ally, now performed his second volte-face in two years. He declared himself opposed to the amnesty and denounced the National Union as a tool of the UPC. Formerly he himself had angled for UPC support by denouncing Pré's repressive policy. Now he called for more effective repression and declared himself the only true friend of France.[1]

The UPC was in fact profiting from Messmer's tolerance to organise its troops in the Bassa country of Sanaga-Maritime (the homeland of Um Nyobé). It also infiltrated the National Union and accumulated votes within it by affiliating all its various front and satellite organisations. In protest against this technique both USC and BDC left the Union after its first congress, in August 1956.[2]

Meanwhile Defferre and his advisers worked on the text of a Cameroun Statute, similar to the one they had just given to Togo. As in Togo, so in Cameroun they intended to consult the elected representatives of the population. The existing ATCAM, elected more than four years before, no longer had sufficient moral authority for so important a deliberation. Defferre therefore ordered new territorial elections, to be held on 23rd December.

This caused a further split in the National Union. Soppo Priso had originally insisted that new elections must be preceded by an amnesty. The UPC wanted to stick to this programme, and therefore called for a boycott, unless the amnesty were granted and the ban on the UPC itself lifted. Soppo Priso now argued that it was better to fight the elections and then use the new Assembly as a platform from which to reiterate these demands. No agreement was reached on this point, and in November the National Union broke up. Soppo Priso sponsored a list of candidates entitled *Action Nationale*. His main ally was **Charles Assalé**, a Boulou leader from Ebolowa in the Ntem region (on the border of Gabon – the Boulou are related to the Gabonese Fang). Assalé had worked with Um Nyobé in the early days of the Cameroun CGT (USCC). Like Bakary Djibo of Niger he had been nominated by the CGT to the French Economic Council in 1947. But when the CGT split he followed the Socialists into FO,[3] and subsequently he became a Socialist member of ATCAM.

---

[1] Ibid. (notably in the open letter to Mbida already quoted).
[2] Ansprenger, p. 202, quoting the USC paper *L'Union*, 22nd October 1956.
[3] Ansprenger, p. 488. For FO, see above, p. 180.

*Elections and Rebellion*

Before the general election came municipal elections in the three full communes which the Municipal Reform Act had created in Cameroun–Douala, Yaoundé and Nkongsamba (capital of the Moungo region). They were held on 18th November, exactly a year after the Act was passed. The low poll in Douala and Yaoundé (12 per cent and 39 per cent respectively, as against 74 per cent in Nkongsamba, a much smaller town) showed the strength of the UPC among the urban workers. But the general election on 23rd December showed that outside the towns only Sanaga-Maritime was really under UPC control. There the poll was 12 per cent and in Wouri (the constituency which included Douala itself ) 21 per cent. But elsewhere it was relatively high, between 50 per cent and 70 per cent.[1]

Only Um Nyobé's fellow-tribesmen, the Bassa, responded massively to his instructions. They did so not merely by abstaining, but also by starting a large-scale terrorist campaign which Messmer's over-trustful policy had given them plenty of time to prepare. On the night of 18th–19th December telephone lines were cut, bridges destroyed, railway lines torn up and houses burnt. Soon there were murders as well. Most conspicuous was the assassination of two moderate nationalist candidates on the day of the election. One of them, **Dr Delangué,** was killed near Um Nyobé's home village, Boumnyebel. He was a man known and respected throughout Southern Cameroun for his professional competence, his saintliness, and his nationalist views. He had never taken any direct part in politics before. Such men were feared and hated by the UPC leaders. If nationalism made progress by legal and peaceful means, the UPC's own influence was bound to decline, whereas violent repression tended to win it sympathisers and adherents. This was what now happened. The government, taken unawares, reacted violently. The whole area between Douala and Yaoundé was filled with troops, mostly paratroopers. Hundreds of Africans were shot on sight, many of them probably innocent and many more who had joined the rebellion only out of fear. The total number of rebels cannot have been more than three thousand, and was probably far less. Most of them were armed only with machetes or hunting-rifles (though a few may have had sub-machineguns). But the government's brutality was of far more value to them than their own weapons.

[1] Ansprenger, p. 205.

244

For many Camerounians the new Assembly was discredited in advance.[1]

As for the Assembly itself, its composition accentuated Cameroun's regional divisons. It was dominated by two groups: Mbida's (Christian) Democratic party–the *démocrates camerounais*, all of whom came from the central tribes (mainly Eton and Ewondo)–and the *Union Camerounaise* of Ahmadou Ahidjo, whose 38 assemblymen included all the representatives of the north and east. Ahidjo himself was the son-in-law of one of the most powerful Moslem rulers, the Lamido of Garoua.[2] He had failed to defeat Ninine in the National Assembly election, but now had Ninine's support and was the accepted leader of all the north. Very few northerners had had any French education, and hitherto the Catholicised coastal regions of Cameroun had had almost a monopoly of modern political activity. Now, by sheer weight of population, the north was going to make itself felt. With those of the thinly populated east and south-east, its representatives made up half the Assembly; and since they were united in a single group, they could hold the balance between the mutually hostile factions of the south-west. Of these Mbida's supporters were the largest group; when the Assembly met they numbered twenty (including, but not for long, Okala's Socialists). The *Groupe d'Action Nationale Camerounaise* (GANC), led by Soppo Priso and Assalé, had only eight members, all of whom came from the regions nearest the coast.[3]

### Birth of a State

In the new year (1957) the Assembly started work. After electing Ahidjo as its president, it at once turned its attention to the new Statute proposed by the French government. The discussion lasted till the end of February. Mbida supported the French draft. Soppo Priso opposed it, insisting that Cameroun be recognised as a fully sovereign state. Ahidjo's supporters adopted a half-way position, and produced an alternative draft, much shorter than the French one. They demanded complete internal autonomy and a transitional period before independence. The final result was a compromise between Ahidjo and Mbida. Some sixty small amendments were made to the French draft, extending the powers of the future

---

[1] *Témoignage Chretien*, 1st February 1957.  [2] Ansprenger, p. 488.
[3] Ibid., pp. 204–6.

Cameroun government and replacing the title 'Territory' with 'State under Trusteeship'.[1] In this form the Statute was accepted by all except Soppo Priso's Group of Eight. It became law by decree of the French government on 16th April 1957.

Cameroun thus acquired a constitution, under which the French High Commissioner remained responsible for its defence, and for its relations both with France and with foreign countries. He also had to choose the prime minister, but the latter then had to be invested by the Assembly. There was a Cameroun citizenship, distinct from that of France (and later in the year there was a flag, a national anthem and a motto). On 9th May the Assembly took the title of *Assemblée Législative du Cameroun* (ALCAM). On the following day–which was to become the national feast-day–Mbida was invested as prime minister. Proudly proclaiming the achievement of *une indépendance à trois quarts*,[2] he proceeded to nominate a cabinet in which Ahidjo was deputy prime minister and minister of the Interior.[3] (The presidency of the Assembly passed to the Bamiléké chief **Daniel Kémajou,** who had his own grouplet of 'Independent Peasants'. The Group of Eight remained in opposition.) In June the Statute was formally inaugurated. Cameroun was now a State, under Trusteeship but outside the French Union[4] (although, like Togo, it continued to be represented in the French parliament).

The UPC, still illegal and unappeased, continued its terrorist activity in the maquis.

[1] Mveng, *Histoire du Cameroun*, op. cit. Ansprenger, p. 206.
[2] Mveng, ibid.      [3] Ansprenger, ibid.
[4] *L'Histoire du Cameroun de la préhistoire au 1er janvier 1960* (Yaoundé 1961).

## Chapter 18

# New Names and New Attitudes,
# February 1956 to January 1957

While the decrees applying the Loi-Cadre to Togo and Cameroun were discussed with the local assemblies of those territories, those applying it to AOF and AEF had to run the gauntlet of the French parliament. At precisely the same time–the end of January and beginning of February 1957–when the Cameroun Statute was being thrashed out in Yaoundé, the Palais Bourbon in Paris was the scene of heated debates between French and African deputies about the form and degree of autonomy which should be conceded to those overseas territories that were constitutionally still part of the 'one and indivisible' Republic. In these debates several of the most prominent African deputies were speaking for the first time under new party labels. A series of dramatic political realignments was beginning, which was to bewilder inattentive observers of the Franco-African scene throughout the next three years.

### A. The Trades Unions

The first phase in this kaleidoscopic process was a general disengagement of African political and parapolitical organisations from their French counterparts, whether left- or right-wing. In the trade union movement it had begun in 1955 (see p. 224). During 1956 and 1957 it gathered momentum. On 15th February 1956, Sékou Touré and others were expelled from the AOF section of the CGT for refusing to accept control from Paris. Encouraged by High Commissioner Cornut-Gentille, who was anxious to weaken Communist influence in AOF, Touré proceeded to organise the *Confédération Générale des Travailleurs Africains* (CGTA), which soon seduced from their allegiance about half the former members of the West African CGT, as well as some from FO. In July the Catholic trade unionists followed suit: the West African CFTC at its congress in Ouagadougou became the CATC–*Confédération Africaine des Travailleurs Croyants*. The substitution of the word *Croyants* (believing) for *Chrétiens* was intended to be significant. The African organisation was to be open to believers of all religions, not reserved for Christians. Its leaders claimed that spirituality was a common African heritage, something that went deeper than the formality of adhering to a religion imported from Europe. Six months later (6th January 1957) a parallel organisation was created in AEF.

The logical next step was for the different African trades unions, having broken their 'vertical' links with France, to establish 'horizontal' ones with each other. For this purpose a Conference was held at Cotonou in Dahomey from 16th to 19th January 1957. Representatives came from the CGTA, the CATC, the various unaffiliated unions, and also from the 'orthodox' CGT, whose African leaders had now been authorised to disaffiliate themselves from the Communist-controlled World Federation of Trade Unions in order to preserve African neutrality in the Cold War. The West African CGT was thus able to break its links with the French CGT, and so to end the disagreement between itself and the CGTA. But its leaders, especially **Abdoulaye Diallo** (founder and leader of the Soudan section), brought their Communist sympathies and terminology with them into the new organisation, the *Union Générale des Travailleurs de l'Afrique Noire* (UGTAN). The CATC leaders took offence at this, and seceded from the new movement within a few months of its creation. The dominant figure at the Cotonou Conference, and subsequently in UGTAN, was Sékou Touré.[1] The Conference's resolution reflected his political views, which now seemed to be closer to those of Senghor than to those of Houphouët. It denounced the Loi-Cadre as 'a mystification, a façade that deceives no one' – and particularly its 'balkanising' aspect, which the UGTAN leaders feared would 'result in the break-up of the workers' unity'.[2]

## B. The IOM in Opposition

The attempt to realise African unity was not confined to the trades unions. Once again it was preoccupying the parliamentary politicians. This time the intiative came from Senghor, who was anxious to make up the loss which his prestige had suffered from the IOM's election

[1] Ansprenger, pp. 222–5.
[2] Quoted in 'Les élus des TOM et la Loi-cadre' (*Présence Africaine*, nos. 17–18, 1958, pp. 122 sq.).

defeat, and to find allies who like himself had a genuine popular following in their own territories rather than being administrative puppets. The disappearance from the parliamentary scene of such IOM deputies as Zodi Ikhia and Mamba Sano, who had been obstacles in the RDA's path to power, should have facilitated a *rapprochement* between the RDA and the remaining hard core of the IOM. Immediately after the election Manadou Dia visited Houphouët in Abidjan to sound out the prospects. But Houphouët was unwilling to abandon the UDSR, which the election result had just put him in virtual control of, and which gave him such excellent hopes of ministerial office; and the IOM were not prepared simply to join the RDA-UDSR (as it was now called). They therefore decided to stay with the MRP, voting for Mollet's cabinet in the first instance, but reserving their attitude for the future.[1]

Their reserves about the Mollet government grew stronger as the year 1956 progressed, mainly because its North African policy proved considerably less liberal than had been hoped. In February, Mollet visited Algiers and allowed himself to be intimidated out of any attempt to impose a liberal settlement in Algeria by a mob of European *sans-culottes* hurling rotten tomatoes. In May, Mendès-France left the government in quiet disappointment. In October it took responsibility for the hijacking of the FLN[2] leaders' aeroplane between Rabat and Tunis (both now capitals of independent states), and in November it attacked Egypt. None of this was likely to dispel African misgivings about France's general attitude, and the IOM, no longer a party of government, felt no obligation to conceal these misgivings. While the RDA voted confidence in Mollet's North African policy on 5th June, the IOM abstained.[3] They abstained again in the vote on the Suez expedition on 31st October. On both occasions they were at variance with their nominal allies, the MRP (but in agreement with Mendès-France). The only important vote during 1956 in which all the IOM deputies supported the government was the passage of the Loi-Cadre itself.[4] They did so not with wholehearted enthusiasm—for Senghor had already attacked the law both for the threat of balkanisation which it implied and for not going far enough in the direction of African autonomy—but because they considered even this reform better than none.

---

[1] Ansprenger, pp. 270–1.
[2] *Front de Libération Nationale*, the Algerian independence movement.
[3] Guillemin, 'Les élus d'Afrique noire . . .' (op. cit.).
[4] Williams, Appendix IVb, p. 501.

## C. The Bloc Populaire Sénégalais

Disappointed for the time being of his hopes of union with the RDA, Senghor worked to broaden his base in other directions. In May the eighth annual congress of the BDS issued a call to 'all local organisations which had freed themselves from dependence on the metropole' to join together in a united front, and instructed the party leadership to prepare a regroupment conference for this purpose.[1] This appeal was aimed principally at Lamine-Guèye; it meant that he had only to break with the SFIO for the BDS to be prepared to submerge its name and organisation in a new movement where he would naturally find a place of honour. At first it seemed that he might well accept. On 13th June the Senegalese SFIO agreed in principle to unite with the BDS and the two rival Senegal sections of the RDA (UDS and MPS).[2] But at the last minute both Houphouët and Lamine-Guèye (the latter under pressure from the French SFIO) forbade their followers to go on.[3] A few young radicals in both parties disobeyed orders, and joined Senghor, but for the time being both SFIO and MPS retained their separate identity. Only the UDS and one regional party, the *Mouvement Autonome du Casamance* (hitherto allied with the SFIO), agreed to merge with the BDS in a new party, the *Bloc Populaire Sénégalais* (BPS).

At first sight it may seem surprising that the UDS, a small band of intellectuals and trade unionists who had followed d'Arboussier's rigid pro-Communist line in and after 1950, should now choose to join Senghor's motley following of Moslem traditionalists, illiterate peasants and wheeling-dealing politicoes. If loyalty to the PCF had overcome loyalty to Houphouët in 1950 and after, why on earth should it succumb to the wiles of Senghor now?

In the first place, the PCF's influence in Africa had shrunk considerably during the last few years, partly owing to the decline of its hopes of seizing power in France, partly as a result of the French CGT's undignified attempts, first to check the rise of Sékou Touré within the CGT, then to prevent its members from joining him in the CGTA.[4] About this time Moscow seems to have abandoned both PCF and CGT as means of penetration in Africa and begun instead to hedge its bets, giving encouragement to groups which favoured African independence and non-alignment rather than to

---

[1] *Paris-Dakar*, 22nd May 1956.  [2] *Condition Humaine*, 19th June 1956.
[3] Morgenthau, p. 160. Ansprenger, p. 171.
[4] Morgenthau, pp. 159 and 229.

ones that were overtly pro-Communist.[1] From this point the pro-d'Arboussier splinter-groups of the RDA lost most of their *raison d'être*. D'Arboussier himself did an unostentatious volte-face and made his peace with Houphouët. The UDS regarded this as a betrayal and refused to follow him.[2] It was not prepared to fall into line behind the MPS, which had been set up as a result of its exclusion from the RDA in 1955–especially since support of Houphouët would now entail support of the Mollet government.

In the second place, the BDS had undergone an important change since the National Assembly elections. Not only was it now more or less in opposition to the French government and therefore receptive to left-wing ideas: it was actually producing such ideas itself. For it had been joined by a group of young Marxist intellectuals, mostly students returned from Paris, who had hitherto held aloof from all political parties. Most prominent of these 'Young Turks' was the historian **Abdoulaye Ly,** who at the May Congress was elected propaganda and organisation secretary of the BDS–an election secured by Dia and Senghor against rumblings of opposition from conservative elements both inside and outside the party.[3] Senghor was wise enough to see that men like Ly would be valuable as a ginger-group and brain-box within the party–which owing to its mainly rural base suffered precisely from a lack of educated cadres–and that their presence would increase its appeal to the younger generation and its plausibility as a nucleus for African unity, whereas their nuisance value if they remained in opposition might well be considerable.

The UDS leaders therefore decided to make common cause with the Young Turks inside the BDS rather than remain in splendid but fruitless isolation or crawl back to Houphouët. So they joined the BPS (whose Founding Congress was held in February 1957).

## D. Writers, Artists and Students

While intellectuals were taking the lead in Senegalese politics, it was appropriate that Senegalese initiative should be making its mark in the intellectual world. The first Congress of Negro Writers and Artists was held in Paris from 19th to 22nd September 1956. It was the culmination of long years of effort by *Présence Africaine* and its founder editor Alioune Diop (see above, p. 135), and it was dominated by Senegalese writers. Both American negroes and English-speaking

---

[1] Ansprenger, pp. 82 and 223–4.    [2] Morgenthau, p. 159.    [3] Ibid., p. 158.

Africans listened with some puzzlement to Diop's attacks on assimilation. The American **Richard Wright** doubted if it were possible for men like himself to go back to an African culture from which their ancestors had been torn three centuries before, while few other Africans had experienced the degree of assimilation to European culture that was common among French-African *évolués* and particularly among the Senegalese. None the less the Congress constituted the boldest and most convincing assertion of an indigenous African culture that had yet been made; and the speakers showed themselves ready to reject not only cultural but political and social domination by European systems. For example, one Senegalese speaker protested against the imposition of French law on traditional Senegalese society.[1] Although the Congress produced no demand for political independence as such, the social and cultural attitudes which were expressed clearly pointed in that direction.

Certainly the subject was not taboo in these Parisian intellectual circles, as it was in Parliament and tended to be in Africa itself. As early as 1952 a *Présence Africaine* publication, 'Les étudiants noirs parlent', had included an article in which **Majhemout Diop** had called for immediate, unequivocal and absolute independence. His views were not necessarily shared by all his fellow-students, but they lived and talked in an atmosphere far more radical than that of party congresses and Territorial Assemblies. It was from this atmosphere that university graduates like Abdoulaye Ly and Majhemout Diop himself were now returning to pull the centre of gravity of Senegalese politics further left. Senghor later remarked that 'our students return from Paris Communist, from Moscow anti-Communist'. In fact few Africans if any were actually Communist Party members – it was not Communist policy that they should be. But many African students in France came to combine Marxist economic arguments for independence with anti-assimilationist cultural ones. These left-wing students were usually the most active in the African students' union – the *Fédération des Etudiants d'Afrique Noire en France* (FEANF). This organisation held its seventh annual congress at the end of December 1956, and passed a resolution which demanded a 'struggle for the *total independence* of the peoples of Black Africa'.[2]

## E. 'Cartierism'

While the idea of independence was still only openly canvassed by

[1] M. Crowder, *Senegal* (op. cit), pp. 58–9.
[2] *Présence Africaine*, December 1956–January 1957.

the boldest of left-wing Africans, it was already acquiring a certain popularity among right-wing Frenchmen. The official reaction to the loss of Indo-China was '*Lâchons l'Asie, gardons l'Afrique*'. But many of those to whom empire was primarily a business proposition began to feel a general disillusionment with the whole enterprise. It seemed ridiculous for France to console herself for being thrown out of the richest part of her empire by pouring more and more money into the least profitable–namely Afrique Noire. There was a resurgence of that economic anti-imperalism which had been the creed of a substantial minority of French politicians at the time the empire was built–the hard-headed anti-romantics who had answered Jules Ferry's turgid breast-beating and ex-post-facto economic sophistry by asking when, if ever, the nation would get its money back.[1]

In August and September 1956 the illustrated magazine *Paris-Match* published a series of three articles whose author, **Raymond Cartier,** pointed the contrast between the desperate natural poverty of France's African possessions and the enormous sums of French taxpayers' money which were being spent on them through FIDES; between the prosperity of Holland, which had lost its empire, and the economic difficulties of France, who was trying to keep hers by an expensive mixture of force and bribery. This attitude became known as '*le Cartiérisme*'. It was perhaps best summed up by a French observer at the Congress of Bamako (in September 1957– see below) who was overheard remarking, after a discussion of economic and social programmes for Africa, 'I demand independence for France'.[2]

Of course it was far from welcome to African politicians, most of whom were determined that French public investment in Africa should continue, whatever other forms of French activity they were anxious to stop. But at the same time it did a good deal to deflate the emotional importance which right-wing circles had hitherto attached to empire as such, and thereby to make possible a more dispassionate discussion of the pros and cons of independence from both French and African points of view.

### F. Municipal Elections

By the autumn of 1956 even the French Socialists realised that there was no future in Africa for French political parties. In October an

[1] See Henri Brunschwig, *Mythes et réalités de l'imperialisme colonial français 1871–1914*, Paris 1960.
[2] A. Blanchet, *L'Itinéraire des partis africains* . . . (op. cit.).

SFIO study group in Paris sanctioned Lamine-Guèye's decision to break the links between the French party and its Senegalese section, and to create an autonomous African Socialist movement. He was thus able to fight the municipal elections of 18th November with a free hand. Senghor, who hoped at last to gain control of the municipality of Dakar, had secured a provision that these elections should be held in the old as well as the new communes. But this stratagem failed. The BPS gained only 16 out of 37 seats on the Dakar town council, and Lamine-Guèye remained safely wrapped in his mayoral scarf.[1]

Elsewhere in Afrique Noire, where these elections were the first local ones to be held in single college and with universal suffrage, they confirmed the strength of the RDA. Modibo Keïta (since Konaté's death the leader of the US-RDA) became the first elected mayor of Bamako, Houphouët of Abidjan, Sékou Touré of Conakry, Lisette of Fort-Lamy. Two local parties recently affiliated to the RDA were also successful: the *Bloc Démocratique Gabonais* (BDG) whose leader Léon Mba became mayor of Libreville, and the *Union Démocratique Dahoméenne* (UDD) which captured Cotonou, the largest town in Dahomey–although Apithy's PRD (*Parti Républicain du Dahomey*) remained securely in control of the territorial capital, Porto Novo.

One veteran RDA leader, Félix-Tchicaya, suffered a humiliating defeat. Even in his home town, Pointe Noire, he was overwhelmed by a coalition of his two main opponents: Opangault's Socialists and Youlou's six-month-old *Union Démocratique de Défense des Intérêts Africains* (UDDIA). Since neither of these groups had an absolute majority on the new town council, they compromised by electing as mayor a former supporter of Tchicaya's who was now Independent and coyly promised his favour to both sides: the Vili station-master **Stéphane Tchitchellé**. He soon succeeded in replacing his former leader as the charismatic leader of the ba-Vili.[2] Meanwhile Youlou became mayor of Brazzaville with a landslide majority–only less conclusive than that of his fellow-priest[3] Boganda in Bangui, where MESAN won 32 out of 37 seats.

But perhaps the most interesting result was in Niamey, capital of Niger. Here Djibo Bakary was elected to the town council with ten

[1] Ansprenger, pp. 242–3.
[2] Ibid., p. 190 and Thompson and Adloff, *Emerging States* . . . (op. cit.)
[3] Although unfrocked (above p. 164) Boganda continued to be known as 'L'abbé'.

other members of his party. Thirteen seats went to the orthodox RDA of Hamani Diori and four to a list headed by Prince Djermakoye, who called himself a Socialist.[1] Like the UDS in Senegal, Djibo's party was isolated by the break-up of the CGT (he had sided with the 'orthodox' CGT against Sékou Touré) and the reconciliation between Houphouët and d'Arboussier; and like the UDS, Djibo now made surprising but useful friends: he suddenly made an alliance with Djermakoye and joined the SFIO, thus securing a majority in the town council and his own election as mayor.

## G. The Mouvement Socialiste Africain

So it came about that a pro-Communist trade unionist arrived, with the style and dignity of Mayor of Niamey, at the founding congress of the *Mouvement Socialiste Africain* (MSA), which met in Conakry on 11th January 1957. Although the purpose of this meeting was to break African links with the French SFIO, it none the less had the French SFIO's blessing, and was attended by its acting General Secretary. With the exception of Djibo, the delegates were long-established leaders of the SFIO's African branches: Lamine-Guèye of Senegal, Sissoko of the Soudan, Opangault of Moyen-Congo, Okala of Cameroun, and the host of the congress, Barry III of Guinea. What they had most conspicuously in common was failure. Only Sissoko was still a deputy, only Lamine-Guèye was a mayor, and both of these were veteran leaders who had now lost control of their territories to the new-style mass parties (BPS and US-RDA respectively). Djibo, by contrast, was an up-and-coming politician– 35 years old–who brought with him the smell of success. His talents as an organiser outweighed his dubious ideological credentials, and he was promptly elected to a deputy general secretaryship in the new movement. (Lamine-Guèye was President, Barry III General Secretary.)

Otherwise the new MSA was very much the old SFIO writ small, and its chief function seemed to consist in backing up the Mollet government. It underwrote the Loi-Cadre, refrained from calling explicitly for African autonomy, proclaimed its disapproval of one-

[1] In 1955 Djermakoye and the other chiefs had broken with Zodi Ikhia, left UNIS, and joined Georges Condat in a new party, the *Bloc Nigerian d'Action* (BNA). Djermakoye took second place on Condat's list in the National Assembly election of 2nd January 1956. Condat was UDSR-RDA in the National Assembly, but Djermakoye was Socialist in the Assembly of the French Union.

party states, accepted representation within the French delegation at the Socialist International, and exchanged three *ex officio* seats on its steering committee with the corresponding organ of the French SFIO.[1] But it did call for a 'free association between metropolitan France and the overseas territories', implying at least a theoretical right to opt for total independence;[2] and it was after all a sign of the times that a group which had so little natural inclination for independence should now feel that to make itself formally independent of its French parent was nothing less than a political necessity.

## H. The Convention Africaine

While Lamine-Guèye and his friends were founding the MSA in Conakry, Senghor and *his* friends were founding the *Convention Africaine* in Dakar. Here too the newest thing about the new party was its name. Its member-parties were precisely the same ones that had belonged to the old IOM, minus the UDD of Dahomey and PSEMA of Upper Volta, both of which had gone over to the RDA. It was, however, a specifically African party, not merely an 'overseas' one as the IOM had been, and it produced a policy statement bolder and clearer than any that either RDA or MSA (both partly muzzled by participation in the French government) had yet committed themselves to. In it Senghor's 'federalist' ideas—in the sense of demanding a Federal French Republic—were combined with 'federalism' in the other sense, soon to be the more important, of defending the AOF and AEF federations against balkanisation. It demanded autonomy for all territories, but 'within the framework of the two federations', which in due course would become two 'states' within the Federal Republic. This Republic in its turn would belong to a 'confederal union of free and equal peoples', to which Cameroun and Togo should belong as independent states (a significant item in a programme to which Aujoulat's and Grunitzky's parties subscribed). In Algeria there should be a ceasefire as soon as possible, followed by negotiations with 'the authentic representatives of the Algerian people'. Suggested goal of these negotiations: 'internal autonomy with the right to independence, in the framework of a Maghreb freely associated to France by confederal links'. Since the other two countries of the Maghreb (Morocco and Tunisia) had become fully sovereign independent states in March 1956, this

[1] Ansprenger, pp. 158–9.  [2] Témoignage Chrétien, 1st February 1957.

proposal would in practice have meant independence for Algeria in all but name, if not in name as well, and was therefore fairly radical.

But the main purpose of the Convention Africaine was to prepare the ground for a wider union of all African parties. Senghor hoped that various unaffiliated local leaders, such as Youlou and Boganda, would join it. In this he was disappointed, although Youlou and Barry Diawadou both sent observers to the Congress, and Gérard Ouédraogo of Upper Volta attended it in person. Ouezzin Coulibaly and Doudou Guèye came as observers from the RDA, but gave only cautious encouragement to the idea of a single African party. Coulibaly invited the new movement to send representatives to the congress which the RDA planned to hold at Bamako. But the date of this was as yet unspecified. First, in March, would come new territorial elections, in which the RDA expected to sweep the board. After that it could enter on any merger-negotiations from a position of strength.[1]

[1] Ibid. and Ansprenger pp. 174–5.

# Chapter 19

## *'La Bombe Apithy'—the Debate on the Loi-Cadre Decrees*

So there was no union of African parties in January 1957. But there was effective co-operation between African deputies in the National Assembly. During the debates on the government decrees taken under the Loi-Cadre, which began on 29th January, Apithy and Senghor mounted a joint attack on the government, and were supported by the RDA. In several divisions the only Africans voting for the government were Diawadou, the Socialists, and Houphouët (who as a minister was obliged to do so but instructed his followers to vote against him).

The main issues were the powers of the Territorial Assemblies and the composition of the new Councils of Government. Africans expected that the T.O.M. would be given a degree of autonomy comparable to that which Togo now had and Cameroun would soon have. Instead, the government produced texts which would have given each territory a status similar to that of Togo under its *previous* Statute, that of 1955. The Council of Government was to be presided over by the colonial Governor, partly nominated by him, and not responsible to the Territorial Assembly. The matters falling within the territorial government's competence were far fewer than in Togo or Cameroun. Those organised federally at the level of the Group (AOF and AEF) were reduced to a minimum. All the most important services were classed as *services d'état*, to be run directly from Paris. How far all this represented Defferre's own policy is not certain. On Algerian policy his views were considerably more liberal than those of most of his colleagues, and it may be that in Black Africa too he was unable to persuade them to go as far as he would have liked. The government included not only some remarkably illiberal Socialists and Radicals, but also some Gaullists. This meant that any government-sponsored text on African policy was bound to be a compromise; it had to give some satisfaction to Bayrou and Malbrant as well as to Houphouët. Probably Defferre was not sorry to see some amendments passed, even though in the name of the government he opposed them.

The campaign against the government text began in Dakar. On 12th December 1956 the Great Council of AOF rejected the federal budget in order to register a protest against the approaching diminution of its powers.[1] It also unanimously passed a motion of protest against the government's failure to consult either it or the Territorial Assemblies during the drafting of the decrees. In this it was supported by six of the eight Territorial Assemblies in AOF.[2]

The next stage was the discussion of the decrees in the T.O.M. Commission. Apithy proposed to amend them so as to give the Territories a real internal autonomy. Each was to have a prime minister elected by the Territorial Assembly. He would then nominate the other members of the Council of Government, which would be collectively responsible to the Assembly. At the same time a number of important matters, such as higher education, radio, police, criminal and administrative justice, labour inspection, and customs, should be classed as *services territoriaux*, and not (as the government proposed) as *services d'état*; also it should be the territorial, not the metropolitan government which had residual powers.[3]

Now at last Apithy's membership of the Conservative group (IPAS) was seen to pay off. Although his proposals were more radical than those of the Communists, he was supported by the chief Conservative spokesman on colonial affairs, **Michel Raingeard,** and the IPAS representatives on the Commission voted in favour of his draft report. So did the Communists, some of the Radicals, and Sékou Touré, who represented the RDA. It was thus carried against the votes of the Socialists and even of Gabriel Lisette (RDA) who was standing in for Hamani Diori;[4] and Apithy was able to present it to the National Assembly in the Commission's name on 29th January. It caused a considerable sensation, and **Max Jalade,** a friendly journalist, christened it 'the Apithy bomb'.

[1] *Paris-Dakar*, 13th December 1956.
[2] See Senghor's speech in the National Assembly, 29th January 1957.
[3] Ibid., Teitgen's speech.
[4] I owe these details to M. Apithy himself. As he put it to me, 'La Loi-Cadre a été ce qu'elle a été, et ceci grâce à ceux qu'on appelle les réactionnaires.' I have it on independent testimony that Apithy was by this time decidedly popular with his Conservative colleagues. If Pinay had succeeded in forming a government in October 1957, he would have been a minister.

'Politically', Apithy told the Assembly, 'it is impossible not to grant to the territories of Afrique Noire at least the status which is enjoyed by Togo, in virtue of the decree of 24th August 1956, and which has just been offered to Cameroun'. The majority in the Assembly thought differently. On the composition of the Councils of Government it went a long way to meet Apithy's views; although the Governor of each Territory was still to preside over its Council, all the remaining members were now to be elected by the Territorial Assembly on a single list, and the head of the list became 'Vice-President of the Council'. He would distribute portfolios among his colleagues, and could have them dismissed by the Governor. In fact he was prime minister in all but name. Each minister was bound to reply to any question or demand for explanation from a member of the Assembly relating to matters within his competence, and the Council as a whole had the 'faculty' of resigning, if it considered that it no longer enjoyed the Assembly's confidence.

But when it came to the *powers* of the Territorial Assemblies and Governments, the National Assembly refused to make any significant concessions. African deputies did succeed in restoring to the federal Governments-General of AOF and AEF a few of the powers which the government text had removed to Paris; but since there was no provisions for elected executives at the federal level – and African deputies were not agreed as to whether or not there should be – this was of more administrative than political significance. What the Assembly would not accept was the transfer of important powers from the list of *services d'état* to that of *services territoriaux*. It was unwilling to give individual territories responsibility for services which they could not afford to maintain, or which could obviously be better organised on an interterritorial scale. Thus, whether or not it was so intended, the decision to create governments at the Territorial and not at the federal level acted as a brake on the transfer of power from French to African hands.

Senghor complained bitterly of the fact that in several crucial votes nearly all the Africans voted on one side, and all the metropolitan groups except the Communists on the other. 'The statute that will emerge from our deliberations', he said, 'will not be a statute freely discussed between the mother-country and the overseas territories; it will be a charter graciously bestowed [*une charte octroyée*]. . . . We are no longer the outsize children that people like to think us, and that is why we are not interested in toys and lollipops (*joujoux et sucettes*).' Realising that there was no danger of the decrees being actually defeated, and Africa thus left without any political reform at all, the IOM decided to demonstrate its profound dissatisfaction by refusing to vote for them.[1]

---

[1] The IOM still existed as a parliamentary group, although dissolved as a 'movement'. The *Convention Africaine* did not form a separate group in the assembly until October 1957.

*Chapter 20*

# The Elections of March 1957

The decrees were formally put into force on 4th April. By that time Ghana had become an independent state (6th March), and the Treaty of Rome had been signed (25th March), creating a European Economic Community with which the French T.O.M., together with Cameroun and the Autonomous Republic of Togo (as well as the Belgian Congo, Ruanda-Urundi, Somalia and Dutch New Guinea) were associated. Annexed to the Treaty was an application convention, valid for five years, whose provisions included a development fund for overseas countries and territories, to which all Six members of the Community would contribute.[1]

On 31st March, French Africa elected the Territorial Assemblies which were to work the Loi-Cadre system. These were the first general elections to be held in single college and with universal suffrage. During April and May the new Assemblies elected the territorial Councils of Government, and African party leaders began for the first time to assume executive responsibilities for their own territories.

The RDA was the principal beneficiary of this process, for the results of these elections reversed those of March 1952 even more decisively than the 1956 National Assembly election had reversed that of 1951. The eight Territorial Assemblies in AOF included 474 members in all. Of these the RDA in April 1957 could claim 236, the MSA 62 and the *Convention Africaine* only 58 (of whom 47 were in Senegal). Of the unaffiliated parties the most successful in AOF were the *Union Progressiste Mauritanienne* (UPM), which won 33 out of 34 seats in Mauritania, and Apithy's PRD which won 35 out of 60 seats in Dahomey (although it had only 45 per cent of the votes: the constituency boundaries ran in its favour). In AEF the

---

[1] *Traité instituant la Communauté Economique Européenne et documents annexes* (Services des Publications des Communautés Européennes, 1963 edition), pp. 111, 213, 273, 278.

RDA was also the largest single party, with 54 out of 200 seats altogether, but in fact its strength was concentrated mainly in Tchad. Boganda's MESAN won all 50 seats in Oubangui-Chari, Youlou's UDDIA 21 out of 45 in Moyen-Congo. The *Convention Africaine* had 18 seats, all in Gabon, and the MSA 14, all in Moyen-Congo.[1]

To understand the pattern of territorial governments which now emerged, we must look at these results in slightly greater detail. In four territories the RDA had a clear majority in the Assembly, and therefore automatically controlled the Council of Government: Sékou TOURÉ became Vice-President in Guinea, and Gabriel LISETTE in Tchad, while Houphouët in the Ivory Coast and Modibo Keita in the Soudan preferred to leave this office to trusted lieutenants, respectively Auguste DENISE and Jean-Marie KONÉ. The RDA's victories in Guinea and the Soudan were particularly striking. In Guinea, where it had been virtually unrepresented until Touré's by-election victory of 1953, it now won all but four of the seats. In the Soudan it had had two out of 30 second-college seats in 1947, 13 out of 40 in 1952, and now it had 57 out of 70–while of the remaining thirteen, seven were won by a tribal party, which was in alliance with, and soon absorbed by, the US-RDA; this left only Sissoko's six Socialists in opposition.

These victories are important because they strengthened the position of radical leaders within the RDA–Sékou Touré and Modibo Keita–and made them less dependent on Houphouët's prestige. This was to be fully apparent at the party congress later in the year.

Lisette, who was Houphouët's loyal follower, also strengthened his position. His party, which had only four (out of 30 second-college) seats in the former Assembly, had 46 out of 65 in the new one. But he could not claim to be master of Tchad in the sense that Houphouët, Touré and Keïta were master of their respective territories. As a negro, he was resented by the Arabs; as an *évolué*, he was suspect to the chiefs; as an interterritorial RDA politician, he was disliked by some Equatorial Africans who saw the RDA as an instrument of West African domination; and as a West Indian, he remained a foreigner to Africans of all sorts. He won the election, not on a straight RDA ticket, but as head of a 'Republican Entente' which included UDIT, the party of Jean-Baptiste. The eleven UDIT members formed a separate group within the majority in the new

[1] Ansprenger, table 6.

Assembly. To safeguard his position, Lisette thought it wiser to form a coalition including both UDIT and his defeated opponents, the Gaullists (AST). In the Council of Government, Jean-Baptiste became Minister of Economic Planning, and **Djibrine Kherallah** (AST) Minister of Finance. There were also two European ministers who sat with the RDA group but called themselves UDSR. Despite the dramatic change of majority, the tone of the new Assembly was surprisingly similar to that of its predecessor which had been dominated by the Gaullists. Chiefs and Europeans remained influential, and the President was **Gontchomé Sahoulba,** a man who had already been elected a Senator by the old majority. No doubt Lisette feared an alliance against him by traditionalists inside and outside his party. If so, events were to prove him right. Meanwhile the only party unrepresented in his coalition was the MSA.[1] Its leader, Koulamallah, had refused to join the Republican Entente, and all his candidates had been beaten by it. But in his own constituency of Chari-Baguirmi the result had been very close, and the MSA disputed the Entente's victory. Koulamallah accused the RDA of rigging the election and appealed to the French Council of State to annul the results. If his application were successful, it would unseat seven RDA assemblymen, including the European Minister of the Interior.[2]

There were two other territories in which RDA leaders became heads of coalition governments (or, to be strictly accurate, Vice-Presidents of coalition Councils): Upper Volta and Gabon. In Upper Volta the *Parti Démocratique Unifié* (PDU-RDA) won 37 out of 70 seats. This party was the result of the slightly improbable fusion, arranged the year before, between the old RDA section of western Upper Volta and Conombo's traditionalist Mossi party (PSEMA). Within this alliance the western RDA emerged from the elections as much the stronger partner. Nazi Boni's group (MPEA-Convention Africaine), which had won all the western constituencies in 1952, now had only five seats, plus the support of two sympathetic independents; whereas Conombo's opponents in the Mossi area, the *Mouvement Démocratique Voltaïque* (MDV) of Michel Dorange and Gérard Ouédraogo, won 26 seats. Rather than rely on their tenuous overall majority the RDA leaders, who were much criticised, especially by left-wing students in Paris, for allying with the feudal

---

[1] Koulamallah had so renamed his party in 1955. But it remained affiliated to the French SFIO not to the West African MSA.
[2] Thompson and Adloff, *Emerging States* . . . , op. cit.

Mossi chiefs, decided to seek a coalition with the MDV. This was arranged at a meeting at Houphouët's home in Yamoussoukro (Ivory Coast). Ouëzzin COULIBALY, deputy for the Ivory Coast but himself a native of western Upper Volta, became Vice-President of the Council. But five of the other twelve ministers were MDV, including Dorange himself (Interior) and **Maurice Yaméogo** (Agriculture), a Catholic trade unionist who had formerly belonged to the *Union Voltaïque*.[1]

In Gabon the Assembly was divided between two rival Fang groups: the *Union Démocratique et Sociale du Gabon* (UDSG-*Convention Africaine*) of deputy Aubame, whose support came from the interior, and especially from the Woleu-Ntem region bordering on Cameroun, and the *Bloc Démocratique Gabonais* (BDG-RDA), whose leader Léon MBA was Mayor of Libreville and hero of the Fang who lived in and near that city.[2] Aubame won 16 seats in the Assembly, Mba and his allies exactly the same number. The last-minute support of five of the six Independents gave Mba the Vice-Presidency of the Council, but like Coulibaly he brought his opponents into the government rather than depend on a precarious majority; the UDSG got three portfolios.[3]

The least conclusive election was that in Moyen-Congo. This was the one territory in which the Socialists had effectively reorganised and increased their membership since the creation of the MSA. They also shrewdly included some ex-Gaullists on their lists, which probably gained them some votes from those for whom 'Ngol' was still a semi-divine hero. At all events, they won 14 seats out of 45, and were joined in the Assembly by six members from the Kouilou-Niari region (where Tchicaya had formerly been popular) and by the one surviving member of Tchicaya's party. This brought them exactly equal with the 21 supporters of Youlou, who was now in alliance with a number of European employers whose work force came from tribes other than the ba-Lari—a circumstance which did not improve inter-tribal relations.[4] The balance between the two groups was held by three Independents. One of them was Tchitchellé, Mayor of Pointe Noire, who was claimed as a member by both and committed himself to neither. The other two sided with the MSA and thus forced Youlou to accept a coalition government in which

[1] Gil Dugué, *Vers les Etats-Unis d'Afrique* (Dakar 1960).
[2] See above, p. 40.      [3] Thompson and Adloff, op. cit.
[4] See anonymous letter to Youlou, November 1957. (German translation in Ansprenger, pp. 470–1.)

OPANGAULT, the Socialist leader, was Vice-President of the Council, and himself only minister of Agriculture.[1]

## The Great Councils

Although the Great Councils of AOF and AEF suffered a relative decline in importance as a result of the Loi-Cadre, the RDA was nontheless anxious to gain control of them, if only for prestige reasons, and to be represented in them by its most effective spokesmen. For this reason it refrained from fighting the territorial election in Senegal (foreseeing the inevitable BPS victory which carried Mamadou DIA to the Vice-Presidency of the Council) and instead had Doudou Guèye elected to the Territorial Assembly of Guinea and the returned prodigal d'Arboussier to that of Niger (where Hamani Diori salvaged 19 out of 60 seats from the landslide victory of BAKARY DJIBO and the MSA). Both these leaders of the MPS (Senegal RDA) could thus be elected to represent their temporarily adopted territories in the Great Council at Dakar.[2]

These secondary elections were held on 15th May. The RDA won 19 of the 40 seats, the MSA and *Convention Africaine* five each. The RDA quickly made a deal with the middle group of unaffiliated Dahomeyans, Mauritanians and Voltaïques, by which it secured the election of Houphouët as President and d'Arboussier as first Vice-President (21st June).

In AEF the situation was less clear. The RDA could count on all five Great Councillors from Tchad and three of those from Gabon. MESAN had the five from Oubangui-Chari. From Moyen-Congo the MSA had three and UDDIA two. Then, in May, the RDA strengthened its position by a piece of brutal *realpolitik*; it made a pact with Youlou. UDDIA replaced Tchicaya's PPC as the Moyen-Congo section of the RDA. Sentimental considerations, such as that Tchicaya was a founder-member of the movement, were not allowed to outweigh the fact that Youlou and not he could now deliver the electoral goods. Youlou's adherence gave the RDA hopes of controlling another territory. It gave Youlou a foothold in interterritorial politics, and generally increased his prestige and respectability. Immediately after the pact was concluded, Tchitchellé, who had once belonged to the RDA as a member of the PPC, came off the fence and rejoined it by throwing in his lot with UDDIA.

The RDA group now controlled exactly half the Great Council.

[1] Ansprenger, p. 190.    [2] Ibid., p. 248n.

266

Against it was Boganda, who had imitated Houphouët in leaving the Vice-Presidency of the Council in his territory to a subordinate (**Abel** GOUMBA), and hoped to imitate him also by becoming President of the Great Council of his Group. The RDA could easily have defeated him if it had allied with the MSA, but the two groups were unable to agree on a candidate. Lisette thought it would be better if Boganda, like Youlou, could himself be brought into the RDA fold. Boganda appeared at first to be favourably disposed. A preliminary agreement was made by which Boganda became President and the RDA got the first and second Vice-Presidencies. Only later did Lisette realise that Boganda had no intention of joining the RDA, but was using the alliance as cover for an attempt to start a MESAN section in southern Tchad.[1]

### The Abidjan Wager

Just after the territorial elections, on 6th April, Kwame Nkrumah visited Houphouët in Abidjan.[2] It was a historic meeting between two men who spoke mutually intelligible African dialects: one the prime minister of a newly independent state, the other the leader of the majority party of French Black Africa, who was himself a minister in the government of France. They seemed to personify opposite solutions to a single African problem, and each was as sure as the other that his own solution was the better. Nkrumah believed that only African effort could develop the African economy and African civilisation. Houphouët believed that France and Africa could only develop in association with each other, in a 'Franco-African Community'.

'You are witnessing the start of two experiments . . .' Houphouët told his compatriots. 'A wager has been made between two territories, one having chosen independence, the other preferring the difficult road to the construction, with the metropole, of a community of men equal in rights and duties . . .'[3]

### End of the Mollet Government

For the French government, and especially for Defferre, it was highly gratifying to hear Houphouët speak in these terms and to

[1] Thompson and Adloff, op. cit.   [2] *Afrique Nouvelle*, 9th April 1957.
[3] Mitterrand, *Présence française et abandon* (op. cit.), pp. 215–16.

contemplate the election results.[1] Whatever its weaknesses the Loi-Cadre had achieved its main purpose, the avoidance of bloodshed. Children or not, Africans had accepted the 'toys and lollipops' which Defferre had offered them. Certainly they would call for further reforms, and no doubt further reforms would soon have to be undertaken, but there was nothing for either side to fight about. Moreover, the results seemed to vindicate France's general colonial policy since 1944. Five of the twelve new Vice-Presidents of Councils of Government and both the new Presidents of the Great Councils, were deputies with French parliamentary experience; and all the Councils of Government included European Frenchmen chosen by African leaders to help them in their new task of government.

Defferre was nothing like so satisfied with the policy his colleagues were pursuing in Algeria, where the war continued to spread and terrorism was now raging in the heart of civilian Algiers. On 21st May, Mollet's government was defeated on its tax policy. The Socialist-Radical coalition continued under the leadership of **Maurice Bourgès-Maunoury,** a Radical and a supporter of the 'tough' policy in Algeria. Houphouët became a full Minister of State, and Modibo Keïta an Under-Secretary.[2] But Defferre and Mitterrand refused to join; Mendès-France resigned the leadership of the Radical party, and both he and the Gaullists went into formal opposition. **Gérard Jaquet,** a Socialist close to Guy Mollet, who had previously had no special interest in overseas affairs, became Minister of France d'Outre-Mer.

### Reconciliation of Senghor and Lamine-Guèye

Meanwhile Senghor continued to hope that he could end his isolation among successful African leaders and realise the union of African parties. The RDA could not be approached until it had digested the fruits of victory. But there were signs that Lamine-Guèye was now ready to accept the subsidiary but still important position in Senegalese politics to which repeated election results had consigned him. (With twelve seats in the Territorial Assembly, he was just able to secure one in the AOF Great Council, and so to welcome the Councillors to Dakar as colleague as well as mayor.) When Houphouët was elected president of the Great Council, the MSA Councillors joined the *Convention Africaine* in abstaining. Then, on 29th June,

---

[1] See *Témoignage Chretien*, 5th July 1957.
[2] Hamani Diori replaced him as Vice-President of the National Assembly.

the two parties held a joint rally in Dakar at which Senghor and Lamine-Guèye appeared side by side and both called for a union of all African parties.[1] Since 1945, when the Mayor of Dakar had first presented the unknown schoolteacher to his electorate, the wheel of Senegalese politics had come full circle.

[1] Blanchet, *Itinéraire* . . . (op. cit.)

# Chapter 21

# The Congress of Bamako, September 1957

## A. Preparations

On its side, the RDA prepared to hold its first party congress since the one which, at Treichville in January 1949, d'Arboussier had held to a firmly pro-Communist line. The party had come a very long way since then. The idea that the French administration should try to crush it out of existence, as it had in Coste-Floret's time, now seemed almost inconceivably remote. The danger now was rather that its participation in government at both metropolitan and colonial levels might diminish its popularity with the African masses, as it already had with African students and intellectuals. Many African trade unionists, from Sékou Touré downwards, were now territorial ministers. But how long would they retain their followers' confidence now that, as the government, they had become the largest employer? It is a problem that faces all labour governments, and African labour leaders could not escape it.

Inevitably, other political leaders were jealous of the RDA's success. Equally inevitably, they cashed in on discontent which had hitherto worked in the RDA's favour. Those who had been obliged to climb on to its bandwagon were on the look-out for jumping-off points. Already during the summer of 1957 there were danger signals. In Upper Volta the government's supporters among the Mossi – Joseph Conombo, nominally within the RDA, and Gérard Ouédraogo outside it – began to draw nearer both to each other and to the opposition, led by Nazi Boni. In August these 'three musketeers' – as they became known – formed a separate group in the Territorial Assembly. 'Solidarité Voltaïque', on which Coulibaly's majority would from now on depend.[1] In Gabon too the coalition showed signs of disintegrating. And in the same month fighting broke out between Arabs and Fulani in the Chari-Baguirmi region of Tchad,

[1] Dugué, *Vers les Etats-Unis d'Afrique*, (op. cit.) Ansprenger, p. 182.

where Lisette was suspected of having rigged the election. Thirty-one people were killed and forty-one wounded. The incident helped to discredit Lisette's government, and to build up the prestige of his opponent Koulamallah, who used his religious authority as local head of the Tijaniyya to settle the dispute according to customary law.[1]

After several postponements the RDA Congress was fixed for 25th September at Bamako, where the movement had been founded nearly eleven years before. By the time it met it was clear what would be the chief point of disagreement between the delegates: the need for federal executives at Dakar and Brazzaville. Houphouët did not believe in it. He had said so often, and earlier in the year had even called for the suppression of the Great Council of AOF, along with what was left of the old Government-General. At first, while UGTAN echoed Senghor's warnings of 'balkanisation', the RDA political leaders, apart from Sékou Touré, had quietly accepted Houphouët's views. In January, Modibo Keïta had told the left-wing Catholic paper *Témoignage Chrétien* that he did not think a federal government at Dakar was necessary, 'for the existing bonds between the territorial political organisation are sufficient to stop the territories being exposed to isolation. Besides, the territories of AOF do not all feel the same degree of solidarity with Dakar.'[2]

But after the election, when the RDA controlled the Great Council, the tune began to change. Sékou Touré launched his 'federalist' offensive in July with a vote of the Guinea Territorial Assembly, demanding a federal executive at Dakar. At the end of August, he astonished everyone by securing a unanimous vote of the AOF Great Council to the same end. The new Great Council thus aligned itself on the policy of its predecessor, in which the *Convention Africaine* had had a majority. Various things were noticeable about this vote. First, the motion was proposed jointly by Touré and **Doudou Thiam,** a BPS-Convention Africaine Councillor from Senegal. Secondly, the MSA group decided to vote for it on the initiative of Bakary Djibo and his colleagues from Niger. Lamine-Guèye only reluctantly concurred. And thirdly, the RDA Councillors voted it in Houphouët's absence, in defiance of his known opinion. But those who were present and did vote included d'Arboussier, Doudou Guèye, and above all the Councillors from the Soudan.[3]

[1] Thompson and Adloff, *Emerging States* . . . , (op. cit.)
[2] *Témoignage Chrétien*, 1st February 1957.
[3] Andre Blanchet, *L'Itinéraire des partis africains depuis Bamako*, Paris 1958. This work is my main source for this and the following chapter, where no other source is given.

Modibo Keïta had completely changed his mind on this issue, and was now Touré's keenest ally.

It was Modibo Keïta's party, the US-RDA, which acted as host to the RDA Congress. Although the federal executive was not on the official agenda, everyone knew that it would in fact be discussed; and the US leaders provocatively prejudged the issue by including the slogan *'Exécutif fédéral'* among less controversial banners (*'liberté'*, *'égalité'*, *'fraternité'* etc.) which festooned the great dormitory of the Technical College where the Congress was to meet.

How strange, then, was Houphouët's situation when he rose, on 27th September, to deliver his 'moral report' to the party. In 1949, when he last appeared before the rank and file of his followers, he had been considered by many as France's leading opponent in Africa. Now he received red-carpet treatment from the French administrators in Bamako, was welcomed by a detachment of troops, lodged at the Governor's palace, and generally treated as one of the most important members of the French government, the living symbol of that 'Franco-African Community' which his speeches so frequently invoked. He addressed an assembly which included 254 delegates, from seven of the eight territories in AOF and three of the four in AEF. It included well-tried party stalwarts like Coulibaly and Lisette, up-and-coming radical leaders like Touré and Keïta, new allies from AEF like Mba and Youlou; and there, back in his place, was the old friend and enemy, d'Arboussier. It also included distinguished guests. Some of them were observers from other African parties: Lamine-Guèye for the MSA, Mamadou Dia for the *Convention Africaine*, Barry Diawadou for the BAG, Gérard Ouédraogo for the MDV. Others, like Houphouët himself, had come all the way from Paris: representatives, for example, of all France's leading political parties except the Poujadists and Communists (yet the latter had been the *only* party represented at the two previous RDA Congresses) and many of her leading newspapers. Mitterrand was there, and so were two former French prime ministers: Edgar Faure was to raise loud applause by preaching the Franco-African Community, Pierre Mendès-France even louder applause by denouncing the past war in Indo-China and the present one in Algeria.

### B. The Franco-African Community

Surely such an occasion should have been Houphouët's apotheosis.

With pardonable self-satisfaction he pointed out the results which his movement had so far obtained: on the one hand, equality of political and social rights between African and Frenchmen; on the other, democratic institutions functioning in Africa itself. The Franco-African Community was already a reality: all that remained was to crown it with a federal constitution. 'We can, with confidence, attempt this bold experiment, the only one of its kind in the world, in partnership with France. But we owe it to ourselves to repeat unceasingly and forcefully to our metropolitan brothers that the federation which we wish to bring about with them will be based on equality or not at all.' And he went on to proclaim the RDA's readiness to collaborate with all African parties, and its desire to encourage investment in order to raise the African standard of living.

During this speech, if not before, Houphouët must have realised that the Congress would not be his apotheosis after all. He aroused applause, but not enthusiasm. Not that the delegates were hostile to the idea of the Franco-African Community: on the contrary, the only speaker who dared to call it in question, and to suggest total independence, was a guest from the African students' organisation in Paris (FEANF).[1] He was listened to in cold but polite silence. Sékou Touré was as anxious as Houphouët himself to see the 'realisation and reinforcement of a democratic and fraternal Franco-African Community based on equality'– to quote the words which Touré inserted into the Congress's final political resolution.

But Touré and his friends were less enthusiastic about the idea of a 'federal government and federal Parliament' on whose inclusion Houphouët for his part insisted. They accepted this formula only at the price of a balancing assertion that *the independence of peoples is an inalienable right* [my italics] which allows them to dispose of the attributes of their sovereignty according to the interests of the mass of the population'. The federal government which they wanted to set up was not that of a putative federal French Republic, in which Africans would inevitably have a secondary rôle, if only for economic reasons, however much the principle of equality was proclaimed. What they wanted was an elected federal government at Dakar (and at Brazzaville) which would enable Africans to manage their own affairs.

[1] See Michael Crowder, 'Independence as a Goal in French West African Politics' in *French-Speaking Africa, the Search for Identity*, edited by William H. Lewis, New York 1965, p. 31.

## C. The Case for the Federal Executive: Democracy and Autonomy

As d'Arboussier, who had presided over the Great Council on the day of the surprise vote, explained: 'On the territorial level, for a budget of three, four or five thousand million francs, the executive is now run with the direct participation of those elected by the population, whereas the federal budget, amounting to 20 or 25 thousand million, is administered by civil servants, who are admittedly subject to control by the Great Council, but take their orders from the High Commissioner.' Or, in Touré's words: 'Our pride requires that we be allowed to choose democratically those who will be entrusted with the management of the common patrimony, instead of being obliged to accept the decisions of a High Commissioner, however human he may be. The executive exists: it must be democratised.'

The passage in Houphouët's report which was least well received by the majority of the delegates was therefore that in which he demanded 'that the intermediate organisms between the territories and the central federal power *be suppressed as soon as possible* and, on the other hand, that the personality and autonomy of the territories be every day more strongly asserted.' The majority of the delegates believed, and knew that the French government believed, that the territories on their own were economically too weak to take over the management of the most important services; and therefore that if the federal Governments-General were dismantled altogether and their functions divided between the territories and the 'central federal power' (i.e. the French government), the latter would inevitably get the lion's share—as the division into *Services d'état* and *Services territoriaux* already indicated.

It should be stressed that few of those who now demanded an elected federal executive wanted it to *replace* the territorial governments already set up (although some of them in the months that followed were to declare their willingness to see these governments suppressed if they could thereby secure a federal executive). Many of them in the years before 1956 had vigorously complained of the interference of Dakar or Brazzaville in the local affairs of their territories, and called for decentralisation. This decentralisation the Loi-Cadre had now given them. In that direction it had gone far enough, whereas in the direction of African autonomy it had not. In their view, there could only be full internal autonomy if and when African governments were set up at the federal level. As long as concessions were made only to individual territories–that is to units containing from one to four million people each–they would always be in the nature of 'toys and lollipops'. Grown-ups' business would go on being managed by France. Whether it was done by Frenchmen in Paris or Frenchmen in Dakar and Brazzaville was of no great importance.

Thus the cry for a federal executive was above all an autonomist one, only secondarily a federalist one. This point, at first sight paradoxical, is worth insisting on because it helps us to understand why Sékou Touré, who only a year later was to lead his territory alone into complete independence, should at Bamako have been the leader of the 'federalists'.

## D. The Case Against It

(i) *Paris not Dakar.* There were several reasons why Houphouët could not share the federalist point of view. In the first place, he was himself a member of the French government. So admittedly was Modibo Keïta, who was federalist. But Houphouët was now a senior and an influential minister, while Keïta was only an Under-Secretary. Houphouët was regarded by his colleagues as an *'interlocuteur valable'*, a politician able to speak for black Africans in general. Moreover, he had much more first-hand experience of the inner workings of French politics than either Keïta or Touré, more even by now than d'Arboussier. The prospect that the French government would continue to have an important say in African affairs was therefore less intolerable to him than to them, for he could see it as the government–in the future no doubt the federal government –of a Franco-African ensemble, a government in which Africans in their turn had their say. Sékou Touré wanted to be able to exert pressure on the French government–which for him remained essentially un-African–as a minister in a West African government at Dakar. Houphouët preferred to exert pressure from within, as a member of a political group in Paris.

(ii) *The bogey of 'secession'.* Houphouët's opponents suspected that this pressure was reciprocal. There were rumours–hotly denied by Houphouët's entourage–that prime minister Bourgès-Maunoury several times telephoned him from Paris during the Congress, adjuring him not to accept at any price the idea of an executive at Dakar. The last day of the Congress (30th September) was also, as it happened, the last of Bourgès-Maunoury's government. It was defeated on a new loi-cadre, designed for Algeria, which would have set up a federal executive at Algiers. The very fact that people like Sékou Touré wanted such an executive in order to secure greater autonomy made it seem to many Frenchmen and some Africans the first step to complete secession; and it is likely enough that Bourgès-Maunoury, harassed by the right wing both inside and outside his cabinet, was anxious to prevent his African colleagues from being identified with any proposal that smacked of disloyalty.

Telephone calls or no telephone calls, Houphouët at this time was certainly sincerely opposed to any form of secession or independence. But even stronger than his loyalty to France was his loyalty to the Ivory Coast, and this more than anything brought him into conflict with the idea of the federal executive. As Auguste Denise, Vice-President of the Ivory Coast Council of Government, later told the steering committee of the PDCI: 'The Ivory Coast delegation would have refused to allow Félix Houphouët to accept the presidency of the movement, if the discussions at Bamako had resulted in the creation at Dakar of a federal executive, a kind of super-council of government which would open the way to seccession.' At the Congress itself Denise bore the brunt of the hostility which respect had held in check while Houphouët himself was speaking. His statement, 'While we have not yet assimilated the Loi-Cadre, we are astonished already to hear demands for a federal executive', was greeted with howls of rage and disapproval.

(iii) *The economic interests of the Ivory Coast and Gabon.* The only delegation which sided with that of the Ivory Coast on this issue was that of Gabon, which consisted only of Léon Mba and two Europeans. There was a fairly close parallel between the situations of the two territories. Both were 'rich' territories as compared to the others in their group: the Ivory Coast produced 38 per cent of AOF's exports in 1956, Gabon more than half those of AEF in 1957, and both contributed a proportionately high share of the federal budget—i.e. a disproportionately high share in terms of their population, for the Ivory Coast contained only one seventh of the people in AOF, Gabon less than one tenth of those in AEF. Yet neither was to any important extent economically dependent on its neighbours. The Ivory Coast admittedly drew part of its labour force from Upper Volta, and did a certain amount of small-scale trade with Guinea and the Soudan. But its main exports, coffee and cocoa, went outside AOF, and a substantial proportion of them went outside the French Union altogether (bringing in 88 per cent of AOF's dollar earnings). This meant that it sold large quantities of these commodities at world prices (whereas, for example, the entire Senegalese groundnut crop was bought at a deliberately inflated price by France) and was therefore particularly sensitive to the internal price-increases, rising sometimes to 30 or 50 per cent, which resulted from federal taxation. As for Gabon, it had virtually no geographical or economic links with its neighbours at all; exports from the rest of AEF reached the sea not at Libreville or Port Gentil but by the Congo-Ocean railway from Brazzaville to Pointe Noire.

Both territories therefore had an obvious interest in the disappearance of the Governments-General and the federal budgets. At the same time it would have seemed ungracious merely to announce their unwillingness to continue subsidising their 'poor relations'. Accordingly in his speech Mba left aside the economic arguments and stressed the purely political ones against the federal executive.

As far as we are concerned, that is we Gabonese in particular, this Loi-Cadre has just brought us what we have been asking for for more than half a century: territorial autonomy. If we are to prepare a Franco-African Federation, in which France is to be one territory among those of the community, we must leap over the too narrow and too restrictive stage of the federal executives of Dakar and Brazzaville. ... If we had to sum up, in a striking phrase, our position on this question, we should say: the Loi-Cadre, the whole Loi-Cadre, and at least for the time being, *nothing but the Loi-Cadre.*

To the majority of delegates this speech seemed flagrantly dishonest. Not only was Mba trying to skate over the real–and in their view selfish–reasons for his choice; he had the face to use against the federal executive what was patently one of the best arguments in its favour, namely the necessity of creating a federal ensemble in which France would not be too overwhelmingly the biggest and most powerful partner. As Senghor was to put it a few days later: 'In the French Federal Republic it will be essential to maintain a certain balance; now, over against a metropolitan France with 44 million inhabitants, an AOF of 20 million and an Algeria of 10 million are already too weak.' How then was Gabon, with its 420,000, to expect France to become merely 'one territory among those of the community'?

### E. D'Arboussier's compromise

Like Denise, Mba was howled down by the Congress. Houphouët
was furious and retired in dudgeon to his quarters in the Governor's
palace on Koulouba Hill, some way outside the town. There he sat,
apparently sulking, for three days. The corridors of the Congress
hummed with rumour, speculation and intrigue. Would the movement split? Would Houphouët resign? (Apparently he offered to,
but none of his opponents was willing to stand for the succession.)
Neither side seemed prepared to give way. Emissaries went to and
fro, and eventually a face-saving compromise formula was worked
out by d'Arboussier, representing the federalists, and Lisette who
was loyal to Houphouët although his personal feelings may have
been mixed:[1]

Conscious of the indissoluble economic, political and cultural bonds
which unite the territories and anxious to preserve the destinies of
the African Community, the Congress instructs its elected representatives to put down a bill tending to democratise the existing federal
executive organs.

So read the political resolution as it was finally and unanimously
passed. The phrasing was deliberately ambiguous. The majority
accepted it with a bad grace, purely out of deference to Houphouët's
prestige and anxiety not to split the movement. Sékou Touré put it
bluntly enough at the closing session: 'Félix Houphouët-Boigny
remains our president, but in the government he will defend not his
own ideas, but those of the RDA.' It was an optimistic statement.
Houphouët had accepted d'Arboussier's formula only after two
days' negotiation, and certainly did not intend to let a federal
executive be imposed on him. Probably he was playing mainly for
time, and hoping that the storm would die down before anything was
done about it. In any case the Ivory Coast was in a strong position
since in the last resort it could simply refuse to pay any more federal
taxes.

---

[1] 'We have never been hostile to federalism,' he had declared shortly before
the congress' 'None of us has defended the stupid thesis that would involve
imagining that in the XXth century Africa can be made up of a multitude of
scattered states; a political federalism is necessary, but it must be rooted in
reality . . . For example, Niger and Dahomey will realise that they complement
each other, while the Ivory Coast and Upper Volta will reunite.' (*Témoignage
Chrétien*, 6th September 1957.) Lisette was of course aware that in Tchad there
was little enthusiasm for continued rule from far-off Brazzaville.

## F. Algeria

But there was no question that Houphouët's authority outside the Ivory Coast was badly damaged by the Congress. In the formal sessions his person had been respected. But many hard things were said about him in the corridors; many young RDA militants regarded him as excessively subservient to the government of which he was a member. Evidence of this was his attitude not only to the federal executive but also to the Algerian war–for he showed no sign of sharing their sympathy with the FLN. Indeed he was ready to summon the Algerian people explicitly to lay down their arms and join the Franco-African Community. Sékou Touré insisted that the resolution should call on the French government to 'negotiate with the authentic representatives of the Algerian people'. But probably if he and his supporters had been left to themselves they would have specified who, in their view, these representatives were.

## G. Regroupment

What of the union of African parties? The distinguished guests– Mamadou Dia, Gérard Ouëdraogo, Lamine-Guèye–all implored the RDA to come to terms with them in the higher interests of Africa. These appeals met with enthusiastic applause from the floor of the Congress, cautious approval from the RDA leaders. 'The Congress confirms the perpetual vocation of the RDA to unite all the living forces of the country, and notes with satisfaction the proposals for negotiations, with a view to regroupment, formulated by all the African political parties; it instructs its Co-ordination Committee to organise these negotiations.' It was none the less apparent that the RDA leaders thought of 'regroupment' principally in terms of integrating the other parties into the RDA, whereas Mamadou Dia, expressing the ideas of Senghor which on this point were shared by the other party leaders, made it clear that the Convention Africaine wanted not a *'parti unique'* but a *'parti unifié'*, i.e. a new party resulting from the fusion of all previous ones. French observers at the Congress were mostly sceptical about the prospects of unity in practice.

## H. The Leadership

Finally, the Congress elected a new Co-ordination Committee; Houphouët remained president. Of the four vice-presidents elected in 1949, Konaté was dead, Um Nyobé had been excluded from the movement in 1955, and Félix-Tchicaya had been virtually repudiated by the agreement with UDDIA; only Doudou Guèye was left. Alongside him the Congress now elected the three most successful territorial leaders: Keita, Touré and Lisette. The post of General Secretary, vacant since d'Arboussier's resignation in 1950, was suppressed. Instead, four secretaries were elected, of whom d'Arboussier was one. The other three were Ouëzzin Coulibaly, Hamani Diori, and **Justin Ahomadegbé** of Dahomey.

Chapter 22

# The Effort to Regroup.
# October 1957–April 1958

## A. The Aftermath of Bamako

The Congress of Bamako ended on 30th September. While Houphouët flew to Paris to play his part in five weeks of negotiation which
preceded the formation of a new French government, less exalted
delegates returned to their home territories. In Abidjan the second
Congress of the Conseil Fédéral de la Jeunesse de l'AOF met from
3rd to 5th October. The organisation shortened its name to *Conseil
de la Jeunesse d'Afrique*, denounced the Loi-Cadre for 'balkanisation'
and 'mystification', and declared that 'The only way to the total
liberation of the oppressed peoples of Africa is the struggle for
national independence'.[1] That this could happen in the city of which
Houphouët was mayor was a sharp reminder of the growing gap
between generations in African politics.

On the issue of the federal executive, it was soon apparent how
little the Bamako compromise was worth. Both sides hardened their
positions. On 3rd October, Houphouët told a journalist in Paris:
'After what happened at Bamako, where its delegation was not
treated with the courtesy accorded to the spokesmen of the other
territories, where the Vice-President of its Council of Government
was hooted at [*conspué*], the Ivory Coast is threatening to withdraw
from the Group of territories.' He also explained that in his view the
first step towards the 'democratisation of the existing federal executive organs' should be the appointment of a resident French minister
at Dakar (as prescribed by the still-born constitution of April
1946). Meanwhile in Gabon, Mba and Aubame temporarily set aside
their differences and joined together in proposing a motion which
the Territorial Assembly voted by acclamation, and which proclaimed 'its formal refusal to make over part of its hard-won rights
to an intermediate organism between the mother country and the

[1] Ansprenger, pp. 227–8.

281

territories . . .' 'If the will of the Assembly is disregarded', it continued, 'the latter is fully determined to take advantage of Gabon's geographical and economic position, which makes possible its direct integration into the French government.'

On his side Sékou Touré, back in Conakry, reaffirmed that in the view of his party, the PDG-RDA, the AOF Great Council should be transformed into a Federal Parliament, which would then elect an executive responsible for all the common services of the Group. The trial of strength between him and Houphouët had been only postponed and not averted. But in AEF there was no such crusading enthusiasm for a federal executive. It seemed that Gabon was less likely than the Ivory Coast to have to put its threats into action. Already in June the Vice-Presidents of the four territories of AEF had met at Brazzaville and had calmly discussed, under High Commissioner Chauvet's chairmanship, which of their economic and technical services could best be jointly administered. They decided to retain existing taxes for the time being, and in the future to consult one another regularly before submitting any fiscal change to their respective Territorial Assemblies.[1] A provisional agreement also divided export duties into those to be fixed by the Great Council and those to be fixed by the individual Territorial Assemblies. This set a pattern for development in AEF, where all the territorial leaders tended to prefer voluntary co-operation to the establishment of a federal government with coercive powers.[2] When the Great Council reassembled in October, President Boganda stated, in his reply to Chauvet's inaugural address, that a federal executive 'might be useful, but is certainly not indispensable at the present moment.'

The unhurried tone of the remark contrasts both with the fiery disputes at Bamako, and with other parts of Boganda's speech, in which he vigorously attacked the administration, both federal and territorial, and demanded a modification and extension of the Loi-Cadre so as to provide full political autonomy, with France contributing only financial and technical aid. 'What we need', he said, 'is fewer civil servants and more technicians . . .'[3] He accused the civil servants of deliberately resisting the transfer of executive power to Africans. This indictment was no doubt partly justified by the facts, but also partly intended to increase Boganda's prestige by putting him in direct conflict with the administration. At any rate,

[1] See *La Vie Française*, 28th June 1957.
[2] Thompson and Adloff, *Emerging States* . . . , op. cit.
[3] See *Afrique Nouvelle*, 29th October 1957.

that was its effect. French officials reacted with sharp protests, which in turn provoked a unanimous vote of confidence in Boganda (16th November). At the same time the Council appealed to Chauvet to punish any civil servant who failed to observe the Loi-Cadre decrees in letter or spirit.[1]

## B. First Moves Towards Regroupment

In Paris, the non-RDA African members of Parliament assembled on 16th October at the Hôtel Lutétia to consider the problem of regroupment. Filyl Dabo Sissoko was given the task of writing to Houphouët and asking for a 'regroupment conference' to be held at Bamako towards the end of December. On 19th October, Senghor and Dia personally approached the RDA leaders with the suggestion that at least 'unity of action' could be achieved for the time being, even if full fusion of the parties had to wait. At the end of the month Sissoko received a reply written by Lisette on behalf of the bureau of the RDA Co-ordination Committee. In form it was favourable, but its content was discouraging. The parties must be regrouped around the existing RDA; they must agree on a common doctrine and programme; minority parties in each territory must be ready to accept the label of the majority party or a new label agreed on with it; each new organisation so formed would become a territorial section of the RDA. On this basis the RDA was prepared to negotiate, but on 9th December and at Paris. This left little time for preparations, and was bound to anger those who had insisted that the reunion of African parties must be achieved on African soil–a point of view which had been urged even within the RDA (notably by Sékou Touré). Sissoko took the letter as a brush-off. It may well have been so intended. The choice of Sissoko as spokesman for the non-RDA parties was tactless, in view of his record of hostility to the RDA since its very beginning. It angered several RDA leaders, especially, of course, those from the Soudan.

When, on 2nd November, the bureau of the Co-ordination Committee met again, this time to consider the Senghor-Dia proposal, it adopted a much more conciliatory line. Senghor was encouraged, and went on to suggest the creation of a 'united political movement of socialist inspiration'. Finally a meeting of unofficial emissaries in Dakar, not including Sissoko, achieved agreement that the regroupment conference should be held in Paris, but not till February.

[1] Thompson and Adloff, op. cit.

## C. Political Crisis in France and Africa, November 1957–February 1958

*The Gaillard Government.* On 5th November, France at last had a government, but one so 'broad and shallow' that 'its energies were mainly occupied in avoiding its own disintegration'.[1] Headed by the Radical **Félix Gaillard,** it contained not only Radicals, Socialists and RDA-UDSR but also MRP and Conservatives, while the Gaullist Chaban-Delmas was installed in the Ministry of Defence. Even the *Convention Africaine* was represented, for Hubert Maga became Under-Secretary of State for Labour–although the group did not propose him for the post, and Senghor had made it known that he personally would not accept office in any French government so long as the war in Algeria went on. Modibo Keïta and Hamadoun Dicko remained Secretaries of State, but were moved from the Rue Oudinot (where Jaquet was left in charge) to the Prime Minister's office and the Ministry of Education respectively. Houphouët, to the delight of French satirists and his own slight embarrassment, became Minister of Public Health and Population.

*Crisis as an Institution.* It was not long before the children of French democracy in Africa–the territorial mini-governments and mini-parliaments–began to exhibit hereditary symptoms. The phenomenon of 'Crisis as an Institution'[2] came all too naturally to African politicians who had learnt their trade from France. In Tchad the RDA's coalition partners prepared to desert it at the earliest favourable moment. In Gabon and Upper Volta they actually did desert. Mba and Coulibaly only managed to preserve their majorities by inducing individual ministers to stay in office and resign from their former parties (respectively UDSG and MDV).

While the RDA fought off these crises, it tried to provoke similar ones in territories which it did not yet control. In Moyen-Congo four UDDIA ministers resigned from Opangault's government and were only persuaded to resume their seats after a month's intensive diplomacy by the Governor and High Commissioner. A public reconciliation between Opangault and Youlou on 24th December was followed on 11th January by a battle between their supporters in which one person was killed and eleven injured. In Niger, Djibo Bakary just forestalled an attempt by the RDA to seduce some of his supporters, and accused it of fomenting a teachers' strike for purely

[1]Williams, pp. 49–50.     [2] Ibid., p. 413.

political reasons. In Dahomey the RDA gave enthusiastic support to a series of violent strikes whose main cause was rising unemployment. Apithy resigned as Vice-President of the Council, hoping to form a broader coalition. But the RDA refused to join it, and some of his former supporters deserted. So he came back into office with a narrower one than before.[1]

Even in Senegal, where the RDA played no significant part in territorial politics, suspicion and bitterness persisted between Socialists and BPS. The first round of negotiations to unite all Senegalese parties was unsuccessful, and Senghor suffered a defeat within his own party when he tried to get Ibrahima Seydou Ndaw replaced by a younger and more progressive figure as president of the Territorial Assembly.[2] In fact the only territorial governments which experienced no serious political difficulties during the winter of 1957–8 were the three 'monochrome' RDA governments of AOF (Ivory Coast, Soudan and Guinea) and the MESAN one in Oubangui-Chari. And only in Guinea did the government really take the initiative.

*Guinea–Birth of a Nation?* As Vice-President of the Council Sékou Touré was in effect already prime minister of Guinea, for Jean Ramadier, who was now its Governor, deliberately effaced himself, allowing Touré to preside at Council meetings (a precedent which embarrassed some of his fellow-Governors) and co-operating in a large-scale local government reform initiated by Touré's party, the PDG-RDA. After a conference of all the Commandants de Cercle in the territory, in July 1957, it was decided to abolish altogether the traditional (or pseudo-traditional) *chefs de canton*, with effect from 31st December. They were replaced by career administrators nominated from Conakry, who in due course were to be assisted by elected *conseils de circonscription*. The chiefs had been too closely associated with the French administration, and in particular with the electoral activities of the BAG, to survive the arrival of the PDG in power. The significance of the reform was indubitably political as well as administrative and social. Yet, all things considered, the change-over went remarkably smoothly. Only in the Fouta Djallon, where the Fula aristocracy had despotised over a number of submerged ethnic groups since the eighteenth century, was it the occasion of some ugly *réglements de comptes*; and everywhere it

[1] Thompson and Adloff, op. cit. Dugué, *Vers les Etats-Unis d'Afrique*, (op. cit.)    [2] Dugué, ibid.

increased rather than diminished the prestige and authority of the Party—as was shown in May 1958 by the results of the elections to the new *conseils de circonscription:* the PDG gained 87·8 per cent of all votes cast.[1]

This reform was only the most spectacular part of an energetic programme on which the PDG government embarked: Africanisation of the upper and middle grades of the civil service (including the 'administrator-mayors' of mixed communes), suppression of native customary courts, creation of a territorial School of Administration, increase in family allowances, extension of social security benefits to day-labourers, expansion of secondary education—and so on.[2] No wonder that, at its territorial congress in January 1958, the PDG displayed a new confidence, that of a party which has experienced the responsibilities of power and knows that it is equal to them. It also revealed new preoccupations: instead of dwelling at length on the virtues of the 'Franco-African ensemble', or even on the problem of the standard of living or the struggle of the African workers for their rights, the reports and motions presented to the congress spoke in terms of Africa as a whole, of the 'African personality', and above all of African unity. In fact, they expressed an African nationalism, even if the words, out of courtesy to France, were still a little minced: 'The African structure of our organisation allows us to adopt the idea of *patrie*, and also to give to the action of Africans a framework, if not of African nationality, at least of African personality.' So ran the 'moral report', and it went on to speak of 'the inevitable retreat of the forces of domination before the rise of the African nationalist movement . . .' The Loi-Cadre was seen as 'a stage on the way to the most complete autonomy, that which will allow the country to associate freely with France and discuss on an equal footing the problems which they have in common . . .' At the same time the Congress reaffirmed unequivocally its determination to build the federal executive, ignoring the terms of a compromise formula on which the bureau of the RDA Co-ordination Committee in Paris had just agreed. 'The decision for or against the federal executive', the report concluded, 'involves a prior decision for or against an African unit' (or 'unity'—the French word is the same). There was no doubt on this point which way the PDG had decided.[3]

---

[1] Ansprenger, p. 295.  [2] Dugué, op. cit.
[3] Text in *L'Expérience guinéenne et l'unité africaine* (*Présence Africaine*, Paris 1959).

*FEANF and PAI.* Sékou Touré was moving rapidly towards an outright assertion of nationalism and a demand for independence. But he was still far from satisfying the aspirations of FEANF in Paris, or of its Senegalese offshoot, the *Parti Africain de l'Indépendance* (PAI), founded in September 1957 by Majhemout Diop, **Oumar Diallo** and **Kader Fall** as an extreme left splinter group from Senghor's BPS.[1] FEANF's periodical *l'Etudiant d'Afrique Noire* printed frequent attacks both on the Guinean government and on Touré himself. The former was 'in violent contradiction with the legitimate desire of Africans to manage the resources of their soil', according to the issue of July 1957; the latter's report on trade union activity at Bamako was 'demagogical and pseudo-analytical', according to that of December. Even as late as May 1958 a student writer asserted: 'To identify M. Sékou Touré with the African working class is a monstrous swindle which must be denounced. Does the Sékou Touré of the Franco-African Community, the Sékou Touré who holds office under the Loi-Cadre, who receives a fat salary taken from the workers' pockets, the Sékou Touré who incites Guineans to murder,[2] does *he* represent the workers? . . . MM. Sékou Touré and co. talk of "liquidating the colonial system", of the "struggle for emancipation", or "decolonisation", but they avoid pronouncing the key-word of our time, "independence".'[3]

The students themselves no longer had any qualms about pronouncing this word. For them the foundation of the PAI–the African Independence Party–was a great step forward in African politics, even though its influence within Senegal remained minimal. On 31st December 1957 the eighth annual congress of FEANF solemnly proclaimed itself the 'historic congress of national independence, which must be won not through illusory reforms, but by the revolutionary struggle of the masses of the African people.'

## D. The Paris Regroupment Conference, February 1958

Not surprisingly, when representatives of the Senegalese parties met again on 1st February 1958, the PAI withdrew from the discussions. Although it professed to desire a union of African parties it was not prepared to sacrifice any of the nationalist or Marxist-Leninist

---

[1] Ansprenger, pp. 177 and 377. Morgenthau, p. 423.
[2] A reference, presumably, to the events in the Fouta Djallon–though it seems unlikely that this writer would have seriously opposed the deposition of the chiefs.
[3] Quoted in Lacouture, *Cinq Hommes et la France*, (op. cit.) pp. 336–7.

principles which had caused it to secede from the BPS in the first place. (As Senghor later remarked: 'the Senegalese have their strengths and their weaknesses. One of their weaknesses consists in the tendency of every malcontent to found his own party and then issue an appeal for unity; it is an unproductive game.')[1] This time, however, BPS and Socialists did agree to merge; and the MPS-RDA also agreed to come in, on the understanding that on the inter-territorial level the MSA and Convention Africaine would merge with the RDA.[2]

*Composition:* Despite all the local conflicts, it was therefore in a relatively hopeful atmosphere that the Regroupment Conference assembled on Saturday 15th February, in the Salle Colbert at the Palais Bourbon. At least the differences between the parties seemed no greater than those within the RDA, whose Co-ordination Committee had just failed to patch up the breach between Houphouët and Touré over the federal executive. If unity could be achieved in Senegal, for long the scene of such bitter polemics, surely it could be achieved in Paris, where African deputies had considerable experience of co-operation across party lines. There was certainly no lack of good will. Even the bitterest of local opponents–such as Coulibaly and the 'Three Musketeers'[3]–travelled to meet each other in Paris, leaving their mutual acrimony at home. Of the twelve Vice-Presidents of Councils of Government in AOF and AEF, only

---

[1] Letter to the PAI quoted in its newspaper *La Lutte*, 24th September 1959.
[2] Dugué, op. cit.
[3] The alliance of Conombo, Nazi Boni and Gérard Ouédraogo had actually put Coulibaly in a minority in the Upper Volta Assembly (14th December 1957). Coulibaly infuriated them, first by refusing to resign, then by persuading four MDV assemblymen, including Maurice Yaméogo the Minister of Agriculture, to join the RDA–thus just restoring its majority (11th January 1958). (Dugué, op. cit.) Nazi Boni circulated a scurrilous pamphlet enumerating 'les dix commandements du Muezzin Coulibaly', of which Blanchet (*L'Itinéraire* ... op. cit.) quotes the following:

> La démocratie tu bafoueras
> Pour le grand bien du RDA.
> Tes adversaires tu attireras
> Par des procédés de scélérat.
> Le fromage tu boufferas
> Et jamais rassasié ne seras.
> La vice-présidence tu garderas
> Et la Haute-Volta se détruira ...

Apithy found his local problems too pressing to let him make the journey. Besides the three interterritorial parties–RDA, Convention Africaine and MSA–there were also respresentatives from:

> the PAI (Majhemout Diop),
> BAG (Barry Diawadou),
> PSEMA (Joseph Conombo),
> MDV (Michael Dorange and Gérard Ouédraogo),
> RDD[1] (Hubert Maga),
> MSUS[2],
> and *Union Républicaine de la Côte des Somalis*.[3]

Vice-President **Mokhtar ould Daddah** of Mauritania led a joint delegation from the various parties of his territory; Vice-President Goumba of Oubangui-Chari was sent by Boganda to represent MESAN but only as an observer; another observer was a Togolese minister sent by Grunitzky.

*Procedure:* The RDA, which was formally the host party, provided an experienced chairman for the Conference, Hamani Diori, who had many times had to preside in the French National Assembly. The first discussions concerned the problem whether organisational regroupment should precede the establishment of a common programme, or vice versa. In so large and heterogeneous an assembly these discussions were not easy to manage. The delegates therefore decided to set up a 'restricted commission' which was to produce both a programme and a formula for regroupment over the weekend. Each of the three main parties chose members of the commission from its left–i.e. federalist and autonomist–wing; perhaps they realised that it was here that they were most likely to discover common ground. The RDA representatives were Touré, Keïta, Abdoulaye Diallo (Minister of Labour in the Soudan), and d'Arboussier, none of whom shared Houphouët's views about the federal executive. The MSA representatives included Bakary Djibo, the Convention Africaine ones Abdoulaye Ly–as well as Senghor, Dia and **Alexandre Adandé** (Dahomey), all of whom were convinced federalists.[4]

[1] *Rassemblement Démocratique Dahoméen*, a north Dahomeyan party formed in August 1957 to unite Maga with his former opponents, the Independents led by Paul Darboux (Morgenthau, p. 417).
[2] *Mouvement Socialist d'Union Sénégalaise*, a splinter-group of Senegalese Socialists who had favoured union with the BPS at a moment when Lamine-Guèye was still opposed to it. Led by Ousman Socé Diop, a well-known novelist, formerly Senator for Senegal and Mayor of Rufisque (Morgenthau, p. 423).          [3] Dugué, op. cit.          [4] Ibid.

*Programme:* In fact the text which the commission brought back to the Conference on Monday 17th was essentially the work of three men: Sékou Touré, Abdoulaye Ly and the Soudanese Socialist **Ya Doumbia.** The 'minimum political programme' which they devised contained two points:

(a) Complete internal autonomy for the Territories; in AOF, AEF and other Groups of Territories there should be 'federations democratically constituted by these territories on the basis of solidarity, equality, and voluntary renunciation of territorial sovereignty.'

(b) A Federal Republic should be set up, joining France to the Groups of Territories, and to the ungrouped Territories, 'on the basis of free co-operation, absolute equality and the right to independence'. The Government of the Federal Republic should retain control of Diplomacy, Defence, Currency, Higher Education and the Magistrature.[1] The Federal Republic could in its turn contract a 'Confederal Union' with other States which were either already independent or becoming so.

*Organisation:* On this basis the parties were to unite, the majority party in each territory absorbing its rivals, but taking a new name to salvage their *amour-propre.* Each united territorial party was to be equally represented on the governing body of the federal movement. But what should this new federal party be called? On this point, and this point only, the Commission was unable to agree. The RDA delegates refused to give up the name 'R.D.A.', whereas the others favoured a new name, even if this should be visibly derived from the 'R.D.A.' (e.g. 'R.P.A.' – *Rassemblement populaire africain*, 'M.D.A.' – *Mouvement démocratique africain*, etc.).

*Secession of the PAI:* After this report was read to the Conference, Majhemout Diop rose to protest, in the name of the PAI, against its excessive moderation, and to demand 'immediate independence'. His speech was noisily supported by representatives of FEANF, who declared their readiness to fight for independence. Sékou Touré, d'Arboussier and Senghor all admonished these young hotheads and urged them to leave if they were not prepared to co-operate. They refused to do so, and the session had therefore to be suspended.[2] When it reassembled, this time in the absence of the PAI, all the other parties adopted the report unanimously and by acclamation.

[1] Ibid.    [2] Ibid.

All delegations were instructed to refer it back to their governing bodies, which were to confirm their acceptance before 5th March. The RDA Co-ordination Committee, which was to meet in the Ivory Coast on 10th March, would then take a final decision. Then a second conference was to be held, at Dakar, when the AOF Great Council session opened at the end of March. This conference was to 'set on foot the effective Unification'. The question of the name was left open for the time being.

Finally the Conference observed a minute's silence in memory of the victims of a bombing raid which the French airforce had just carried out on Tunisian territory, and 'asked the French government to take all possible steps to put an immediate end to the Algerian war'.

These results were as much as anything a defeat for Houphouët. Sékou Touré had brought in reinforcements from outside the RDA to support his campaign for a federal executive, and built a platform for a united African party in which the federal executive was an essential plank. Admittedly the sacrifice of territorial sovereignty was to be voluntary; there was therefore no question of forcing the Ivory Coast into a federation against her expressed will. But this did not make Houphouët's position much easier. If African unity were achieved around this programme, anyone refusing to enter a federation would be automatically branded as a traitor to the united African party. For Houphouët, who would presumably be the leader of that party, this was not an encouraging prospect.

### E. The Dakar Regroupment Congress: Formation of the PRA (March–April 1958)

*Preliminaries:* The crisis within the RDA remained unresolved, and the meeting of the Co-ordination Committee was inconclusive. It was held during the celebrations of the opening of a new bridge, the *pont Félix Houphouët-Boigny*, which now links Abidjan to its suburb of Treichville.[1] Minister Jaquet, who performed the ceremony, took occasion to make a tour of AOF.[2] He was welcomed at Bamako by his colleague Modibo Keïta with a speech that was cordial but blunt: 'Africa has chosen. France still hesitates. The chances of

[1] The Common Market Commission was invited to this ceremony, and thus had its first opportunity to make direct contact with African leaders on African soil. (See Communauté Economique Européenne, Commission: *Premier rapport général sur l'activité de la Communauté*, Brussels 1958, p. 111.)

[2] Dugué, op. cit.

291

building the Franco-African Community diminish every day. . . . If France were to let slip the opportunity of realising the Franco-African Community, Africa would inevitably set out upon the only free road compatible with its dignity, the road of independence. . . .' A few day later, in Conakry, he heard a similar speech from Sékou Touré; if France did not soon make its choice, Africa would resign itself to the 'leap into the unknown'.[1] These remarks were no doubt intended primarily as a criticism of the French National Assembly's continued failure to make up its mind to any large-scale constitutional reform; they none the less took the form of a threat. To be in a position to utter such a threat was no doubt exhilarating; but the idea of carrying it out must also have seemed increasingly exciting to politicians who now felt themselves on the threshold of realising African unity, and who watched–surely with a certain envy–the preparations for the first Conference of Independent African States, which was to open on 15th April at Accra.[2]

*Division into blocs:* It was in this mood that the younger West African leaders arrived in Dakar for the Regroupment Congress, which was held on 26th March. To achieve the union of parties, there remained only the question of the name to be settled. But no compromise on this point had yet been found, and in the event none was. The RDA remained unwilling to sacrifice its name, the symbol of so many years of struggle, which now indeed was almost the only thing that still held it together. Doubtless it was also unwilling to sacrifice the advantages which it enjoyed as a majority party in AOF. As for its opponents, having now achieved unity among themselves, they felt able to continue opposing it with greater confidence. The Great Council session was to open the next day. Already the Councillors were forming into two opposing blocs. The RDA would have 18 members including Houphouët; the 'Unionists' (who now included Apithy and his supporters from Dahomey) would have 17. The balance was held by the five Mauritanians, who had so far maintained an impenetrable reserve.[3]

*Deadlock:* When the Congress opened, at 4.30 in the afternoon, neither Houphouët nor Touré had yet arrived. Hamani Diori was again in the chair. The RDA spokesmen announced their refusal to

[1] Both speeches quoted in Lacouture, op. cit., p. 343.
[2] Ansprenger, p. 429.
[3] Dugué, op. cit., is the main source for the rest of this chapter.

alter their name. The 'Unionists', in a last bid for compromise, suggested at least the addition of the word '*Parti*' – to make 'P.R.D.A.' Nothing doing. Thereupon, on Lamine-Guèye's initiative, the other parties decided to regroup with or without the RDA. The Mauritanians were on the point of joining them, then decided to abstain.

In the evening Sékou Touré arrived. He was expected to come with Houphouët. But Houphouët, who had already decided to give up the Presidency of the Great Council, now suddenly announced that his health would not permit him to leave the Ivory Coast. Already he seemed to be repudiating the federal institutions of AOF. So Sékou Touré came alone, only to find that the African unity on which he pinned his hopes had not been realised after all. During the night the RDA's opponents founded their new party, the *Parti du Regroupement Africain* (PRA). Its career was to be short but dramatic.

*A two-party system?* Next morning the Great Council met. Sékou Touré managed to get the session suspended for twenty-four hours 'so that perhaps we can resume our work in unity'. A further day and night of negotiations followed. In the previous session the RDA had had an easy majority in the Great Council because, while the MSA and Convention Africaine had opposed them, the middle group of Dahomeyans, Mauritanians and Voltaïques had voted with them. Now that the Dahomeyans and the non-RDA Voltaïques had agreed to join the PRA everything was thrown into doubt: if they were to persuade the Mauritanians to join them, the RDA would find itself in a minority. The RDA tried to keep the old alliance in being; but Dahomeyans and Voltaïques would only come into the coalition if the rest of the PRA were brought in too. So the RDA tried instead to seduce Djibo Bakary and the Socialists, but they too were loyal to their new party. Finally, after some intensive horse-trading, it was the Mauritanians who agreed to support the RDA. D'Arboussier was elected President of the Council, in return for which the Mauritanians got the first Vice-Presidency and various other plum offices. The majority thus constituted proceeded to evict the Senegalese Great Councillors from the governing bodies of various federal institutions situated in Senegal (such as the port of Dakar). Touré, as majority leader, explained this policy as follows: 'The representation of the AOF Group is a political option, like all the acts of this session. It is time to do away with territorial and regional characteristics. We are agreed that these appointments should now be made in this way, according to the political option of this Assembly.' In other words, the politicisation of these appointments was intended as a step towards a responsible federal government. Since the effort to achieve a single party had failed for the time being, Touré was prepared to govern AOF on a two-party parliamentary system. Senghor was cast as leader of the opposition, a rôle which, as a good federalist, he meekly accepted. 'We are against . . .', he declared, as each set of appointments was announced. 'But we submit, and that will not prevent us from working co-operatively in the service of Africa.'

*Demand for a federal executive:* On one point majority and opposition were agreed. On the same day, 5th April, that the political appointments were made, a resolution was presented jointly by all three groups (RDA, PRA, and Mauritanians) and voted unanimously, asserting the 'urgent necessity of creating the federal executive' and demanding 'internal autonomy for the AOF Group of Territories'. Unanimously? Yes, but only one Councillor from the Ivory Coast was present, and he was rapidly called to order by his colleagues. Three days later all the Ivory Coast Councillors together issued a statement dissociating themselves from the motion; and on 12th April in Abidjan the Ivory Coast Territorial Assembly retaliated by expressing the determination of that territory 'to integrate directly into the Franco-African Community' and to achieve autonomy as quickly as possible on its own. Whereupon Touré at once issued a communiqué stating that the RDA group in the Council still backed the motion of 5th April 'with all its weight'.[1] Houphouët then summoned another meeting of the RDA Co-ordination Committee (which had never had so much co-ordinating to do) for 24th April, in Paris. Once again the differences were formally patched up. But each time this happened it was a little less convincing. Touré and Keïta were clearly still reluctant to break with the founder-president of their movement. But it was now equally clear that if they were forced to choose between him and the federal state of AOF, they would choose the latter.

If they decided to postpone the crisis in the RDA, that may have been partly because yet another crisis was by now in progress in France. The Gaillard government had been overthrown on 15th April by a revolt of right-wingers who considered its Algerian policy was not tough enough. As a series of more or less '*Algérie Française*' politicians–Soustelle, Bidault, Pleven–tried and failed to form

[1] See *La Semaine en AOF*, 12th and 19th April 1958.

cabinets, and civilians and soldiers in Algiers became increasingly restive, the Fourth Republic entered on its final paroxysm. Now was perhaps not the moment for an African party to break up.

*Situation in AEF:* At the end of the Fourth Republic, then, there was in AOF a two-party line-up, even though few people believed in the virtues of a two-party system as such. While the RDA held tenuously together, its rivals in the different territories hastily amalgamated into territorial sections of the PRA. A similar though less clear-cut situation was developing in AEF. Tchicaya had left the RDA in February, and on 28th March his party decided to co-operate with the MSA in opposition to Youlou. In the Great Council both MSA and *Convention Africaine* supported Boganda against the RDA, which now opposed him, so that he was just re-elected to the presidency by 10 votes to 9. In Tchad Socialists, UDIT and AST (Gaullists) amalgamated into a single anti-RDA party, the *Union Socialiste Tchadienne* (UST). In Gabon, Aubame's party affiliated to the PRA and students at Libreville College went on strike to demonstrate their support for him against Mba's government (which was supported by the teachers). The college had to be closed.[1]

## F. Towards Independence

But the apparent division of African politicians into two opposing teams was misleading. There was no general issue of principle dividing one party from the other. Both sides were more or less accidental coalitions of heterogeneous local interests. The most intensively canvassed issue of the moment–the federal executive– tended to unite (for example) Senghor and Sékou Touré across party lines, while it divided the former from Apithy, the latter from Houphouët, within their own parties. Another issue which was rapidly coming into prominence–that between federal and con-federal links with France–also cut across party lines. And before long it was to be the same with the allied questions of Independence and how to vote in the Referendum. Already it was apparent that Touré and Keïta were moving towards a demand for independence; but the leader who was closest to their attitude, and indeed was ahead of them in his public statements, was Bakary Djibo, the hated foe of the RDA in Niger, and himself one of the dominant person-alities in the PRA. In May 1958, at the very moment when the

[1] Thompson and Adloff, op. cit.

Algiers mob was dealing the death-blow of the Fourth Republic, Djibo attempted to define the policy of the PRA as follows: 'There is no other way to salvation than the constitution of a confederal union which will unite . . . on an equal footing the French Republic, the North African federation that is still to be created, the federation of A.O.F., the federation of A.E.F., and the Malagasy federation; each of these last must . . . accede progressively to independence, or in any case must be accorded the right to self-determination.'[1] It remained to be seen whether such a policy would be accepted by the official founding congress of the PRA, but intelligent French observers of the African scene predicted that it would be. They knew that the word 'independence' had a power over African emotions too strong to be resisted even by such fundamentally moderate politicians as Senghor and Lamine-Guèye. Once it had been adopted as a serious political slogan no African politician could long afford to hold out against it.

[1] Blanchet, op. cit., p. 149.

*Chapter 23*

---

# New Governments in Togo and Cameroun

## A. The Victory of Olympio (April 1958)

Even before the dramatic events of May 1958 reopened the whole French constitutional question, the idea of independence received a considerable fillip from an event which occurred outside, but only just outside, the French Republic: the Togo elections of 27th April. These elections were held as a result of the report of the UN mission which visited Togo in June 1957. It pointed out that the existing Territorial Assembly had been elected in 1955, i.e. before the Loi-Cadre and therefore without full universal suffrage (only 190,000 registered voters as against 491,000 in 1958); that the referendum of October 1956, unlike that in British Togoland, had been held without UN control; and that the 1956 Togo Statute still fell short of complete autonomy. In view of this the UN General Assembly decided to impose two conditions for the ending of Trusteeship: further powers should be conceded by France to the 'Autonomous Republic', and a new territorial assembly should be elected with UN control and universal suffrage. These terms were accepted by the French delegation in November 1957.[1]

Grunitzky and his party thus found that their policy, which the referendum had apparently crowned with success, was once more in question. The very fact did a good deal to undermine their prestige; and they saw that it was going to be increasingly difficult to resist the cry for independence which was so insistently raised by the CUT and JUVENTO. In fact, they began to echo this cry themselves. During the negotiations at the UN they expressed the wish that Togo be admitted to the UN as a full member with equal rights. Olympio quickly pointed out (in a speech before the Trusteeship Council) that this implied sovereign and independent status. By the end of the

[1] Cornevin, *Le Togo, nation pilote*, (op. cit.)

year Grunitzky's party, the PTP, was itself openly demanding independence, qualifying the demand only with warnings that Togo would continue to depend economically on France.[1] Of course Olympio and the CUT in their turn gained prestige from the fact that they had now succeeded not only in imposing their views on the UN, but also in imposing their policies on their political opponents.

By decree of 22nd February 1958 the French government duly made over to the Togolese government all powers except the control of currency, defence and foreign policy. There was now nothing short of full independence left to demand. The wind was in Olympio's sails, even though he himself was legally disqualified from being a candidate in the elections. (He had been convicted of a currency offence in 1954.) The Grunitzky government betrayed its lack of confidence, first by delaying the arrival of the UN observers, then by complaining when they caused 100,000 voters, so far illegally dis-franchised, to be added to the lists at the last moment. None the less it affected to be sure of winning, and asserted that only the Ewe would vote for the CUT, which would therefore gain a maximum of 15 to 20 seats.[2] The CUT itself was unsure of the result, and took care to point out that constituency boundaries were drawn in the government's favour. Probably Olympio was surprised by the extent of his victory. Out of 46 seats altogether the CUT got 29, the UCPN (Grunitzky's northern allies) ten, Independents four and the PTP only three.[3]

Governor **Spénale** realised that, disqualified or not, Olympio was now the unquestioned political leader of Togo, and therefore invited him to form a government. He became prime minister on 13th May (the very day of the *coup d'état* in Algiers). Sékou Touré telegraphed his congratulations, urging the new leader to rejoin, sooner or later, the Franco-African association[4]–a clear indication that he considered the latter should be composed of more or less independent states. For there could be no doubt of Olympio's intention to lead Togo to independence. FEANF was overjoyed at his success, and predicted that Grunitzky's fate would soon be shared by all the other 'Franco-African' leaders.[5] By September,

[1] Ansprenger, p. 214.
[2] Cornevin, 'Les élections à l'Assemblée togolaise' in *Encyclopédie mensuelle de l'Afrique*, July 1958.
[3] Cornevin, *Histoire du Togo* (op. cit.).
[4] Lacouture, *Cinq Hommes et la France* (op. cit.), p. 343.
[5] Blanchet, *Itinéraire* . . . (op. cit.).

Olympio was negotiating with the new French government to fix the date of complete independence in 1960.[1]

## B. The Bamiléké Revolt and the Fall of Mbida

The UPC was to have no triumphant vindication like that of the CUT. Its opponents did indeed take over its original programme, but they also managed to pocket its political rewards.

The first phase of Cameroun's history as a 'State under Trusteeship' coincided with a sharpening of the conflict between the authorities and the UPC. Despite repression, the terrorist campaign in Sanaga-Maritime mounted in intensity throughout 1957. On 23rd September, Um Nyobé stated the terms on which his followers would lay down their arms: the dissolution of the existing Assembly, followed by a new general election, a complete amnesty for all political prisoners and suspects, and immediate independence.[2] The announcement of a Cameroun national anthem, which occurred the following month, was scarcely to be taken as an answer. The real answer came on 9th November, when Prime Minister Mbida went to Um's home village of Boumnyebel and made a fiery speech denouncing the UPC as a 'clique of liars and demagogues' and threatening 'severe measures' against all who failed to 'come out of the forests within ten days and return to their villages'.[3]

Within a few weeks of this speech violence had spread to another area, the Bamiléké region. Here there was a growing social conflict between the peasants and the chiefs. The latter were traditionally entrusted with the management of the common land, a trust which under the influence of modern economic phenomena (production for the market, plantation agriculture etc.) they tended to abuse. The land-hunger of the peasants became acute, partly owing to a very rapid rise in population. The privileges of the chiefs were more and more resented, until in November 1957 a kind of *jacquerie* was sparked off by the administration's decision to depose a young reforming chief, who had just returned from college in France, in favour of his more traditionally minded rival. Needless to say the UPC immediately supported and claimed credit for the revolt. On the night of 13th–14th December a member of the Legislative Assembly (ALCAM) was murdered. From then on the region was

[1] Cornevin, *Le Togo, nation pilote* (op. cit.).
[2] Mveng, *Histoire du Cameroun* (op. cit.).
[3] Mbida, *Discours prononcé le 9 novembre 1957 à Boumnyebel*, Yaoundé 1957.

in a state of perpetual guerrilla warfare; the administration retained nominal control during daylight, but by night the terrorists were supreme, burning church property and murdering chiefs, missionaries and Europeans. Troops sent to suppress the rebellion only provided it with new targets. During the next two years it spread to the big towns, Yaoundé and Douala, where Bamiléké immigrants were a large and economically important minority.[1]

Meanwhile Mbida flew to Paris to ask for military reinforcements. He suggested that the battalion now fighting the UPC should be supplemented with two or three extra companies. As the UPC's own troops were estimated at a mere 300 in Sanaga-Maritime, perhaps 200 in the Bamiléké region, French politicians were unwilling to believe this was necessary. They were far from anxious to get involved in yet another large-scale colonial war, and continued to hope that a peaceful settlement with the UPC could be reached. This hope was shared by many Camerounians, including the Bishop of Douala, who actually managed to see Um Nyobé in person, but failed to persuade him to accept a cease-fire.[2] Jaquet, Minister of France d'Outre-Mer, took a personal dislike to Mbida and began to think that his government was the principal obstacle to peace. But Mbida was backed up by the High Commissioner, Messmer, who, like Roland Pré before him had been converted by the course of events from leniency to a tardy and heavy-handed repression. Like Buron in 1954 and Defferre in 1956, Jaquet decided that a new High Commissioner would stand a better chance. At the end of 1957 he promoted Messmer to be High Commissioner of AEF, and replaced him in Cameroun with Jean Ramadier, who had just come back from Guinea. He instructed Ramadier to sound out the political possibilities and then report back.

Ramadier exceeded these instructions spectacularly. Virtually his first action on arrival in Yaoundé was to persuade Ahidjo's *Union Camerounaise* to desert Mbida's government. Left without a majority, Mbida resigned, and on 18th February Ahidjo was elected prime minister in his place. Mbida again flew to Paris, and filled the lobbies of the Palais Bourbon with his complaints. Jaquet telegraphed desperately to Ramadier for an explanation. Ramadier replied vaguely, and the unfortunate minister was left to carry the can before the National Assembly for an action which fundamentally he approved but of whose details he was still totally ignorant. Ramadier, still embroiled in political intrigues in Yaoundé, replied

<hr />

[1] Mveng, op. cit.      [2] Ansprenger, p. 207.

evasively to a series of increasingly formal demands that he should return and explain himself. Finally his disobedience resulted in his replacement by a more orthodox administrator (**Xavier Torré**), although his distinguished Socialist pedigree saved him from formal dismissal.[1]

## C. The Ahidjo Government and the Death of Um Nyobé

But Ramadier would not have been able to do what he did if Mbida had not already made himself thoroughly unpopular in Cameroun, and the results of his brief term of office were not reversed. Mbida and his party (the *Démocrates Camerounais*) went into opposition, while the Group of Eight (Soppo Priso and Assalé) came into Ahidjo's government, which adopted Soppo Priso's old strategy: to win the UPC back to legal methods by taking over its principal demand–independence. On 12th June 1958 ALCAM voted to ask the French government (now headed by de Gaulle) to 'transfer to the State of Cameroun all competences which relate to the management of internal affairs'–i.e. to give it complete internal autonomy such as Togo had acquired in February; and moreover 'to recognize ... its option for independence at the end of trusteeship'.[2] De Gaulle replied favourably, and negotiations between the two governments went ahead.[3]

But reconciliation with the UPC was not achieved. Its leaders appear to have been incensed that politicians whom they regarded as puppets and traitors should now steal the credit for an independence which was really the fruit of their own efforts. In their view, a country ruled by such men would not be independent in more than name. So there was no cease-fire, and no peace-talks. Um Nyobé himself remained in the maquis until, on 13th September 1958, he was shot by a government patrol near Boumnyebel. The description of his death given by his secretary, Mayi Matip,[4] suggests that he intended himself to be killed. Possibly he saw himself as an obstacle to national reconciliation as long as he lived. Once dead, he became a national hero to whom even supporters of the government could afford to pay lip-service. Mayi Matip came out of the maquis, claiming to be Um Nyobé's political executor, and declared himself ready to return

---

[1] Jaquet, conversation with the author in April 1967.
[2] Mveng, op. cit.
[3] Ansprenger, p. 393.
[4] In *France-Observateur*, 26th March 1959.

to legal opposition even before the UPC was officially re-legalised or a full political amnesty granted. The government wisely allowed him to do so, and the terrorism in Sanaga-Maritime came to an end. But his action was immediately disowned by Moumié and the other UPC leaders in exile, and the fighting in the Bamiléké region went on.[1]

[1] Ansprenger, p. 395.

# Chapter 24

# An Eventful Summer

General de Gaulle was elected prime minister on 1st June 1958 by 329 votes to 224.[1] No Africans voted against him. Those who voted for him were: from the RDA Houphouët, Hamani Diori and Modibo Keïta, from the PRA Apithy, Tchicaya, Maga, Sissoko, Dicko and Ninine. The remainder did not vote but in most cases this was because they were not in Paris. In general the RDA's attitude was more positive than that of the PRA. Houphouët at once agreed to join the government, and immediately telephoned all RDA deputies asking them to come to Paris. The PRA was offered a ministry, which some of its leaders (Lamine-Guèye, Diawadou, Conombo, Sissoko) would have liked to accept. Others, notably Abdoulaye Ly, were strongly against it, and Senghor could not make up his mind until it was too late. But both parties voted for the government on 3rd June when de Gaulle asked for authority to draft a new Constitution and have it ratified by referendum.[2]

## A. The Constitutional Problem

Africans wept few tears for the Fourth Republic. They were glad enough to see the constitutional question taken out of the hands of an assembly which had for so long shown itself unable or unwilling to cope with it. It was now three years since Title VIII had been declared '*révisable*', but it had still not been revised. In fact the only progress the Assembly had made was to realise that to revise Title VIII by itself would not be possible. Any new text which took account of the results of the Loi-Cadre and of African aspirations to autonomy would not fit into the existing Constitution. It would have to create a 'very broadly decentralised French Republic',[3] which would be almost the antithesis of the one described in the Con-

---

[1] Williams, p. 501.    [2] Dugué, op. cit.
[3] Coste-Floret, report on behalf of the Universal Suffrage Commission of the National Assembly, March 1957. (Quoted in Coret, 'Le Problème de la révision du Titre VIII . . .', op. cit.)

stitution of 1946. By October 1957 the Convention Africaine deputies were proposing to declare *'révisable'*, not merely the 23 articles of Title VIII but 71 other articles as well as the preamble and even the title of the Constitution itself. From the French side (Professor **Luchaire**) came a less drastic suggestion: Title VIII should simply be excised from the Constitution, and the relations between France and her former colonies should be 'deconstitutionalised'. This would mean that the T.O.M. would no longer be considered part and parcel of the Republic, and their evolution would no longer be delayed by what one might call the 'indivisibility complex'. The suggestion was taken up by some of Edgar Faure's supporters, who said they preferred 'a reasoned empiricism to an outdated dogmatism'.[1]

Another suggestion which found much favour with Africans was a revival of one they had made themselves in 1946: a 'Constituent Assembly of the French Union'. This was explicitly advocated in an article in *Le Monde* by **Maurice Duverger,** the celebrated political scientist (20th March 1958), but Assembly and government were already groping towards something like it. Mitterrand proposed, on 4th February 1958, 'the meeting of a conference which will bring together the qualified representatives of the Government of the Republic with the elected representatives of the populations of French Africa, with a view to the creation of the Franco-African Community, and in order to define the general and specialised institutions of that Community';[2] and Jaquet was working on the preliminaries of such a conference behind the scenes.[3]

This was the point which the constitutional problem had reached when de Gaulle came into power. The unstated reason why it had still not been dealt with was that most French politicians were unwilling to accept the full implications of either of the possible solutions: on the one hand, a federal, egalitarian constitution involving a partial sacrifice of French sovereignty; on the other, a loose confederation, or 'French Commonwealth', in which the former T.O.M. would be virtually independent. This was one of many political nettles, so far avoided, which de Gaulle would have to grasp. With good reason, Africans believed he would be more able and more willing to grasp it than the Assembly had been. Once they were reassured that he was not going to put the clock back, nor yet

[1] Coret, ibid.
[2] Assemblée Nationale, 3rd legislature, motion no. 6487.
[3] Jaquet, in an interview with the author, April 1967.

maintain the *status quo*, but like them was convinced of the need for a community whose individual members would be genuinely autonomous, they were glad to co-operate with him. Senghor, on emerging from an interview with the new prime minister just after his arrival in Paris, felt able to announce that there was 'no essential difference between the General's ideas and the programme of the PRA on the question of constitutional reform'. And on 13th June an interministerial committee was set up to start work on constitutional revision. Two members of it were particularly entrusted with Title VIII: Pflimlin and Houphouët.[1] They were assisted by a team of civil servants in the Rue Oudinot, now under the command of Cornut-Gentille, whom de Gaulle had recalled from the post of Ambassador in the Argentine to be his Minister of France d'Outre-Mer.[2]

Which then was it to be – Federal Republic or Confederal Commonwealth? Interestingly enough, Senghor, the originator of the former idea, was now less unequivocally in its favour than Houphouët and the RDA. On 9th July he and Mamadou Dia published a memorandum on behalf of the PRA which stated: 'There can be no question of a classical federalism, but only of a light and loose federalism.' The Federal Republic should be composed of individual republics, which should delegate to it some executive but no important legislative powers: i.e. the Federal President (whose name, it was not hard to guess, would be de Gaulle) would be a genuine central executive, but the federal assembly (or 'congress') would not be a real parliament but essentially a forum in which parliamentarians from overseas and from metropolitan France could meet and discuss matters of common interest. The RDA, on the other hand, wanted a federal parliament to which the federal government would be responsible.[3]

Despite this apparent difference between their policies, the two parties were able, on 18th July, to issue a joint declaration setting out the general attitude of the overseas peoples. It insisted on the 'recognition of the right of the overseas peoples to self-determination' and specified that 'the Federal Republic is composed of autonomous

---

[1] Dugué, op. cit. Pflimlin was now the leader of the MRP, which under his guidance had become increasingly hostile to the Algerian war. His nomination as prime minister at the beginning of May had sparked off the Algiers coup, news of which rallied support to him in the Assembly and helped to ensure his investiture on 14th May. He resigned on 28th May to make way for de Gaulle (Williams, pp. 55–6).

[2] Ansprenger, p. 262.    [3] Ibid., p. 263.

states'. The powers of the federal government were to be confined to diplomacy, national defence, higher education, and 'economic and social solidarity'. It also mentioned the possibility of a 'Confederal Union' in which the Federal Republic would in its turn be linked to 'states that are already independent or acceding to independence'.[1] This suggested that the 'autonomous states' might hope eventually to become independent without thereby breaking all links with France.

As for Sékou Touré, the style of his remarks was rather different, but their content surprisingly similar. 'We shall not give up our independence', he told a PDG Congress at the beginning of June, 'we shall not give up our freedom. We are willing, thanks to our independence, to resign the exercise of certain attributes of that independence to a more vast ensemble, in order that our state of freely accepted interdependence may confer on our acts a value and a scope that are in accordance with our interests. We have already stated that France remains the nation with which we mean to link our destiny, provided that she realises that such a political option results neither from fear, nor from opportunism, but is the precise expression of a deliberate and enlightened will.'[2]

## B. The Congress of Cotonou, 25th–27th July

This language seems very moderate when set alongside the speeches made by the PRA leaders at their founding Congress, which was held at Cotonou (an odd choice, for the town was solidly RDA and the delegates were greeted with hostile demonstrations) from 25th to 27th July. It was for Senghor what the Bamako Congress had been for Houphouët: the moment of painful realisation that his 'followers' had left him behind. Like Houphouët he read a report setting out the ideas and demands which had always won him applause in the past, only to find that the audience wanted something else. His statement that 'independence has no positive content, it is not a solution' was disavowed in the name of the *Union Progressiste Sénégalaise* (UPS– the Senegal section of the PRA) not only by Abdoulaye Ly–which might have been expected–but even by Mamadou Dia, usually his faithful lieutenant. 'Senghor displays a certain optimism about the Government of General de Gaulle', said Dia, 'the UPS does not

---

[1] Ibid., p. 264. (German version of full text pp. 475–6.)
[2] Text in *L'Expérience guinéene et l'unité africaine*, (op. cit.)

agree. The respect which we owe him does not necessarily entail confidence. The Government itself leads us to pose the problem of Independence [sc. by its inadequate constitutional proposals–see below]. . . . In colonial matters France is always one reform behind.' Dia objected to the one-sided procedure by which France proposed to confront Africa with a cut-and-dried, take-it-or-leave-it constitution. 'For all sorts of reasons, both cultural and economic, we are resolved to enter into a confederation with the Metropole, but we too have proposals to make to France.'

But it was Bakary Djibo who took the Congress by storm, with a few short sentences which contrasted refreshingly with Senghor's convoluted rhetoric. 'You can only associate when you're already independent,' he said. 'National independence first, the rest later.' The Niger delegation rose to its feet to applaud its leader (who was later elected General Secretary of the PRA), and the whole Congress followed suit.

Djibo represented the Hausa-speaking people of south-eastern Niger, who had much more in common with Northern Nigeria than with any other people in AOF. He represented a territory whose natural trade-routes to the sea lay at least as much through Nigeria as through Dahomey. 'Historically,' he said, 'we are linked to other States which will be independent in 1960'. And his lieutenant **Mamani Abdoulaye** went further: 'There is no doubt that after listening to the messages of friendship [sc. from English-speaking countries], the meeting has already chosen: the right to withdraw from the French ensemble. Niger demands freedom to confederate with Nigeria or other territories.'

Not surprisingly this found an echo from Zinsou, the old advocate of 'horizontal' contacts. 'We must immediately make English a compulsory language in our schools, and French must be made one in the British territories. In so doing we shall take the first step towards the United States of Africa.'[1] What *was* surprising was that the cry for independence was taken up by the former Socialists, who until lately had been the group most favourable to assimilation and most hostile to anything that smacks of secession. Sissoko said: 'If we demand Independence, France should be convinced that we do so for her own good. In international gatherings Black Africa should be there in person and not have to speak through an intermediary . . .' Hamadoun Dicko suggested that the Congress should send a message

---

[1] This speech must have given pleasure to George Padmore, the apostle of Pan-Africanism, who was present at the Congress.

to the French government, adjuring it 'to proclaim the independence of the peoples of Africa'. And Lamine-Guèye himself declared: 'I am for Independence without conditions.'

The delegates were even prepared to take the economic consequences of independence in their stride. Mamadou Dia said: 'Given the direction which we are taking, there can no longer be any question of FIDES, or of the Common Market. . . . That will involve on our side much austerity and a sense of national discipline.' Or, as a Soudanese delegate, **Bass Madiop,** put it: 'Up to now we have called on France, but now we shall have to call on ourselves.' Abdoulaye Ly was more optimistic: 'As for investments, once we are independent we shall find it easier to attract capital.' Only Apithy and the delegates from Guinea, representing the two territories which stood to lose most if the FIDES credits were cut off, raised a warning note amidst all this enthusiasm and self-denial. They were ignored.

It may well be imagined that in this atmosphere Houphouët's greetings telegram, expressing hope that the Congress would 'bring realistic elements construction Franco-African Community', was met with howls of derision; and that incessant references to Olympio's glorious victory, as well as applause for a telegram from JUVENTO, deterred Grunitzky from attending after the first day. More surprising –at any rate in view of what happened afterwards– is the loud applause which greeted Nazi Boni's suggestion that volunteers should go and conduct a propaganda campaign against the RDA in Guinea. Evidently Sékou Touré was still far from being the darling of the Left.[1]

The Government's preliminary constitutional draft was not in fact published until 30th July, three days after the Congress ended. But some information about it had already leaked out, and this partly–but only partly–explains the sudden outburst of separatism among hitherto pro-French leaders. De Gaulle proposed a Federation (so-called) whose members, although they 'enjoy autonomy and dispose of their own affairs' would not be specifically recognised as states. Instead of a separate federal assembly there was merely to be representation for the overseas territories in the French Senate. And Africans must choose once and for all between membership of this Federation and secession. Once they had accepted the constitution

---

[1] This account of the Cotonou Congress is closely based on that in Dugué, op. cit., which I believe is the fullest in existence. There is no official transcript of the proceedings, so accuracy of the quotations cannot be guaranteed.

there was to be no more question of self-determination, still less of the Right to Independence.[1]

This news incensed the delegates at Cotonou. They passed a resolution condemning de Gaulle's draft, and announced the convocation of a 'National Constituent Assembly ... to organise the new nation, a federation based on equality and on voluntary sacrifices of sovereignty by the present territories, which must immediately and without delay be given internal autonomy, purely to enable them to prepare rapidly for this national constituent assembly.' The nation in question was of course not France but Africa (or at least Afrique Noire). Only after the constituent assembly had met would they consider 'the negotiation with France of a multinational confederation of free and equal peoples, without thereby abandoning the African will to federate all former colonies into a United States of Africa.' Finally the Congress 'adopts the password [*mot d'ordre*] of Immediate Independence, and decides to take all necessary measures to mobilise the African masses around this password and to translate into fact this desire for independence.'

This remarkable text was the work of Senghor himself.[2] It was skilfully worded so that he apparently bent before the storm, but yet avoided taking any irrevocable step at once. No date or place was fixed for the 'National Constituent Assembly'–and it was France who was asked to 'help facilitate its rapid meeting'. As for Independence, although 'Immediate', it remained a 'password', i.e. apparently a goal to be struggled for rather than something that was really expected to happen at once. As Senghor inscrutably explained to a journalist who asked whether he really intended to take immediate independence: 'L'Indépendance Immédiate, certes oui, mais non pas dans l'immédiat.' A Consultative Constitutional Committee was about to meet in Paris to consider de Gaulle's draft. It was composed mainly of parliamentarians, and would certainly include some Africans, notably Senghor himself. He had at least secured a breathing space during which it could try and persuade the government to accept a more liberal Constitutional formula for the Franco-African Community.

## C. The Consultative Constitutional Committee

The Committee held its first session on 29th July. The African members of it were Senghor and Lamine-Guèye for the PRA, and

---

[1] Ansprenger, p. 265.    [2] Dugué, op. cit.

Lisette for the RDA; there was also **Philibert Tsiranana,** head of the government of Madagascar. For a moment it was thought that Sékou Touré might also take part; he came to Paris, and was chosen by the RDA deputies to see de Gaulle on their behalf and explain the party's point of view. But in the end Lisette was left as the only RDA representative on the Committee—which meant that it was Houphouët's views rather than those of the majority of the party which were represented.[1]

Senghor also had a private interview with de Gaulle on his return from Cotonou, in which it seems the General took no pains to conceal his dissatisfaction with the proceedings at the Congress. A leader, he pointed out acidly, should lead his troops, not follow them. As for the anti-colonial polemics that were now in fashion, he did not think much of them. Why could Africans not admit that French colonialism had done them good? After all, had it not been for Roman colonialism 'who would have taught us Gauls to wash?' These *boutades* might have been less painful had not Senghor himself been more than half convinced of their truth. He emerged from the Presence with his tail between his legs.

Nonetheless it was clear that after Cotonou he could not accept the tight federal formula proposed by de Gaulle—whereas Lisette, representing Houphouët, was generally satisfied with it. Luckily for Senghor the MRP representatives on the Commission—Teitgen and Coste-Floret—were now in favour of the 'confederal' solution. On 5th August a working-group on overseas institutions, chaired by Lamine-Guèye, adopted an amendment of Coste-Floret's which would have given the Territorial Assembly of each territory the choice between the maintenance of its *status quo* as T.O.M. and any one of four other options: it could become a fully assimilated Department of the French Republic, a member of the Federation as defined by the government draft, an independent state within the 'Community of Free Peoples' (also included in the government draft, but intended for the former protectorates, which were already independent), or—in between the last two—an independent state within a Confederation, linked to France by a 'freely concluded agreement'. The choice should not be irrevocable; territories would later be able to move from one category to another.

De Gaulle was having none of this. He saw that if the Confederation was allowed, the Federation would soon be a dead letter, for it would be intolerable for its members to see other territories,

[1] Lacouture, *Cinq Hommes et la France* (op. cit.), pp. 345–6.

who had opted for the Confederation, enjoying the same advantages as them together with a much greater degree of independence. Therefore, one or the other, but not both: "Federation" or "Confederation", these are only words. I, de Gaulle, say "Federation" and there we stop.'

*A fortiori*, it was impossible to offer the territories the option of joining the 'Community of Free Peoples'. To de Gaulle it seemed that the Africans were trying to have it both ways. They wanted to shirk the responsibilities of the Federation, but to keep its advantages. If they wanted independence let them take it by voting 'No'– and good luck to them. But if they voted 'Yes,' they were committing themselves to a federation in which all the partners (France included) must accept some sacrifice of sovereignty.

'All of us here together', he explained to the Committee, 'are engaged on an immense and novel task . . . We are going to build a modern federal State, on the basis of spontaneous acceptance by the overseas peoples and by France. Of course I understand the attractions of independence and the lure of secession . . . The referendum will tell us whether secession carries the day. But what is inconceivable is an independent state which France continues to help. If the choice is for independence, the government will draw, with regret, the conclusions that follow from the expression of that choice.'

To the Africans and their supporters in the Committee this policy amounted to blackmail. They objected, first to being forced to choose between independence and the Franco-African Community–whereas the confederal formula would have enabled them to enjoy the advantages of both; and secondly to having to choose once and for all, so that by voting 'Yes' in the referendum they would turn their backs on independence for good. As Coste-Floret said, it was undesirable that the T.O.M. should only be able to achieve independence by voting 'No'. 'It would be better to offer them this possibility through a Yes-vote as well.'

Both Senghor and Lamine-Guèye rose up in sorrow and in anger against de Gaulle's policy, as they had against Bidault's in 1946. Indeed their remarks were closer on content and in style to those of 1946 than to their recent declarations at Cotonou. 'I implore you,' said Lamine-Guèye, 'do not put weapons in the hands of those who really favour secession. . . .' (This from a man who only a few days before had cried 'I am for Independence without conditions'!) 'We can only be Frenchmen like you if you are willing to be Frenchmen with us. . . . Since you are creating an association of free peoples, at least leave us the right to enter it one day: we will never do so without your consent, only by unanimous agreement.'

Both Lamine-Guèye and Senghor stressed their credentials as Frenchmen in order to convince France of their good will, while asking at the same time for recognition of their human dignity as Africans. Lamine-Guèye said that the Senegalese were proud to have been French for longer than the inhabitants of Savoy, but 'we demand not to be barred from all evolution'. Senghor alluded–just as in 1946–to the decree which abolished slavery in 1848: 'It contains on every line the phrase "human dignity". For Africans, the recognition of their right to independence is a question of dignity. . . .' And again: 'If you do not give us the option which we demand, certainly we shall remain French in our civilisation, but nonetheless we shall vote against the Constitution. Have the Bretons been told that if they vote "No", *they* will be Separatists? Why then should that be said to us? . . . If I refuse a federal association and pronounce for a confederal one, the alternative stated by General de Gaulle means that confederation equals secession.'

The committee was not insensitive to these entreaties. Although it accepted de Gaulle's veto of the 'Confederation', it transformed the 'Federation' into a 'Community' (this was Tsiranana's suggestion), and the 'Community of free peoples' into an 'association of free (i.e. independent) states'. Members of the former were to have the opportunity of transferring to the latter after a five-year interim; and even while they remained in the Community they were to be expressly recognised as 'states'. Instead of being represented in the French Senate, they would send delegates from their own parliaments to an 'Assembly of the Community' which would have some genuine powers over economic and foreign policy. There would also be an 'Executive Council' of the Community, composed of all the prime ministers of member-states, plus one other minister for each state whose special responsibility would be Community affairs. This Council was to exercise the powers reserved for the Community, which would cover currency, defence, diplomacy, common economic and financial policy, and (saving special agreements to the contrary) justice, higher education, transport and telecommunications.[1]

[1] *Travaux preparatoires de la Constitution–avis et debats du Comité Consultatif Constitutionnel* (Documentation Française, Paris 1960).

## D. The Final Text

These proposals were set out in an official letter from the Committee to de Gaulle, dated 14th August. By the 21st the government had produced its final text,[1] which incorporated most of the Committee's proposals. The most important alterations were the following:

(a) The option after five years disappeared; it was stated (Articles 86 and 87) that Member-States of the Community could change their status in the future; but if they became independent, they would thereby cease to be members of the Community.

(b) The 'Assembly of the Community' was renamed 'Senate of the Community'; it would only have decisive powers on such matters (if any) as should be delegated to it by the legislative assemblies of the member-states (Article 83).

(c) It was not made clear whether the executive powers of the Community fell to the Executive Council (which was to 'organise the co-operation of members of the Community at Government and administration levels' (Article 82)), or to the President of the Republic (who was also President of the Community, elected by an electoral college which included overseas representatives (Articles 76 and 80)).

Such was the Constitution to be submitted to the French and African peoples on 28th September. It did not go all the way to meet the aspirations of the 'confederalists'—since independence and membership of the Community were stated to be incompatible. But it stopped short only at that point, and the right to proceed to independence even after an initial Yes-vote was recognised, albeit grudgingly. As for the vexed question of the federal executive at the level of the Group of Territories, it was left open: the T.O.M. could become member-States of the Community 'either in groups or as single units'. On the face of it, the draft might reasonably be expected to satisfy Sékou Touré, but those who had called for 'Immediate Independence' at Cotonou might logically be expected to vote 'No', for de Gaulle had said that any territory where there was a majority of 'Noes' would be considered from that moment as a foreign country.

But few Africans (and probably few Frenchmen) based their decision how to vote purely on the text. Apart from anything else,

[1] Not quite final, in fact. Some further amendments were made in the light of the legal opinion given by the Conseil d'Etat on 29th August. (Ansprenger, p. 269).

313

the text was not published until 4th September, and by then most people's attitudes had already begun to crystallise. For de Gaulle himself the campaign started on 21st August, and it started with a tour of Madagascar and Africa. In a series of speeches, at Tananarive on 22nd August, at Brazzaville on the 24th, at Abidjan and Conakry on the 25th, and Dakar on the 26th, he explained his conception of the Franco-African Community, and of the choice which he was asking Malagasies and Africans to make.

## E. De Gaulle's Tour of Africa (August 21st–26th)

What was still not clear, at the time when de Gaulle left Paris, was the answer to what was for most Africans the most important question: would they preserve the Right to Independence if they voted 'Yes'? If not, it would be difficult, if not impossible, for them to do so. Yet few of them were really anxious to take immediate independence by voting 'No', for they feared the economic consequences. As Tsiranana put it, in a press conference at Tananarive on 21st August: 'When I let my heart talk, I am a partisan of total and immediate independence; when I make my reason speak, I realise that it is impossible.'[1]

As always, de Gaulle indicated his intentions by grandiose but elliptical phrases rather than precise undertakings. For example, he answered Tsiranana's plea for independence within the Community by pointing at the ancient palace of Queen Ranavalo and telling the vast crowd which packed the Tananarive city stadium: 'Tomorrow you will again be a state, as when this palace was inhabited.'[2] The value of this promise depended on one's opinion of the nineteenth-century Hova monarchy. The listening crowd apparently took it as an affirmative reply to Tsiranana's request, for it was greeted with thunderous applause. African leaders were less certain.

De Gaulle managed to avoid giving any clear indication as to what, if any, evolution would be possible for member-states within the Community. But one all-important promise he did make, in his speech at Brazzaville: 'If within this Community a given territory in the course of time, after a certain period which I do not specify, feels itself able to undertake all the burdens and duties of independence, that is its affair, for it to decide through its elected

[1] Crowder, 'Independence as a Goal . . .', (op. cit.), p. 32.
[2] De Gaulle's main speeches on his tour of Africa were printed in *Chroniques d'Outre-Mer*, October 1958.

representatives.... I guarantee in advance that in such a case metropolitan France will raise no obstacles.' This declaration followed private conversations with President Boganda, who had apparently convinced de Gaulle that at least five territories (Oubangui-Chari, Guinea, Senegal, Dahomey and Niger) could be relied on to vote 'No,' if a Yes-vote was taken to imply an irrevocable renunciation of independence.[1] Moderate African leaders heaved a great sigh of relief. Most of them were still not fully satisfied with de Gaulle's Constitution, but they could now reasonably ask their peoples to vote for it as a step towards, not an alternative to, independence.

At Abidjan, all was smiles and cheers. Houphouët did not hesitate to assure the General that the RDA, and all the RDA, would vote 'Yes'. Unfortunately, he was out of touch with the Guinea section. Sékou Touré had been infuriated to hear of de Gaulle's ruling that a territory which voted 'No' would automatically be taken to have seceded. 'General de Gaulle has said that we can take independence with all its consequences,' he had declared on 9th August. 'I shall reply, for my part, that the consequences are not exclusively African but may be French as well.' He seems to have felt that a challenge had been issued, which African dignity could not afford to ignore. More than ever he was determined not to accept any constitution which did not explicitly confirm the Right to Independence; and the right to secede and take the consequences was not good enough. If a choice must be made, sooner or later, between independence and France's continued friendship, better to make it now.

But Touré made it abundantly clear that he did not want to have to make this choice at all. If de Gaulle had only been prepared to say, in so many words, that France recognised the African states' right to independence and would not attempt to penalise them if and when they became independent, there can be little doubt that Touré would have voted 'Yes'. But de Gaulle would not go beyond his formula of 'raise no obstacles'. 'I say it here,' he declared in Conakry, 'even louder than elsewhere: independence is at Guinea's disposal. She can take it by saying "no" to the proposal which is made to her, and in that case I guarantee that metropolitan France will raise no obstacles. Naturally she will draw the conclusions, but she will raise no obstacles ...' 'Draw the conclusions'—how could this be interpreted, other than as a threat to withdraw all forms of

[1] Boganda, *Enfin on décolonise* ... (Brazzaville 1958): speech at Bangui, 7th September 1958.

aid? And how could a man as proud as Sékou Touré be expected to renounce independence under duress?

The conflict between the two men was partly personal. Unlike other African leaders like Boganda and Houphouët, Touré failed to sugar his speech of welcome with phrases of admiration for de Gaulle's genius and his historic career, of gratitude for what France had done for Africa, or of respect for her senior statesman. He made a speech remarkably similar to the one he had made to Jaquet five months before. It did contain references to friendship with France, and expressions of hope that the association between France and Africa would continue; but it also contained harsh criticisms of France's colonial abuses, and glowing references to Africa's united and independent future. It was these that provoked loud cheers from the Guinean audience at whom the speech was plainly directed, for Touré spoke with his back half turned to his distinguished guest; and when he declared rhetorically, 'We prefer poverty in freedom to wealth in slavery!', there was deafening applause which was to echo round the entire world.

De Gaulle was offended by this language, and he must also have been offended by the fact that the crowd's enthusiasm was evidently directed only at Touré, while he himself was the object of polite indifference. This contrasted with the euphoric atmosphere in which he had basked at Brazzaville, where the return of 'Ngol' had provoked transports of delight, and at Abidjan, where he had been hailed as a bringer of friendship and freedom. In Conakry the crowd which thronged and danced along the road from the airport to the town set up a rhythmic and disciplined chant of 'Sily'— meaning 'elephant', the symbol of the RDA. It seemed to have come not to welcome de Gaulle but to make him realise that Sékou Touré was the leader of a united and determined people.

After Touré's speech, de Gaulle refused to make any gesture which would make it easier for him to vote 'Yes'. He regarded it as a cause already lost. 'Well, gentlemen', he is said to have remarked to his entourage, 'there is a man we shall never get on with. Come now, the thing is clear: we shall leave on 29th September, in the morning.' From then on everything was done to humiliate the Guinean leader: an invitation to come in the General's aeroplane to Dakar was withdrawn; he was informed that the General would not meet him at the party given that evening by the Governor; Cornut-Gentille, Minister of France d'Outre-Mer, would not stay the night with him as arranged, but would go to a hotel. Next morning the General took leave of him with a disdainful 'Good luck to Guinea'.[1] It seems almost as if he was deliberately trying to discourage any inclination which Touré might still feel to vote 'Yes'. Perhaps he had decided that such a man would only be a nuisance if he came into the Community, but that Guinea might be valuable outside it as an example of the effects of France's displeasure—*pour encourager les autres*.

Touré was not the only African leader who was thinking of voting 'No'. The PRA Congress at Cotonou had after all 'adopted the password of Immediate Independence', and de Gaulle had now made it clear that those who voted 'No' would have Immediate Independence on the day after the referendum. It was rather as if he had suddenly opened a door which the PRA had assumed would take several years to break down. Now it would be seen which of the speakers at Cotonou had really meant what they said. Predictably enough this caused an embarrassing split in Senghor's party, the UPS. The established leaders—Senghor himself, Mamadou Dia, and Lamine-Guèye—all back-pedalled on their ill-considered statements at Cotonou, and argued for a 'Yes', while Abdoulaye Ly and most of the 'Young Turks' were insistent for a 'No'. De Gaulle's visit to Dakar on 26th August was the occasion of ugly anti-French demonstrations organised jointly by the 'Young Turks and the Marxist PAI.' There were shouts of 'A bas de Gaulle' and 'L'Assassin de Tiaroye'.[2] A tape of Senghor's speech at Cotonou, in which he had called for 'independence by September', was played over a loudspeaker.[3] Senghor and Dia themselves were conspicuously absent from the meeting, but Lamine-Guèye bravely appeared on the platform alongside de Gaulle, as did d'Arboussier (president of the Great Council), Ndaw (President of the Territorial Assembly), and **Valdiodio Ndiaye** (Minister of the Interior). A substantial claque of war-veterans stood between the platform and the demonstrators, whose sentiments they evidently did not share.[4]

## F. The Referendum

### (i) *UGTAN*: *The Decision to Vote No*

As it turned out, Guinea was the only territory in which the mass of the population was mobilised for a No-vote, and there the result

---

[1] Lacouture, op. cit., pp. 348–53.   [2] See above, p. 60.
[3] Morgenthau, p. 162.   [4] *Le Monde*, 28th August 1958.

was entirely attributable to Touré's personal prestige. Of those few West African leaders who eventually committed themselves to a No campaign, most were closely associated with the UGTAN group of trades unions: Touré himself in Guinea, Bakary Djibo in Niger, Abdoulaye Guèye and **Alioune Cissé** in Senegal, Abdoulaye Diallo in the Soudan. These men met in Dakar on the day after de Gaulle's visit, and decided provisionally to call for a 'No', subject to the approval of a special 'cadre conference' which would be held at Bamako on 10th September.[1] They knew that the desire for independence was strong among trade union militants–and especially among the teachers, the most effectively unionised profession.[2]

Immediately after the meeting, Sékou Touré announced: 'Between voting Yes to a constitution which infringes the dignity, the unity and the freedom of Africa, and accepting, as General de Gaulle says, immediate independence, Guinea will choose that independence without hesitating. We do not have to be blackmailed by France. We cannot yield on behalf of our countries to those who threaten and put pressure on us to make us choose, against heart and reason, the conditions of a marriage which would keep us within the complex of the colonial regime ... We say "no", unanimously and categorically, to any project which does not cater for our aspirations.'[3]

Bakary Djibo flew back to Niger for the founding congress of the Niger section of the PRA, which took the overtly nationalist name *Sawaba*–a Hausa word meaning 'homeland'.[4]


## (ii) *The RDA*

Both Touré and Djibo were anticipating the decisions of their parties–the RDA and the PRA. Both had up to now been ardent federalists, yet now they were prepared to lead their territories into independence without waiting to see if the rest of AOF would follow. In fact they must have known that this would mean the break-up of AOF, for the Ivory Coast at least was certain to vote 'Yes'. Houphouët went so far as to declare, on arriving back in Paris on 26th August: 'All Territories will vote Yes ... Africans are not madmen.' He seems to have assumed that once again his opponents would give in, after a short resistance, rather than break up the RDA. Yet this time he was not prepared to risk an open showdown with Touré. A meeting of the Co-ordination Committee, which had been fixed for

[1] Ansprenger, p. 283.  [2] See Crowder, op. cit., p. 35.
[3] Lacouture, op. cit., p. 353–4.  [4] Morgenthau, p. 312.

3rd September, at Ouagadougou, was postponed at the last moment until after the referendum.[1]

One reason for this was that Ouezzin Coulibaly, at whose insistence the meeting had been summoned, and who would have acted as its host, was desperately ill in hospital in Paris. And he alone seems to have realised the urgency of the situation. Houphouët and d'Aroussier refused to believe that Touré would really vote 'No'. His party, the PDG, was to take its final decision at a territorial conference on 14th September. They were sure that by then Touré would find some excuse to call for a 'Yes' after all, and they saw no reason to pander to his self-importance by going all the way to Conakry to talk him round.[2]

*The Soudan:* Oddly enough, this attitude seems to have been shared by Modibo Keïta, although he was still in Bamako and could easily have made the trip. Keïta and the other Soudan leaders must have been strongly tempted to call for a 'No' themselves, but only Abdoulaye Diallo actually did so. The others were more cautious. Although the Soudan had ethnic and political ties with Guinea, it had economic ones with Senegal, the most important of which was the Dakar-Niger railway. Keïta and his colleagues did not want to risk being cut off from the outside world if, as seemed probable, Senegal voted 'Yes'. They still hoped to preserve AOF as a federal Group and to endow it with a federal executive. If they now left the Franco-African Community, their last hope of getting Houphouët to accept this would disappear. Independence would be more valuable if attained by a federal AOF and not by several 'balkanised' territories; and within the terms of the Constitution it would be possible for AOF to enter the Community as a Group, and then demand independence when the federal executive had been set up. It is even said that Houphouët secretly promised to drop his opposition to such an executive, if the RDA sections would vote 'Yes'.[3]

Moreover, there was always the risk that if the US-RDA called for a No, it might be defeated.[4] Its opponents had after all won more than 25 per cent of the votes in the March 1957 elections (whereas those of the PDG in Guinea had won less than 20 per cent). If Sissoko now campaigned against it for a 'Yes', he would again have

[1] Lacouture, p. 355. Ansprenger, p. 279.
[2] Lacouture, p. 355–6.
[3] I. Wallerstein, 'How Seven States Were Born in Former French West Africa', in *Africa Report*, March 1961.
[4] Ibid.

the full weight of the administration on his side. This was still no negligible factor–as the result in Niger was to show.

Anyway, Modibo Keïta agreed–for the last time–to accept Houphouët's lead, and persuaded his party to follow suit. But he was apparently unwilling to beg Touré to do likewise,[1] either because he feared Touré would convert him rather than the other way round, or because he thought party loyalty should be a sufficient argument in itself.

Ouezzin Coulibaly died on 7th September, and the last hope of preserving RDA unity died with him. By the 11th all RDA sections except those of Guinea and Senegal had committed themselves to voting 'Yes'. In Senegal the MPS-RDA waited to see which side the UPS would come down on before taking a final decision (21st September), but there was little doubt that this time both Doudou Guèye and d'Arboussier would support Houphouët. Doudou Guèye actually did go to Guinea to try and persuade Touré, in the name of federalism, to change his mind. So did Mamadou Dia, on behalf of the Yes-party within the PRA.[2]

But the Guinea section of the PRA, which held its Congress from 4th to 7th September, decided to vote 'No'. Diawadou and Barry III seized the chance to be ahead of the PDG for once instead of behind it. On the 11th the UGTAN 'cadre conference' at Bamako ratified its steering committee's call for a 'No'.[3] Bakary Djibo publicly associated himself with this decision. Since he was the leader of the majority party in Niger, this seemed to ensure that at least one territory would vote 'No'. Next day Touré put an end to speculation about his intentions. Guinea would vote 'No', because 'to vote No is to spare ourselves a war' (*faire l'économie d'une guerre*). Two days later this decision was ratified by the PDG territorial conference. 'We shall vote "no" to inequality, we shall vote "no" to irresponsibility. As from 29th September, we shall be an independent country.'[4] Unanimous applause. Since there was no opposition, the PDG did not even have to campaign; and this time the French administration was powerless to influence the result.

[1] Lacouture, op. cit., p. 356, says he 'telephoned in a particularly sharp tone, from Bamako, to warn his comrades against any temptation to give way to the Guinean leader's pressure.'
[2] Ansprenger, pp. 279 and 281.
[3] Ibid., pp. 281 and 283.
[4] *L'Experiénce guinéenne* . . . , op. cit.

## (iii) *The PRA*

On the same day, 14th September, the PRA steering committee met in Niamey. It failed to reach any agreement, for Djibo, the General Secretary, was already committed to voting 'No', while Senghor, the President, was equally determined to vote 'Yes'. Senghor claimed that this was compatible with the Cotonou Resolution, since the Congress had only 'adopted the password of Immediate Independence', rather than actually demanding immediate independence. It was meant only as a formula with which to 'mobilise the African masses'. Not surprisingly, this argument failed to convince his opponents. The committee decided to leave each territorial section to decide how to vote 'according to local circumstances'.[1]

*Niger:* Djibo immediately announced that *Sawaba* would vote 'No'. Niger would become independent, and then join, not the Community, but the Association of Free States–without prejudice to a possible future federation with Nigeria.[2] One may reasonably wonder whether Djibo paid enough attention to 'local circumstances'. Unless and until federation with Nigeria was achieved–and that could hardly be before Nigeria became independent in 1960–an independent Niger would be little more than a 'hole in the desert'. And if such a federation were achieved, Niger's $2\frac{1}{2}$ million citizens, with their tiny French-speaking élite, would inevitably become the underprivileged cousins of the English-speaking 'giant of Africa', whose population was then estimated at about 35 million and is now thought to be nearer 60 million. *Sawaba* was likely to find little favour with the rulers of independent Nigeria. Both the federal prime minister and the prime minister of the Northern Region belonged to a strongly aristocratic, traditionalist party. They had actually succeeded in *postponing* Nigeria's independence by four years, and they were firmly opposing the rise of a 'Northern Elements' Progressive Union' which was trying to mobilise the Hausa peasantry against the Fula Emirs, and whose rallying cry was, precisely, '*Sawaba*'.[3]

But Djibo did not have to look so far afield for his enemies. True, since the end of 1956 he had been in alliance with the chiefs, but it was an alliance of interest, not of the heart. Prince Djermakoye, their

---

[1] Ansprenger, pp. 279 and 281.
[2] *La Semaine en AOF*, 20th September 1958.
[3] See James Coleman, *Nigeria: Background to Nationalism* (Los Angeles 1958).

political leader, had formerly co-operated with the French administration (in the days when he ran UNIS), and felt little enthusiasm for
Djibo's radical policies. He suspected him of wanting to abolish
chiefs, as Touré had done in Guinea – and not without reason: seven
chiefs had already been deposed at the beginning of 1958. So perhaps
Djibo should not have been surprised when, immediately after he
announced his No campaign, the chiefs suddenly seceded from
*Sawaba* and called for a 'Yes'.[1] Only the deputy Georges Condat,
formerly Djermakoye's ally, remained faithful to his new allegiance –
perhaps because he knew that the programme of independence and
union with Nigeria was popular among the Hausa of Maradi (his
birthplace) and Tessaoua (his constituency) on the Nigerian border.

Djibo and Condat had a formidable coalition ranged against them:
there was the RDA, led by Hamani Diori, strong throughout the
west of the territory; there was governor **Jean Colombani,** now ready
to scourge the enemies of the RDA in Niger as his fellow-Corsican
Ignacio Colombani had once scourged the RDA in Tchad (see pages
198–9); and there were the chiefs and administrators, in allegiance
once again: both were still powerful in this backward, strongly
traditionalist territory, especially among the nomadic tribes of the
north. There were ominous movements of French troops into Niger
from the Algerian Sahara. Even in alliance with the chiefs in March
1957, the MSA had only had 60 per cent of the votes in a 29 per cent
poll. The chances of reversing this result were obviously good.

Djibo's downfall could be foreseen by those who read the signs.
More cautious PRA leaders refused to follow him, and all territorial
sections of the PRA except those of Guinea and Niger decided to
vote 'Yes'. Neither Apithy in Dahomey nor the 'Three Musketeers'
in Upper Volta were anxious to pit their weakly built coalitions
against both France and the RDA at once. Nor were they really
eager for Immediate Independence. Few Dahomeyans wanted to
cut themselves off from France, for French money and French
engineers were about to build a harbour at Cotonou which could
transform the Dahomeyan economy; and few Voltaïques wanted
to cut themselves off from the Ivory Coast, on which their economy
largely depended. As for Sissoko in the Soudan, despite his cries of
'Independence' at Cotonou he had no desire to court a defeat by the
RDA even more decisive than that of March 1957, and thereby
destroy any hopes of a political comeback.

[1] Ansprenger, p. 282.

*Senegal:* Only in Senegal could there be any serious doubt about the PRA's decision. If Senghor had campaigned all out for a 'No', he could probably have got a majority. But he was a recent and uncertain convert to the idea of independence, and a man to whom membership of the French Community meant much. He sympathised with the criticisms levelled at the Constitution by Touré, Djibo, and the left wing of his own UPS. But he wanted to keep the door open for federalism, and he hesitated to cut Senegal off from France. Apart from more sentimental considerations, Senegal depended on France to maintain the artificially high price of its groundnuts (an argument which must have weighed heavily with Mamadou Dia, despite his bold words at Cotonou). 'Independence will have to be paid for', said Senghor. 'That is no reason to renounce it, but it is a reason to see that it is well organised. . . . My "Yes" will be a stage on the road to independence.'[1]

Senghor and Dia knew that their party was divided on the referendum. Neither choice would please everybody. But finally they thought it safer to alienate the 'Young Turks' than the traditional Moslem leaders, who were in much closer touch with the mass of the peasants. On 20th September–with only eight days to go before polling-day–the UPS Executive Committee decided to vote 'Yes'. Abdoulaye Ly and two other members of it who had already committed themselves to a 'No' immediately resigned, proclaiming their loyalty to the PRA and to the 'revolutionary positions' of the Cotonou Congress. They formed a separate party, the *PRA-Sénégal*, which attracted nearly all the left-wingers who had joined Senghor in 1956, whether they had originally belonged to FEANF, the UDS-RDA, or the *Mouvement Autonome du Casamance*. The UPS was left with those who had belonged to the two main parties before 1956–the BDS and the SFIO.

Three parties in Senegal campaigned for a 'No': the PAI, the *PRA-Sénégal*, and another new party, the *Mouvement de Libération Nationale* (MLN), whose leaders were Catholic ex-members of FEANF from Upper Volta and Dahomey who happened to be living in Dakar. Between them, these three contained nearly all of Senegal's young intellectuals and many of its leading trade unionists. On Senghor's side were the French administration, the traditional and religious leaders, the experienced politicians, and (for what it was worth) the MPS-RDA.

Throughout AOF the results revealed the isolation of the in-

[1] *Afrique Nouvelle*, 26th September 1958.

tellectuals and the trade union leaders. Universal suffrage had ensured the electoral pre-eminence of the political parties against all other types of organisation, for they alone were in contact with the rural masses. 97·6 per cent of Senegalese voters voted 'Yes', and this was a relatively low figure. In Upper Volta it was 99·1 per cent, in the Ivory Coast 99·9 per cent (in a 98 per cent poll!–These figures seem a little too good to be true). In Guinea 95·2 per cent voted 'No'. Every other territory in AOF voted 'Yes', and everywhere except in Niger the majority was 94 per cent or more. In Niger it was 78 per cent. Condat's fief of Tessaoua was the only constituency with a majority of 'Noes'. (In Maradi it was fifty-fifty.)[1] The overall poll in Niger was 37·4 per cent–low, but still higher than in 1957; it looked as if Colombani's subordinates had succeeded in keeping a number of *Sawaba* voters away from the polls, as well as mobilising many pro-French voters who had previously been non-political.[2]

## (iv) *AEF*

In AEF the issue was never really in doubt. The RDA leaders, Lisette, Youlou and Mba, were all for a 'Yes'. The PRA had no real organisation. Aubame had attended the Cotonou Congress, and so had Vice-President Goumba of Oubangui-Chari; but neither considered himself committed to the demand for Immediate Independence. Boganda would certainly have carried his territory if he had called for a 'No', but once de Gaulle had assured him that the door to independence would not be irreversibly closed he was quite happy to vote 'Yes'. No other leader was in sufficiently sure control of his territory to risk a 'No' campaign. Tchicaya and Opangault were fighting tooth and nail against the rise of Youlou (whose party had won a crucial by-election in July), and anyway they knew that Moyen-Congo depended on French aid for the construction of an important dam on the river Kouilou. Similar considerations prevailed with Aubame; and in Tchad no opposition leader wanted to drive the traditionalists, who were about to desert Lisette, back into his arms. Lisette's majority was already down to 13, after Koulamallah had won the seven seats of Chari-Baguirmi in a new election ordered by the French Council of State (1st June). Now, in September, nine members of the RDA group in the Assembly joined a new chiefs' party, the *Groupement des Intérêts Ruraux du Tchad* (GIRT), whose leader was the president of the Assembly, Gontchomé Sahoulba.

[1] Dugué, op. cit.     [2] Figures from Ansprenger, Table 7.

Koulamallah and Jean-Baptiste, the opposition leaders, wanted to woo this party (which was pro-French) rather than to alienate their own Gaullist allies by calling for a 'No'. Koulamallah was still nominally a Socialist, but he had nothing in common with Bakary Djibo. As an Arab religious leader he had been accused of favouring the FLN in Algeria, and was anxious to counteract this smear by proclaiming his loyalty to France. Both he and Sahoulba favoured keeping Tchad as a T.O.M. for the time being rather than applying for membership of the Community as a State. 'Our vocation is independence', said Koulamallah on 23rd August, 'but it would be of no benefit for us to obtain it right now. Independence would mean a multiplication of the burdens that the people of Tchad would have to bear. The MSA favours maintaining the *status quo* until independence is achieved.' His underlying motive was no doubt a feeling that French rule was preferable to that of the French-educated negroes in the PPT-RDA.

AEF seems to have almost totally lacked the emotional radicalism which made some West African leaders vote 'No' and many more wish that they could. Many Equatorial Africans had grievances against the colonial administration, and these were often voiced outspokenly, especially by Boganda. But he and almost everyone else retained a strong affection for France as an idea, and a respect for the person of General de Gaulle. The only political group in AEF which actually campaigned for a 'No' was a small splinter-group in Gabon, the *Parti d'Union Nationale Gabonaise* (PUNGA). It contained a number of youth leaders, trade unionists and students, most of whom belonged to minor tribes who resented the domination of the Fang. (One of its leaders was a tribal prince who demanded a stricter application of the treaties which France had signed with his ancestors in 1839.)[1] As a result Gabon had the largest number of No-votes in AEF: about 15,000–or 8 per cent of the total.

[1] Thompson and Adloff, *Emerging States* . . . , op. cit.

# PART FIVE

Independence,
September 1958 – August 1960

# Chapter 25

# Guinea (2nd October 1958 . . .)

Although the Guinean leaders proclaimed their desire for independence in the months before the referendum, it is not clear that they fully realised what independence meant. Certainly it did not mean the same to them as it did to de Gaulle. When de Gaulle said that anyone could take independence by voting No, he meant that they could choose whether to cut themselves off completely from France or not. For Sékou Touré it was a choice how his relationship with France should be defined. 'I shall say "NO" to the constitution but "YES" to France.' Already before the referendum actually took place he approached Governor **Mauberna** (24th September) with an informal application for Association with the Community under the terms of Article 88 of the Constitution – the same status which Djibo hoped to achieve for Niger. After the referendum and the proclamation of Guinean independence (2nd October) he attempted to present the first government of the new state to the representative of the French government, Governor **Jean Risterucci,** as if to an acting head of state. But Risterucci had been sent to replace Mauberna only for the purpose of organising the departure of French personnel. He was greatly embarrassed by Touré's gesture. Had he not already declared, on the day after the referendum, that 'Guinean independence is now a fact?'[1] He was now the representative of a foreign power, and it was quite impossible for him to take note of, or in anyway ratify, the existence of the new government. All he could do was offer the ministers a drink.[2]

Had the matter rested there it might have been no more than a joke. But de Gaulle aimed to show that voting against him was no laughing matter. Through Risterucci, the French government notified the Guinean government that it intended to transfer all French civil servants out of Guinea within two months, and that Guinea

[1] Lacouture, *Cinq Hommes et La France* (op. cit.), pp. 357–8.
[2] I was told this by M. Max Jalade, who was told it by Risterucci himself.

would receive no further public investment or budgetary aid from France.

The Guinean leaders had not believed that this would really happen. **Alioune Dramé,** the Minister of Finance, had said shortly before 28th September: 'France will not dare. It's not in her interests. It would cost her more than it would us. . . .'[1] How, he asked, could France sever itself completely from a country which had till now been so tightly integrated into its own institutions? 'Take my own case: I'm a French civil servant, ranked as clerk of the treasury [*commis du trésor*] at Rouen.' 'Believe me', replied the French journalist[2] to whom he was talking, 'you don't know General de Gaulle. Tomorrow you won't be anything any more. You'll be Guinean.' But Dramé did not believe him. Nor did Touré himself, who said to a British journalist about the same time: 'How can a mother abandon her children?'

Even after Risterucci's note they still thought de Gaulle was bluffing. The following telegram was sent to René Coty, President of the French Republic, with a copy to de Gaulle himself:

PRESIDENT REPUBLIC GUINEA
TO PRESIDENT FRENCH REPUBLIC
HEAD OF FRENCH GOVERNMENT – PARIS

CONAKRY 2.10.1958

HONOUR INFORM YOU PROCLAMATION SECOND OCTOBER 1958 REPUBLIC GUINEA BY NATIONAL ASSEMBLY – STOP – GUINEAN GOVERNMENT CONSTITUTED TODAY – STOP – INDEPENDENT AND SOVEREIGN STATE, GUINEA WISHES ESTABLISHMENT RELATIONS DIPLOMATIC LEVEL AND ON BASIS INTERNATIONAL CO-OPERATION WITH FRENCH REPUBLIC – STOP – REASSURE YOU IN NAME NATIONAL ASSEMBLY AND GOVERNMENT REPUBLIC OF GUINEA OUR SINCERE WISH FOR PRESERVATION AND DEVELOPMENT FRATERNAL FRIENDSHIP AND COLLABORATION IN COMMON INTEREST OUR TWO PEOPLES.

SIGNED: SÉKOU TOURÉ

The French government replied five days later with a bare acknowledgment. A second telegram from Touré (9th October) did elicit a fuller reply, which oddly enough was sent through the Ministry of France d'Outre-Mer – although France had declared on the very day of the referendum that relations between the two countries would from now on be governed by international law. This

[1] Lacouture, p. 358.    [2] M. Jalade.

telegram stated that France's attitude would depend not only on the nature of the agreement that Guinea desired, but also on 'the proofs that the present government of Guinea could give as to its chances of coping effectively with the expenses and obligations of independence and sovereignty', and on the advice of 'the organs of the Community when they have come into existence'.[1]

De Gaulle's attitude was not the result of pure pique. As this telegram shows, he was anxious about two things. First, could Guinea in fact stand on its own feet as an independent country, or would 'co-operation' turn out to mean merely French aid on a larger scale, and less effectively applied, than before independence? Secondly, if independent Guinea were to be treated as a returned prodigal and feasted on the fatted calf almost before it had left home, what would be the reaction of the faithful elder sons who had voted 'Yes'? De Gaulle was thinking particularly of Houphouët-Boigny, who felt humiliated and angered by Touré's breach of discipline, which he rightly saw was the beginning of the end of the federal Franco-African Community. Houphouët felt that the only hope of holding the Community together lay in a convincing demonstration of the advantages of being inside it as opposed to outside. The spectacle of Guinea languishing in poverty and chaos might be useful from this point of view. The spectacle of it receiving much the same advantages as the Member-States within the Community would be fatal.

For by taking independence Guinea had acquired an unquestionable glamour. Before, few people outside the French Union had ever heard of it. Now suddenly it was known all over the world, and Sékou Touré became a pan-African hero. Young men in Nigeria were wearing 'Sékou Touré' hats.[2] His glory dimmed the brightness of the more cautious leaders who had voted 'Yes'. Inevitably they would be tempted to follow his example in order to regain lost prestige. In Houphouët's view it was therefore essential to provide a correspondingly strong disincentive.

This view was not shared by the Soudanese leaders, who had been close to voting 'No' themselves. Abdoulaye Diallo, who had actually done so, left the Soudan and immediately became a minister in Guinea. This was a reminder of the close ties between the two territories, and particularly between their respective RDA sections.

[1] Diabate Boubacar, *Porte Ouverte sur la Communauté Franco-Africaine*, Brussels 1961.
[2] Crowder, 'Independence as a goal . . .'. (op. cit.), p. 36.

Modibo Keïta and his colleagues strongly resented Houphouët's anti-Guinean propaganda. For one thing, they realised that the further Guinea was pushed away from the Community, the less hope there would be of its eventually joining a federal West African State. The same considerations influenced Senghor, who wanted to smooth over, not accentuate, the differences between African rulers. He came out in favour of accepting the Guinean demand for 'Association'. So too did Apithy, who wisely remarked that though a sentiment of indignation against Guinea was understandable in the circumstances, 'on ne fait pas de la politique avec des sentiments'.[1]

But it was Houphouët who had de Gaulle's ear, and it was no doubt of Houphouët that the leader-writer of *Le Figaro* was thinking, when he wrote on 17th October: 'To keep M. Sékou Touré's head under water for a moment is understandable; it is an indispensable example for the sake of the territories who voted Yes.' But, the same editorial continued 'to leave the Guinean leader and Guinea itself to drown would be worse than mistake, for someone else would be found to throw him a lifebelt, and then we should have lost out on all levels.' By 'someone else' was clearly meant the USSR. This bogey failed to scare de Gaulle, whose attitude to the problem seems to have been almost Cartierist: France had no intention of wasting its resources on a state which was probably neither economically nor politically viable. If other powers wished to do so, good luck to them. 'As far as we are concerned', he declared in a press conference on 23rd October, 'Guinea is on its way and we don't know where to.[2] We are watching to see what it will be and what it will do under its present Council of Government, from the point of view of its external tendencies and connections and from the point of view of its capacity as a State, if a State really does emerge there . . .'[3] He could not have been more Olympianly aloof.

None the less Touré persisted in his efforts to reach an understanding. Early in November he sent a personal representative to Paris. It was an absurd situation. France, which had itself proclaimed the 'fact' of Guinean independence on 29th September, still refused to recognise the new Republic *de jure*, or to establish diplomatic relations with it–even when twenty other states, including Great Britain, the USA, and those of the Soviet Bloc, had already done so. As for the 'agreement of association' under Article 88, for which

---

[1] Lacouture, pp. 359–60.
[2] 'La Guinée est pour nous un devenir et nous ignorons lequel.'
[3] Lacouture, p. 362.

Touré had originally asked, there was no longer any question of it. Just as *Le Figaro* had predicted, Guinea turned elsewhere for support. On 18th November she concluded a commercial and cultural agreement with East Germany. On the 23rd a 'Union' between the states of Guinea and Ghana was declared, and the latter promised the former a loan of £10 million. Abdoulaye Diallo became Guinea's permanent minister-resident in Accra. Yet Touré took care to inform Paris of this agreement, and to assure the French government that it did not alter his desire to conclude an association with France. He even asked France to sponsor Guinea's candidature for membership of the United Nations. No reply. So this honour fell to Japan and Iraq, seconded by Ghana and Haiti. On 9th December the Security Council, on the 13th the General Assembly, voted *nem con.* for Guinea's admission. In each case there was one abstention: France.[1]

Meanwhile, on 30th November, Risterucci's mission had come to an end and the two-month time limit for the departure of French civil servants had expired. The President of the Republic moved into the former Governor's Palace, which till now he had insisted on reserving for the representative of France. He found an absurd scene of desolation: furniture and pictures had all been removed, the cellars emptied, the crockery smashed. The safe was intact–but no one knew the combination. Even the telephones had gone.[2] It was the same all over Guinea. Only 150 French government employees remained in the country, and 110 of these were teachers who did so as volunteers (thereby losing their seniority in the French academic hierarchy). All army units were of course withdrawn, but this also involved the departure of all the army doctors, who had been largely responsible for the health of the civilian population. They left abruptly, taking their medical supplies with them. The police force left after smashing the furniture and windows of its barracks. Officials took with them anything portable that belonged (by the Loi-Cadre division) to the French state, and fouled or broke anything that was too cumbersome to take.[3] At the same time Guinean students in Paris and Dakar lost their French government scholarships, French public investment in Guinea ceased altogether, and the French government tried to get private firms to stop investing there too (on the whole, unsuccessfully).[4]

[1] Ansprenger, p. 301.　　　[2] Ibid., p. 299.
[3] Lacouture, p. 364. See *Le Monde*, 3rd June 1959.
[4] *The Economist*, 4th October 1958.

In these circumstances it is not surprising that a mission sent to Guinea in December to investigate the possibility of re-establishing relations, and even of signing economic and financial agreements, was coldly received in Conakry. Touré and his colleagues did not want to seem to be negotiating under duress, and they resented the fact that the mission was headed by a colonial administrator rather than a politician or career diplomat. They felt insulted by France's continued failure to accord them formal *de jure* recognition. The whole procedure seemed to make nonsense of de Gaulle's promise that France would 'raise no obstacles' to Guinea's independence.

On the other hand, the Guinean leaders were still anxious to reach an understanding of some sort with France. They knew they would have to go on recruiting French doctors and teachers for the time being, if only for linguistic reasons. At the beginning of January 1959, therefore, they agreed to a compromise by which co-operation agreements were signed and diplomatic representation exchanged simultaneously. (Hitherto they had insisted on *de jure* recognition before signing anything.) Three agreements were signed on 7th January. By one, French was stated to be the official language of the Guinean Republic, and France undertook to provide teachers. By another, Guinea was kept within the franc zone. And the third made her eligible for French technical assistance. On 21st January the first Guinean ambassador presented his credentials to de Gaulle, who had just become first President of the Fifth French Republic. 'We hope', telegraphed Touré once again, 'that your term of office will bring not only greatness to France but a tightening of the bonds of co-operation and friendship between our two countries.' 'Greatly touched by your message', replied de Gaulle, 'like you I express my satisfaction at the protocols regulating our agreements. I send you my best wishes for the Guinean Republic, which is recognised by the French Republic, and I hope the bonds of co-operation between Guinea and France will grow tighter.'[1]

On which note one would like to end this chapter. But to do so would be misleading, unless the reader gives considerable weight to the omission of the word 'friendship' in de Gaulle's reply. Friendship was not re-established between France and Guinea, and in an unfriendly atmosphere co-operation proved impossible. Not until the summer of 1959 did a mission headed by **Roger Seydoux** arrive in Conakry to work out the practical application of the agreements. By then the atmosphere had worsened considerably, partly because

[1] Lacouture, p. 366.

334

Touré had begun to receive military aid from Czechoslovakia, partly because he was urging the African states within the Community to demand independence. No doubt the strengthening of their ties with the Soviet Bloc, and their promising relations with the United States, made the Guinean leaders feel less dependent on France. At the same time they were angered by the continued departures of French businessmen and other residents, the unconcealed hostility of many Frenchmen to their régime (whose totalitarian aspects have always received more attention from the French press than its democratic ones), and the continuation of the war in Algeria. At all events, they showed little anxiety to reach agreement, first extending the subjects of negotiation beyond Seydoux's terms of reference (so that he had to make a special trip back to Paris for further instructions), then breaking the negotiations off when only one out of twelve points of difference remained to be settled. Seydoux finally left Conakry in August 1959. By March 1960 no further progress had been made, and France then excluded Guinea from the franc zone. Trade between the two countries came practically to a stop. In April a conspiracy to overthrow the Guinean government with the help of arms smuggled in from Senegal was discovered. Almost certainly some individual Frenchmen were involved, and the Guineans asserted that the whole thing was organised by the French secret service. A further French financial mission was as unsuccessful as the last.[1]

Since then political relations between France and Guinea have never been really good (although the French company Péchiney has played an important part in exploiting Guinea's mineral resources). They improved somewhat at the end of the Algerian war (after Touré had quarrelled with the Russians), only to deteriorate again to a complete rupture at the end of 1965.

[1] Ibid., p. 368.

## Chapter 26

# Cameroun (1st January 1960)

On 24th October 1958 the Legislative Assembly of Cameroun (ALCAM) solemnly proclaimed the desire of the Camerounian people to see their State achieve complete independence on 1st January 1960. It demanded reunification of the French and British zones before that date, and invited the French Government to inform the UN General Assembly of its intentions during the current session, so that the abrogation of the Trusteeship Agreement could be timed to coincide with independence.[1]

On 22nd November ALCAM accepted a new Statute proposed to it by the French government to cover the transitional period before independence. This Statute was promulgated as an *Ordonnance* on 30th December, and came into force on 1st January 1959. Under it, Cameroun acquired complete internal autonomy such as Togo had had since February 1958. It was no longer represented in French assemblies, and its elected authorities took over all powers of legislation, administration and justice. Camerounian nationality was internationally recognised. France retained responsibility only for currency, foreign policy, frontier control and defence, and in practice she associated the Camerounian authorities with her in the management of these.[2]

Ahidjo's policy was thus vindicated by French acceptance of it. Mbida, who had formerly posed as France's only true friend in Cameroun, now suddenly left the country (23rd January) and went to Guinea, where he joined the exiled leaders of the UPC. They were sufficiently opportunist to accept his support despite the violently anti-UPC policy he had pursued when he was prime minister. On 20th February a new round of debates on Cameroun began at the UN. Mbida joined the UPC petitioners, Moumié and Madame **Ouandié**, in demanding that ALCAM be dissolved and new elections

[1] Mveng, *Histoire du Cameroun* (op. cit.).
[2] *Histoire du Cameroun, de la préhistoire au 1er janvier 1960* (op. cit.).

336

held before independence, and that the trusteeship continue until the new institutions were set up after independence. Ahidjo, who headed the official Cameroun delegation sponsored by France, wanted the existing ALCAM to continue until a few months after independence. He wanted trusteeship to end on the same day that independence was proclaimed – 1st January 1960. And he now suggested that reunification should come later, after a plebiscite in the British zone.

The western powers supported Ahidjo, the Soviet Bloc opposed him, and the Afro-Asians were divided. Even his opponents disagreed as to whether reunification should precede, coincide with, or follow independence; and the representatives of the British zone disagreed as to whether reunification should take place at all. Some of them favoured the immediate annexation of the Northern Cameroons to Northern Nigeria, without waiting for a plebiscite.[1]

On 12th March the Trusteeship Council, and on 14th March the General Assembly, decided to support Ahidjo. In Togo the UN had insisted on holding new elections before granting the end of Trusteeship. (See above, p. 297.) In Cameroun this demand was waived, for various reasons. Unlike Togo in 1957, Cameroun in 1959 already had full internal autonomy, no longer belonged to the French Union (for the French Union no longer existed), and was going to be granted complete independence. In these circumstances it was much easier for the French delegation to argue that the ends of Trusteeship had been fulfilled. Also, Ahidjo was fighting a civil war in the Bamiléké country against a more or less Communist enemy. Consequently the United States, followed by most non-Communist nations in the UN, were unwilling to let his position be undermined as Grunitzky's had been in 1957. The result might be something much worse than a mere nationalistic victory in the elections.

Fortified by this decision, Ahidjo continued with his efforts to draw the UPC's sting. By-elections were held in Sanaga-Maritime on 12th April, and Mayi Matip and his friends were allowed to win them although the UPC as a party was still illegal, and they concealed neither their membership of it, nor the part they had formerly played in the terrorist campaign under Um Nyobé's leadership. (It was of course because of this, not in spite of it, that people voted for them.) Once elected, they carried on a vociferous opposition both inside and outside ALCAM, but condemned the violent methods of the Bamiléké revolt and the exiled leaders. Ahidjo made his attitude to

[1] Mveng, op. cit.

Mayi Matip a showpiece of government tolerance, while turning the force of his wrath on the Bamiléké. In May he obtained special powers from ALCAM (curfew, internal pass system, censorship of private letters as well as publications, arrest on suspicion, and so on, and so forth). This did not succeed in preventing a new outbreak of terrorism in Douala on 27th June. The prime minister began apparently to distrust all Bamiléké, even those within the government. **Michel Njine,** Minister of Education, was dismissed on 12th September, and Daniel Kémajou was removed from the presidency of ALCAM by the Union Camerounaise majority on 13th October.[1]

But this may have been intended to conciliate the Bamiléké peasants, for Kémajou did after all represent the chiefly caste against which they had originally revolted. Cameroun could not live without the Bamiléké. It might be necessary to kill some of them and imprison or disgrace others, but the main body of the tribe would have to be won over. Ahijdo toured the Bamiléké region trying desperately to convince the population of his good intentions. But he was still unable to overcome the combination of fear (of the terrorists), loyalty (to the UPC), and resentment (of government repression) which kept the rebellion going. Much of the violence, especially in the towns, seems to have had no other purpose than to sow doubt at the UN as to whether Trusteeship should be ended while Ahidjo was in power.[2]

In vain. On 30th October ALCAM elected a consultative commission to help the government prepare a Constitution. On the 31st it voted full powers to the government and went into recess. On 19th November the UN Trusteeship Council rejected a motion proposed by India and Ghana demanding that one last mission be sent to Cameroun. And on 1st January 1960, in the presence of the UN General Secretary, Dag Hammarskjöld, the independence of Cameroun was proclaimed. On that day alone forty Africans and three Europeans were killed.[3]

On 21st February Ahidjo's constitution was ratified by referendum. It was carried by the votes of the north against the almost unanimous opposition of the south-west. (Overall totals: 797,000 'Yes', 531,000 'No'.) It was a constitution modelled on that of the Fifth French Republic, with a government chosen by and responsible

[1] Ansprenger, p. 398.    [2] Ibid., p. 397.
[3] *Le Dossier Afrique*, ed. Jean-Jacques Schellens and Jacqueline Mayer, Verviers 1962, p. 259.

to the President of the Republic, who, however, was elected by the National Assembly (ANCAM). Moumié, Mayi Matip and Mbida all opposed it, protesting that it had been worked out by the executive, which had no democratic mandate to do such a thing, and that its patent object was to safeguard the power of one party and even of one man. Mayi Matip demanded a directly elected Constituent Assembly. Even the Catholics opposed the Constitution, for they considered its Moslem and Socialist authors had gone further in separating Church and State than a country which relied so extensively on mission education could afford.

Undeterred, Ahidjo proceeded with his plans for national reconcilation. Four days after the referendum the decree of 13th July 1955, banning the UPC, was at last repealed. Thenceforth there were two UPCs: the legal, led by Mayi Matip, and the illegal, led from exile by Moumié. On 10 April general elections were held. ANCAM, like its predecessors, was composed of political groups which corresponded fairly exactly to regional blocs. Out of a hundred seats, the Union Camerounaise, representing the north and east, had 53. The Bamiléké 'Popular Front' had 18. The Démocrates Camerounais had 11, all in central Cameroun where Mbida was still popular, although he had just performed his fourth political somersault, by coming back from exile and breaking with the UPC. The Progressistes – an alliance of Okala's Socialists with what was left of Soppo Priso and Assalé's *Action Nationale* – won 9, in areas inhabited by Okala's and Assalé's tribes (respectively Bafia and Boulou). The legal UPC won 8, mainly in Bassa country. And there were two Independents from Douala: the former deputy, Prince Douala Manga Bell (who unexpectedly defeated Soppo Priso) and Dr **Marcel Bebey Eyidi,** a former associate of Aujoulat's who was sympathetic to, but not a member of, the UPC.[1]

On 5th May Ahidjo was elected first President of the Cameroun Republic. Assalé became prime minister and Okala foreign minister. Mbida's followers and the Popular Front were also brought into the government. Only the UPC and the two Independents remained in opposition. The illegal UPC did not of course take part in the elections. Its adherents demonstrated their opinion of them by burning part of the town of Douala. A month later they were attacking shops and burning them down in broad daylight. In July the government undertook a large-scale military campaign in the Bamiléké region, and succeeded in killing 130 rebels. At the same

[1] Ansprenger, pp. 400–1.

time Ahidjo prepared to bring about the achievement of the only item in the original UPC programme which was still outstanding: reunification. He visited Buea, capital of the (British) 'Southern Cameroons' and reached agreement with the prime minister, **John Foncha,** on a form of loose federation. On 11th and 12th February 1961 the Southern Cameroons voted in favour of reunification. (The Northern Cameroons, which were not contiguous with the Southern –though they were with the north of ex-French Cameroun–voted to join Northern Nigeria.) The federal state of Cameroon came into existence on 1st October 1961. It continued to benefit from French military, economic and cultural co-operation under the terms of an agreement signed by France and the Republic of Cameroun in November 1960, and from associate membership of the European Economic Community.[1]

[1] See Williard R. Johnson, 'The Cameroon Federation: Political Union between English- and French-speaking Africa' in Lewis (ed.), *French-Speaking Africa and the Search for Identity*, op. cit.

# Chapter 27

# *Togo (27th April 1960)*

The independence of Togo was fixed by the UN General Assembly, at Olympio's request, for 27th April 1960 – the second anniversary of his electoral triumph over Grunitzky. He devoted two years of preparation to making Togo as economically self-sufficient as possible, for he wished his country to be independent in fact as well as name. Cheated of his original pan-Ewe hopes, he firmly opposed Nkrumah's hints that the Ewe could still be reunited if Togo were incorporated into Ghana. Relations between the two states grew worse when Nkrumah began to accuse Olympio of fomenting discontent among the Ewe of former British Togoland. Togo drew away from Ghana, and Olympio held aloof from Nkrumah's pan-African schemes. He also drew closer to France, and even talked of the possibility of a 'commonwealth français'[1] – though he showed no interest in joining the existing French Community, or any of the African groupings within it.

Olympio's isolationist foreign policy and lack of ideological commitment won him enemies on the Left of his own party. JUVENTO, which had started as the CUT youth movement, broke away from the CUT during 1959 and went into opposition. At the same time his old enemies on the Right drew together: Grunitzky merged his party with that of the Northern chiefs in a *Union Démocratique des Populations du Togo* (UDPT). This party won respectable minorities of seats in three of Togo's six communes when municipal elections were held in November 1959 (a month after its foundation). In January 1960 **Antoine Méatchi,** who was now Grunitzky's main northern ally, was manhandled by CUT militants. But Olympio was not personally responsible for this, and in general he seems to have allowed his opponents a degree of freedom rare in any part of Africa.[2]

His idea seems to have been to adopt an attitude of benevolent

---

[1] *La Monde*, 2nd August 1958.     [2] Ansprenger, p. 408.

detachment before all groups and alliances, and so to make himself the honest broker of inter-African diplomacy–a rôle which his personal charm and his fluency in both French and English well fitted him for. At the time of Togo's independence many regarded him as the outstanding success story of democratic African politics. His assassination, on 13th January 1963, by soldiers of the tiny national army which he was trying to disband because he considered it a pointless expense, came as a considerable shock to Africa and the world. But it did not damage Togo's relations with France. On the contrary, for the soldiers recalled Grunitzky and Méatchi to power, and they pursued a consistently pro-French foreign policy. Togo has remained an associate member of the E.E.C., and a recipient of substantial economic aid both from France and from West Germany.

# Chapter 28

## The French Community: Balkanisation[1]

### A. Niger

The situation of Niger immediately after the referendum was anomalous. It had a government which had come out firmly for a 'No', and which still had a majority in the Territorial Assembly, but which had apparently been repudiated by the result of the referendum. Prince Djermakoye, who had played an important part in creating this situation, now attempted to profit from it by starting a 'third force' party which would hold the balance in the Assembly between PRA and RDA. He failed. Only seven other PRA assemblymen resigned from the party along with him, and this still left Djibo with an overall majority of six.

None the less on 14th October Djibo agreed to resign, in view of the referendum result, in order to form a coalition government. This manoeuvre failed too, for the opposition knew that the tide had now turned in their favour and made no serious efforts to reach a compromise. Governor Colombani, whose aim was now the removal by hook or crook (and mainly, as it turned out, crook) of Djibo's government, took advantage of the deadlock and temporarily assumed the powers of government in person. Several of Djibo's ministers were immediately prosecuted for misappropriating government petrol during the referendum campaign.

Then, on 14th November, the French Council of Ministers issued a decree dissolving the Territorial Assembly. It was easy to foresee what would happen next. Vainly did Senghor and Lamine-Guèye attempt to come to Djibo's rescue (for surprisingly enough PRA party loyalty survived the battle between 'Yes' and 'No'). A press conference which they held in Paris on 19th November, to protest against the administration's blatant electoral and pre-electoral manoeuvres, was loftily ignored by the government. Senghor then went in person to Niamey to confer with the local PRA leaders. But his

[1] For all but the last section of this chapter, the main source where not otherwise stated, is Dugué, *Vers les Etats-Unis d'Afrique* (op. cit.).

protests only drew counter-objections from Djermakoye and Hamani Diori. New elections were held on 15th December. The RDA and the dissident PRA formed joint lists which included 25 chiefs and sons of chiefs (out of 60 candidates), and were easily the victors. Only in the six-seat constituency of Zinder–an old stronghold of Djibo's party–the list headed by Hamani Diori himself was defeated by the *Sawaba* one of Mamani Abdoulaye. This did not stop the new Assembly from electing Hamani as first prime minister of the Republic of Niger, which became a Member-State of the Community on 18th December.[1]

'Morally', commented Senghor, 'I sometimes wonder if we were right to vote "Yes". The acts perpetrated throughout the election campaign take us back to the time of the *indigénat*. I refuse to believe that General de Gaulle would approve of the inhuman methods which were used during the election campaign in Niger, and which are contrary to France's interests. The determination to crush Djibo Bakary at all costs has made him a martyr.' But it was useless to speculate what General de Gaulle would or would not approve of. He was not available for comment.

### B. The Primary Federation

Senghor's concern was not of course purely altruistic. What was at stake in Niger was not so much abstract democratic principles as the future political geography of West Africa. Bakary Djibo was well known as a passionate advocate of the federal executive. His failure to lead Niger to independence had only made him more anxious to form a strong federal West African State which would soon be able to take independence even if this meant leaving the Community. Hamani Diori, on the other hand, although his section had supported the federalist line at Bamako (Niger was after all one of the poorest territories, and therefore particularly dependent on federal expenditure), was above all a loyal RDA man and a loyal French citizen. His political position was now such that he could ill afford to offend either France or Houphouët. Once his government was installed in office, there was little prospect of Niger joining a new West African federation.

Such a federation–a 'primary federation' which would come between the individual West African territories and the federal Community itself–was now Senghor's main political aim. The arguments

[1] Ansprenger, Table 1.

for and against it were of course substantially the same as those for and against the federal executive had been in the time of the Loi-Cadre. But the balance between the two sides had shifted. Sékou Touré, once the leader of the federalists, had gone out into outer darkness, and had thereby demonstrated that a single territory could become independent on its own. Within the RDA his departure (for the PDG ceased to be an RDA section in October 1958) removed the main focus of opposition to Houphouët. Any hope that the Ivory Coast might be pushed into joining a federation by pressure from inside the RDA vanished overnight. Houphouët would go his own way now, that was certain. A suggestion that the three remaining RDA-controlled territories (the Soudan, Upper Volta and the Ivory Coast) should form a federation by themselves was quickly scotched. The question that remained was: could a federation be formed without Houphouët, and if so, how many territories would join?

Clearly the Great Council, which Sékou Touré had tried to turn into a federal parliament, remained the most convenient meeting-point for negotiations. On 12th November its bureau assembled, with President d'Arboussier in the chair. The Ivory Coast was not represented, but RDA members from Upper Volta and the Soudan were there, as well as two UPS leaders from Senegal and one Mauritanian. To this informal meeting d'Arboussier submitted a paper in which he discussed three main problems. The first was that of the relations between the putative Primary Federation and the Community. On this point he had already sounded out the French government, and had been told 'that once the Primary Federations were set up, and if the territories which compose them so desire, the said Federations could join the Community as States'. This answer was in conformity with the Constitution, Article 76 of which stated that the T.O.M. could become Member-States of the Community 'either in groups or as single units'. In fact the French government was not very keen on the idea of a Primary Federation in West Africa. It considered that such a Federation lost most of its point once Guinea and the Ivory Coast were excluded from it, and it rightly suspected that some of the federalist leaders, particularly Bakary Djibo and Modibo Keïta, intended to use the Federation as a stepping-stone to independence, possibly even to a reunion with Guinea outside the Community. But rather than oppose it overtly, de Gaulle and his ministers contented themselves with encouraging Houphouët and exercising discreet pressure on waverers to follow him rather than the federalists. The latter were at a disadvantage inasmuch as it would take time to set up the Primary Federation, and time was not on their side. Every month that passed reinforced the habits of autonomy within the different territories, and made them less anxious to give up the powers they had acquired. Indeed the federalist leaders almost sold the pass before they had even captured it, for they had to agree to let the individual territories enter the Community in the first instance as 'Autonomous Republics'. (The Soudan did so on 24th November, Senegal on the 25th, Mauritania on the 28th, Dahomey and the Ivory Coast on 4th December.)[1]

The second problem was that of the powers which these Republics would eventually resign to the Primary Federation. D'Arboussier considered it indispensable that they should include customs, tax-collection, control of the civil service, enforcement of the Labour Code, development programmes, and judicial organisation. Other services such as the struggle against endemic diseases and migrant insects, aerial and maritime security, and mining research, might be regrouped more gradually in the interests of greater efficiency. There should also be a concentration of higher education and specialised schools since these were too expensive to be maintained by individual territories. All these services should be under the authority of a Federal Assembly composed of an equal number of members elected by the Legislative Assembly of each territorial state – like the existing Great Council. What form the executive should take d'Arboussier was uncertain. It was suggested that there should be a Federal Executive Committee composed of all the territorial Prime Ministers and one other minister from each territory, delegated to deal with federal affairs (on the model of the projected Executive Council of the Community). These minister-delegates should form a standing commission to manage the common services, and would be responsible to the Federal Assembly.

Thirdly, what form should the Federal Assembly's decision take? D'Arboussier thought it should have sovereign power in matters within its competence, as well as the right to make recommendations on other matters submitted to it by the Assemblies of the individual States.

The opponents of this programme were not unfavourable to any sort of interstate co-operation, or even to the idea of poor states being subsidised by rich ones. But they were unfavourable to any sacrifice of sovereignty, advocating instead a purely economic

[1] Ibid.

*Entente*. Political federation, they said, would only mean high expenditure on federal services, and particularly on an unnecessary 'super-Assembly' and 'super-Government'.

The clash between these points of view came out clearly at a meeting of the bureau of the RDA Co-ordination Committee on 15th November. Modibo Keïta defended the federalist position; Houphouët and Hamani Diori pleaded the cause of the non-political *Entente*. There seemed to be no prospect of agreement, and the full meeting of the Co-ordination Committee, which had been fixed for 27th November at Brazzaville, was again cancelled. The RDA was now openly split. Both wings competed for the support of the Mauritanians, formerly the RDA's allies in the Great Council. First Modibo Keïta and Doudou Guèye, then a delegation from the Ivory Coast, visited the new Mauritanian capital, Nouakchott. The Ivory Coast leaders were prepared to make quite big concessions in order to defeat the political federation: **Philippe Yacé,** who led the delegation, proposed not only an annual conference of Presidents of Legislative Assemblies and Prime Ministers to discuss common problems, but also a federal treasury which should receive one tenth of each member-state's budget, and from which the *ristournes* should be in inverse proportion to the amounts paid in–the very principle which the Ivory Coast respresentatives had formerly refused to accept in the AOF Great Council (but then of course the Ivory Coast's contribution to the federal budget had been very much more than 10 per cent of her global revenue).[1]

The Mauritanians declined, for the time being, to commit themselves, and both sides pushed ahead with their plans. At this point four territories appeared to be favourable in principle to the Primary Federation, and agreed to send representatives to a meeting at Bamako on 29th December. Two were PRA-controlled (Senegal and Dahomey), one RDA (the Soudan), and in the fourth (Upper Volta) the internal political situation was thoroughly confused.

## C. Upper Volta

On the death of Ouezzin Coulibaly, Maurice Yaméogo became acting head of government in Upper Volta. (He was the Minister of Agriculture whose timely defection from MDV to RDA had saved

[1] See Elliot Berg, 'The Economic Basis of Political Choice in French West Africa', in *The American Political Science Review*, June 1960.

Coulibaly from defeat in January.) In October he presented himself for election by the Territorial Assembly, with an all-RDA list of ministers. The opposition, strongly backed by the Moro Naba, demanded a 'government of union', but eventually agreed to vote for Yaméogo on condition that he succeeded in forming such a government within thirty days. A week later (26th October) an RDA conference rejected this idea and demanded a Constitution, followed by new elections. It also came out in favour of a Primary Federation. Yaméogo ostensibly accepted the conference's decisions; this gave him an excuse not to form a coalition government. But on the federal issue he back-pedalled hard, for he considered economic links with the Ivory Coast more important to Upper Volta than political ones with Senegal and the Soudan. After consulting personally with Houphouët he showed his hand at the end of November by dismissing two ministers who were known to be leading federalists. One of them, **Ousman Bâ,** was Soudanese by birth and had formerly been Coulibaly's right-hand man.

For a moment it looked as if Yaméogo had over-reached himself. There was a real possibility that the Bobo-Dioulasso wing of the RDA, which was uniformly federalist, would join forces with the PRA against him. After a visit from Modibo Keïta on 3rd and 4th December the Bobos were even talking of demanding detachment from Upper Volta and union with the Soudan, if the Upper Volta Assembly should oppose federation. On the 6th the Moro Naba again called for a union government, and he too now declared himself in favour of the Primary Federation. Just in time Yaméogo bent before the storm. By 10th December he had formed a coalition, with six RDA ministers and five PRA. The Assembly invested this government with only two votes against and one abstention; and on 11th December, the Republic of Upper Volta entered the Community as an apparently united state, with Yaméogo as its first prime minister.

It was generally thought that Yaméogo had now accepted the federalist programme. A motion was proposed by which 'The Republic of Upper Volta decides to form a Federation with the States of Afrique Noire, members of the Community, who will have made their choice.' This was then amended, by 34 votes to 32, to read 'The Voltaic Republic decides to form with the States of Afrique Noire, members of the Community, a Federation which shall protect the interests of the Voltaic State and guarantee African Unity.' The result was publicised as a vote in favour of the Primary

Federation. But in Paris, on December 18th, Yaméogo informed General de Gaulle that the Assembly had voted by 34 votes to 32 in favour of co-ordination with the Ivory Coast and against an unconditional political Federation with the other neighbouring Republics.

In fact, his sudden acceptance of the coalition seems to have been not a capitulation to the federalists at all, but the prelude to an attempt to turn their flank by finding anti-federalist allies among the former opposition (i.e. the PRA). As such it succeeded brilliantly. As early as 20th December the Moro Naba modified his position considerably: 'We could not', he said, 'submit blindly to a Federation which would be a dangerous weapon in the hands of subversive elements who would irremediably jeopardise the peace and prosperity of our country and our peoples.' Somebody – either Yaméogo or the French, or both – must have pointed out to him that in a Federation dominated by the Soudan RDA his chiefly privileges (the most extensive in Afrique Noire) would be unlikely to last long. But that did not mean that those PRA leaders who *favoured* social reform among the Mossi were necessarily federalist. The founders of the MDV – Gérard Ouédraogo (who was one of those to whom Yaméogo had just given a portfolio) and Michel Dorange – were still officially Gaullists, and out of sympathy with the PRA's federalist programme. Ouédraogo did not conceal his preference for close contacts with Abidjan.

## D. The Birth of Mali

On 27th December, Yaméogo returned from Paris and put up a further smokescreen of ambiguous statements. Evidently a fierce argument was going on within his government between federalists and Houphouëtists. On the 28th the French High Commissioner in Upper Volta sent a telegram to Bamako saying no official Upper Volta delegation would attend the federalist conference, which was to open there next day. Sure enough, on the morning of the 29th only Soudanese, Senegalese and Dahomeyans were present. But then came a telephone call from Ouagadougou: the Voltaïques were coming after all. At 3 p.m. their plane arrived. On it were three ministers (two RDA and Gérard Ouédraogo for the PRA) and fifteen assemblymen, including Nazi Boni (PRA), Joseph Conombo (PRA), Ousman Bâ (federalist RDA) and Djibril Vinama, the Mayor of Bobol Dioulasso, an RDA militant since 1946 and now

349

an ardent federalist. The most conspicious absentee was Yaméogo himself. Otherwise the delegation was reasonably representative.

As for the other territories, there was of course a strong RDA delegation from the Soudan, as well as d'Arboussier and Doudou Guèye from Senegal. The PRA was represented by all its most important leaders in Senegal and Dahomey: Senghor, Dia, Lamine-Guèye, Apithy, Zinsou, Adandé, Maga. There were also observers from Mauritania. The atmosphere was hopeful, if tense. 'Each time the Africans gather at Bamako', cried Zinsou poetically, 'they feel the beating of their collective heart. Even if I were to be classified as a foreigner in Dakar and in Niamey, it would make no difference, I feel at home in Bamako and there is nothing you can do about it.'

Apithy, who presided at the first session, was more sober in his approach. He was in favour of the Federation, he said, 'in so far as it will allow Dahomey to maintain flexible relations with its immediate neighbours. It is unthinkable that we should be penalised by our neighbours for our adhesion.' It was not surprising that Apithy, who in the years before 1956 had been one of the most determined advocates of the decentralisation of AOF, should display reserves about the new Federation; and it was traditional that Dahomey should be preoccupied by its relations with Togo and Nigeria as much as with the other territories of AOF. But when Apithy spoke of being 'penalised by our neighbours' ('*que nous subissions de la part de nos voisins les conséquences de notre adhésion*') he must surely have been referring to the attitude of the Ivory Coast, where Dahomeyan immigrants had been the principal victims of some horrible xenophobic pogroms at the end of October. Houphouët might deplore these events. It was none the less true that they had been partly inspired by Ivoiriens' resentment of the federalist attempt to encircle their territory and defy their leader.[1] Apithy did not wish to defy Houphouët. Nor did he wish to defy France—and France had been hinting that the Cotonou harbour project might be jeopardised if Dahomey insisted on joining the Federation.

But neither Upper Volta nor Dahomey was ready to reject Federation out of hand; the grass-roots appeal of African unity was too strong for that. All four delegations signed a proclamation 'expressing the will to form between the states of West Africa,

[1] Morgenthau, p. 217.

members of the Community, a Primary Federation'. It was decided that each State's Assembly should nominate representatives to a Federal Constituent Assembly which would meet at Dakar on 14th January 1959.

For Yaméogo this was going a little far. He now announced that the delegates of the Upper Volta government had been sent only as observers. None the less, under pressure from federalist demonstrations in Bobo-Dioulasso, he agreed to submit the conclusions of the Bamako Conference to the Upper Volta Assembly. Then, confronted with a federalist majority in the Assembly which was now demanding his resignation, he was able to save his government only by promising to attend the Dakar meeting in person.

Apithy suffered a similar defeat at the hands of the federalists in the Dahomey Assembly, led by Alexandre Adandé. He thereupon resigned his place in the delegation to Dakar. Two places in it were offered to the opposition (the UDD-RDA), but Ahomadegbé refused them. He was already committed to the Houphouët line. Dahomey was therefore represented in the Federal Constituent Assembly by a delegation which included neither the prime minister nor any member of a party which had won 27 per cent of the votes in the 1957 elections, and had been growing in strength since.

The Upper Volta delegation was greeted on its arrival in Dakar by the news that a new French High Commissioner to Upper Volta had just been appointed. His name was **Masson,** and he was already known in the territory, for he had been *chef de cabinet* to Governor Mouragues. His appointment was a political favour to the MRP (and Pflimlin in particular), and probably not intended as a deliberate act of African policy at all. But Mouragues' rule was too well-remembered for Africans to be indifferent to his subordinate's return. They saw it as an ominous reminder that there were Frenchmen who knew how to run an election in an African territory where chiefs were still powerful and political parties weak. Would a federalist government in Upper Volta go the way of Bakary Djibo? It seemed at least possible.

For the moment these forebodings were set aside. In three days a Federal Constitution was worked out under the chairmanship of Modibo Keïta (who had just replaced d'Arboussier as President of the Great Council), and on 17th January the Federation of Mali was solemnly proclaimed. The name was one already endowed with historical resonance. In the fourteenth century the Mandé empire of Mali had controlled the whole Western Sudan from Cape Verde to the edge of modern Nigeria.[1] Its founder Soundiatta Keïta (died 1255) was a hero of African romance to whose family Modibo Keïta was proud to belong. At Modibo's bidding all the delegates rose and swore 'on their honour, in the name of respect for African dignity, to defend the Mali Federation everywhere.'[2]

## E. A Federation of Two

The Federal Constitution was ratified by the Soudan Assembly on 22nd January, by those of Senegal and Upper Volta on the 28th. On 29th it was discussed by the steering committee of the Dahomey PRA. Apithy now openly opposed it, on the grounds that it encroached too far on Dahomeyan autonomy. Besides, he said, it was geographically absurd for Dahomey to federate with Senegal, the Soudan and Upper Volta, when her most important economic links were with Togo and Niger. But he was unable to persuade his colleagues to repudiate the oath they had just sworn in Dakar. On the 31st, therefore, he resigned from the PRA. But he was still prime minister of Dahomey.

On 3rd and 4th February the prime ministers of the Member-States assembled in Paris for the first meeting of the Executive Council of the Community. Apithy was able to declare before his colleagues and before de Gaulle[3] that he could 'not agree to join the Mali Federation in its present form'. Meanwhile in Dakar Dahomeyan students were demanding his resignation, and in Porto Novo–where the influx of refugees from the Ivory Coast had swelled the ranks of the unemployed–there were riots outside the Assembly. Fifteen people were injured, and the RDA leader, Ahomadegbé, demanded dissolution. His request was ignored and on 6th February the Assembly met, protected by the *Garde Républicaine du Dahomey*. It appointed a Consultative Constitutional Commission which was to produce a constitution by 15th February. Apithy still had a majority. He remained in office and did not dismiss his federalist ministers. But he reconstituted his old party, the PRD, outside the PRA and in opposition to Mali. While some northern

[1] Its power, wealth and organisation are admiringly recorded in the *Travels* of Ibn Battuta.
[2] Ansprenger, p. 336.
[3] De Gaulle had been elected President of the French Republic and hence *ex officio* of the Community, on 21st December 1958. The electoral college included 2488 electors in Afrique Noire (as against 76,359 in metropolitan France). Ansprenger, p. 321.

federalists talked wildly of seceding from Dahomey and joining Upper Volta, the PRD majority in the Assembly voted through a Constitution which contained no reference to any Primary Federation, still less to Mali as such. 'Now and in the future', declared Apithy, 'I say "No" to the Mali Federation–in the form in which it is proposed to us.'

Upper Volta was soon to follow suit. True, the Territorial Assembly (which had now renamed itself 'Constituent') accepted the Federal Constitution unanimously. But eleven deputies were absent at the time, and one of them, Michel Dorange, immediately resigned from his party (the PRA). As for Prime Minister Yaméogo, he had sworn the oath to Mali at Dakar, but it seems as if he had done so only in order to put his opponents off their guard. During February he carried his anti-federalist plans into action with Machiavellian skill. First of all he obtained special powers for his coalition government (although 18 PRA deputies abstained), and prorogued the Assembly until further notice. Then, on 25th February, by which time the federalist deputies (most of whom in both parties came from the west) were well away from Ouagadougou, he suddenly reconvened it for two days later. On the 27th only 31 out of 70 deputies were present–less than a quorum. The government had therefore to prorogue the Assembly once again–but did so for the minimum time allowable, until five minutes past midnight the next morning. At dawn on the 28th the Constitution of the Republic of Upper Volta was voted by 37 votes to 2: it defined the Republic's place in the Community without once mentioning the Mali Federation. Indeed it might well have been drafted in Abidjan. Yaméogo had clearly worked hard on members of both parties during the recess–and the hard-line federalists arrived furious but too late. Yaméogo left for Paris, where the second meeting of the Executive Council was held on 2nd and 3rd March, leaving his embarrassed friends to explain that he hadn't actually sworn the oath at Dakar, but merely raised his arm to adjust his coat.[1] He himself attributed his change of front to the 'contacts which I made and the conversations I had–both in Africa and in Paris'. In fact there could be little doubt that he was influenced principally by Houphouët. 'The Mali Federation', he said (in perfect Houphouëtese), 'would be a wall between us and the Community'. And he went on to stress the vital economic links, such as the railway, which attached Upper Volta to Abidjan rather than Dakar.

[1] 'Perhaps he was already wanting to turn it', suggests M. Dugué.

On 15th March the Upper Volta Constitution was submitted to the people by referendum and obtained a four-fifths majority. Nearly all the Noes were in the west–the area closest to Bamako. The federalists were hampered in organising opposition by the fact that they were still divided between the two parties.

So two states were detached from the Mali Federation before it had even started. Similar attempts were made to sabotage federalism in the remaining two–Senegal and the Soudan. But there the party leaders, unlike Apithy and Yaméogo, were whole-hearted federalists from the start: the only hope was to bring about their defeat. In Senegal some of the pro-French traditionalist leaders, including Ibrahima Seydou Ndaw, were first drawn into a semi-political *Association pour la Cinquième République*. When this was suppressed on the grounds that the Republic of Senegal was now separate from the Fifth French Republic, they resigned from the UPS and formed an opposition party, the *Parti de la Solidarité Sénégalaise* (PSS), which then negotiated with the existing Left opposition (PRA-Sénégal and PAI) in the hope of forming an anti-federalist front. In the Soudan it was the PRA, under Hammadoun Dicko's influence, which turned anti-federalist, in alliance with the pro-French Cadi (Moslem ruler) of Timbuktu. Both these efforts collapsed when put to the test in general elections. On 8th March the US-RDA secured 76 per cent of the votes and all the seats in the Soudan Legislative Assembly. Dicko did not have a majority even in his own village. In Senegal the alliance between pro-French *marabouts* and 'immediate independence' extremists not surprisingly failed to materialise. Senghor and Dia were able to retain or win back the support of the most important religious leaders,[1] and in the elections on 22nd March the PSS made no significant showing at all. The PRA-Sénégal had a respectably large minority vote in the Casamance, but elsewhere was equally unsuccessful. The MPS-RDA, under pressure from Bamako, had now merged with the UPS, so that the federalists presented a united front and d'Arboussier was elected on a UPS ticket.

### F. Mali in Action

Senegal and the Soudan were now ready to bind themselves in the federal harness which Apithy had found too tight. On 24th March

[1] To do so they made a number of concessions, notably agreeing to include some Moslem scholars on the list of UPS candidates.

the two governing parties (UPS and US) held a joint conference in Dakar. Also present were the leaders of federalist opposition movements in other territories: the RDA and PRA of western Upper Volta (Ali Barraud and Nazi Boni), *Sawaba* of Niger (Bakary Djibo and Georges Condat), and the rump of the PRA in Dahomey (Adandé and Zinsou). All agreed to unite their parties in a new interterritorial movement: the *Parti de la Fédération Africaine* (PFA). Modibo Keïta thus at last broke with the RDA, which henceforth would be simply the party of Houphouët-Boigny and his supporters. The Senegalese and Soudanese also agreed that their Federation should be represented in the Executive Council of the Community, preferably as well as, but failing that instead of, their individual states.

Both now proceeded to a preliminary reorganisation of their territorial governments. Sissoko and the Soudan PRA, reconverted to federalism after their electoral defeat, agreed to merge with the US as a section of the PFA (leaving the discredited anti-federalist Dicko out in the cold). At the same time Modibo Keïta took over the presidency of the government in person (Koné stepping down to vice-president). In Senegal the Assembly met for the first time in Dakar (which had just replaced Saint-Louis as the territorial capital) and appropriately elected Lamine-Guèye, the mayor of Dakar, its president. Mamadou Dia remained at the head of the government.

On 5th April the Great Council of AOF met for the last time, and handed over its buildings to the Federal Assembly of Mali. This body, which had 20 Soudanese and 20 Senegalese members, proceeded to elect Senghor its president. Then it elected the first Federal Government, which was intended to be a 'symbiosis at the federal level of the executives of both States'. Thus Modibo Keïta headed it, with Mamadou Dia as vice-president. There were six other ministers: three from the Soudan cabinet (including Ousman Bâ, formerly minister of Public Works in Upper Volta) and three from the Senegal one. Since each cabinet had only 14 members altogether (whereas by May 1959 that of Upper Volta had 16 and that of the Ivory Coast 21) the 'super-government' was not so absurdly expensive after all.

## G. The Conseil de l'Entente

While the federalists closed their ranks to fill the gaps left by desertion, Houphouët set about marshalling his growing number of followers in a looser formation. He summoned them to membership of a 'Conseil de l'Entente':

This Council would be a meeting of the Prime Ministers of all the states, assisted by the Ministers concerned with common affairs, to whom would be added the Presidents and Vice-Presidents of Legislative Assemblies. The Council would sit by turns in the capital of each state ... It would take decisions, either by unanimous vote, or by a specified majority–that is a question to be discussed–and these decisions would be enforceable. In case of dispute we shall have recourse to the Court of Arbitration of the Community.[1]

*Upper Volta* was the first state to answer the call. First the Moro Naba, then Yaméogo, visited Abidjan for discussions, and an agreement was concluded on 4th April. Fortified by this, Yaméogo proceeded to hold general elections under his new Constitution on 19th April. By skilful use of a strange electoral law which he drafted himself in virtue of the powers voted to him two months before, he succeeded in producing an overwhelming RDA majority which was also predominantly anti-federalist. Meanwhile on 12th April the *Ivory Coast* affirmed its confidence in Houphouët's policy by a massive turn-out at the polls to elect the single list of PDCI-RDA candidates to the Legislative Assembly. On 2nd May, Houphouët himself replaced Denise as prime minister, simultaneously resigning as 'Ministre d'Etat' in the French cabinet. He still hoped that the Community would develop into a 'real multinational state, with a federal government and central federal assemblies'.[2] There was little sign of this happening in the near future, but in the meantime he continued to oppose political federation on the West African level, and to pursue the construction of the Conseil de l'Entente. *Niger* came into it soon after Upper Volta, and *Dahomey's* adherence was delayed only by the confusion of its internal politics. Here elections were held on 2nd April. Apithy jerrymandered them so successfully that the PRD won 37 seats although it actually had fewer votes than the UDD-RDA, which won only 11 seats. After a predictable outcry there was a partial re-election and Apithy was forced to resign. There was then a three-cornered political crisis lasting about a month, and finally on 21st May Hubert Maga emerged as head of a three-party coalition. He duly appeared at the first meeting of the Conseil de l'Entente, which was held at Abidjan on 29th May.

[1] This body was provided for in the Constitution, but it never actually met.
[2] *Le Monde*, 26th May 1959.

The Conseil agreed to set up a joint treasury (whose real function would be the canalisation of financial aid from the Ivory Coast to the other States), and to maintain the customs union between its members. (A few days later an agreement was signed in Paris with representatives of Mali and Mauritania, by which all former AOF except Guinea was kept as a free trade area.) The basis of a common social and economic policy was discussed. The port of Abidjan and the Abidjan-Ouagadougou railway were placed under joint administration.[1] The policy of economic co-operation without sacrifice of sovereignty could now be tested in practice, and its achievements compared with those of the Mali Federation.

## H. Equatorial Africa

The Federation of AEF, like its sister AOF, was condemned by the silence of the 1958 Constitution. The Equatorial territories too had to decide whether or not to group themselves federally before asking for membership of the Community. Except in Gabon, the desperate poverty of the territories predisposed their leaders to seek some kind of federal solution. But there were political and ethnic differences between them which made it difficult to reach agreement. Youlou was preoccupied not with the future of AEF as such but with that of the ba-Kongo people. He dreamed of an Equatorial State, which would unite, under his leadership, the ba-Kongo now divided between French, Belgian and Portuguese rule. This objective was of course of little interest to the leaders of other territories, or to Youlou's own political rivals. In Gabon, Aubame, who had previously supported Mba's government in its opposition to the idea of a federal executive, seems to have come round to a federalist point of view after the Cotonou Congress. At the end of August 1958 he proposed a meeting of AEF leaders at Brazzaville to 'study the possibility of creating a state of Equatorial Africa'–but one unlike that proposed by Youlou. He was able to persuade Mba to modify his extreme territorialist line. In October, Mba reshuffled his government to accommodate Aubame's party, and agreed to send a representative to confer with heads of government in the other territories. Later he went so far as to say, 'Gabon is not hostile to a secondary community of AEF states'.

Meanwhile Boganda produced his own formula for a 'Central African State', and gained the support of the PRA leaders in Moyen-

[1] Ansprenger, p. 362.

Congo (Opangault and Tchicaya). But this very fact assured him of Youlou's opposition, and that in turn made it difficult for Lisette and Mba, who were officially allied with Youlou in the RDA, to support him. In any case neither of them was very keen to help Boganda assume the leadership of all AEF, which was what he evidently hoped to do. At the beginning of November, therefore, Boganda re-defined his plan: 'In proposing the Central African State, our aim is to reconstitute the Congo and to form a Great Congo, which would be open to all and whose capital would be at Brazzaville. We should like to preserve AEF in a form more efficacious and less costly than the old one. . . . Faced with reservations on the part of Tchad and Gabon, this single state will for the time being be confined to Oubangui-Chari and Moyen-Congo.'[1]

Even this limited union proved impossible to realise. Opangault's government was too weak to carry Moyen-Congo into it against Youlou's opposition. As in AOF, the different territories decided to become separate Member-States of the Community in the first instance. On 28th November the Autonomous Republics of Tchad, Gabon and the Congo were proclaimed.[2] In the Congo (ex-Moyen-Congo) the proclamation provided the occasion for the collapse of Opangault's government–and therefore indirectly of Boganda's hopes. A former MSA assemblyman, **Georges Yambot,** suddenly announced his conversion to UDDIA, which thereby acquired an absolute majority in the Assembly. Youlou claimed the right to form a government and demanded the transfer of the state capital from Pointe Noire to Brazzaville. The motive of this demand was immediately apparent when the MSA militants of Pointe Noire invaded the Assembly and tried to seize the 'traitor' Yambot. The UDDIA group produced a draft constitution, but the MSA assemblymen refused to discuss it and walked out. The UDDIA group, left in possession of the chamber, now exactly made up the quorum of 23; it therefore proceeded to invest Youlou as prime minister and voted the transfer of the capital to Brazzaville. The MSA then returned in force and a remarkably undignified hand-to-hand battle ensued. The UDDIA assemblymen succeeded in escaping to Brazzaville, but riots continued in Pointe Noire for some time.[3]

[1] *Afrique Nouvelle*, 7th November 1958.
[2] Ansprenger, Table 1.
[3] In the following year there was a series of very violent riots in Brazzaville. First, in February, there were battles between ba-Kongo and Mbochi: 98 killed, 170 wounded, 350 arrests (including Opangault and other Socialist leaders). Then, after an election in which UDDIA won 51 out of 61 seats, the

So when on 1st December Boganda proclaimed his 'Central African Republic', this was in fact no more than a new name for Oubangui-Chari. He still saw it as the core of a future 'United States of Latin Africa', which would first be formed by a union of French-speaking countries (AEF, Cameroun and the Belgian Congo), then extended to include Portuguese Angola, and finally also Spanish Guinea. But this was no more than a pipe-dream. On 6th December, Boganda became prime minister of the new Republic. (Abel Goumba stepped down to Minister of Finance.) On the 15th he was in Paris at a round-table conference with the other three prime ministers of AEF: Lisette, Mba and Youlou. Also present were the presidents of the four Legislative Assemblies, and the leaders of the main political parties. The Conference decided to reject the idea of a federal parliament and executive, opting instead for co-ordinated activity in the economic and technical spheres; so doing, it anticipated the West African Conseil de l'Entente. On 17th January 1959 it was agreed to maintain the customs union and a common administration for transport and communications. On 26th March a committee of representatives from each state was convened in Brazzaville by the French High Commissioner, **Yvon Bourges,** to wind up the AEF Federation and dispose of its property.[1] Although as late as February Boganda was still talking hopefully of the United States of Latin Africa, all real prospect of political unity in AEF had vanished by the time of his tragic death in an air crash on Easter Sunday, 29th March 1959. The Federation officially ceased to exist on 30th June.[2]

---

UDDIA supporters among the ba-Kongo attacked the orthodox Matsouanists, whose organisation was smashed after a bitter struggle (June-August). The riots gave Youlou an excuse to suppress political opposition and have himself voted special powers. They appear to have little or no connection with the great anti-European riots across the river in Leopoldville (January 1959), which shook the Belgian government into its sudden decision to give the other Congo independence. In the Brazzaville riots Europeans were left completely unmolested.

[1] Thompson and Adloff, *Emerging States* . . . (op. cit.).
[2] Ansprenger, p. 390.

# Chapter 29

## The French Community: Disintegration

### A. The 'Federal' Institutions

Was the Community of 1958 merely a mask for continued French control over France's former colonies? Or was it a genuine attempt at federal organisation? It is difficult to answer this question with any certainty, for detailed minutes of the sessions of the Executive Council have not been published. We cannot tell whether de Gaulle modified his policy in any important respect on the advice of the Council, or of its individual members.

But even if his government was federal, it was not clearly seen to be federal. The Executive Council met only seven times between February 1959 and March 1960. The day to day management of the Community's affairs was inevitably the work of the French Council of Ministers. Once the African states ceased to be 'T.O.M.' and became Autonomous Republics within the Community, they were no longer subject to the Ministry of France d'Outre-Mer. But those of their affairs which were still the responsibility of the Community as a whole came under the authority of its President, de Gaulle. Under him was the prime minister of the French Republic, **Michel Debré.** He had to answer for the government's policy before the National Assembly. Therefore he could scarcely help taking responsibility for its management of foreign affairs, etc., even though these were notionally the concern of the Community as a whole.

Some of Debré's colleagues were particularly concerned with the African states. One was Jacques Soustelle, who until January 1960 was *Ministre délégué auprès du Premier Ministre*, with special responsibility for the Sahara. He ran the *Organisation Commune des Régions Sahariennes* (OCRS) which had been set up by Mollet's government in January 1957. Its object was partly to detach the Algerian Sahara from the rest of Algeria. But the problems with which it dealt ran across the frontiers into Mauritania, the Soudan, Niger and Tchad. Under the Fourth Republic these territories had

360

sent representatives from their Territorial Assemblies to OCRS meetings in Paris.[1] Now, as Autonomous Republics, they were asked to surrender part of their sovereignty over the Saharan parts of their territory to OCRS. One reason for the French government's hostility to Bakary Djibo was that he refused to do this, thus threatening to disrupt the organisation and create a 'hole in the desert'. The campaign to get rid of him was believed to have been carried out under Soustelle's orders. And when Hamani Diori's government brought Niger back into the OCRS (11th May 1959), the federalists hinted that this was in the nature of a *quid pro quo*. Soustelle was in any case unpopular with Africans because he was known to be the leader of the *Algérie Française* lobby. Mamadou Dia had given his appointment as a reason for distrusting de Gaulle's government as early as the Cotonou Congress.[2] As long as he was believed to be influential with dc Gaulle it was difficult for many Africans to think of the French government as representing them. Yet it was Soustelle who inherited what was left of the Rue Oudinot's power in Afrique Noire.

There was also a *Ministre d'Etat* with responsibility for 'questions of co-operation between the French republic and other Member-States in the economic, financial, cultural and social domaines': **Robert Lecourt** (MRP). In other words, he was in charge of FIDES, which was now rechristened 'FAC' (*Fonds d'Aide et de Co-opération*). After Soustelle's fall in January 1960 he became Minister of the Sahara, and **Jean Foyer** (Gaullist) was appointed 'Secretary of State for relations with the States of the Community'. The Secretariat of the Community itself was headed successively by two close personal associates of de Gaulle: **Raymond Janot** until February 1960, and thereafter **Jacques Foccart**.[3]

These were the men who to all appearances ran the Community. In the summer of 1959 de Gaulle did also appoint four *Ministres-Counseillers*, one from each of the Community's main territorial blocs (Madagascar, AEF, Mali and the Conseil de l'Entente). These were:

---

[1] See Thompson and Adloff, *Emerging States*, op. cit., for the wrangle over this in the Tchad territorial assembly in January 1958, when Lisette insisted on sending two faithful PPT-RDA assemblymen and not the representative of the region concerned, who belonged to UDIT.

[2] Dugué, *Vers les Etats-Unis d'Afrique* (op. cit.).

[3] Ansprenger, pp. 321–2.

Tsiranana (Defence)
Lisette (Economic and Social Policy)
Senghor (Culture)
Houphouët-Boigny (Foreign Affairs).

But they had no direct executive powers, only advisory ones, and it seems probable that the appointments were intended as marks of de Gaulle's personal esteem for these individuals rather than as an undertaking to be guided by their advice.

The Community would only have taken on a genuinely federal appearance if, as the RDA had originally advocated, there had been a federal parliament with a federal government responsible to it. But this was far from being the case. The Senate of the Community was composed of delegations from the Legislative Assemblies of the Member-States, and had no power at all. 'Il s'est réuni deux fois, pour la naissance et pour l'enterrement' (It has met twice, for its birth and for its funeral), scoffed Georges Bidault, now the leader of *Algérie Française* opposition to de Gaulle, in the National Assembly in June 1960.[1] The jibe was fair enough: the Senate met for the first time in July 1959, for the second and last in June 1960. And the 'Court of Arbitration of the Community' never met at all.

## B. The Independence of Mali

Even if all the African members of the Community had been dedicated to the federal idea at the start, it would not have been surprising if they had ended by demanding independence when they saw that de Gaulle did not intend to let his government be responsible to the Community as a whole (or indeed to anybody but himself). But in fact the leaders who took the initiative in breaking up the federal structure–Senghor, Modibo Keïta and Tsiranana–had all taken up a more or less overtly confederalist stand at the time the Constitution was being worked out. They accepted de Gaulle's federal formula, not as a permanent substitute for a confederation of independent states, but as a necessary stepping-stone towards it. This was the reason for Houphouët's increasing bitterness towards the leaders of Mali. He knew that their principal aim in building a West African federation was to escape as soon as possible from the Community in its federal form–the form on which he himself had

[1] Quoted in Rene Viard, *La Fin de l'Empire colonial français*, Paris 1963, p. 119.

staked his reputation, and to which he felt they were not giving a fair chance.

At first de Gaulle supported Houphouët, and refused to recognise Mali's existence. At the third meeting of the Executive Council (Paris, 4th May 1959) Modibo Keïta was absent, and a communiqué was issued saying that Mali was not yet a State. 'The States (Senegal and the Soudan) entered the Community separately; Mali could only have been represented in the Executive Council if the States composing it had decided to group themselves as a single State at the time of their option.'[1]

The only effect of this was to encourage the Malian leaders to push ahead with their demand for independence. The Constituent Congress of the *Parti de la Fédération Africaine* (PFA), which was held at Dakar from 1st to 3rd July, decided that Mali should now seek independence and retain only confederal links (if available) with France.[2] Houphouët was furious. On 7th July he arrived in Tananarive, where the fourth meeting of the Executive Council was held, declaring huffily to a correspondent from *Le Monde*: 'Let's have no more duplicity. Are we or are we not committing ourselves to the construction of a Community which will last? If not, we who are members of the Conseil de l'Entente will refuse to belong to a Community which would be nothing more than a Commonwealth.' (A *Commonwealth a la française* was precisely what Senghor was demanding.)[3] Although de Gaulle agreed, under pressure, to a further step in 'federalising' the Community–the inclusion of Africans and Malagasies in French diplomatic missions–Houphouët merely commented bitterly: 'I don't see the point of trying to organise the Community, while some members are still talking of leaving it.' In fact, so far from drawing the Community together, the Tananarive meeting widened the gap between its African members. De Gaulle listened in melancholy silence while Hamani Diori complained to the PFA leaders of illegal activity by the PFA-Sawaba in Niger,[4] and Boganda's successor **David Dacko** accused the RDA of interfering in the Central African Republic.[5]

At the beginning of September, Houphouët held an RDA Congress

---

[1] Dugué, op. cit.

[2] Crowder, 'Independence as a Goal . . .' (op. cit.), p. 37.

[3] Ansprenger, p. 344.

[4] Hamani's government had just dissolved the Niger section of UGTAN. *Sawaba* itself was banned three months later, after which Bakary Djibo fled to Mali.

[5] Dugué, op. cit.

in Abidjan. This time there was no danger of a conflict between him and the other territorial leaders. Those who had led the opposition in 1957–Touré, Keïta and d'Arboussier–had now left the RDA. Those who remained were his staunch supporters: Yaméogo, Lisette, Hamani Diori, Mba, Youlou, Ahomadegbé. All accepted the de Gaulle Community, and Houphouët's leadership within it. Yaméogo even went so far as to call Houphouët 'notre Général à nous'. There was loud applause for this, as there was when Houphouët once again expounded his belief in the federal Community: 'We wish to create a State like the USSR or the United States . . . a multi-national or intercontinental ensemble'.[1]

But on their side the Malians, egged on by Sékou Touré (who now had a 'National Committee for the Liberation of the Ivory Coast' under his patronage in Conakry),[2] pushed ahead with their demand for independence. On 10th September, at the fifth session of the Executive Council (in Paris), the prime ministers of Senegal and the Soudan reported that their Federation, which France still did not recognise, now desired independence within the Community. A few days later, at a Congress of the PDG in Conakry, the guest-representative of the PFA referred 'to the outstanding success of Guinea's independence' as one of Mali's principal sources of inspiration. Even Apithy's party (PRD), which was still part of the governing coalition in Dahomey, sent a representative who declared that independence must be achieved, 'while preserving France's friendship'. The confederalist formula had its adherents even within the Conseil de l'Entente.

On 24th September the PFA steering committee decided that at the next meeting of the Executive Council (which was to be held in December at Saint-Louis-du-Sénégal) the Malian representatives should demand the transfer to the Malian government of all the powers hitherto reserved to the Community.[3] They would base their demand on Article 78 of the Constitution, which said 'Special agreements may . . . regulate any transfer of jurisdiction from the Community to one of its members', and not on Article 86, by which a Member-State could become independent, but only after a referendum, and would thereby leave the Community. By using the 'transfer of jurisdiction' formula they gave the Community a chance to turn itself into a Confederation. On 28th September the two prime ministers–Mamadou Dia and Modibo Keïta–signed a joint letter to de Gaulle informing him of this decision.

[1] Ibid.          [2] *Le Monde*, 6th August 1960.          [3] Dugué, op. cit.

It might have been expected that de Gaulle would reply by repeating his offer of 1958; any state could leave the Community if it chose, but if it remained within the Community it must accept the sacrifices involved. This is certainly the reply that Houphouët would have liked him to give. But by the autumn of 1959 Houphouët seems to have realised (as many Frenchmen were realising) that de Gaulle could not be relied on to resist the 'wind of change' in Africa, whose existence Mr Macmillan was soon to proclaim (4th February 1960). In early November, Houphouët addressed the UN General Assembly, as a member of the French delegation. 'It may be', he said, 'that one day the thirteen Republics which form the Franco-African Community will come to the UN as independent nations; that would in no way weaken the bonds which unite them with the French Republic.' This amounted virtually to an acceptance of the Malian confederalist thesis. Houphouët was forced to recognise that the centrifugal forces were proving too strong for the federal Community. His only consolation was the thought that they would certainly be too strong for Pan-Africanism too: 'L'Unité africaine ne se réalisera jamais'.

A few days later, on 10th November, de Gaulle referred to the Community in a television broadcast. 'In this Community,' he said, 'all the states that compose it are in it because they have chosen it, and all can leave at any moment they choose. It is effective independence and guaranteed co-operation.'[1]

At last he was moving from a federalist to a confederalist conception. And when he arrived at Saint-Louis on 10th December he at last recognised the Primary Federation with the words 'je salue ceux du Mali'.[2] The Executive Council now admitted the fact of Mali's existence, and conceded in principle that it could become independent without forfeiting its membership of the Community. On 13th December, de Gaulle publicly confirmed this before the Federal Assembly at Dakar: 'This state of Mali will take what is called Independence, but I prefer to call International Sovereignty.'[3]

On 18th December, Tsiranana presented de Gaulle with a similar demand on behalf of Madagascar. Negotiations with both states were held in Paris during January and February 1960, and brought to a successful conclusion on 2nd April (Madagascar) and 4th April (Mali). It only remained to amend the French Constitution so as to

[1] Ibid.     [2] Ansprenger, p. 345.
[3] *Chronique de la Communauté*, December 1959.

allow for the changed character of the Community. This was done by a docile French parliament on 10th May. As some opposition deputies plaintively pointed out, since the agreements with Mali and Madagascar had created a *fait accompli*, Parliament had little choice but to regularise the situation—for as the Constitution stood the agreements were certainly unconstitutional. Debré replied that the agreements would in due course be presented to Parliament for ratification.[1] But in the circumstances it would have been difficult for Parliament to refuse. In any case, it did not try, for there was a comfortable Gaullist majority in both houses. From henceforth, therefore, 'a Member-State may, by way of agreements, become independent without thereby ceasing to belong to the Community.' (Article 86, as amended by Constitutional Law of 4th June 1960). A 'Renewed Community' came into existence, which was in fact a confederation, without common citizenship or common nationality.[2] The institutions of the Community (Executive Council, Senate, Court of Arbitration) were not formally abolished but the transfer of the remaining powers from the Community to its individual members would evidently deprive them of even their theoretical importance. All that was left was de Gaulle's title of 'President of the Community', the joint secretariat headed by Foccart, and the *Fonds d'Aide et de Co-opération*.

So Mali became an independent State within the Community on 20th June, and Madagascar on 26th June. What they got was certainly not less than what Touré had demanded in 1958. Why had de Gaulle changed his mind?

The reasons were beyond doubt largely personal. The General had taken Touré's speech in Conakry, and his subsequent No-vote, as a personal snub. He could not take protestations of friendship for France seriously, when they came from a man so blatantly lacking in respect for France's senior statesman. On the other hand, the behaviour of Tsiranana, Senghor, and even Modibo Keïta, was well calculated to flatter de Gaulle's *amour propre*. He knew that all three men had to cope with a strong desire for independence, both among their followers and in their own hearts. Yet all three were able to overcome this desire on 28th September 1958, and to subordinate it to their appreciation of the value of continued association with France. For de Gaulle, the 'Yes' or 'No' given by Africans on

[1] Viard, op. cit., pp. 104–5.
[2] See Bidault's speech in the National Assembly, 9th June 1960 (quoted by Viard, p. 118).

that day did not really concern a particular constitutional formula: it was a 'Yes' or 'No' to France. Those who voted 'Yes' were France's friends. Those who voted 'No' had turned their backs on her.

Of course, there were also changes in the political situation during 1959. By the time de Gaulle promised independence to Mali, he had already offered the option of independence to Algeria, and alienated the colonialist Right in France which had formerly supported him. Politically, he no longer had anything to lose by adopting a liberal policy in Afrique Noire. Then, too, there was the fact of Guinean survival, and Guinea's growing friendship with other powers, especially the Soviet Bloc. France had little interest in driving more African nations into alliance with Russia, by refusing to underwrite or even smile upon their independence. If she excluded Mali from the Community, it could only be a matter of time before the other states would pluck up their courage and leave it too.

## C. The Conseil de l'Entente

As de Gaulle had seen in 1958, once some states were allowed to have a confederal relationship with France it was impossible to expect others to maintain a federal one. The agreements with Mali and Madagascar meant the end of the federal Community, the Community which Houphouët had long preached and which de Gaulle had promised in 1958. In private, Houphouët was bitterly disappointed. 'General de Gaulle is a great liar', he is said to have exclaimed. But in public he put a bold face on it. On 2nd April, the day of the agreement with Madagascar, he announced that the Conseil de l'Entente states would in their turn demand independence.[1]

He still had one card to play. He stuck to the formula which he had produced at Tananarive the year before: 'Nous nous refuserons, nous, ... à être d'une Communauté qui ne serait plus qu'un Commonwealth'. If the Community was not federal, he said, he saw no point in having it. On 3rd June the four Conseil de l'Entente prime ministers – Maga, Hamani Diori, Yaméogo and Houphouët himself – demanded independence without any prior conditions or agreements (such as had been negotiated in Mali's case). Their states would leave the Community, and only then, from a position of complete independence, would they negotiate such bilateral agreements with France (or any other country) as they wished.

[1] *Le Monde*, 5th April 1960.

Politically, this was a master-stroke. On the eve of Malian independence, Houphouët turned the tables on the Malian leaders and made it appear that *they* were neocolonialist French puppets and *he* the believer in real independence. His prestige in other parts of Africa, which had sagged badly since the independence of Guinea, was restored overnight. When the independence of the Ivory Coast was proclaimed on 7th August (after those of Dahomey, Niger and Upper Volta on the 1st, 3rd and 6th) Sékou Touré himself sent a congratulatory telegram. The 'National Committee for the Liberation of the Ivory Coast' was disbanded.[1]

But in practical terms Houphouët's gesture was pure showmanship. He knew that de Gaulle could hardly penalise him for having meant what he said about the Franco-African Community. The spectacle of Mali basking in French friendship while the Ivory Coast had a dose of the Guinea treatment would have been too grotesque. Although the states of the Conseil de l'Entente (sometimes known as the *Union du Bénin-Sahel*) did not rejoin the Community, they all did sign bilateral co-operation agreements with France, remained within the franc zone, had associate membership of the European Economic Community, and received liberal financial assistance from the FAC. The effect of this was to make what was left of the Community quite meaningless, since there was no longer any discernible difference between African states which were members of it and those which were not. It became simply a face-saving device, in whose name France could keep troops in those states whose governments desired it.

## D. The Equatorial States

The leaders of the four republics which had formerly composed AEF decided, after de Gaulle promised independence to Mali, that they too would ask for independence within the Community. Once again they debated whether they should not do so as a group rather than as individual states. In February 1960 the four prime ministers – Youlou, Mba, Dacko and Tombalbaye[2] – met at Bangui to discuss

---

[1] Ansprenger, pp. 368–70.

[2] Lisette's government had fallen in February 1959 when its traditionalist supporters (GIRT) at last deserted. Six weeks later the RDA was back in power, this time with Socialist support, but it was François Tombalbaye (see p. 198) who became prime minister. He had fewer personal enemies than Lisette and unlike him was a native African. (See Thompson and Adloff, op. cit.)

the question. They agreed that their states were so small and impoverished as to make international sovereignty for each one of them by itself a daunting, if not a ridiculous, prospect, and that therefore an effort should be made 'to carry on to the political level the relations which already exist in the sphere of economic, social and cultural co-ordination' and to 'reconcile the demands of internal political autonomy with a common international sovereignty'. But in the event these demands proved irreconcilable. Mba was still very suspicious of anything like a federal executive, and was unwilling to go further than a joint defence force and inter-governmental co-ordination of foreign policy (combined, of course, with the existing customs and currency union). The other three considered this an inadequate interpretation of 'common international sovereignty'. Gabon therefore dropped out of the scheme. At a second meeting, at Fort-Lamy, on 17th May, the other three states agreed to join the Renewed Community as a 'Union of Central African Republics'. But this too collapsed at the end of July when Youlou withdrew, realising that he would not after all be able to dominate it and fearing that it might get in the way of any future projects for ba-Kongo unity. (He was keenly watching the events across the river in the ex-Belgian Congo, which had just become independent and showed promising signs of breaking up, owing to the opposition of President Kasavubu's ba-Kongo party (ABAKO) to the centralising policy of Prime Minister Lumumba.) He also reasoned, no doubt, that if Gabon, with 400,000 people, could be an internationally sovereign state, there was no reason why Congo-Brazzaville, with 750,000, should not be one too. So, on the 11th, 12th, 14th and 17th August, Tchad, the Central African Republic, Congo (Brazzaville) and Gabon became four separate independent states.[1]

### E. Senegal

The final stage of balkanisation came only three days later: on 20th August the Republic of Senegal suddenly seceded from the Mali Federation and expelled the Soudanese ministers from its territory. The break-up of Mali apparently vindicated its critics, such as Houphouët, who had been against any kind of federation, and Apithy, who had considered this particular federal constitution too restrictive. But it was also partly their responsibility, for by refusing to join it they had left it as a two-state federation, in which tensions

[1] Ansprenger, pp. 390–1 and Table 1.

were inevitably polarised and concessions to the federal government were seen as benefiting the other partner in particular rather than the common weal.

The immediate cause of the crisis seems to have been a dispute over the approaching election of a President of the Federal Republic. The Soudanese had at first opposed the creation of this office, but the Senegalese had insisted on it, assuming that it would be given to Senghor. The Soudanese then agreed to the office, but refused to commit themselves to supporting Senghor. They believed in the need for a strong federal government, and were afraid that it would be weakened if it had to cope with so powerful a figure as Senghor as head of state. Rumour had it that they would put up a Soundanese candidate, or possibly support Lamine-Guèye, a move which would be sure to reopen old divisions among the Senegalese.

The Senegalese on their side considered that the office fell to Senghor by right as one of Africa's most internationally prestigious leaders. Also, they wanted to place some effective check on Modibo Keïta's government. In general they resented Modibo's centralising federal policy, which they feared would defeat the main purpose of Mali– to attract other African states into a wider union–and which they saw as a Soudanese bid to take over Senegal. Every time that a desirable villa on Cape Verde came into the possession of a Soudanese minister or official, the fact was immediately noted and commented on by the Senegalese. The Soudanese also manoeuvred for influence within Senegalese political parties, while in their own territory they organised a monolithic one-party state. Not only Senegal's material interests, but her long-standing tradition of political freedom and diversity, seemed to be threatened. The rigorous, Marxist-inspired traditions of the Soudan RDA found little sympathy among the easy-going, Frenchified Senegalese. (As one Frenchman put it to me: 'Les Sénégalais, ce sont des Méridionaux'–the Senegalese are southerners.)[1]

Disillusioned with the federal experience, Senegal became an independent republic and was immediately recognised as such by France. The Soudanese leaders were humiliated and angry, and accused France of deliberately sabotaging the federation. The Soudan was renamed *République du Mali*. It kept the Mali flag and the Mali national anthem (although the words had been written by Senghor). But the *Parti de la Fédération Africaine* was dissolved and the

[1] These impressions are drawn partly from conversation with M. Fernand Wibaux, who was French Consul-General in Bamako at the time.

Soudan party resumed the name of 'US-RDA'. Mali broke off agreements with France, formed a national political union with Guinea and Ghana (December 1960) and later left the franc zone – only to rejoin it in 1967. For three years it refused to recognise Senegal's existence.

So, in September 1960, France sponsored the admission to the United Nations of twelve independent Black African republics.[1] The attempt to find a formula which would rationally unite the lands and peoples irrationally conglomerated by French colonial expansion, which would end colonialism but preserve the empire, was at last abandoned.

[1] They were: Ivory Coast, Dahomey, Upper Volta, Niger, Senegal, Mali, Tchad, Central African Republic, Congo (Brazzaville), Gabon, Cameroun and Togo. Mauritania, which became independent on 28th November, was vetoed for UN membership by the Soviet Union, because Morocco (which in those days pursued an actively pro-Communist foreign policy) claimed that Mauritania was part of its national territory.

# Index

# Index

Samory (Touré), 200 n.
Sanaga (river—Cameroun), 216
Sanaga-Maritime region (Cameroun), 125, 218, 243–4, 299–300, 302, 337
San Francisco, 55
Sanmarco, Governor, 202
Sano, Mamba, 112, 131, 142, 188, 200, 205, 227–8, 249
Sanogo, Sékou, 170, 175 n., 190–1, 209, 228
Santos, Anani, 205
Sarr, Ibrahima, 134
Savoy (France), 312
Sawaba, 318, 321–2, 324, 344, 355, 363
Schachter, Ruth: see Morgenthau
Schellens, Jean-Jacques, 338 n.
Schuman, Robert, 119, 129–31, 188, 209
Second College: see Double College
Second Empire, 77
Second Republic, 33
Secretaries of State, 149, 155, 189–90, 201, 209–10, 213, 284, 361
Seine (river), 109 n.
*La Semaine en AOF*, 294 n., 321 n.
Senate, Senators: 57, 80, 101, 170, 181, 186, 215, 264, 289 n., 308, 312. *See also* Council of the Republic
Senate of the Community, 313, 362, 366
Senegal (river), 33, 132–3
Senegal (territory), 19, 23–4, 32–3, 36, 39–47, 56, 59–61, 63, 68, 73, 85, 87, 100, 104, 120–2, 131–6, 141–2, 155, 162, 164, 166, 169, 172, 174, 176–8, 180, 187–8, 191, 199, 203, 219–20, 224, 227, 238, 250–2, 254–5, 266, 268–9, 271, 277, 285, 287–8, 289 n., 293, 306, 312, 315, 318–20, 323–4, 335, 345–50, 352, 354–5, 363–4, 369–71
Senghor, Léopold Sédar (photo facing p. 80), 23, 56–7, 61, 64, 68–70, 72–3, 77–8, 80, 85, 87–8, 92, 97–8, 105–6, 112, 121–2, 128, 130–6, 143, 151–2, 157, 164, 171, 185, 188–93, 195–6, 207, 209–10, 215, 221, 224, 227, 231, 235, 237–9, 248–52, 254, 256–60, 268–9, 271, 277, 279, 283–5, 287–90, 294–6, 303, 305–7, 309–12, 317, 321, 323, 332, 343–4, 350, 354–5, 362–3, 366, 370

Sérère tribe (Senegal), 134 n.
Services d'état, 237–8, 258–60, 274
Seydoux, Roger, 334–5
SFIO: see Socialists
Silvandre, Jean, 107, 111–12, 130, 229 n.
Sine-Saloum region (Senegal), 121, 133
Singapore, 30
Sissoko, Fily-Dabo (photo facing p. 65), 50, 64–5, 68–9, 72, 97, 105, 107–8, 110–2, 129, 141, 143, 177, 209, 229, 255, 263, 283, 303, 307, 319, 322, 355
Slave Coast, 194
Social Republicans: see RS
Socialist International, 256
'Socialist Party of Guinea', 112
Socialists (SFIO), 44–5, 61, 63, 71–3, 75, 77, 79–80, 87–8, 91, 94, 96–7, 105–7, 108 n., 109, 111–13, 116–17, 120–3, 126, 128–32, 134–6, 140, 143, 149, 151, 154–5, 167, 171–2, 174, 176–7, 180, 182, 186, 201–2, 205–6, 209, 212, 215–16, 223, 229–31, 233–4, 243, 245, 250, 253–6, 258–9, 264 n., 268, 284, 301, 307, 323, 325, 339, 368 n.
Sognigbé, 42
'Solidarité Voltaïque', 270
Somalia, 262
Somaliland (Côte Française des Somalis), 21, 29 n., 101–2, 112, 171, 216, 228
Songhay tribe (Niger), 175 n.
Soppo Priso, Paul, 43, 126, 215–16, 218, 229, 242–3, 245–6, 301, 339
Soucadaux, J. L., 215–16
Soudan, 21, 23, 64–5, 73, 86, 90, 107–8, 111–12, 117, 141, 143, 156, 167, 171–2, 174, 176–8, 180, 185, 227, 229, 231 n., 248, 255, 263, 271, 276, 283, 285, 289–90, 308, 318–20, 322, 331, 345–50, 352, 354–5, 360, 363–4, 369–71
Soudan Democratic Party, 107
Soudanese Bloc, 107
Soumah, David, 181–2
Sou Quatre, 170, 228
Soussou tribe (Guinea), 64
Soustelle, Jacques, 71, 74–5, 208, 294, 360–1
South West Africa, 35
Soviet bloc, 115, 332, 335, 337, 367

387